World War II and Its Origins

World War II and Its Origins:

A Select Annotated Bibliography of Books in English

Marty Bloomberg
California State College,
San Bernardino

Hans H. Weber
University of California,
Riverside

1975

Libraries Unlimited, Inc. - Littleton, Colo.

Library of Congress Card Number 74-81959
International Standard Book Number 0-87287-089-8

LIBRARIES UNLIMITED, INC.
P.O. Box 263
Littleton, Colorado 80120

TABLE OF CONTENTS

Introduction   xiii

CHAPTER 1–REFERENCE MATERIALS, 1

Bibliographies of World War II   1
General History Bibliographies with Sections on World War II   1
General Bibliographies of Books with Sections on World War II   2
Book Reviews   3
Periodical and Newspaper Indexes   3
Government Document Indexes   5
Miscellaneous Reference Works   5
    Atlases   5
    Battlefields   6
    Biographies   6
    Chronologies   6
    Encyclopedias   7
    Language and Code Names   7
    Sources   7
    Statistics   8
    Yearbooks   8

CHAPTER 2–PRE-WAR YEARS, 1919-1939, 10

General Histories, 1919-1941   10
Special Topics   16
    Treaty of Versailles, 1919   16
    League of Nations   17
    Disarmament and Arms Limitations   18
    German Reparations   19
    Occupation of the Ruhr, 1923   20
    Corfu Incident, 1923   20
    Locarno Conference, 1925   20
    Kellogg-Briand Pact, 1928   20

Japan and Manchuria, 1931-1932 21
Four-Power Pact, 1933 22
Saar Plebiscite, 1935 22
Italo-Ethiopian War, 1935-1936 22
Spanish Civil War, 1936-1939 23
Sino-Japanese War, 1937-1941 25
Anschluss Movement 26
Appeasement 27
Munich Conference, 1938 28
United States—Isolationism and Neutrality 30
United States and Lend-Lease 32
Final Crisis, 1939-1941 32
Individual Countries 33
Australia 33
Austria 33
Belgium 34
China 34
Czechoslovakia 34
France 35
Germany 36
Great Britain 43
Hungary 47
Italy 47
Japan 48
Poland 50
Russia 51
United States 53
Yugoslavia 58
Relations Between Two or More Countries 58
Baltic States 58
Central Europe 58
Czechoslovakia and Germany 59
Eastern Europe 59
Far East 59
France and Germany 60
France and Russia 60
Germany and Italy 60
Germany and Japan 60
Germany and Poland (Including Danzig) 61
Germany and Spain 61
Germany and Russia 62
Great Britain and France 63
Great Britain and Germany 63
Great Britain and Japan 64
Great Britain and the Far East 64
Great Britain and the United States 64
Poland and France 65
Poland and Russia 65

Russia and China 65
Russia and the Far East 65
United States and China 66
United States and France 66
United States and Germany (and the Americas) 66
United States and Japan (Including Events Leading Up to
    the Attack on Pearl Harbor) 67
United States and Russia 69
United States and the Far East 69

CHAPTER 3–GENERAL INTRODUCTORY WORKS ON THE WAR, 1939-1945, AND WORKS ON STRATEGY, 71

The Total War 71
The War in Europe–The Mediterranean–North Africa 73
The War in the Far East 74
Pictorial Histories 75
Strategy 76

CHAPTER 4–THE WAR YEARS, 1939-1945: MILITARY ASPECTS, 83

Ground War in Europe 83
General Works 83
Germany-Poland, 1939 88
Russia-Finland, 1940 88
Germany-Norway, 1940 89
Germany-France, 1940 89
Dunkirk–Battle of Britain, 1940–Operation Sea
    Lion–Commando Raids 90
The Balkans, 1941 92
Germany-Russia, 1941-1945 93
Germany and Italy–Anglo-Americans and Allies 98
    The Defeat of Italy, 1943-1945 98
    The Defeat of Germany, 1944-1945 100
        General, 100; Normandy Invasion, 1944, 100;
        Liberation of France, 1944, 102; Final Defeat of
        Germany in the West, 1944-1945, 103
The War in North Africa and the Mediterranean 106
The War in the Far East 111
General 111
Pearl Harbor 113
Japanese Advance and Allied Victory 114
The War in the Air 121
General 121

Europe, North Africa, and the Mediterranean 124
Far East 128
The War on the Seas 130
General 130
The Atlantic, Arctic, and Mediterranean 133
The Pacific 138

CHAPTER 5—WEAPONS, 142

General Works 142
Individual Countries 145
Canada 145
Germany 145
Great Britain 147
Japan 149
Russia 150
United States 150
Atomic Bomb 153

CHAPTER 6—THE WAR YEARS, 1939-1945: POLITICAL ASPECTS, 156

Comprehensive Works 156
General Works 157
General Accounts 157
General Diplomacy 158
Peace 159
Propaganda 162
Unconditional Surrender 164
Individual Countries 165
Australia 165
Burma 165
China 165
Czechoslovakia 167
Finland 168
France 168
Germany 171
Great Britain 177
Greece 180
Hungary 181
Iran 181
Italy 181
Japan 183
Lithuania 185
New Zealand 185

Norway 185
Philippines 186
Poland 186
Romania 187
Russia 187
Spain 189
Switzerland 189
Turkey 189
United States 189
Vatican 197
Yugoslavia 198
Relations Between Two or More Countries 198
China and Japan 198
Czechoslovakia and Poland 198
Eastern Europe 198
Finland and Russia 198
Germany and Great Britain 199
Germany and Japan 199
Germany and Russia 199
Germany and the Arabs 200
Great Britain and Poland 200
Great Britain and Spain 200
Hungary and Germany 200
Italy and Germany 201
Japan and Russia 201
Middle East 201
Poland and Russia 202
Russia and China 202
United States and China 202
United States and France 204
United States and Great Britain 204
United States and India 204
United States and Russia 204
United States and Spain 206
United States and Switzerland 207
United States and the Vatican 207
United States, Great Britain, and Russia 207
Vatican and Germany 208
Yugoslavia and Russia 209

CHAPTER 7—THE WAR YEARS, 1939-1945: ECONOMIC ASPECTS, 210

General Works 210
Individual Countries 210
Australia 210
China 211

x / Table of Contents

France 211
Germany 211
Great Britain 212
India 214
Japan 214
Norway 215
Russia 215
United States 215
Relations Between Two or More Countries 220
Australia and New Zealand 220
Canada and the United States 220
Great Britain, United States, and Canada 220
Middle East 220

CHAPTER 8–THE WAR YEARS, 1939-1945:
SOCIAL AND CULTURAL ASPECTS, 222

General Works 222
Individual Countries 223
Germany 223
Great Britain 224
Italy 225
United States 225

CHAPTER 9–OCCUPATION AND RESISTANCE, 230

Occupation and Military Governments 230
General 230
Africa 230
Belgium 230
Burma 230
Czechoslovakia 231
Estonia 231
Europe 231
Far East 232
France 232
Great Britain (Channel Islands) 232
Greece 232
Indonesia 233
Italy 233
Netherlands 234
Philippines 234
Russia 234
Resistance and Underground Activities 235
General 235
Albania 235

Burma 235
China 236
Czechoslovakia 236
Denmark 236
Europe 237
France 237
Italy 239
Malaya 239
Netherlands 239
Norway 240
Philippines 240
Poland 241
Russia 241
Thailand 242
Yugoslavia 242
Anti-Fascist, Anti-Nazi, and Anti-Soviet Movements 243
Anti-Fascist Movements in Italy 243
Anti-Nazi Movements in Germany 243
Anti-Soviet Movements in Russia 248

CHAPTER 10—ESPIONAGE, 249

CHAPTER 11—THE "FINAL SOLUTION," CONCENTRATION CAMPS AND OTHER MAJOR ATROCITIES, 261

The "Final Solution" and Concentration Camps 261
Atrocities and Prison Camps 268
Europe 268
Far East 270

CHAPTER 12—WAR CRIMES TRIALS, 272

General 272
German 273
Eichmann Trial 278
Japanese 278

Author-Title-Biographee Index 281

INTRODUCTION

This bibliography was compiled to help provide a selected body of literature on the origins of World War II and on the military, political, social, cultural, and technological events of the war years, from 1939 to 1945. The books selected are limited to those originally published in English or translated into English. The number of books being published on World War II remains at a floodtide, and many of these new books will undoubtedly supersede some of the earlier works included in this bibliography. However, the authors made every effort to include works that will stand the test of time.

In order to keep the size of this bibliography manageable, it was necessary to exercise great care in the selection of books to be included. The authors are only too well aware that many good books have been omitted, but it is hoped that the ones included will prove to be the most reliable for introducing the reader to the whole spectrum of events leading to the war and to the events of the war years. For most topics more than one book has been included to give the reader some choice. What may be the best book for one person may be pure boredom for another. Selecting the right materials is a most important learning experience. One educator has noted that "an essential part of the learning process consists in hunting out useful materials for oneself and just as essential is the recognition that there is no one book, no one writer, no one text, which neatly dispenses necessary knowledge."[1]

Certain genres and topics have been excluded from this bibliography. Among them are: fiction, poetry, juvenile literature, unit histories (with a few exceptions), registers of the dead, escape accounts, medical history, and works on postwar problems (except for the peace treaties). Biographies, autobiographies, and memoirs have been included where they specifically relate to pre-war events or to the war years. No attempt has been made to include works covering individuals' whole lives unless that work is the only source on their role in the war. The authors purposely limited the number of personal memoirs, which exist in great number but which are generally of limited scope.

Under each topic books are entered alphabetically by author. With a few exceptions, these author entries are Library of Congress entries. It may be necessary to look under several topics listed in the Table of Contents to find a particular

---

[1] Fay Blake, "Teaching Is a Funny Business," *California Librarian* 33:201.

work, but the author and title index will also be of help. Many of the books, because they cover several topics and could easily have been placed several places in the outline, were difficult to classify. It was decided not to have a separate section for biographies and memoirs but to place biographies in the various subject categories. Some, therefore, will be classed under military history, some under social and economic topics, and some, like Churchill's *The Second World War*, under general histories of the war.

Each entry includes the following bibliographical information: author's name, title, edition if necessary, place of publication, publisher, date of publication, paging, and an indication of maps and bibliography when they are included in the book. The abbreviation "bibliog." is used to indicate not only bibliographies *per se* but any kind of bibliographic footnotes or references. Following the bibliographic description is a brief annotation describing the subject of the book, the author's viewpoint when appropriate, and, when pertinent, some information about the author. When several editions of a book are available the American edition has been cited unless the foreign edition is more authoritative or more complete.

In compiling this bibliography the authors tried to examine each book and at least two critical reviews of the book. The final selections were based on the authors' personal readings, citation frequency of the books in other bibliographies, and citations of books in well-known scholarly books on specific aspects of the war, as well as on critical book reviews. In some cases books were included simply because their authors played an important part in the war, without regard to the book's literary merit or accuracy. An effort was made to include books on several sides of a topic when appropriate. Finally, many books labelled "popular history" have been included, to balance the scholarly and official publications.

The authors want to thank all those who read sections of the manuscript and offered many valuable suggestions. The research on the manuscript was performed primarily in three libraries—California State College, San Bernardino, University of California, Riverside, and University of California at Los Angeles. Our appreciation goes especially to Linda Evans, who read, criticized, and typed the entire manuscript from handwritten copy that at times resembled hieroglyphics. Any errors in this book are the responsibility of the authors. We would appreciate readers' comments about mistakes and about books that should or should not have been included. Finally, our appreciation to our wives, who for over a year accepted our excuse that work on the manuscript took precedence over a multitude of household chores.

Riverside, California
December 1973

M.B.
H.H.W.

CHAPTER 1—REFERENCE MATERIALS

BIBLIOGRAPHIES OF WORLD WAR II

1   Morton, Louis. **Writings on World War II**. Washington, Service Center for Teachers of History, 1967. 54p.

A brief bibliographic essay covering some of the standard titles most suitable for classroom use at the high school and college undergraduate levels. An excellent selection of primary and secondary sources within its limited scope.

2   **The Two World Wars: Selective Bibliography**. New York, Pergamon Press, 1964. 246p.

A bibliography limited to 466 entries. The books cited are in several foreign languages with only a few titles in English. There are sections on photographs, transparencies, and records and films.

3   Ziegler, Janet. **World War II: Books in English, 1945-1965**. Stanford, Calif., Hoover Institution Press, 1971. 223p.

A comprehensive non-selective bibliography listing 4,519 titles of books published in English. The table of contents is an excellent comprehensive outline of the war. This is an essential bibliography, and a useful starting place for a bibliographic search on almost any aspect or phase of the war. It is helpful to examine this bibliography to get an idea of the scope of the war and the quantity and variety of books on the war.

GENERAL HISTORY BIBLIOGRAPHIES WITH SECTIONS ON WORLD WAR II

4   American Historical Association. **Guide to Historical Literature**. New York, Macmillan, 1961. 962p.

Section "AG—The Two World Wars" lists 258 books on both World War I and World War II. About 130 titles are on World War II. The titles were selected by Basil H. Liddell Hart and Hugh M. Cole, two noted scholars of the wars. The selections are excellent, but the scope is limited, and the bibliography has not been revised in over 12 years.

5   **Foreign Affairs Bibliography: A Selected and Annotated List of Books on International Relations, 1919/1932—**. New York, Harper, 1933—.

Four volumes have been published to date and each, except the first, covers a ten year period: 1919-1932, 1932-42, 1942-52, and 1952-62. The entries are annotated and based on the bibliographies of the journal *Foreign Affairs*. The books listed are in several languages, but most are in English. There are special sections on World War II in the last two volumes. It is necessary to look under related subjects or under the names of individual countries to get a more complete idea of the materials available.

6   **The Foreign Affairs 50-Year Bibliography: New Evaluations of Significant Books on International Relations, 1920-1970.** New York, R. R.
Bowker, 1972. 936p.

The titles included in this bibliography were selected from the *Foreign Affairs
Bibliography* cited above. There is a special section on World War II. The books
selected were ones whose scholarship and importance have stood the test of time
and have not yet been superseded. All entries have long critical annotations.

7   Handlin, Oscar, and others. **Harvard Guide to American History.**
Cambridge, Mass., Belknap Press, 1954. 689p.

A comprehensive bibliography of American history which includes a section on the
role of the United States in World War II. The entries include both primary and
secondary sources. Most of the primary sources are still among the best available.
However, some of the secondary sources and monographs have been superseded as
the bibliography is now 20 years old.

8   Higham, Robin, ed. **A Guide to the Sources of British Military History.**
Berkeley, University of California Press, 1971. 630p.

A select bibliography with critical bibliographic essays. Six chapters are devoted to
the events leading to World War II and to the war itself: "The Development of the
Royal Air Force, 1909-1945," "The Inter-War Years," "The Royal Navy, 1939-
1945," "The Second World War on Land," "Britain in the Second World War,"
and "Science and Technology, 1914-1945." These chapters list over 1,300 citations
to books, archival materials, and other primary source materials.

9   Higham, Robin, ed. **Official Histories: Essays and Bibliographies from
Around the World.** Manhattan, Kansas State University Library, 1970.
644p.

A guide to the official military histories of over 50 countries. An essay on the
origins and preparation of the histories is included for most countries. Useful for
the listings of all official histories of a particular country. A section "Why Official
History" is a helpful introduction to the whole field of official history.

GENERAL BIBLIOGRAPHIES OF BOOKS WITH
SECTIONS ON WORLD WAR II

10   **Bibliographic Index: A Cumulative Bibliography of Bibliographies,
1937–** . New York, H. W. Wilson, 1938– .

Lists bibliographies on all subjects including biographies and the sciences. The
bibliographies included are: 1) separately published books, 2) those included in
books, and 3) those in about 1,500 selected periodicals. Bibliographies relating to
the war can be found under the subject entry "World War, 1939-1945" and its subdivisions, and under the names of individuals and countries.

11   **Cumulative Book Index.** New York, H. W. Wilson, 1898– .

A comprehensive international bibliography of books published in English. It does
not include government documents, pamphlets under 40 pages, most paperbound
books, maps, music scores, and material of a local or ephemeral nature. Books are

entered by author, title, and subject. Books on the war can be found under the subject heading "World War, 1939-1945" and its subdivisions, and under the names of individuals and countries.

12   **Essay and General Literature Index, 1900/33– .** New York, H. W. Wilson, 1934– .
An index to essays and articles found in collections and anthologies. Entries are listed under the author and the subject. Works on the war can be found under the subject entry "World War, 1939-1945," and under subject entries for individuals and countries.

13   **Subject Guide to Books in Print.** New York, R. R. Bowker, 1957– .
A subject bibliography of books in print published in the United States. Books on the war can be found under the subject entry "World War, 1939-1945," and under subject entries for individuals and countries. A related work, *Paperbound Books in Print* (New York, R. R. Bowker, 1955–) is useful for finding paperbound books in print.

14   U.S. Library of Congress. **Books: Subjects: A Cumulative List of Works Represented by Library of Congress Printed Cards, 1950– .** Washington, Library of Congress, 1955– .
A listing by subject of books cataloged by the Library of Congress, or one of a number of cooperating libraries. The books are in many languages. Books on the war are listed under the subject entry "World War, 1939-1945" and its subdivisions, and under the names of individuals and countries. A useful work because of the comprehensiveness of the Library of Congress collection, and because of the great number of foreign language books.

BOOK REVIEWS

15   **Book Review Digest.** New York, H. W. Wilson, 1905– .
A digest of book reviews for about 5,000 fiction and non-fiction titles annually. Book reviews are listed alphabetically by author and give bibliographic citations to the original sources of the reviews. To be included books must be reviewed in several of the periodicals whose reviews are included in *Book Review Digest.* Because a book does not have a review included does not mean it is not valuable and useful. The subject index simplifies locating books on the war.

PERIODICAL AND NEWSPAPER INDEXES

16   **Historical Abstracts: Bibliography of the World's Periodical Literature, 1775-to Date.** Santa Barbara, Calif., American Bibliographical Center, ABC-Clio Press, 1955– .
An abstract, international in scope, of important periodical articles in all areas of history. There is a section in each issue on World War II. Articles are abstracted in English, French, German, Spanish, and Russian. Complete bibliographic citations

are given so the user can refer to the original article. Starting with volume 17, *Historical Abstracts* is in two parts, and it is necessary to check both.

17   **The New York Times Index, 1851– .** New York, The New York Times, 1913– .
An alphabetical subject index to the contents of the *New York Times*. Entries are listed chronologically under each subject and include the date published, page and column. Many of the entries give a brief summary of the articles. Materials on the war can be found under the subject entry "World War, 1939-1945," and under the names of individuals and countries. There are cross references to related subjects. It is necessary to search the volumes both before 1939 and after 1945 to find pre-war information and post-war analysis.

18   Public Affairs Information Service. **Bulletin.** New York, Public Affairs Information Service, 1915– .
A subject index to periodicals, books, pamphlets, government documents, and special reports. Some entries are annotated. Materials on the war can be found under the subject "World War, 1939-1945" and its subdivisions, and under related subjects which are cross referenced.

19   **The Readers' Guide to Periodical Literature, 1900– .** New York, H. W. Wilson, 1905– .
This guide indexes about 130 titles of popular non-technical periodicals. The index is arranged alphabetically with entries for authors, subjects, and sometimes titles. Articles on the war can be found under the subject entry "World War, 1939-1945" and its subdivisions, and under related subjects which are cross referenced. Materials will also be found under the names of individuals and countries. An *Abridged Readers' Guide to Periodical Literature* is available and may be found in many school libraries and small public libraries.

20   **Social Sciences & Humanities Index, 1907– .** New York, H. W. Wilson, 1916– .
An index to about 200 scholarly American and English periodicals. The entries are arranged alphabetically by subject and title and include a complete bibliographic citation. Until 1965 the title of the index was *International Index*. Articles on the war can be found under the subject entry "World War, 1939-1945" and its subdivisions, and under related subjects which are cross referenced. Articles can also be found under the names of individuals and countries. The periodicals indexed in this work are generally more scholarly than those in *Readers' Guide.*

21   Times, London. **Index to the Times, 1906– .** London, The Times, 1907– .
The title of this index has varied over the years and during the war it was titled the *Official Index.* The indexing methods and subject headings changed during the war years and it is necessary to read the instructions in each annual volume to locate materials on the war. The *Times* during the war years was an excellent source of articles, maps, and statistics. It is also a most valuable primary source for studying wartime England.

GOVERNMENT DOCUMENT INDEXES

22   Great Britain. Public Record Office. **The Second World War: A Guide to Documents in the Public Record Office**. London, H. M. Stationery Office, 1972. 303p.

A guide to the official records of Great Britain's role in the war. These records were only recently made public and this book is not a complete listing of materials. This volume is primarily helpful for research. Four appendices add to the value of the work: a dictionary of code names used during the war, abbreviations used in the Official Histories of the war, an index to war cabinet committees and a list of Official Histories of the war.

23   U.S. National Archives. **Federal Records of World War II**. Washington, National Archives, 1950-51. 2v.

Indexes the records of many federal departments and agencies available in the National Archives. The first volume indexes the records of civilian agencies, and the second volume indexes the records of military agencies.

24   U.S. Superintendent of Documents. **Monthly Catalog of United States Government Publications**. Washington, Government Printing Office, 1895– .

An index and bibliography of the publications of the United States government. Restricted, administrative, and "processed" (i.e., mimeographed, dittoed) documents are not included. Monthly issues have an index which is cumulated annually. Each index includes author, title and subject entries. The documents are arranged by issuing department. Most documents relating to the war are cited under the subject "World War, 1939-1945." The title of the *Monthly Catalog* has varied and from 1940 to 1950 the title was *United States Government Publications: A Monthly Catalog.*

MISCELLANEOUS REFERENCE WORKS

Atlases

25   Brown, Ernest Francis. **The War in Maps: An Atlas of the New York Times Maps**. 4th ed. rev. and enl. New York, Oxford University Press, 1946. 197p.

A useful compilation of maps.

26   Stembridge, Jasper Harry. **The Oxford War Atlas**. New York, Oxford University Press, 1941-46. 4v.

A detailed collection of maps covering all aspects and theaters of the war.

27   U.S. Military Academy, West Point. Department of Military Art and Engineering. **The West Point Atlas of American Wars**. New York, Praeger, 1959. 2v.

A section on World War II can be found in the second volume. There are 168 maps of campaigns in both the European and Pacific theaters. Each map is accompanied by a short narrative account of the campaign or battle. Maps cover only action of land forces.

Battlefields

28   Chandler, David G., ed. **A Traveller's Guide to the Battlefields of Europe.** Philadelphia, Chilton Books, 1965. 2v. Bibliog.
Volume one gives information on battlefields of Western Europe, and volume two the battlefields of Central and Eastern Europe. Battles from all periods of European history are included and not just battles of World War II. For each battle the following information is given: date, location, war and campaign, object of the action, opposing sides, forces engaged, casualties, result, nearby accommodations, suggested readings, and a short narrative description of the battle.

29   Harbottle, Thomas Benfield. **Dictionary of Battles.** Rev. and updated by George Bruce. New York, Stein and Day, 1971. 333p.
A comprehensive work including information for battles in all periods of history. Includes information for all major battles of World War II.

Biographies

30   **Biography Index: A Cumulative Index to Biographical Material in Books and Magazines.** New York, H. W. Wilson, 1946– .
An index to biographical information in books and over 1,500 selected periodicals. All materials are in English. No biographical information is included in the index, but only references to sources of information.

31   **Current Biography.** New York, H. W. Wilson, 1940– .
A monthly publication giving short biographical sketches of prominent or newsworthy persons. The volumes for 1940-1945 have nearly 2,400 biographical sketches of wartime personalities. Each sketch usually includes a portrait and bibliographical references.

32   Tunny, Christopher. **Biographical Dictionary of World War II.** New York, St. Martin's Press, 1973.
This work gives short biographical sketches for over 400 persons important in some way for their part in the war. Includes military leaders, political leaders, journalists, scientists, consciencious objectors and other assorted heroes and villains. Useful for determining the person's official position or his particular role during the war.

Chronologies

33   Royal Institute of International Affairs. **Chronology of the Second World War.** London, Royal Institute of International Affairs, 1947. 374p.
Covers events for the years 1938-1945.

34   U.S. Office of Naval History. **Chronology of the Navy's War in the**

Pacific, World War II. Washington, U.S. Office of Naval History, 1947. 116p.
A useful chronology with emphasis, of course, on the navy's role.

35   Williams, Mary H., comp. **Chronology, 1941-1945**. Washington, Office of the Chief of Military History, Department of Army, 1960. 660p.
Chronology of the war with emphasis on the activities of the U.S. Army.

Encyclopedias

36   Dupuy, Richard Ernest, and Trevor N. Dupuy. **The Encyclopedia of Military History: From 3500 B.C. to the Present**. New York, Harper & Row, 1970. 1,406p. Bibliog.
A comprehensive work with information on all aspects of military history. Two sections are devoted to World War II: "World War II in the West" and "World War II in Asia and the Pacific." Brief descriptions are given for important events and battles. Includes a select bibliography.

Language and Code Names

37   Greet, William Cabell. **World Words, Recommended Pronunciations**. 2nd ed., rev. and enl. New York, Columbia University Press, 1948. 608p.
Lists some 12,000 names, places, battles, geographic terms, and air force objectives with their recommended pronunciations. All terms are associated with the war. This work is an expansion of the author's earlier work, *War Words*.

38   Partridge, Eric, ed. **A Dictionary of Forces' Slang, 1939-1945**. Freeport, N.Y., Books for Libraries, 1970. 212p.
This volume is divided into three sections: "Naval Slang," by Wilfred Granville, "Army Slang," by Frank Roberts, and "Air Force Slang," by Eric Partridge. This book is a reprint edition of a work first published in 1948.

39   Ruffner, Frederick G., and Robert C. Thomas, eds. **Code Names Dictionary: A Guide to Code Names, Slang, Nicknames, Journalese, and Similar Terms**. Detroit, Gale Research, 1963. 555p.
An indispensible guide for locating information on many of the official code names used during the war. Besides official code names many unofficial nicknames for military operations and geographic areas are included.

40   Taylor, Anna Marjorie, comp. **The Language of World War II: Abbreviations, Captions, Quotations, Slogans, Titles, and Other Terms and Phrases**. Rev. and enl. ed. New York, H. W. Wilson, 1948. 265p.
An excellent work which attempts to be comprehensive in its coverage.

Sources

41   Langsam, Walter Consuelo, ed. **Historic Documents of World War II**. Princeton, N.J., Van Nostrand, 1958. 192p.
Contains 47 important documents relating to some aspect of the war. Includes

"treaties, pacts, laws, decrees, governmental acts, armistices," and other types of documents. Examples of documents are "The Naming of the War," "Assumption of Power by Donitz," "Four Freedoms Speech," and the "Italian Peace Treaty."

42   U.S. Congress. Senate. Committee on Foreign Relations. **A Decade of American Foreign Policy: Basic Documents, 1941-49.** Washington, Government Printing Office, 1950. 1,381 p.

A selective compilation of documents relating to U.S. foreign policy. There are 313 documents included, most of which relate to the war. A convenient source for many important wartime documents. Some examples of documents are "Armistice with Rumania, September 12, 1944," "Rio de Janeiro Meeting of the Ministers of Foreign Affairs of the American Republics, January 15-28, 1942," and "Zones of Occupation and the Administration of the City of Vienna . . . July 9, 1945."

Statistics

43   Gt. Brit. Central Statistical Office. **Statistical Digest of the War.** London, Her Majesty's Stationary Office, 1951. 247 p.

A compilation of social, economic and military statistics relating to the war years, September 1939-August 1945. Some topics covered include manpower, vital statistics, social conditions, fuel and power, production, and many others.

44   U.S. Bureau of the Census. **Statistical Abstract of the United States.** Washington, Government Printing Office, 1878– .

An annual summary of important statistical data supplied by all the statistical agencies of the United States government and by some private agencies. The statistics are arranged in 33 broad categories, and the emphasis is on national statistics rather than state or local statistics. The statistics usually include current data and retrospective data for 15 to 30 years. Useful for wartime statistical date for the United States.

Yearbooks

45   **The Annual Register of World Events: A Review of the Year.** London, New York, Longmans, Green, 1758–.

An annual general review of world events. Includes summaries of events and developments for most countries. Particularly good coverage of Great Britain and the Commonwealth countries. The arrangement is alphabetical by country.

46   **Brassey's Annual: The Armed Forces Yearbook.** New York, Praeger, 1886– .

A standard yearbook of military affairs. This work is especially useful for the war years. Includes articles on all aspects of the war, on technical naval problems, statistics of all kinds, and pictures and silhouettes of ships. From 1936 to 1949 the title was *Brassey's Naval Annual.*

47   **The Statesman's Yearbook: Statistical and Historical Annual of the States of the World.** New York, St. Martin's Press, 1864– .

An annual publication giving detailed information about important events and the government of most countries. A brief history of the country is given along with relevant data on area, population, religion, education, judicial system, finance, defense, agriculture, industry, commerce, etc. Includes select bibliographies.

48   **World Almanac and Book of Facts.** New York, World Telegram, 1868-1966; New York, Doubleday, 1960– .

One of the best known ready reference books. Includes a variety of statistical information on industry, agriculture, government, education, etc. Most statistical information is for the United States. It can be especially useful for its chronology of events for the preceding year and for lists of world leaders and rulers.

CHAPTER 2–PRE-WAR YEARS, 1919-1939

GENERAL HISTORIES, 1919-1941

49   Armstrong, Hamilton Fish. **Peace and Counterpeace: From Wilson to Hitler; Memoirs of Hamilton Fish Armstrong.** New York, Harper & Row, 1971. 585p. Bibliog.
The editor of *Foreign Affairs* relates of his contacts with many of the leading political personalities of the 1920s and 1930s with assessments of these figures and the events they helped shape. Included are detailed accounts of his interviews with Hitler and Mussolini in 1933 and his travels in Eastern Europe, especially the Balkans.

50   Arndt, H. W. **The Economic Lessons of the Nineteen Thirties.** Issued under the auspices of the Royal Institute of International Affairs. London, Oxford University Press, 1944. 314p.
A discussion of the interdependence of international and national economics through detailed studies of U.S., British, German and French economics in the 1930s. Stressed are the causes, effects and lessons of pre-war economic developments among the great powers.

51   Carr, Edward Hallett. **International Relations Between the Two World Wars, 1919-1939.** London, Macmillan, 1947. 302p. Maps.
A compact survey and interpretation from the European and British point of view of international relations in the interwar era. The study is divided into four sections: 1) the period of enforcement and alliances from 1920 to 1924; 2) the period of pacification and the League of Nations spanning 1924 to 1930; 3) the period of crisis and return to power politics in the years 1930 to 1933; and 4) the re-emergence of Germany and the end of the treaties which dominated the years from 1933 to 1939.

52   Carr, Edward Hallett. **The Twenty Years' Crisis, 1919-1939: An Introduction to the Study of International Relations.** 2nd ed. London, Macmillan and Co., Ltd., 1946. 243p. Bibliog.
Presenting a wealth of historical evidence, the author discusses the relationship of power to morality in international relations. Nationalism is seen to be the dominant force in international society. This is a stimulating study on the theories, principles and practices of international affairs and their relation to geographical, economic and political factors.

53   Carsten, Francis Ludwig. **The Rise of Fascism.** Berkeley, University of California Press, 1967. 256p. Bibliog.
A good study on the origins of fascism and its development, especially during the 1920s and 1930s. The principal countries considered are Italy and Germany, but several other European countries with fascist movements are also discussed. The reasons for its success or failure in various countries are investigated and related to prior intellectual and political doctrines versus existing social and economic conditions.

54   Cave, Floyd Augustine, and associates. **The Origins and Consequences of World War II.** New York, Dryden Press, 1948. 820p. Maps. Bibliog.
Examines the economic and political affairs which contributed to the causes of the Second World War. The causes of the First World War and the resultant treaties are discussed as a background to the events precipitating the second major world conflict.

55   Churchill, Winston Leonard Spender. **The Gathering Storm.** Boston, Houghton Mifflin, 1948. 784p. Maps.
Volume one of his work on the Second World War, this is one of the outstanding documents of the time. It carries a profound sense of history and a brilliant gift for language. The first part covers the years 1919-1939 and is a narration of the mistakes of the Allies after the First World War, the rise and rearmament of Germany and Italy, the Spanish Civil War and its consequences, and the lack of resolution to protect Austria and prevent the dismemberment of Czechoslovakia. The second part covers the period of the phoney war of 1939-1940 and emphasizes military developments.

56   Colvin, Ian Goodhope. **None So Blind: A British Diplomatic View of the Origins of World War II.** New York, Harcourt, Brace and World, 1965. 360p. Bibliog.
Based on the papers of Sir Robert Vansittart, the British Permanent Under-Secretary of State for Foreign Affairs, 1930-1938, this is a description of the intricate diplomatic involvements in Europe during the period of his tenure in office. This survey on the causes of World War II also discusses Vansittart's opinions and their lack of effect on the Foreign Office.

57   Craig, Gordon Alexander, and Felix Gilbert. **The Diplomats: 1919-1939.** Princeton, Princeton University Press, 1953. 700p. Bibliog.
An authoritative commentary on the methods and activities of the diplomats in the conduct of international relations during the interwar period. Provides an increased understanding of the diplomats' role in policy making and in their efforts to achieve these goals.

58   Delzell, Charles F., comp. **Mediterranean Fascism, 1919-1945.** New York, Walker, 1971. 364p. Bibliog.
A documentary history of the advent and course of fascism in Italy, Spain and Portugal. Connecting notes and narrative place the selections in their proper historic context. The Italian section includes documents and speeches from the birth of fascism through its successive paths to totalitarianism and its end in the Italian Social Republic. The Spanish Falange movement is carried from its inception and subordination by Franco during the Spanish Civil War to its problems with the Axis in World War II. Portugal's smaller section sets forth the dictator Salazar's political and economic philosophy of his clerico-cooperative government.

59   Eubank, Keith. **The Origins of World War II.** New York, Crowell, 1969. 194p. Bibliog. Pap.
This is a good basic study of the origins of World War II. Two of the author's

main theses are that people were under the illusion that they were safe from a world war due to the security of the League of Nations and various international treaties and that appeasement rose out of public demand to avoid war at almost all cost.

60   Eubank, Keith, comp. **The Road to World War II: A Documentary History**. New York, Crowell, 1973. 284p. Bibliog.
A representative selection of pertinent documents indicating policy decisions, recording negotiations and disclosing plans, all serving to provide a background to the events which led to World War II. This work is primarily intended to supplement the author's *Origins of World War II*. The documents are each prefaced with an explanatory introduction and many also have a brief analysis at the end.

61   Gantenbein, James Watson, ed. **Documentary Background of World War II, 1931-1941**. New York, Columbia University Press, 1948. 1122p.
Traces the story of the foreign policies of the United States, the leading European states and the League of Nations through official publications, diplomatic correspondence and speeches of major political personages.

62   Gathorne-Hardy, Geoffrey M. **A Short History of International Affairs, 1920-1939**. 4th ed. London, Oxford University Press, 1950. 540p. Map.
Considered to be one of the best summaries of international relations between the two world wars.

63   Gatzke, Hans Wilhelm, ed. **European Diplomacy Between Two Wars, 1919-1939**. Chicago, Quadrangle Books, 1972. 277p.
A collection of essays previously published in scholarly journals and books focusing on the key events and major issues of interwar diplomacy. Most of the essays involve Germany and its foreign policy in the 1920s and 1930s.

64   Germany. Auswartiges Amt. **Documents on German Foreign Policy, 1918-1945, from the Archives of the German Foreign Ministry**. Washington, GPO, 1949-1966. (Series C: January 30-Aug 1937; 5 vols. out of 6 published to date, Series D: September 1937-Dec 1941, 13 vols.)
The title is somewhat misleading since the English translation only covers the period from January 30, 1933, to December 1941, after the declaration of war on the U.S. by Germany. The documents are from the captured archives of the German Foreign Ministry and the Reich Chancellery. They establish the record of German foreign policy and serve as source material for the pre-war period as far as the English translation is concerned. They are printed in chronological order with a topical list at the beginning of each volume.

65   Great Britain. Foreign Office. **Documents on British Foreign Policy, 1919-1939**. London, H.M. Stationery Office, 1946-1961. 43v. Maps.
The most important documents in the British Foreign Office archives relating to foreign policy between 1919 and 1939 have been selected for this comprehensive series. The emphasis is on a subject arrangement but the documents do cover given periods of time from the signature of the Treaty of Peace on June 28, 1919, to the declaration of war upon Germany on September 3, 1939.

66 Haines, Charles Grove, and Ross J. S. Hoffman. **Origins and Background of the Second World War.** 2nd ed. New York, Oxford University Press, 1947. 729p. Maps, Bibliog.
Covering the period from 1900 through 1941, the authors summarize the political conditions and events leading to World War II. This is an authoritative and well-balanced work showing the effects and repercussions of the new European ideologies of fascism, national socialism and communism on international affairs.

67 Howe, Quincy. **The World Between the Wars: From the 1918 Armistice to the Munich Agreement.** New York, Simon and Schuster, 1953. 784p. Maps, Bibliog.
A review of the changes in the old order and of the influences and the effects of new ideologies. A well reasoned analysis with vivid sketches of the major personalities.

68 Lafore, Laurence Davis. **The End of Glory: An Interpretation of the Origins of World War II.** Philadelphia, J. B. Lippincott Co., 1972. 280p. Bibliog.
The author contends that it was a crisis in the operation of the European state system in that the smaller states were still under the impression of the myth of their individual supremacy to determine international events. That it was this crisis rather than German aggression or a failure of the democracies to stand up to the totalitarian states that brought about the subsequent conflict. He further contends that French weakness and indecision was a key to the breakdown in the European system.

69 Langer, Robert. **Seizure of Territory: The Stimson Doctrine and Related Principles of Legal Theory and Diplomatic Practice.** Princeton, N.J., Princeton University Press, 1947. 313p. Bibliog.
The doctrine's purpose was to deny diplomatic recognition of territorial changes as a result of force or the threat of it. A detailed study of the failure of this principle in discouraging aggression.

70 Lee, Dwight Erwin. **Ten Years: The World on the Way to War, 1930-1940.** Boston, Houghton Mifflin, 1942. 443p. Maps, Bibliog.
A careful and coherent record of the main diplomatic and political events of the decade. Somewhat chronological rather than interpretive, it does provide, however, an analytical clarification of the immediate causes of the war.

71 Mosley, Leonard. **On Borrowed Time: How World War II Began.** New York, Random House, 1969. 509p. Maps, Bibliog.
A narrative of the diplomatic, political and military events and moves between Munich and the outbreak of war by the chief correspondent for the *London Sunday Times.* The author feels that stupidity, cowardice and petty self-interest caused many opportunities to which the western powers could have acted and reacted against totalitarian pressure, to be ignored or mismanaged. The policies of appeasement of Britain and France are seen to have been one of the major causes of the war.

72   Namier, Lewis Bernstein. **Diplomatic Prelude, 1938-1939**. London,
        Macmillan, 1948. 502p.
Diplomatic history of the period between Munich and the outbreak of World
War II. The classic study is based on official collections of documents, memoirs and
newspaper reports from the United States and Great Britain.

73   Namier, Lewis Bernstein. **Europe in Decay: A Study in Disintegra-
        tion, 1936-1940**. London, Macmillan, 1950. 329p.
A collection of book review essays and summaries of documents important for an
understanding of European diplomacy. They consist of material published since
the author's book *Diplomatic Prelude, 1938-1939*.

74   Newman, Karl John. **European Democracy Between the Wars**. Translated
        by Kenneth Morgan. London, Allen and Unwin, 1970. 475p. Bibliog.
The conflict of political ideologies in Europe is laid to the basic differences
between the aims of the democracies and national socialism and nazism. The total
breakdown of the democracies is seen to be due to their failure to recognize the
danger and threat of totalitarianism.

75   Newman, William J. **The Balance of Power in the Interwar Years, 1919-
        1939**. New York, Random House, 1968. 239p. Bibliog.
An in-depth study of the balance of power in Europe with special emphasis on the
Locarno Pact of 1925 to its collapse in the 1930s. The complexities of balance of
power politics and some of its features are seen in the light of the negotiations
between the states that produced varying degrees of this balance.

76   Nolte, Ernest. **Three Faces of Fascism: Action Francaise, Italian Fascism,
        National Socialism**. Translated from the German by Leila Vennewitz. New
        York, Holt, Rinehart and Winston, 1966. 561p. Bibliog.
A study of the three major fascist movements of the 1920 and 1930s stressing
their conservative nationalism and anti-Marxist doctrine. Describes the intellectual
origins, economic, social, and political institutions and the psychological motivations of these different fascist movements.

77   Orton, William Aylott. **Twenty Years' Armistice 1918-1938**. New York,
        Farrar and Rinehart, Inc., 1938. 305p. Maps, Bibliog.
Concentrating on central and eastern Europe this is a review of the situation in
Europe, the years under the Versailles Treaty. The author assumes that Chamber-
lain's peace with honor was necessary.

78   Rappard, William Emmanuel. **The Quest for Peace Since the World War**.
        Cambridge, Mass., Harvard University Press, 1940. 516p.
Traces the quest for peace through the twenty years from its evolution during
World War I, its handling at the Peace Conference and its post-war developments.
Presents this quest in relation to three major ideas on which the League of Nations
stood, that of arbitration, collective security and disarmament. Criticizes the
concepts of neutrality and isolation as bringing upon many peoples the specter of
war and loss of freedom.

79   Renouvin, Pierre. **World War II and Its Origins: International Relations,**
      1929-1945. Translated by Remy Inglis Hall. New York, Harper and Row,
      1969. 402p. Bibliog.
Good insight into the origins of World War II by a French diplomatic historian.
He presents stimulating hypotheses in his explanations, with critical interpreta-
tions of the reactions of the major powers in regard to their diplomatic negotiations.

80   Robertson, Esmonde Manning, comp. **Origins of the Second World War:**
      Historical Interpretations. London, Macmillan, 1971. 312p. Bibliog.
A collection of essays occasioned by the publication of A. J. P. Taylor's *The
Origins of the Second World War.* The Ethiopian crisis and Japanese foreign policy
are just two of the areas covered. There is also a discussion of the range of materials
open to historians and the areas still to be explored.

81   Salvemini, Gaetano. **Prelude to World War II.** Garden City, N.Y., Double-
      day, 1954 (i.e., 1953). 519p. Bibliog.
A critical survey of international relations in Europe with special emphasis on the
period between Italy's role in the Corfu incident in 1923 and her invasion of
Ethiopia in 1935. The author castigates those foreign governments and international leaders who either just stood by or actively helped keep Mussolini in power.

82   Schuman, Frederick Lewis. **Europe on the Eve: The Crisis of Diplomacy,**
      1933-1939. New York, Knopf, 1939. 573p. Map, Bibliog.
The history of Europe from the rise of Hitler in 1933 to January 1939. Stimulating
analysis of Great Britain's position, Germany's plans, the Soviet Union's policy and
the position of the central European states.

83   Sontag, Raymond James. **A Broken World, 1919-1939.** New York, Harper
      and Row, 1971. 415p. Maps, Bibliog.
An excellent work centering around the thesis that World War I created an era of
violence and upheaval spawning totalitarian states which the democracies found
themselves in confrontation with. Includes social and economic developments with
excellent discussions of the Paris Peace Conference, the Czechoslovak crisis,
Hitler's objectives, Soviet foreign policy and their relation to the causes of World
War II.

84   Taylor, Alan John Percivale. **The Origins of the Second World War.** 2nd
      ed. with a reply to the critics. Greenwich, Conn., Fawcett Publications,
      1966. 304p. Maps.
A revisionist account of the causes of World War II. The primary thesis is that
Hitler did not wish war but only a peaceful revision of the Treaty of Versailles.
This is a vigorous rebuttal against past indictments of Hitler as having the over-
whelming war guilt. Considers that blunders were made by both sides and that
Chamberlain and Halifax for Britain and Daladier and Bonnet for France were
responsible for the eventual destiny of Europe while minimizing Hitler's role.

85   Thorne, Christopher G. **The Approach of War, 1938-1939.** New York,
      St. Martin's Press, 1967. 232p. Maps, Bibliog.

Well documented coverage of the diplomatic activity in the two years preceding World War II. Examines the motives, character, strengths and weaknesses of the leaders of Europe. Reassesses Hitler's opportunities and methods in terms of the policies of appeasement of the West.

86   Wiskemann, Elizabeth. **Europe of the Dictators, 1919-1945**. New York, Harper and Row, 1966. 287p. Maps, Bibliog.

A brief study of the political and diplomatic history of Europe. The primary emphasis is on central European developments with only those dictators pictured who were prominent during the period covered.

SPECIAL TOPICS

Treaty of Versailles, 1919

87   Birdsall, Paul. **Versailles Twenty Years After**. New York, Reynal and Hitchcock, 1941. 350p. Bibliog.

A well documented and comprehensive discussion of the Treaty, the forces which shaped its general character and the personal and political factors which determined its subsequent effects.

88   Headlam-Morley, James. **A Memoir of the Paris Peace Conference, 1919**. London, Methuen & Co. Ltd., 1972. 230p. Bibliog.

The experiences and reflections of a number of the British Delegation to the Paris Peace Conference. He was actively involved in most of the important and controversial problems of territorial settlements in regard to Germany, the Saar, Danzig and the Polish corridor. The book includes a useful appendix of biographical information of many of the lesser known participants.

89   Keynes, John Maynard. **The Economic Consequences of the Peace**. New York, Harcourt, Brace and Howe, 1920. 298p.

A prophetic criticism of the impracticability of the economic terms of the Peace Treaty, especially in its lack of provisions for the economic reintegration and rehabilitation of Europe. He discusses the difficulties of imposing huge reparation payments and the failure to keep the terms from being politically dominated by an atmosphere of revenge.

90   Luckau, Alma Maria. **The German Delegation at the Paris Peace Conference**. New York, Columbia University Press, 1941. 522p. Bibliog.

A comprehensive presentation with documentation of German preparation and attitudes regarding the Peace Conference. A scholarly survey that had the help of a former Chief Justice of Germany who was also the Commissioner-General of the German delegation.

91   Mantoux, Etienne. . . . **The Carthaginian Peace: Or the Economic Consequences of Mr. Keynes**. London, Oxford University Press, 1946. 210p. Bibliog.

The author attempts to show with relevant facts and figures how, in his view,

Mr. Keynes misinterpreted the effects of the Versailles Treaty. This is a political rather than an economic work that maintains that Mr. Keynes' thesis was an important factor in causing World War II due to the subsequent scaling down of the stringent measures of the Peace Treaty.

92   Mayer, Arno J. **Politics and Diplomacy of Peacemaking: Containment and Counterrevolution at Versailles, 1918-1919.** New York, Knopf, 1967. 918p. Map, Bibliog.

An account of the drafting of the Treaty and of the pitfalls, distractions and movements influencing the decisions made by the Big Four (Wilson, Lloyd George, Clemenceau and Orlando) at the Paris Peace Conference. The interplay of domestic and foreign policies of the Allies in relation to each other and to the underlying structure of Europe is described in detail.

93   Nicolson, Harold George. **Peacemaking 1919.** New York, Harcourt, Brace, 1939. 378p.

An indictment of the victors and their peace by a member of the British delegation. In a tone of objectivity the author recreates the realistic impression of the confusion, disorganization, mistakes and misunderstandings during the intense conflicts of national emotions.

94   Tillman, Seth P. **Anglo-American Relations at the Paris Peace Conference of 1919.** Princeton, N.J., Princeton University Press, 1961. 442p. Bibliog.

The patterns of Anglo-American conflict and cooperation which were to manifest themselves again in the post-Versailles years had their start in large part at the Paris Peace Conference. Areas of cooperation centered around the measures to maintain a permanent peace through an ordered society and peaceful redress of grievances. Fundamental conflicts related to sea power, colonies and mandates and reparations and economic settlements.

League of Nations

95   Barros, James. **Betrayal from Within: Joseph Avenol, Secretary-General of the League of Nations, 1933-1940.** New Haven, Yale University Press, 1969. 289p. Bibliog.

The author attributes many of the weaknesses and failures of the League of Nations to the ideological motives and reactions of the Secretary General, Joseph Avenol. The book provides a chronological examination of the major crises faced by the League and the blunders and incompetence it was subjected to.

96   Dexter, Byron Vinson. **The Years of Opportunity: The League of Nations, 1920-1926.** New York, Viking Press, 1967. 264p. Map, Bibliog.

Emphasizes the mechanizations of the European powers more than the functioning of the League of Nations. The main theme is that it was an effective organization with its share of successes and failures but that it was weakened by the Locarno Treaties.

97   Fleming, Denna Frank. **The United States and the League of Nations, 1918-1920.** New York, G. P. Putnam's Sons, 1932. 559p. Bibliog.

A detailed documented study of the struggle of President Wilson to establish the League and to convince the U.S. Senate to approve U.S. membership. Records the parts played for and against the League by the major American political figures of the period.

98   Fleming, Denna Frank. **The United States and World Organization, 1920-1933.** New York, Columbia University Press, 1938. 569p. Bibliog.
An extended carefully documented account of the various crises in the life of the League, during the crucial period covered by the book, as centered around the League and U.S. policies toward it.

99   Walters, Francis Paul. **A History of the League of Nations.** London, Oxford University Press, 1952. 2v.
A definitive history of the League of Nations from its founding in 1919 to 1946. The account of the organization's political accomplishments, frustrations and failures is by a member of the League's Secretariat.

100   Zimmern, Alfred Eckhard. **The League of Nations and the Rule of Law, 1918-1935.** New York, Russell and Russell, 1969, 542p.
A discussion of the successful accomplishments in the economic and social areas of the work of the League, examines it in the context of the international relations of this period and shows the influence of war-time ideas upon its subsequent activities. This is a reprint of the 1939 edition.

Disarmament and Arms Limitations

101   Hoag, Charles Leonard. **Preface to Preparedness: The Washington Disarmament Conference and Public Opinion.** Washington, American Council on Public Affairs, 1941. 205p. Bibliog.
A study of the Washington Conference on the Limitation of Armament of 1921-1922 and its basic presuppositions such as the probability of war is in proportion to armaments. The work traces the development of U.S. public opinion on disarmament and its relation to the Conference.

102   Morgan, John Hartman. **Assize of Arms: The Disarmament of Germany and Her Rearmament (1919-1939).** New York, Oxford University Press, 1946. 357p. Map, Bibliog.
One of the best accounts on the revival of German militarism, the tactics of the Reichswehr during the crises of the early 1920s, and the efforts of the Germans to deceive on compliance with disarmament. General Morgan was a British member of the Inter-Allied Commission of Control in Germany from 1919 to 1923.

103   O'Connor, Raymond Gish. **Perilous Equilibrium: The United States and the London Naval Conference of 1930.** Lawrence, University of Kansas Press, 1962. 188p.
The limited success of the approach to arms control is shown to be due to inherent difficulties and inadequacies of effective supervision and control. The situation in the Pacific was only temporarily stabilized. Continental Europe was a different

matter and the competitive arms race continued due to a somewhat lessened reliance on the need for sea power for security.

104   Roskill, Stephen Wentworth. **Naval Policy Between the Wars**. London, Collins, 1968. 639p. Maps, Bibliog.
This, the first of two volumes, covers the period from 1919 to 1929 and is by one of Great Britain's outstanding naval historians. Based on official British records, it details the efforts to limit armaments and prevent aggressive war by the Western democracies. The author provides concise portraits of the personalities involved in Anglo-American naval competition and discusses the struggle for control of British naval air power between the Air Ministry and the Admiralty.

105   Tate, Merze. **United States and Armaments**. Cambridge, Harvard University Press, 1948. 312p. Bibliog.
A scholarly study of U.S. participation in disarmament conferences with special emphasis on the naval conferences from 1921-22 to 1935-36.

106   Wheeler-Bennett, John Wheeler. **Disarmament and Security Since Locarno, 1925-1931: Being the Political and Technical Background of the General Disarmament Conference, 1932**. London, G. Allen & Unwin, 1932. 383p.
A clear and unbiased portrayal of each stage in the long development toward disarmament since 1925. The political and technical background of the Geneva conference includes accounts of the 1930 London Naval Conference and the work of the Security and Arbitration Committee of the League of Nations from 1927 to 1930.

107   Wheeler-Bennett, John Wheeler. **Information on the Reduction of Armaments**. London, G. Allen and Unwin, 1925. 216p. Bibliog.
A history of the multi-faceted movements for arms limitation during the period 1919 to 1925. The events span the time from the Paris Peace Conference to the eve of the Locarno Conference and include the Washington Naval Conference of 1921-1922 and the early attempts of the League of Nations to guarantee the world's security by peaceful adjustments of disputes.

108   Wheeler-Bennett, John Wheeler. **The Pipe Dream of Peace: The Story of the Collapse of Disarmament**. New York, W. Morrow and Company, 1935. 302p.
A thorough documentation and account of the General Disarmament Conference which opened in 1932 and the international negotiations which bear upon it. Describes the conflict of forces which caused the repeated failures of the deliberations and resultant impasse.

German Reparations

109   Felix, David. **Walter Rathenau and the Weimar Republic: The Politics of Reparations**. Baltimore, Johns Hopkins Press, 1971. 210p. Bibliog.
A description of the controversial German reparations problem and of the resulting international conferences and negotiations. The efforts of the German Reconstruction Minister and subsequent Foreign Minister to build up trade surpluses in order

to enable Germany to pay reparations within the framework of a stable economy
are detailed.

110   Wheeler-Bennett, John Wheeler. **The Wreck of Reparations: Being the
        Political Background of the Lausanne Agreement, 1932.** London, G.
        Allen and Unwin, 1933. 295p. Bibliog.
A summary of events from the Hague Conference of 1930 to the Lausanne Agreement of 1932 showing the causes of the breakdown of reparations and the interrelationship of the attendant political problems.

Occupation of the Ruhr, 1923

111   Schmidt, Royal Jae. **Versailles and the Ruhr: Seedbed of World War II.**
        The Hague, Martinus Nijhoff, 1968. 320p. Bibliog.
A major premise of this work is that the occupation of Germany's Ruhr in 1923,
mainly by France, was instrumental in shaping the attitudes of Germany in future
European policies and actions. The book discusses the applications of the reparations clause of the Peace Treaty to the Ruhr question and the significance of this
geographical area to the economic and political situation of Europe.

Corfu Incident, 1923

112   Barros, James. **The Corfu Incident of 1923: Mussolini and the League of
        Nations.** Princeton, N.J., Princeton University Press, 1965. 339p. Maps,
        Bibliog.
A detailed analysis of the occupation of the Greek island of Corfu by Mussolini and
the negotiations and actions among the major European countries and the League
of Nations resulting in a peaceful settlement of the crisis.

Locarno Conference, 1925

113   Jacobson, Jon. **Locarno Diplomacy: Germany and the West, 1925-1929.**
        Princeton, N.J., Princeton University Press, 1972. 420p. Bibliog.
Explores the fundamental rivalries, objectives and strategies of France, Great
Britain and Germany with an historical interpretation of the roles of these respec-
tive countries in the diplomacy of the 1920s. The author presents the main points
of conflict and focuses on the differing objectives of the main personalities involved.

Kellogg-Briand Pact, 1928

114   Ferrell, Robert H. **Peace in Their Time: The Origins of the Kellogg-
        Briand Pact.** New Haven, Yale University Press, 1952. 293p. Bibliog.
A penetrating history of the Pact, and the shrewd self-serving diplomacy supported
by a naive public seeking peace which produced this treaty to outlaw war.

115   Shotwell, James Thomson. **War As an Instrument of National Policy and
        Its Renunciation in the Pact of Paris.** New York, Harcourt, Brace and
        Co., 1929. 310p.
One of the best analyses of the Pact, its diplomatic history and its implications

especially in the fact that wars become a means of national self-destruction. The appendices list the official papers bearing on the Pact.

116   Wheeler-Bennett, John Wheeler. **Information on the Renunciation of War, 1927-1928.** London, G. Allen and Unwin, 1928. 191p.
An account of events leading up to the Pact of Paris and worldwide opinion to this, then, new standard of international conduct.

Japan and Manchuria, 1931-1932

117   Bassett, Reginald. **Democracy and Foreign Policy; A Case History: The Sino-Japanese Dispute, 1931-1933.** New York, Longmans, Green, 1952. 654p. Bibliog.
Using the Sino-Japanese conflict as a case history the author shows the effect of British public opinion on foreign policy in the lack of support for sanctions against the Japanese.

118   Jones, Francis Clifford. **Manchuria Since 1931.** London, Royal Institute of International Affairs, 1949. 256p. Map, Bibliog.
An emphasis on the international developments concerning Japan's establishment of its vassal state of Manchukuo.

119   Ogata, Sadako. **Defiance in Manchuria: The Making of Japanese Foreign Policy, 1931-1932.** Berkeley, University of California Press, 1964. 259p. Map, Bibliog.
A discerning analysis of the origins, nature and effects of the Manchurian conflict. Discusses the military radicalism in the Japanese officer corps and the evolvement of Japan's Pan Asian ideology which became the rationale for its imperialistic policies.

120   Smith, Sara Rector. **The Manchurian Crisis, 1931-32: A Tragedy in International Relations.** New York, Columbia University Press, 1948. 281p. Map, Bibliog.
Based on official documents this is a detailed study of the events culminating in the Mukden incident and the subsequent armed conflict of the Japanese and the Chinese. Especial attention is given to the policies of the U.S. and the League of Nations in the crisis.

121   Snow, Edgar. **Far Eastern Front.** New York, H. Smith & R. Haas, 1933. 336p. Map, Bibliog.
A condemnation of Japanese imperialism in Manchuria. This is an eyewitness and graphic account of the undeclared war waged by Japan against China from the Mukden incident to the Tangku armistice.

122   Thorne, Christopher. **The Limits of Foreign Policy: The West, the League and the Far Eastern Crisis of 1931-1933.** London, Hamilton, 1972. 442p. Maps, Bibliog.
A comprehensive assessment of the events leading to Japan's conquest of Manchuria and of the subsequent international repercussions. Extensive footnotes

support detailed evaluations of the foreign policies of Great Britain, France, the U.S., China and Japan in regards to the crisis. The author contends that Japan's defiant action was a major turning point in the decline of the West's influence and power in Asia.

123   Willoughby, Westel Woodbury. **The Sino-Japanese Controversy and the League of Nations.** Baltimore, Johns Hopkins Press, 1935. 733p. Bibliog.
A detailed analysis of the Manchurian incident, the Lytton report on it and the resultant international crisis with an emphasis on the actions of the League of Nations.

124   Yoshihashi, Takehiko. **Conspiracy at Mukden: The Rise of the Japanese Military.** New Haven, Yale University Press, 1963. 274p. Maps, Bibliog.
Based on Japanese and English language sources, this is a description of the Mukden incident and the subsequent seizure of power by the Japanese in Manchuria.

Four-Power Pact, 1933

125   Jarausch, Konrad Hugo. **The Four Power Pact, 1933.** Madison, State Historical Society of Wisconsin for Department of History, University of Wisconsin, 1965. 265p. Bibliog.
An account of early attempts to placate Hitler and Mussolini by Britain and France in spite of double dealing on the part of the dictators. France is pictured as depending on Great Britain to solve its problems in these matters and Britain continues to rely on the premise of signed agreements between gentlemen.

Saar Plebiscite, 1935

126   Wambaugh, Sarah. **The Saar Plebiscite, with a Collection of Official Documents.** Cambridge, Mass., Harvard University Press, 1940. 489p. Maps, Bibliog.
A well documented study dealing with the administration of the Saar by the League of Nations and its eventual transfer back to Germany.

Italo-Ethiopian War, 1935-1936

127   Baer, George W. **The Coming of the Italian-Ethiopian War.** Cambridge, Mass., Harvard University Press, 1967. 404p. Map, Bibliog.
A scholarly study of the origins of the conflict in the context of the political, diplomatic, and military decisions of Europe's borders. Examines Italy's preparation for the war and Ethiopia's defense efforts.

128   Barker, A. J. **The Civilizing Mission: A History of the Italo-Ethiopian War of 1935-1936.** New York, Dial Press, 1968. 383p. Maps, Bibliog.
The book deals with the international diplomacy and the military aspects of the crisis, examines its causes and details the consequences. The ineffectiveness of the League of Nations and the concomitant diplomatic maneuvers of Great Britain and France are also studied.

129   Boca, Angelo del. **The Ethiopian War, 1935-1941**. Translated by P. D.
       Cummins. Chicago, University of Chicago Press, 1969. 289p. Maps, Bibliog.
The author draws upon personal experience and uses numerous interviews to describe the war itself. He shows a genuine feeling for Ethiopia and its people.

130   Dugan, James, and Laurence Lafore. **Days of Emperor and Clown: The
       Italo-Ethiopian War, 1935-1936**. Garden City, N.Y., Doubleday, 1973.
       382p. Map, Bibliog.
A work of military, political and social history relating the events that played a
significant role in shaping opinions which determined subsequent maneuverings of
world leaders. The specific reasons for Mussolini's war to inspire respect for his
government are detailed against a background of Ethiopian history.

131   Harris, Brice. **The United States and the Italo-Ethiopian Crisis**. Stanford,
       Calif., Stanford University Press, 1964. 187p. Bibliog.
A well documented narrative of the role of the United States in the conflict and
its attempts to cooperate with the League of Nations on the matter of sanctions in
the face of continued U.S. isolationist policies.

132   Laurens, Franklin D. **France and the Italo-Ethiopian Crisis 1935-1936**. The
       Hague, Mouton, 1967, 1968. 432p. Bibliog.
A day-by-day account of the crisis, giving its diplomatic background, the reactions
of the League of Nations, and British and French public opinion. Studies the role
of the French government and the impact of the crisis on its internal affairs and on
its position internationally.

Spanish Civil War, 1936-1939

133   Bowers, Claude Gernade. **My Mission to Spain: Watching the Rehearsal for
       World War II**. New York, Simon and Schuster, 1954. 437p.
The U.S. Ambassador to Spain from 1933 to 1939 recounts his impressions of
Spain's leaders under the stress of events and of the establishment of Franco Spain.

134   Brome, Vincent. **The International Brigades: Spain, 1936-1939**. New
       York, Morrow, 1966. 317p. Map, Bibliog.
The story of the foreign volunteers of the international Loyalist (Republican)
brigades in the Spanish Civil War, as seen through their eyes, in their battles with
Franco's Nationalist forces.

135   Broue, Pierre, and Emile Temime. **The Revolution and the Civil War in
       Spain**. Cambridge, M.I.T. Press, 1973. 413p.
First appearing in French in 1961, the authors describe the domestic politics and
foreign policies and alignments of France and Great Britain as they related to
Spain. Also well treated are the descriptions of Spanish labor organizations,
anarchistic trends and the Loyalist war effort.

136   Carr, Raymond, ed. **The Republic and the Civil War in Spain**. New York,
       St. Martin's Press, 1971. 275p. Bibliog.

The problems of rival armies and foreign intervention, the non-intervention and anarchist agrarian movements, and the role of Spain's political parties in the Civil War are among the topics covered in this study.

137   Cattell, David Tredwell. **Communism and the Spanish Civil War.** Berkeley, University of California Press, 1955. 290p. Bibliog.
The first part in a two-part study of the extent and nature of the Soviet Union's intervention and participation in the Civil War.

138   Cattell, David Tredwell. **Soviet Diplomacy and the Spanish Civil War.** Berkeley, University of California Press, 1957. 204p. Bibliog.
The second part in a two-part study of the Soviet Union's actions during the Spanish Civil War in the framework of the diplomacy of Europe. Focuses on the consistent attempt of Russia to apply the doctrine of collective security to her foreign policy.

139   Esch, Patricia A. M. van der. **Prelude to War: The International Repercussions of the Spanish Civil War, 1936-1939.** The Hague, Nijhoff, 1951. 190p. Bibliog.
The international repercussions of the Spanish Civil War are seen to be centered in the powerless nature of the League of Nations to prevent foreign intervention and in the real failure of the Non-Intervention Committee to stop the incursion of men and supplies to both sides, but especially to the Nationalist faction. The diplomatic and strategic positions of England and France were tested to the extent that their virtual inaction led to Hitler's determination to continue his challenges to the political body of Europe.

140   Jackson, Gabriel. **The Spanish Republic and the Civil War, 1931-1939.** Princeton, N.J., Princeton University Press, 1965. 578p. Maps, Bibliog.
A history of the Second Republic and the Civil War. Analyzes the aspirations and frustrations of the leaders of the Republic and their places in Spanish history as seen from within Spain.

141   Johnston, Verle B. **Legions of Babel: The International Brigades in the Spanish Civil War.** University Park, Pennsylvania State University Press, 1968, c.1967. 228p. Maps, Bibliog.
A succinct history of the men of 53 nations who volunteered to fight with the Republican forces against Franco's Nationalists. Analyzes the military, political and propaganda roles and the difficulties encountered due to language, education, training and ideology of the international brigades.

142   Kleine-Ahlbrandt, William Laird. **The Policy of Simmering: A Study of British Policy During the Spanish Civil War, 1936-1939.** The Hague, M. Nijhoff, 1962. 161p. Bibliog.
A chronological account of British policy towards the conflict. British relations with France, Italy and Germany, the formation and activities of the Non-Intervention Committee, the influence of British business interests in Spain and the shifting position of the British Labour Party all combine to depict a somewhat unheroic part played by Great Britain.

143   Landis, Arthur H. **Abraham Lincoln Brigade**. New York, Citadel Press, 1967. 677p. Maps, Bibliog.
An examination of the events of the Spanish Civil War, in terms of the participation of the American volunteer group, through interviews with the survivors.

144   Padelford, Norman Judson. **International Law and Diplomacy in the Spanish Civil Strife**. New York, Macmillan, 1939. 710p.
A study of the diplomacy and international legal problems arising from the civil war. Describes the roles of the non-intervention system and the League of Nations, and the legal aspects of belligerency and interference with foreign shipping by the participating parties.

145   Puzzo, Dante Anthony. **Spain and the Great Powers, 1936-1941**. New York, Columbia University Press, 1962. 296p. Bibliog.
A clear review of the diplomatic, strategic and economic interests and roles played by the great powers that intervened in the civil war and those that also influenced the outcome by their non-intervention.

146   Taylor, Foster Jay. **The United States and the Spanish Civil War**. New York, Bookman Associates, 1956. 288p. Bibliog.
The author views the conflict as a dress rehearsal for World War II. He describes American public opinion and official policy in terms of conflicting isolationist, religious and ideological pressures generated for and against each side of the civil war.

147   Thomas, Hugh. **The Spanish Civil War**. New York, Harper, 1961. 720p. Bibliog.
A balanced comprehensive and unbiased military, political and diplomatic history of the Spanish Civil War by a former member of the British Foreign Office. The narrative covers the background from its origins in the 1920s and early 1930s to the fall of Barcelona in 1939. The author writes well in describing the interacting forces in almost every aspect of this emotion laden conflict.

148   Traina, Richard P. **American Diplomacy and the Spanish Civil War**. Bloomington, Indiana University Press, 1968. 301p. Bibliog.
A review of U.S. relations with Spain from July 1936 to late 1938. Assesses the responsibility of the Roosevelt Administration in detail for U.S. policies and actions in regards to the international problems of the Spanish Civil War.

Sino-Japanese War, 1937-1941

149   Bisson, Thomas Arthur. **Japan in China**. New York, Macmillan, 1938. 417p. Maps.
The personal observation in China and Japan of the author as a representative of the Foreign Policy Association. A scholarly study of the background and origins of the Sino-Japanese conflict. An analysis of the conditions created by the policies and events of the conflict since 1933. The author emphasizes two major developments, Japan's progression toward fascism and China's toward political unity.

150   Bunker, Gerald E. **The Peace Conspiracy: Wang Ching-Wei and the China War, 1937-1941**. Cambridge, Mass., Harvard University Press, 1972. 327p. Bibliog.

Relying on Chinese and Japanese sources and studies, the author presents an accounting of men and events leading up to and including the first year and a half of the Chinese puppet government under the Japanese. The subject was Chief of State and architect of the Japanese-sponsored regime. A major disciple of Sun Yat-sen, he later broke with Chiang and established the Chinese puppet government in 1940.

151   Quigley, Harold Scott. **Far Eastern War, 1937-1941**. Boston, World Peace Foundation, 1942. 369p. Maps, Bibliog.

Traces the diplomatic, economic, and strategic moves of the major powers and the circumstances regarding the outbreak of the war. Details the political and economic consequences of the conflict in China, Japan and in the West. Relevant official documents are included.

152   Snow, Edgar. **Battle for Asia**. New York, Random House, 1941. 431p. Maps.

An exhaustive and penetrating account of the situation in China during the years 1938-1940. A searching analysis of China's economic and social problems and her need for democratic reforms. Mass mobilization and guerrilla warfare are urged as the only way to win the Sino-Japanese War. The author's brilliant descriptive reporting presents a revealing picture of internal conditions in China and the forces at work between the Communist movement, the Nationalist Kuomingtang and the Japanese invaders.

153   Taylor, George Edward. **The Struggle for North China**. New York, International Secretariat. Institute of Pacific Relations, 1940. 250p. Map.

Deals with the complex factors of foreign rights and interests in China, of the guerrilla struggle in Northern China and of the impact of the Japanese-sponsored Provisional Government at Peking.

Anschluss Movement

154   Ball, Mary Margaret. **Post-War German-Austrian Relations: The Anschluss Movement, 1918-1936**. Stanford, Calif., Stanford University Press, c.1937. 304p. Bibliog.

Based on existing documentation, the study includes quotations from German and Austrian party leaders with the addition of surveys of accounts from the contemporary Austrian press.

155   Gehl, Jurgen. **Austria, Germany and the Anschluss, 1931-38**. London, Oxford University Press, 1963. 212p. Maps, Bibliog.

Based on German, Austrian and British documents, the author concentrates on the diplomatic moves of the powers and the international aspects of the Austrian problem.

156   Schuschnigg, Kurt von. **The Brutal Takeover: The Austrian Ex-Chancellor's Account of the Anschluss of Austria by Hitler.** Translated by Richard Perry. London, Weidenfeld and Nicholson, 1971. 383p. Bibliog.

A political autobiography documenting his dealings with Hitler and the chief Nazi agent in Austria. The ex-chancellor relates the events and discusses the issues of blame and responsibility.

157   Shepherd, Gordon. **The Anschluss: The Rape of Austria.** London, Macmillan, 1963. 222p.

A clear documented narrative of the crucial events leading to and resulting in Austria's incorporation into the German Reich. A good critical study of the aspirations and shortcomings of the Austrian Chancellor and of Hitler's character and methods. The study covers the first three months of 1938 and describes Austria's dilemma of choosing between historic German ties and that of independent nationhood.

Appeasement

158   Bruegel, Johann Wolfgang. **Czechoslovakia Before Munich: The German Minority Problem and British Appeasement Policy.** New York, Cambridge University Press, 1973. 334p. Bibliog.

Well written account of the appeasement story in light of the opening of the papers of the British Foreign Office and the Cabinet and those of the German Foreign Office. The author describes the mistakes, missed opportunities, frictions and tensions of German-Czech relations and the role of the German activist parties in developing the crisis. British efforts to provide for a peaceful coexistance and cooperation of the three million German minority in Czechoslovakia are fully documented.

159   Furnia, Arthur Homer. **The Diplomacy of Appeasement: Anglo-French Relations and the Prelude to World War II, 1931-1938.** Washington, University Press, 1960. 454p.

Neville Chamberlain and Georges Bonnet are blamed for their part in bringing about the dismemberment of Czechoslovakia. The divergent Anglo-French policies and the shortsighted ignorance of these two western powers were important factors in this debacle.

160   Gilbert, Martin, and Richard Gott. **The Appeasers.** Boston, Houghton Mifflin, 1963. 444p.

The British policy of appeasement toward Germany, and primarily Hitler, is discussed in terms of its formation and application and of the men responsible for it. In spite of warnings from experienced diplomats and politicians, the study describes the methods the leaders of appeasement were prepared to use to attain their ends.

161   Gilbert, Martin. **The Roots of Appeasement.** London, Weidenfeld and Nicolson, 1966. 254p. Maps, Bibliog.

A study of British policy from 1918 to 1939 showing the different phases of appeasement in the political and British Foreign Office arenas. In the author's opinion, appeasement over the years was a constructive and rational approach but that it was dominated by fear and weakness after 1933.

162   Keith, Arthur Berriedale. **The Causes of the War.** London, New York, T. Nelson and Sons, 1940. 554p.
Takes the matter of appeasement back to the Italo-Ethiopian War emphasizing the lack of moral courage in Britain and France in that confrontation and in subsequent ones with the likes of Mussolini and Hitler. The author believes that while the policies of appeasement were fundamental errors and blunders it was worth trying since, in the final analysis, it strengthened the moral case.

163   Offner, Arnold A. **American Appeasement: United States Foreign Policy and Germany, 1933-1938.** Cambridge, Belknap Press of Harvard University Press, 1969. 328p. Bibliog.
A study faulting the passive acceptance of German aggression by many U.S. diplomats who also failed to understand the serious dangers of German expansions to U.S. security. Ambassador William Dodd is singled out as one of the few exceptions of this attitude.

164   Rock, William R. **Appeasement on Trial: British Foreign Policy and Its Critics, 1938-1939.** Hamden, Conn., Archon Books, 1966. 365p. Bibliog.
The positions adopted by the Conservatives, Liberals and Labourites in successive debates in Parliament on the government's handling of the various crises are described in relation to the opposition to appeasement. Examines the effect of public opinion on British policy.

165   Rowse, Alfred Leslie. **Appeasement: A Study in Political Decline, 1933-1939.** New York, Norton, 1961. 123p.
The arguments of the supporters of appeasement are disputed and criticized in this partisan statement of the opposite side of the case. The author, an English historian, provides some significant insights into the thinking of the proponents of appeasement.

166   Thompson, Neville. **The Anti-Appeasers: Conservative Opposition to Appeasement in the 30's.** Oxford, Clarendon Press, 1971. 256p. Bibliog.
The opposition to appeasement by members of Chamberlain's Conservative Party is seen to have had no real organized cohesive direction. Centrally focused on Churchill, the problem was one of the difficulties in providing a viable alternative.

Munich Conference, 1938

167   Eubank, Keith. **Munich.** Norman, University of Oklahoma Press, 1963. 322p. Maps, Bibliog.
An examination of the pressures on Britain and France with regard to the Czech crisis. Feels that the unpreparedness of Great Britain made the Munich compromise a military necessity.

168   Lammers, Donald N. **Explaining Munich: The Search for Motive in British Policy.** Stanford, Calif., Hoover Institution on War, Revolution

and Peace, Stanford University, 1966. 73p. Bibliog.
An attempt to disprove the anti-red hypothesis of British policy in regard to
Munich. The hypothesis postulated that appeasement was built on western hostility
to the Soviet Union and that giving Germany a free rein in Eastern Europe would
serve to destroy the advances of communism.

169   Loewenheim, Francis L., ed. **Peace or Appeasement? Hitler, Chamberlain,
       and the Munich Crisis.** Boston, Houghton Mifflin, 1965. 204p. Bibliog.
Source material about events leading up to the meeting between Hitler and
Chamberlain. This is a combination of documents, portions of the memoirs of
some of the participants and four essays which consider the crisis in historical
perspective.

170   Nogueres, Henri. **Munich: "Peace for Our Time."** Translated from the
       French by Patrick O'Brian. New York, McGraw-Hill, 1965. 423p. Maps,
       Bibliog.
A view of the Munich crisis by a French historian and journalist tracing the background, politics and agreements from the Auschluss to the events of the Conference.

171   Ripka, Hubert. **Munich; Before and After: A Fully Documented
       Czechoslovak Account of the Crisis of September 1938 and March 1939
       with a Detailed Analysis of the Repercussions of the Munich Agreement
       on the Situation of Europe As a Whole and of Central Europe in Particu-
       lar, Together with an Essay on the Reconstruction of a Free Europe.**
       London, V. Gollancz, 1939. 523p. Maps.
A Czech account of the situation surrounding the Munich agreements.

172   Robbins, Keith. **Munich 1938.** London, Cassell, 1968. 398p. Maps,
       Bibliog.
An informative and critical review of the events from April to September 1938,
in the development of the Munich crisis. The author's aim is to view the situation
without the impediment of the concept of appeasement. He feels that far-reaching
concessions by the Czech government to the Sudeten Germans would have kept
them loyal.

173   Rothstein, Andrew. **The Munich Conspiracy.** London, Lawrence and
       Wishart, 1958. 320p. Bibliog.
The communist viewpoint of the Munich crisis. Declares that the leaders of the
West, abetted by Benes of Czechoslovakia, conspired with Hitler to attack the
Soviet Union. Eventually Czechoslovakia was sacrificed in order to provide the
Germans with a base for their move against Russia.

174   Thompson, Lawrence Victor. **The Greatest Treason: The Untold Story
       of Munich.** New York, Morrow, 1968. 298p. Maps, Bibliog.
An account of the development of the Czech-Sudeten crisis with a reassessment of
Neville Chamberlain's policies and the attitudes of the French leadership of Daladier
and Bonnet. Finds validity to the grievances of the Sudeten Germans.

175   Werth, Alexander. **France and Munich: Before and After the Surrender.**
        New York, Harper and Brothers Publishers, 1939. 447p.
A clear and objective examination of French foreign policy, politics and public
opinion during this period. A moderate and well-reasoned indictment of Munich.

176   Wheeler-Bennett, John Wheeler. **Munich, Prologue to Tragedy.** London,
        Macmillan, 1966. 507p. Maps, Bibliog.
A good interpretation of the immediate causes of World War II in relation to the
background, development and aftermath of the Munich crisis. Very well written
classic diplomatic history.

United States—Isolationism and Neutrality

177   Chadwin, Mark Lincoln. **The Hawks of World War II.** Chapel Hill, Univer-
        sity of North Carolina Press, 1968. 310p. Bibliog.
The origins and tactics of the Fight for Freedom Committee, an account of the
interventionist movement prior to the U.S. entry into World War II. Their goal was
to more deeply commit the U.S. on the Allied side of the conflict and supported
any move to aid the British despite frustrations from F.D.R.'s policies.

178   Challener, Richard D., comp. **From Isolation to Containment, 1921-
        1952: Three Decades of American Foreign Policy, from Harding to
        Truman.** New York, St. Martin's Press, 1970. 184p. Bibliog.
The evolution of U.S. foreign policy, from the rejection of international commitments to isolation, then to partial and subsequently full-scale involvement in world
affairs, illustrated through documentary evidence.

179   Cole, Wayne Stanley. **America First: The Battle Against Intervention,
        1940-1941.** Madison, University of Wisconsin Press, 1953. 305p. Bibliog.
A key work on the isolation side of the great debate on the direction of U.S.
foreign policy. Based on the records of the leading non-interventionist pressure
group, the study reviews their origins, leadership, program and support. This is a
well-documented account of domestic influences on foreign policy.

180   Divine, Robert A. **The Illusion of Neutrality.** Chicago, University of
        Chicago Press, 1962. 370p. Bibliog.
A sound and comprehensive treatment of U.S. foreign policy in the latter half of
the 1930s showing the interplay of politics and policies. Traces the entire scope of
the pacifist legislation of the period and highlights the parliamentary tactics of the
Roosevelt administration. Blames FDR for the evolution of the neutrality enact-
ments of the time due to delaying too long in more closely directing U.S. foreign
policy because of the press of domestic problems.

181   Divine, Robert A. **The Reluctant Belligerent: American Entry Into World
        War II.** New York, Wiley, 1965. 172p. Maps, Bibliog.
A chronicle of FDR's foreign policy in relation to the isolationist mood of the
1930s. Shows FDR as gradually understanding the dangers facing the U.S. and
reluctantly leading it into war to protect its security. In spite of U.S. withdrawal
from the international scene it became a prisoner of events abroad.

182   Drummond, Donald Francis. **The Passing of American Neutrality, 1937-1941**. Ann Arbor, University of Michigan Press, 1955. 409p. Bibliog.
A chronological narrative of the diplomacy of the Roosevelt administration taking into account the changing aspects of public opinion on the question of U.S. neutrality.

183   Johnson, Walter. **Battle Against Isolation**. Chicago, University of Chicago Press, 1944. 269p. Bibliog.
Describes the formation and activities of the Committee to Defend America by Aiding the Allies and relates the activities of its head, William Allen White. Covering the two years preceding the attack on Pearl Harbor, the author concentrates on the personalities and groups involved in the fight against isolationism.

184   Jonas, Manfred. **Isolationism in America, 1935-1941**. Ithaca, N.Y., Cornell University Press, 1966. 315p. Bibliog.
An intellectual history of U.S. isolationist thought based on the letters, papers, and published writings of the leading proponents. Describes the transient triumph and subsequent decline of isolationism. The study finds that two basic premises emerge in isolationist thrust, that of blind faith in unilateralism and an overriding fear of war.

185   Langer, William Leonard, and S. Everett Gleason. **The Challenge to Isolation, 1937-1940**. New York, published for the Council on Foreign Relations by Harper, 1952. 794p. Bibliog.
A factual, well documented and detailed presentation of U.S. foreign policy for 1937-1940. Unpublished materials as well as official documents are used in this authoritative and balanced study.

186   Martin, James Joseph. **American Liberalism and World Politics, 1931-1941: Liberalism's Press and Spokesmen on the Road Back to War Between Mukden and Pearl Harbor**. New York, Devin-Adair, 1964. 2v. Bibliog.
A transcript showing the major shift of the liberal mind and public opinion from pacifism and isolationism to a strong stand for intervention.

187   Smith, Geoffrey S. **To Save a Nation: American Countersubversives, the New Deal, and the Coming of World War II**. New York, Basic Books, 1973. 244p. Bibliog.
The main thesis is that the extremist organizations such as the German-American Bund, contaminated the more moderate anti-interventionist groups such as the America First Committee. The author contends that the more extreme groups eventually aroused opposite sentiments from what they tried to create and caused the moderate advocates of isolationism and non-intervention to be tarred with the same brush in the public mind.

188   Sobel, Robert. **The Origins of Intervention: United States and the Russo-Finnish War**. New York, Bookman Associates, 1961, c.1960. 204p. Bibliog.
The American reaction toward the Russo-Finnish winter war of 1939-1940 resulted

in a shift of public attitudes from isolation and non-intervention to open aid to
the Allies. Also described are the actions of the U.S. Congress, the Roosevelt
administration and the opinions of the press.

United States and Lend-Lease

189 Goodhart, Philip. **Fifty Ships that Saved the World: The Foundation of
the Anglo-American Alliance.** Garden City, N.Y., Doubleday, 1965. 267p.
Map, Bibliog.
The author writes of the tangle of party politics, national pride and fears, along
with the complex negotiations resulting in the basic destroyers for bases agreement
between the United States and Great Britain.

190 Kimball, Warren F. **The Most Unsordid Act: Lend-Lease, 1939-1941.**
Baltimore, Johns Hopkins Press, 1969. 281p. Bibliog.
An excellent study of the American legislative process in relation to the Lend-Lease
Act with an analysis of the roles and concerns of the participants, both domestic
and foreign.

191 Stettinius, Edward Reilly. **Lend-Lease, Weapon for Victory.** New York,
Macmillan, 1944. 358p. Maps.
An account of the origins and progress of Lend-Lease before and after U.S.
belligerency, whom it helped and how it was funded.

Final Crisis, 1939-1941

192 Aster, Sidney. **1939: The Making of the Second World War.** London,
Deutsch, 1973. 456p. Maps, Bibliog.
The declassification of British state papers has made it possible to gain new perspectives and understanding of the events leading up to the outbreak of war. The
author sees the invasion of Czechoslovakia on March 15, 1939, as the critical point
whereby war became inevitable. He describes the collapse of the Western guarantees
to Poland, the courting of the Soviet Union by both sides, and the actions of the
British cabinet just prior to the war.

193 Ball, Adrian. **The Last Day of the Old World: 3rd September, 1939.**
London, F. Muller, 1963. 291p.
An examination of the decisions and reactions of the leaders of Great Britain,
France, Germany, Poland and Italy, and of the belligerents and neutrals during the
twenty-four hours of September 3rd, 1939.

194 Barron, Gloria J. **Leadership in Crisis: FDR and the Path to Intervention.**
Port Washington, N.Y., Kennikat Press, 1973. 145p. Bibliog.
A study of the difficult and crucial pre-war period of 1939-1941. The author sees
FDR's slow and deliberate moves to sustain British morale and war efforts, while
appearing to lag behind public opinion on the matter, as politically astute in the
face of strong Congressional opposition. The President is seen as publicly maintaining that steps toward involvement were efforts in search of peace while privately
realizing the inevitability of U.S. entry into the war.

195   Dahlerus, Johan Birger Essen. **The Last Attempt.** Translated by Alexander
       Dick. London, Hutchinson, 1948. 134p. Map.
Relates the efforts of a well-known Swedish industrial engineer during the summer
of 1939 to avert World War II. He attempted to bring together the leaders of Great
Britain, Chamberlain and Lord Halifax, and of Germany, Hitler and Goering,
either personally or in providing a contact through his services, in desperate
attempts to continue negotiations.

196   Gafencu, Grigore. **The Last Days of Europe: A Diplomatic Journey in
       1939.** Translated by E. Feltcher-Allen. New Haven, Yale University Press,
       1948. 239p.
An account of the European travels in 1939 of the Foreign Minister of Rumania. He
attempted to discover the likelihood of peace or war in discussions with the men
who were guiding Europe's destiny.

197   Hofer, Walther. **War Premeditated, 1939.** Translated by Stanley Godman.
       London, Thames and Hudson, 1955. 227p. Bibliog.
A good study of the immediate background of World War II by a Swiss historian.

198   Schuman, Frederick Lewis. **Night Over Europe: The Diplomacy of
       Nemesis, 1939-1940.** New York, Knopf, 1941. 600p. Bibliog.
A clear explanation of the causes which led to World War II. This scholarly review
provides a careful analysis of world diplomatic events for the years 1939 and
1940.

199   Toynbee, Arnold Joseph, and Veronica Toynbee. **The Eve of War, 1939.**
       London, Oxford University Press, 1958. 744p. Maps, Bibliog.
An exhaustive examination of British and German documents on their foreign
policy for the five and a half months between Hitler's entry into Prague and the
German invasion of Poland.

INDIVIDUAL COUNTRIES

Australia

200   Andrews, Eric Montgomery. **Isolationism and Appeasement in
       Australia: Reactions to the European Crisis, 1935-1939.** Columbia,
       University of South Carolina Press, 1970. 236p. Maps, Bibliog.
An assessment of the patterns of Australian foreign policy and public opinion on
each major European event of the period. Describes the apathy, confusion and
loyalties inherent in Australian responses to foreign problems and pressures.

Austria

201   Gulick, Charles Adams. **Austria from Hapsburg to Hitler.** Berkeley, Univer-
       sity of California Press, 1948. 2v. Bibliog.
A well documented study of the period from 1918 to 1938 of the economic, social
and political aspects of Austria and their effects on the rest of Europe.

Belgium

202   Miller, Jane Kathryn. **Belgian Foreign Policy Between Two Wars, 1919-1940.** New York, Bookman Associates, 1951. 337p. Bibliog.
This is a study of a nation's search for security among the great powers tracing the diplomatic aspects of Belgian foreign policy from the Peace Conference, the reparations problems and Belgium's shift toward more independence of action.

China

203   Liu, Chih-pu. **A Military History of Modern China, 1924-1949.** Princeton, N.J., Princeton University Press, 1956. 312p.
A balanced portrayal, by a former Chinese Nationalist army officer, of the rise of Kuomintang military power and its subsequent fall due to inept leadership and corruption.

204   Schurmann, Herbert Franz, and Orville Schell, comps. **Republican China: Nationalism, War, and the Rise of Communism, 1911-1949.** New York, Random House, 1967. 394p. Bibliog.
This second of three volumes, whose overall title is the *China Reader*, provides a vivid focus on the highlights of China's modern history through the quotation of selected passages from works of scholars, journalists, literary men and political leaders. Introductory essays highlight the major theses and provide a framework for the selections that focus on the fortunes of the Kuomintang, the struggle for power of the Chinese Communists, and the war with Japan.

205   Shewmaker, Kenneth E. **Americans and Chinese Communists, 1927-1945: A Persuading Encounter.** Ithaca, N.Y., Cornell University Press, 1971. 387p. Map, Bibliog.
Focuses on the writings and experiences of Americans who travelled in China, describing and analyzing their reactions to the Chinese Communists. This good introduction to the subject shows that the conspiracy theory against Americans of the 1950s was totally inadequate to deal with the complexities of this hybrid oriental version of Marxism, a movement that was conceived in opposition to Chiang's regime.

Czechoslovakia

206   Kennan, George Frost. **From Prague After Munich: Diplomatic Papers, 1938-1940.** Princeton, N.J., Princeton University Press, 1968. 266p. Maps.
The tragic dissolution of Czechoslovakia and the first 18 months of German occupation are detailed from Mr. Kennan's reports to the U.S. State Department and from his diary notes.

207   Olivova-Pavava, Vera. **The Doomed Democracy: Czechoslovakia in a Disrupted Europe 1914-38.** Translated by George Theiner. London, Sidgwick and Jackson, 1972. 276p.

The author, a Czech historian, discusses the history and international problems of the first Czechoslovak Republic from its origins and development out of the Austro-Hungarian Empire to one of the most democratic and socially progressive states in Europe and to its final betrayal by the Entente.

208   Vondracek, Felix John. **The Foreign Policy of Czechoslovakia, 1918-1935.** New York, Columbia University Press, 1937. 451p. Maps, Bibliog.
A chronological narrative of Czechoslovak foreign policy from the country's inception through President Masaryk's resignation.

France

209   Albrecht-Carrie, Rene. **France, Europe and the Two World Wars.** New York, Harper, 1961. 346p. Bibliog.
The main premise is that the peace of 1919 was based, in part, on the myth of French power and that what strength she had between the wars was asserted when no real danger existed, but not used to any advantage when the threats became serious. The illusions of French hegenomy began to collapse after 1936 when French foreign policy retreated in the face of Hitler and opted for the British leadership.

210   Bankwitz, Philip Charles Farwell. **Maxime Weygand and Civil-Military Relations in Modern France.** Cambridge, Harvard University Press, 1967. 445p. Bibliog.
An impressively researched study of the politicization of the French military command. This study of civil-military relations examines the successive crisis stages and growing distrust between the army and the government during the 1930s through the views of Weygand, the Chief of the French General Staff for the period 1930 to 1935 and the leader of the French army in 1940.

211   Cameron, Elizabeth Ripley. **Prologue to Appeasement: A Study in French Foreign Policy.** Washington, D.C., American Council on Public Affairs, 1942. 228p. Bibliog.
The period covered is between 1933 and 1936, one which determined the shape of the forthcoming emphasis on the policies of appeasement.

212   Dreifort, John E. **Yvon Delbos at the Quai D'Orsay: French Foreign Policy During the Popular Front 1936-1938.** Lawrence, University Press of Kansas, 1973. 273p. Bibliog.
An examination of the development of French foreign policy prior to Munich and its relationship to European developments. The study focuses on the role of the French Foreign Minister in establishing and fulfilling French foreign policy with its many contradictions and problems during this critical period.

213   Reynaud, Paul. **In the Thick of the Fight, 1930-1945.** Translated by James D. Lambert. New York, Simon and Schuster, 1955. 684p.
The story of Reynaud's role in the affairs of France during the years of indecision and disaster. The author presents a picture of men in government who would rather lose a war than an argument. He also attempts to rebut the interpretation of events

put forward to General Weygand and supporters of the 1940 armistice through new testimony supporting Reynaud's views of the catastrophe.

214   Sherwood, John M. **Georges Mandel and the Third Republic**. Stanford, Calif., Stanford University Press, 1970. 393p. Bibliog.
An analysis of a controversial French political figure assassinated by French Fascists in 1944. A fair assessment of the tensions of French politics. His opposition to the Nazis in the 1930s, his efforts to force Germany to abide by the Treaty of Versailles, and refusal to accept defeat in 1940, has shown him to be a courageous patriot.

215   Wandycz, Piotr Stefan. **France and Her Eastern Allies, 1919-1925: French-Czechoslovak-Polish Relations from the Paris Peace Conference to Locarno**. Minneapolis, University of Minnesota Press, 1962. 454p. Maps, Bibliog.
An outstanding treatment of the efforts of France to keep Germany and the Soviet Union apart. An objective analysis of a complex area of European diplomatic history.

216   Werth, Alexander. **The Twilight of France, 1933-1940**. New York, H. Fertig, 1966. 368p. Bibliog.
Vivid contemporary journalism of a critical period by the Paris correspondent of the Manchester *Guardian*. Excellent portraits of French political leaders with a description of the polarization of French politics and its effects on French foreign policy. The author suggests that war-weary pacifism was a major cause for the French national attitude and contributed to eventual defeat in 1940. First published in 1942.

Germany

217   Abel, Theodore Fred. **The Nazi Movement: Why Hitler Came to Power**. New York, Atherton Press, 1965. 320p.
A new introduction is included in this reprint of the 1938 edition of an interesting sociological approach to an analysis of the Nazi mentality. The author endeavors to provide a causal pattern for the development and success of the Nazi movement in terms of the social factors that determined its rise. The methodology consists of securing life-histories, called biograms, from members of the National Socialist Party or its sympathizers. The author's conclusions are that for a movement to succeed it needs: adherents who are motivated by persistent widespread discontent with a nation's affairs that is seen to be a threat to personal or general social values, goals based on deeply rooted sentiments, and a charismatic leader with an organized group of dedicated followers.

218   Allen, William Sheridan. **The Nazi Seizure of Power: The Experience of a Single German Town, 1930-1935**. Chicago, Quadrangle Books, 1965. 345p. Map, Bibliog.
Valuable inside view of how the Nazis solidified their power through the pressures of economy, conformity, and the ever-present threat of terror thus creating a

disruption of normal human ties and a helpless confusion in possible areas of opposition such as the middle class.

219   Bennett, Edward W. **Germany and the Diplomacy of the Financial Crisis, 1931**. Cambridge, Harvard University Press, 1962. 342p. Bibliog.
A study of the German reparations-debt problem. The effects of the Young Plan, the German efforts for reparations revision and the proposed German-Austrian customs union on European and American foreign policies are discussed in some detail.

220   Bretton, Henry L. **Stresemann and the Revision of Versailles: A Fight for Reason**. Stanford, Stanford University Press, 1953. 199p. Maps, Bibliog.
Essentially of a biographical nature, the study seeks to fill in the documentary coverage of Stresemann's policy of peaceful revision of the Treaty of Versailles. Based on his papers, the work shows the role he personally played and the sequence of his attacks against the Treaty and the political order resulting from it.

221   Burden, Hamilton Twombly. **The Nuremberg Party Rallies: 1923-1939**. New York, Praeger, 1967. 206p. Maps, Bibliog.
Capturing the mood and atmosphere of these rallies and the hypnotic personality of Hitler, the author goes on to show how these demonstrations were transformed from the amateurish meetings of the 1920s to the pageants of the 1930s. Chronicles their role in the history of the Nazi party's organization and propaganda. The author reconstructs the key elements of the Nazi rise to power and shows how the paramilitary organizations were used to threaten and intimidate.

222   Carr, William. **Arms, Autarky and Aggression: A Study in German Foreign Policy, 1933-1939**. London, Arnold, 1972. 136p. Bibliog.
A study of the successive stages of Hitler's foreign policy. His efforts to expand the German armed forces and provide Germany with self-sufficiency for its peacetime and war economy are seen as indispensable objectives to his aggressive foreign policy. The author contends that the failure of German domestic opposition to Hitler and the ineffectiveness of the Western appeasement policies provide the keys to the origins of the war.

223   Carsten, Francis Ludwig. **The Reichswehr and Politics: 1918-1933**. Oxford, Clarendon Press, 1966. 427p. Bibliog.
A political history of the German military in the Weimar Republic, along with an analysis of the leading personalities of the Reichswehr. Relations between the German military and the Soviet army are summarized in some detail.

224   Dirksen, Herbert von. **Moscow, Tokyo, London: Twenty Years of German Foreign Policy**. Norman, University of Oklahoma Press, 1952. 276p.
A German career diplomat's account of Germany's foreign relations between the world wars. A behind-the-scenes report from three leading ambassadorial posts of the events which shaped pre-war history.

225   Dorpalen, Andreas. **Hindenburg and the Weimar Republic**. Princeton, N.J., Princeton University Press, 1964. 506p. Bibliog.
A valuable study of the events leading to the appointment of Hitler. The author

views Hindenburg as a person of indecision with a reluctance to accept responsibility. Provides a very good picture of the social and political history of the last years of the Weimar Republic.

226   Eyck, Erich. **A History of the Weimar Republic.** Cambridge, Harvard
       University Press, 1962-1963. 2v. Bibliog.
This is an objective interpretation by a German liberal democrat of the political and parliamentary history of the Weimar Republic. A well written, thorough chronicle with excellent characterizations of leading political figures. Volume one covers the period from the collapse of the empire to Hindenburg's election and volume two proceeds from the Locarno Conference to Hitler's seizure of power.

227   Gatzke, Hans Wilhelm. **Stresemann and the Rearmament of Germany.**
       Baltimore, Johns Hopkins Press, 1954. 132p. Bibliog.
A realistic portrait of a great statesman and friend of peace and democracy, the Foreign Minister of the Weimar Republic from 1923 to 1929.

228   Gordon, Harold J. **Hitler and the Beer Hall Putsch.** Princeton, N.J.,
       Princeton University Press, 1972. 666p. Bibliog.
An extensive historical accounting of the unsuccessful attempt by the National Socialist Party to seize control of the Baravian government in 1923. A good analysis of the events behind the start of Hitler's ten-year climb to power. It is also a good sociological study of the class composition of the early Nazi Party.

229   Gordon, Harold J. **The Reichswehr and the German Republic, 1919-
       1926.** Port Washington, N.Y., Kennikat Press, 1972. 478p. Bibliog.
A scholarly account first published in 1957 of the Reichswehr during its formative years. The author feels that the army was not as disruptive a force in the affairs of state of the young republic as was previously believed.

230   Halperin, Samuel William. **Germany Tried Democracy: A Political History
       of the Reich from 1918-1933.** Hamden, Conn., Archon Books, 1963.
       567p. Bibliog.
An informative narrative of the sequence of political events of the Weimar Republic. The author's main point is that behind the democratic facade the old authoritarian spirit still lived on. First published in 1946.

231   Harris, Charles Reginald Schiller. **Germany's Foreign Indebtedness.**
       London, Oxford University Press, 1935. 124p. Bibliog.
A non-technical approach to the German reparations problem and the financial complications of Germany's economic situation since the Treaty of Versailles.

232   Heiden, Konrad. **Der Fuehrer: Hitler's Rise to Power.** Boston, Houghton
       Mifflin, 1944. 788p.
A socio-political analysis of the roots and growth of Hitlerism up to June 1934. This incisive work provides a picture of Hitler as a person and as a power with interesting sidelights of his top associates. A good understanding of the period is provided with clarity of expression and an abundance of detail.

233   Hitler, Adolf. . . . **Mein Kampf.** New York, Reynal and Hitchcock, 1939.
       993p. Map.
A revelation of the potentialities, if not the precise plans of Hitler, including a
discussion of the effects of propaganda and terrorism. This edition is fully
annotated to supply historical background, text clarifications and to relate his
statements to the subsequent course of events.

234   Hitler, Adolf. **The Speeches of Adolf Hitler, April 1922-August 1939: An
       English Translation of Representative Passages.** New York, Oxford Univer-
       sity Press, 1942. 2v. Bibliog.
Prepared by the Royal Institute of International Affairs, these volumes constitute
an important source of Hitler's thoughts. Volume one is devoted to domestic affairs
and volume two to foreign policy.

235   Hunt, Richard N. **German Social Democracy, 1918-1933.** New Haven,
       Yale University Press, 1964. 292p. Bibliog.
A description of the policies, leadership and the electorate of the German Social
Democratic Party. The party's failure to meet the challenges of communism and
Nazism are laid to the stagnation of its leadership causing loss of public support.
This is contrasted to the active agitation of the National Socialists in its successful
mobilization of the support of the electorate.

236   Klein, Burton H. **Germany's Economic Preparations for War.** Cambridge,
       Harvard University Press, 1959. 272p. Bibliog.
Despite appearances, the author finds that Germany never did completely mobilize
its economic resources for total warfare and that the preparations for war were not
particularly complete enough for sustained conflict. The formulation and coordination of public policy, together with an analysis of national production, is deemed
to be of prime importance in national economics.

237   Maser, Werner. **Hitler: Legend, Myth and Reality.** New York, Harper and
       Row, 1973. 433p. Map, Bibliog.
The author is the Director of the University of Munich's Institute of Contemporary
History and is considered to be Germany's foremost authority on Hitler. Drawing
on archival and newly discovered private material, the author presents a detailed
account of his life. The first half of the book covers Hitler's early years and
intellectual background. The latter half is subject oriented and includes chapters on
his health, his role as a politician and that of a strategist.

238   Maser, Werner. **Hitler's Mein Kampf: An Analysis.** London, Faber and
       Faber, 1970. 272p. Bibliog.
This excellent analysis is divided into two parts. The first describes the origins and
background of Hitler's primary work and investigates the facts and fictions
associated with his early career as noted in *Mein Kampf.* The second part comments
and analyzes Hitler's statements in *Mein Kampf* and discusses their consequences.
The author shows that the more important ideas of Hitler and their background
are to be found in his detailed program for a new German ideology.

239   Mason, Herbert Molloy. **The Rise of the Luftwaffe: Forging the Secret German Air Weapon, 1918-1940**. New York, Dial Press, 1973. 402p. Maps, Bibliog.

A fascinating portrayal of the recreation of Germany's air force. The account details the subterfuge and ingenuity that went into the rebuilding of the Luftwaffe from its initial circumventions of the Inter-Allied Control Commission, the training of fighter pilots in Russia in 1927, its participation in Spain in 1936 to its major efforts at rearmament prior to World War II.

240   Mosse, George Lachmann. **The Crisis of German Ideology: Intellectual Origins of the Third Reich**. New York, Grosset and Dunlop, 1964. 373p. Bibliog.

The author proposes that the Nazi movement was an outgrowth of German thought and tradition, rooted in specifically Germanic history, emphasizing sentiment, nature and the *voelkisch* oneness of the German people. The conception of the similarities between German Fascism and other varieties is questioned by the author who feels that the differences are greater than the similarities.

241   Namier, Lewis Bernstein. **In the Nazi Era**. London, Macmillan, 1952 203p.

A continuation of his earlier books on the diplomatic history of pre-war Europe. This volume is divided into two main sections. The first part deals with the men who served and advised Hitler on the military and diplomatic fronts. The second part is concerned with the crisis of 1938.

242   Nicholls, Anthony James, and Erich Matthias, eds. **German Democracy and the Triumph of Hitler: Essays in Recent German History**. London, Allen and Unwin, 1971. 271p. Bibliog.

The failure to produce a lasting parliamentary democracy is laid to the continual structural crisis of the state and the problem of establishing firm loyalties to this type of government due to the uncertain development of its institutions.

243   Nicholls, Anthony James. **Weimar and the Rise of Hitler**. New York, St. Martin's Press, 1968. 203p. Map, Bibliog.

A concise account of German political history from September 1918 to March 1933. A chronicle of the events from the formation to the final demise of the Weimar Republic.

244   O'Neill, Robert John. **The German Army and the Nazi Party, 1933-1939**. New York, Heineman, 1967, c.1966. 286p. Maps, Bibliog.

Explains and analyzes how the Reichswehr gradually became the tool of the Nazi state by isolating and neutralizing the influence of the generals and at the same time, exploiting their professionalism and patriotism. Shows why the generals supported Hitler as long as this led to a militarily powerful and respected Germany.

245   **Path to Dictatorship, 1918-1933: Ten Essays**. Theodor Eschenberg, and others. New York, Praeger, 1967. 217p. Bibliog.

Ten essays by German scholars on the reasons for the consolidation of Nazi power
and the resultant collapse of the Weimar Republic.

246   Poole, Kenyon Edwards. **German Financial Policies, 1932-1939.**
       Cambridge, Harvard University Press, 1939. 276p. Bibliog.
A discussion of the results of the combination of deflationary and inflationary
tactics used by the German government since 1932 through its use of tax
remission along with public works programs. The financial problems and the effects
of the government's intervention in production and prices provide an interesting
economic facet to the picture of pre-war Germany.

247   Pridham, Geoffrey. **Hitler's Rise to Power: The Nazi Movement in
       Bavaria, 1923-1933.** London, Hart-Davis, MacGibbon, 1973. 380p.
       Map, Bibliog.
A detailed illustration and analysis of the Nazi rise to power on the local and
regional level. Using particular examples at the grassroots level to give a more
realistic picture of the organization propaganda and popular appeal of the Nazi
movement, the work provides a better understanding of the national mood.

248   Rauschning, Hermann. **Revolution of Nihilism: Warning to the West.** New
       York, Alliance Book Corp., Longmans, Green, 1939. 300p.
A former Nazi party member's analysis of the Hitler regime with particular
emphasis on its foreign policy. Formerly the President of the Danzig Senate, the
author also gives a searching analysis of Hitler and the future plans of the Nazi
leader.

249   Rauschning, Hermann. **The Voice of Destruction.** New York, G. P.
       Putnam's Sons, 1940. 295p.
A report of the author's confidential talks with Hitler from 1932 to 1934. It
provides an intimate personal picture and a devastating impression of Hitler and
his movement, and reveals his demonic character and power.

250   Robertson, Esmonde Manning. **Hitler's Pre-War Policy and Military Plans,
       1933-1939.** New York, Citadel Press, 1967, c.1963. 207p. Bibliog.
The argument that Hitler's diplomacy was not really a systematic execution of a
preconceived plan but that he was more an impulsive opportunist with short term
plans is explored here. However, his long-term general aims were continually
pursued as with his Lebensraum fixation. There is also a discussion of the relation
between his military planning and his political and foreign policies.

251   Schmokel, Wolfe. **Dream of Empire: German Colonialism, 1919-1945.**
       New Haven, Yale University Press, 1964. 204p. Bibliog.
A discussion of German attempts during the Weimar Republic and under Hitler to
resurrect Germany's colonial ambitions in terms of economic self-sufficiency and
national prestige. French and British attitudes to colonialism portray their willing-
ness to consider the matter of colonies as pawns in the international game.

252   Schoenbaum, David. **Hitler's Social Revolution: Class and Status in Nazi
       Germany, 1933-1939.** Garden City, N.Y., Doubleday, 1966. 336p. Bibliog.

An extensively documented socio-economic history describing the effects of National Socialism on various groups such as labor, business, agriculture and women. A significant major interpretation holding the view that National Socialism was a consistent extension of German history.

253 Shirer, William Lawrence. **Berlin Diary: The Journal of a Foreign Corres-**
pondent, 1934-1941. New York, A. A. Knopf, 1941. 605p.
One of the most illuminating and absorbing books giving the reader a graphic picture of events in Germany before the war and during its first year and a half. A necessary work for an understanding of the political and psychological aspects of the situation inside Germany prior to and following the start of the initial phase of World War II.

254 Stern, Fritz Richard. **The Politics of Cultural Despair: A Study in the**
Rise of the Germanic Ideology. Berkeley, University of California Press,
1961. 367p. Bibliog.
A discussion of the influence on German thinking of the intellectual progenitors of National Socialism. Their roots lay in Germanic historical romanticism and nationalism which, however, degenerated into Nazism. The author notes that almost every Nazi doctrine was extant decades before Versailles.

255 Waite, Robert George Leeson. **Vanguard of Nazism: The Free Corps Move-**
ment in Postwar Germany, 1918-1923. Cambridge, Harvard University
Press, 1952. 344p. Bibliog.
A well written and documented general picture of the movement from a sociological viewpoint that served as the immediate background to National Socialism.

256 Watt, Richard M. **The Kings Depart: The Tragedy of Germany; Versailles**
and the German Revolution. New York, Simon and Schuster, 1969. 604p.
Map, Bibliog.
Biographical sketches of the major political personalities of the period are enhanced with character analyses and suggestions for motivation. The events of the post-Versailles period are seen to be closely bound up with the provisos and political legacies of the Treaty.

257 Weinberg, Gerhard L. **The Foreign Policy of Hitler's Germany: Diplomatic**
Revolution in Europe, 1933-36. Chicago, University of Chicago Press,
1972. 397p. Map, Bibliog.
A nation-by-nation survey and analysis of Hitler's foreign policy. The author's argument is that Hitler did have a definite foreign policy plan from the beginning which included an ultimate plan for resorting to war.

258 Wheaton, Eliot Barculo. **Prelude to Calamity: The Nazi Revolution, 1933-**
1935. Garden City, N.Y., Doubleday, 1968. 523p. Maps, Bibliog.
A political analysis of the factors that enabled Hitler to consolidate his power. The emphasis is on Hitler's ruthlessness, luck, bluff, and the mistakes of individuals and groups that contributed to his achievements. The author provides valuable chronologies and statistics and also a background survey of the Weimar era.

259   Wheeler-Bennett, John Wheeler. **The Nemesis of Power: The German Army in Politics 1918-1945**. 2nd ed. New York, St. Martin's Press, 1964. 831p. Bibliog.
A well organized and documented study of the German army's influence and involvement in domestic politics and foreign policy.

Great Britain

260   Carlton, David. **MacDonald Versus Henderson: The Foreign Policy of the Second Labour Government**. New York, Humanities Press, 1970. 239p. Bibliog.
A survey of the main problems in Britain's relations with Germany and France between 1929-1931. The questions of reparations, frontiers, security, disarmament and arbitration are discussed in the light of the conflicts and interplay of the policies and personalities of the period.

261   Carter, Gwendolen Margaret. **The British Commonwealth and International Security: The Role of the Dominions, 1919-1939**. Toronto, The Ryerson Press, 1947. 326p.
The role of the British Dominions in the search for security after the Treaty of Versailles is shown to be one of less concern with European matters than with more world-wide questions, such as the Suez Canal. The nature and problems of the Commonwealth nations are woven into the general framework of the diplomacy of the time.

262   Churchill, Winston Leonard Spencer. **The Aftermath**. New York, C. Scribner's Sons, 1929. 502p. Maps.
Volume four of the World Crisis, 1911-1929 continues the personal narrative of the part taken by the author as British Chancellor of the Exchequer, from 1924 to 1929, in dealing with world politics. Presents a graphic description of the struggle with the problems of peace and reconstruction.

263   Churchill, Winston Leonard Spencer. **Step by Step, 1936-1939**. New York, Putnam's Sons, 1939. 323p.
A collection of articles by Churchill which appeared in the press covering home defense and foreign affairs. The main theme is the need for Britain's rearmament. They present a running commentary of events as they developed especially in international affairs. Also evident are his views on non-intervention in Spain and the maintenance of a strict neutrality for Britain in the Spanish Civil War.

264   Eden, Anthony. **Facing the Dictators: The Memoirs of Anthony Eden, Earl of Avon**. Boston, Houghton Mifflin, 1962. 746p.
Reflections of British diplomacy in the mid-1930s with a commentary on his 15 years of public office from 1923 to February 1938. He accounts for his actions and policies during his first period as Great Britain's Foreign Secretary from 1935 to 1938 when he resigned following differences with Neville Chamberlain on policy towards Fascist Italy.

265   Gannon, Franklin Reid. **The British Press and Germany, 1936-1939**.
        Oxford, Clarendon Press, 1971. 314p. Bibliog.
An assessment of the policies and reactions of leading British newspapers from
their initial inability to understand the potential dangers of Nazism to their final
realization of the political and military dangers of Hitler's Germany. The study
provides a better understanding of some of the forces behind Britain's policy of
appeasement.

266   George, Margaret. **The Warped Vision: British Foreign Policy, 1933-1939**.
        Pittsburgh, University of Pittsburgh Press, 1965. 238p. Bibliog.
An indictment of British foreign policy of the period with an emphasis on the
motives and role of the Conservative Party. The book concentrates on the men who
dealt with Hitler and Mussolini and were responsible for the policies of
appeasement.

267   Graves, Robert, and Alan Hodge. **The Long Week End: A Social History
        of Great Britain, 1918-1939**. New York, Macmillan, 1941. 455p.
A significant work which grasps and records the spirit of the period in the social
field, literary and artistic fashions, political arguments of the day, and of the international influences on politics, behavior and business.

268   Higham, Robin. **Armed Forces in Peacetime: Britain 1918-1940; A Case
        Study**. Hamden, Conn., Archon Books, 1962. 332p. Bibliog.
An account of how the army and navy fared in the interwar years in the face of
indifference and a stagnant industrial situation. Shows the neglect and lack of
planning and foresight in Britain's rearmament and defenses against submarines
and aircraft.

269   Higham, Robin. **The Military Intellectuals in Britain, 1918-1939**. New
        Brunswick, N.J., Rutgers University Press, 1966. 267p. Bibliog.
An analysis of the shortcomings of Great Britain's military posture and thought
in the period between World War I and World War II. Contains a good account of
the conflict between the advocates of sea and land power and those in favor of
greater emphasis on airpower.

270   Ironside, Edmund. **Time Unguarded: The Ironside Diaries, 1937-1940**.
        New York, D. McKay Co., 1963, c.1962. 434p. Maps.
These well edited diaries serve to provide further information and clarification
regarding British military and foreign policy in the 1930s. Ironside was one of the
few highly placed British generals who was convinced in 1937 that war with Germany
would follow in two to three years.

271   James, Robert Rhodes. **Churchill: A Study in Failure, 1900-1939**. New
        York, World Pub., 1970. 400p. Maps, Bibliog.
A critical examination of Winston Churchill's career from his election to Parliament
in 1900 to the start of World War II. This revisionist study contends that
Churchill's setbacks were due to his arrogance, vanity and fixed beliefs. The author
reconstructs the climate of opinion of the period and sees Churchill also as a man
of courage and resiliency, but somewhat mistrusted by his Conservative Party

colleagues due to his earlier changes of party from Conservative to Liberal and back again. The study also examines Churchill's record on the major Dardanelles fiasco and on his later actions on rearmament and appeasement.

272   Kennedy, John Fitzgerald. **Why England Slept**. New York, W. Funk, 1961.
       252p. Bibliog.
An objective study of the complex foreign and domestic considerations which influenced Britain's failure to rearm during the 1930s.

273   Liddell Hart, Basil Henry. **The Liddell Hart Memoirs**. New York, Putnam,
       1965-66. 2v. Bibliog.
The memoirs of one of the great modern British military theorists. He attempted to modernize the British army during the pre-war years while serving as an advisor to the British War Minister Hore-Belisha. The second volume covers the period up through the start of the war.

274   Macleod, Iain. **Neville Chamberlain**. New York, Atheneum, 1962. 319p.
       Bibliog.
The author, a leader of the British Conservative Party, seeks to refute the myths grown up around Chamberlain. The emphasis is on the political career before he became Prime Minister, portraying him as a man with more understanding, humanity and intelligence than is usually accepted. However, the author does note the price paid by Chamberlain's misjudgments regarding the true nature of totalitarian governments.

275   Macmillan, Harold. **Winds of Change, 1914-1939**. New York, Harper and
       Row, 1966. 584p. Bibliog.
The first volume in the memoirs of the former Prime Minister of Great Britain. His developing political views prior to and during the period that he was a Conservative member of Parliament are set against the changing background of domestic and foreign affairs.

276   Medlicott, William Newton. **British Foreign Policy Since Versailles**.
       London, Methuen, 1940. 316p. Bibliog.
A well organized discussion of the development of British foreign policy since 1919. The main factors influencing foreign policy and the reasons for the ineffectiveness of Britain's diplomacy are clearly described. The clash between ideology and realism is seen to be a factor whose recognition is necessary to provide a better understanding of Great Britain's domestic and foreign policy.

277   Mowat, Charles Loch. **Britain Between the Wars, 1918-1940**. Chicago,
       University of Chicago Press, 1955. 694p. Bibliog.
British history between the two world wars is reflected in the mood of the times and in the meaning of the events and developments in domestic and foreign fields.

278   Nicolson, Harold George. **Curzon: The Last Phase, 1919-1925: A Study
       in Post-War Diplomacy**. New York, Harcourt, Brace, 1939. 416p. Maps.
A careful analysis of the relations between diplomacy and policy, a study in diplomatic method. The author provides a careful analysis of the men and events

in the immediate post-war period and of the confusion of objectives and actions in settling European affairs. Emphasis is placed on the influence and personality of Lord Curzon, Great Britain's Foreign Secretary from 1919 to 1924.

279   Nicolson, Harold George. **Diaries and Letters, 1930-1939**. Edited by Nigel Nicolsen. London, Collins, 1966. 448p. Maps.

Volume one of these diaries covers the critical decade leading to World War II. The author, a close associate of Eden and Churchill, comments on foreign affairs and domestic politics of Great Britain.

280   Northedge, F. S. **The Troubled Giant: Britain Among the Great Powers, 1916-1939**. New York, Praeger, 1966. 657p. Maps, Bibliog.

Describes the foreign relations and policies of Great Britain during the successive international problems from the middle of World War I to the start of World War II. The author feels that the peace negotiations of the Treaty of Versailles need to be understood in the context of the diplomacy of the last years of World War I. The picture is presented of Great Britain as being unsure of its resources and uncertain of its commitments.

281   Parkinson, Roger. **Peace for Our Time: Munich to Dunkirk—The Inside Story**. New York, McKay, 1972. 411p. Bibliog.

The conduct of British defense and foreign policies from September 1938 to May 1940 is the primary emphasis of this study. The weaknesses and strengths of Churchill and Chamberlain are discussed and judged.

282   Reynolds, Philip Alan. **British Foreign Policy in the Inter-War Years**. New York, Longmans, Green, 1954. 182p. Maps, Bibliog.

The pursuit of traditional policies under changed circumstances and of conciliation to the extent of not recognizing the inherent dangers of attempting to continually satisfy aggressive powers, are seen to have been major causes in the failure of British foreign policy.

283   Selby, Walford. **Diplomatic Twilight, 1930-1940**. London, J. Murray, 1953. 210p.

Faults British policy during the 1930s due to confusion in the government machinery, with special blame being placed on Lord Robert Vansittart of the Foreign Office. The work includes accounts of the British Missions to Vienna (1933-37) and to Portugal (1937-40) to which the author was the British Representative. The author maintains that Britain should have continued to consolidate her relations with France which Great Britain had emphasized during the period from 1924 to 1931.

284   Seton-Watson, Robert William. **Britain and the Dictators: A Survey of Post-War British Policy**. New York, Macmillan, 1938. 460p.

Dealing with the period from 1919 to 1938, the study covers British relations with the countries of Europe, particularly those ruled by dictators, and of these, mainly the relations with Germany. This is contemporary history by an authority on Central Europe written with care and objectivity.

285   Taylor, Alan John Percivale. **English History, 1914-1945.** New York,
       Oxford University Press, 1965. 708p. Maps, Bibliog.
A well balanced discussion of the political background and basic strategies of two
world wars and the concomitant economic mobilization and social welfare programs. This work of an outstanding historian presents some controversy only with
his discussions of Hitler.

286   Templewood, Samuel John Gurney Hoare. **Nine Troubled Years.** London,
       Collins, 1954. 448p.
Presents a good picture of official British policies during the period from 1931 to
1940. As a high government official (from Secretary of State for Air, Secretary of
State for Foreign Affairs, Home Secretary and Ambassador to Spain) he was in
close touch with the other ministers of the government and with the heads of
various European governments. He fought desperately for peace and while admitting
mistakes of method, he holds to the basic purpose. He contends that the turning
point in the history of the period occurred when Hitler occupied the Rhineland
and Britain and France did not counter the move, though he feels that public
opinion in both countries would not have tolerated a war over a clause in the
Versailles Treaty. The work can be essentially considered a defense of Chamberlain's policies.

287   Watkins, K. W. **Britain Divided: The Effect of the Spanish Civil War on
       British Political Opinion.** London, T. Nelson, 1963. 270p. Bibliog.
This work on British public opinion includes many contemporary quotations that
serve to underscore the accuracy of many of the criticisms of British policy at the
time. Two chapters dealing with the opinions of the British Right and the Left are
of particular importance.

Hungary

288   Macartney, Carlile Aylmer. **Hungary and Her Successors: The Treaty of
       Trianon and Its Consequences, 1919-1937.** London, Oxford University
       Press, 1937. 504p. Maps, Bibliog.
An analysis of the complex relations and conditions created in the territories
ceded by Hungary to Austria, Czechoslovakia, Rumania and Yugoslavia, by the
Treaty of Trianon and of Hungary's demand for treaty revision.

Italy

289   Binchy, Daniel A. **Church and State in Fascist Italy.** London, Oxford
       University Press, 1970. 774p. Bibliog.
A reprint of the 1941 edition with a new preface, it sets the background of the
Lateran Treaties of 1929 between the Papacy and the Fascist government of
Italy. A well documented history, scrupulous in its impartiality and with frank
criticism, that provides both the political and religious sides of the settlement.

290   Cassels, Alan. **Mussolini's Early Diplomacy.** Princeton, N.J., Princeton
       University Press, 1970. 425p. Map, Bibliog.
Covering the period from October 1922 to the end of the 1920s, the study traces

Mussolini's progressive control over Italian foreign policy and his efforts to gain an equal status with the European powers such as England, France and Germany, as well as his designs to gain Italian supremacy in the Near East.

291 Ciano, Galeazzo, Conte. **Hidden Diary, 1937-1938.** Translated with notes by Andreas Mayor. New York, Dutton, 1953. 220p.
A highly biased chronicle of Fascist policy and the nature of Italian politics. Provides a vivid picture of Italian intrigue along with portraits of important personalities in the Fascist leadership.

292 Lyttelton, Adrian. **The Seizure of Power: Fascism in Italy, 1919-1929.** New York, Charles Scribner's Sons, 1973. 544p. Map, Bibliog.
A comprehensive and detailed study of the stages in the Fascist seizure of power in Italy during the decade of the 1920s. The relationship between the party and the state is examined in the context of the decisive role of the party in Italian government and society. The author describes the open-ended character of Fascist ideology which facilitated its growth and its political methods of exploiting irrational instricts among the populace.

293 Macartney, Maxwell Henry Hayes, and Paul Cremona. **Italy's Foreign and Colonial Policy, 1914-1937.** London, Oxford University Press, 1938. 353p.
A scholarly study based on facts and documents explaining in chronological order the fundamental motives and prominent features of Italy's foreign relations.

294 Mussolini, Benito. **Fascism: Doctrine and Institutions.** New York, H. Fertig, 1968. 313p. Bibliog.
The work, a reprint of the 1935 edition, is divided into two main sections. The first concerns the doctrine of Fascism and its fundamental precepts. They detail the origins and philosophic concepts of Fascism, the role, essence and aims of the state, the conception of the Corporate State, and general political and social doctrines relating to the state. The second part lists some of the major laws promulgated concerning the Corporate System and its general political, economic, social and educational aspects.

295 Villari, Luigi. **Italian Foreign Policy Under Mussolini.** New York, Devin-Adair, 1956. 396p. Bibliog.
The work is primarily a defense of Mussolini's foreign policies.

296 Wiskemann, Elizabeth. **Fascism in Italy: Its Development and Influence.** New York, St. Martin's Press, 1969. 141p. Maps.
A clear and concise study of the essential aspects of Italian Fascism—its origins, doctrines, domestic and foreign policies, and its influence abroad.

Japan

297 Bamba, Nobuya. **Japanese Diplomacy in a Dilemma: New Light on Japan's China Policy, 1924-1929.** Vancouver, University of British Columbia Press, 1972. 440p. Bibliog.
A study of the influence of the personalities and cultural identities of Shidehara

Kujuro and Tanaka Giichi on Japanese diplomacy. These two Japanese diplomatic leaders were centrally involved in directing Japan's policies during her struggles to develop a national cultural identity in a modern world. The former represented peaceful internationalist civilian diplomacy and the latter an aggressive traditionalist military foreign policy.

298   Bergamini, David. **Japan's Imperial Conspiracy**. New York, Morrow, 1971.
         1239p. Bibliog.
A controversial account of the Japanese Emperor's supposed major role in planning, shaping and determining the aspects of Japan's conflict with the Western powers. A revisionist study of Japan's prewar, wartime and post-war activities and of the responsibility of the Emperor in the attendant conspiracies.

299   Butow, Robert Joseph Charles. **Tojo and the Coming of the War**. Princeton,
         N.J., Princeton University Press, 1961. 584p. Bibliog.
An objective interpretation of the role of the Japanese army up to and during World War II as seen through the career of General Tojo. A detailed account from the Japanese point of view based on official documents, records, trial documents and the Japanese press.

300   Craigie, Robert Leslie. **Behind the Japanese Mask**. London, Hutchinson,
         1945. 172p.
Observations of the British Ambassador to Japan of events from his September 1937 appointment by Neville Chamberlain through his repatriation in 1942 after seven months of internment. Sketches and analyzes prominent Japanese statesmen and describes the situation and changes in Japanese attitudes as they developed. Craigie was convinced that only through timely concessions to the Japanese could there be hope of peace in Asia.

301   Crowley, James B. **Japan's Quest for Autonomy: National Security and
         Foreign Policy, 1930-1938**. Princeton, N.J., Princeton University Press,
         1966. 428p. Bibliog.
Japan's foreign policy during its period of expansion in the 1930s is the subject of this scholarly study. Delves into the reasons and purposes of the Japanese leaders and maintains that foreign policy was determined only after rational deliberation. The material is drawn from Japanese military position papers and examines the Mukden crisis, London Naval Conference of 1930, the war with China, and Japan's withdrawal from the League of Nations.

302   Ike, Nobutaka, ed. **Japan's Decision for War: Records of the 1941 Policy
         Conferences**. Stanford, Calif., Stanford University Press, 1967. 306p.
         Map, Bibliog.
Pictures the thinking of the representatives of the army, navy, and the cabinet as they discussed the domestic and foreign policy issues of peace and war at the highest levels of decision making in the months before war with the U.S.

303   Jones, Francis Clifford. **Japan's New Order in East Asia: Its Rise and Fall,
         1937-1945**. London, Oxford University Press, 1954. 498p. Bibliog.

A diplomatic history of the events leading up to Japan's attack on Pearl Harbor, of the war years and up to her defeat. The study denies the existence of a Japanese master plan for the conquest of Asia and the Pacific, but that each aggressive move was motivated by a specific set of circumstances.

304   Lu, David J. **From the Marco Polo Bridge to Pearl Harbor: Japan's Entry into World War II**. Washington, Public Affairs Press, 1961. 274p.
Attempts to explain Japan's determination to defeat China in spite of the dangers of war with the United States. Provides a deeper understanding of Japanese diplomacy, policy and actions in the period between the start of full-scale war in China and war with the U.S.

305   Maxon, Yale Candee. **Control of Japanese Foreign Policy: A Study of Civil-Military Rivalry, 1930-1945**. Berkeley, University of California Press, 1957. 286p. Bibliog.
The factional disputes within the Japanese government between the Ministry of Foreign Affairs and the military culminated in the subversion of constitutional authority by the military power structure. Shows the responsibility of the military in expanding Japan's imperialistic actions and at times pursuing a virtual foreign policy on their own.

306   Morley, James William, ed. **Dilemmas of Growth in Prewar Japan**. Princeton, N.J., Princeton University Press, 1971. 527p. Bibliog.
This sixth seminar of the Conference on Modern Japan consists of 13 contributions that survey the political, economic and foreign policy problems faced by Japan during the 1930s and 1940s. The three main sections cover political and military, economic and social, and intellectual areas. The general question involved is whether the political systems of modernizing nations need to resort to repression and even war to solve their problems of growth, or can studies of difficulties that they would likely encounter provide alternative choices to take to prevent massive violence.

307   Young, Arthur Morgan. **Imperial Japan: 1926-1938**. New York, W. Morrow & Company, 1938. 328p.
An authoritative work on Japanese militarism by the editor of the British owned *Japan Chronicle*. Analyzes the background to Japan's aggression in China. The author evinces a strong dislike for Japanese imperialism and militarism.

Poland

308   Cienciala, Anna M. **Poland and the Western Powers 1938-1939: A Study in the Interdependence of Eastern and Western Europe**. London, Routledge and K. Paul, 1968. 310p. Maps, Bibliog.
A reevaluation and analysis of Poland's role between the interests of the major western states and her determination to play a dominant role in Eastern Europe against Germany and the Soviet Union. The author's main thesis is that Poland owed her existence to the temporary weakness of her two major neighbors.

309   Debicki, Roman. **Foreign Policy of Poland, 1919-39: From the Rebirth of the Polish Republic to World War II**. New York, Praeger, 1962. 192p.
A survey of the shaping of Polish foreign policy by a member of the Polish diplomatic service. Describes Poland's quest for stability and security amid the provocations and expansionist policies of Germany and the Soviet Union. Provides a description of Poland's search for a system of alliances in the interwar period. Explains the background and origins of World War II from the Polish point of view.

310   Korbel, Josef. **Poland Between East and West: Soviet and German Diplomacy Toward Poland, 1919-1933**. Princeton, N.J., Princeton University Press, 1963. 321p. Bibliog.
Focuses on the problems of Poland's frontiers with Germany and the Soviet Union and the attitudes and actions of the Polish leadership to this matter.

311   Polonsky, Antony. **Politics in Independent Poland 1921-1939: The Crisis of Constitutional Government**. Oxford, Clarendon Press, 1972. 572p. Maps, Bibliog.
An interpretation of the events, personalities, foreign relations, and economic and social conditions in Poland from the end of the Russo-Polish War to Poland's dismemberment in 1939. A major emphasis is the conflict between the autocratic regime of Marshal Pilsudski and his democratic opponents.

Russia

312   Beloff, Max. **The Foreign Policy of Soviet Russia, 1929-1941**. London, Oxford University Press, 1947-49. 2v. Maps, Bibliog.
A British study considered to be one of the best accounts of Soviet foreign policy for the period covered. Strong emphasis is placed on the Soviet search for collective security under the threat of Germany and Japan. Also covered is the attitude of the Soviet Union to the League of Nations and an examination of Soviet nationalism. The study includes long appendices dealing mainly with Soviet activities in China and Mongolia.

313   Degras, Jane (Tabrisky), ed. **Soviet Documents on Foreign Policy**. London, Oxford University Press, 1951-53. 3v. Bibliog.
A standard work covering the period from 1917-1941. Gathers together in chronological order Soviet speeches, interviews, articles and documents never before translated into English.

314   Erickson, John. **The Soviet High Command: A Military-Political History, 1918-1941**. New York, St. Martin's Press, 1962. 889p. Maps, Bibliog.
A perceptive study detailing the development of Soviet military doctrine and power and the role of the political administration of the communist party and its relation to the army through the commissar system. The study also deals with the early years of the Soviet armed forces and with Soviet-German military cooperation during the Weimar Republic.

315   Eudin, Xenia Joukoff and Robert M. Slusser. **Soviet Foreign Policy, 1928-1934: Documents and Materials**. University Park,

Pennsylvania State University Press, 1966-67. 2v. Bibliog.
This excellent work is a continuation of Eudin and Fisher's *Soviet Russia and the West, 1920-1927: A Documentary Survey* and Eudin and North's *Soviet Russia and the East, 1920-1927: A Documentary Survey.* These works provide the most important points of Soviet interpretation and evaluation of their foreign policies. The works for 1928-34 cover a period when major decisions were made and fundamental changes were introduced and effected in Soviet domestic and foreign policies. A substantial narrative summary serves as an introduction to the documents listed.

316   Fischer, Louis. **Russia's Road from Peace to War: Soviet Foreign Relations, 1917-1941.** New York, Harper and Row, 1969. 499p. Bibliog.
The author recounts and explains the course of Russia's foreign relations as basically determined by national interests with its reactions to external events and moves.

317   Fischer, Louis. **The Soviets in World Affairs: A History of the Relations Between the Soviet Union and the Rest of the World, 1917-1929.** 2nd ed. Princeton, N.J., Princeton University Press, 1951. 2v. Maps.
A key work first published in 1930 providing extensive treatment of Bolshevik foreign policy from the Treaty of Brest-Litovsk. The author based his work on Russian sources and documents and writes with a sympathetic bias of the communist regime.

318   Kennan, George Frost. **Russia and the West Under Lenin and Stalin.** Boston, Little, Brown, 1961. 411p.
A top American specialist in Russian affairs documents the illusions and blunders of the West in dealing with the Soviet Union. The study sees the true aim of communism as the organization of destructive forces within the capitalist states and the fact that western society is not prepared to properly contend with this challenge.

319   Rubinstein, Alvin Z., ed. **The Foreign Policy of the Soviet Union.** New York, Random House, 1960. 457p. Maps, Bibliog.
Almost half of this analytical and historical examination of Soviet foreign policy since 1917 is concerned with the period to 1946. The essays are on the key developments in the origin and evolution of Soviet foreign policy objectives and on the changing character and behavior of the Soviet leadership. These excerpts from important writings and official pronouncements provide an insight into Soviet rationale for its actions.

320   Ulam, Adam Bruno. **Expansion and Coexistence: The History of Soviet Foreign Policy, 1917-1967.** New York, Praeger, 1968. 775p. Bibliog.
An analysis of the personal, ideological and political factors that have shaped Soviet foreign policy. The main theme is that Soviet foreign policy has been actually more consistent than otherwise realized.

United States

321   Adler, Selig. **The Uncertain Giant: 1921-1941; American Foreign Policy Between the Wars.** New York, Macmillan, 1965. 340p. Bibliog.
A review of American attitudes and how they developed and influenced U.S. foreign policy in the context of the interaction between the policies of the great powers. Surveys the diplomacy of F.D.R., the rise of Fascism and Nazism and the gradual but seemingly inexorable involvement of the U.S. in world affairs and conflict.

322   Alsop, Joseph Wright, and Robert Kintner. **American White Paper: The Story of American Diplomacy and the Second World War.** New York, Simon and Schuster, 1940. 107p.
A personal interpretation by two Washington correspondents of the record of the semi-secret foreign policy moves of the Roosevelt administration after Munich.

323   Barnes, Harry Elmer, ed. **Perpetual War for Perpetual Peace: A Critical Examination of the Foreign Policy of Franklin Delano Roosevelt and Its Aftermath.** Caldwell, Ida., Caxton Printers, 1953. 679p. Map, Bibliog.
A revisionist approach to the histories of New Deal historians in a critical survey and appraisal of the development of F.D.R.'s foreign policies.

324   Beard, Charles Austin. **American Foreign Policy in the Making, 1932-1940: A Study in Responsibilities.** New Haven, Yale University Press, 1946. 336p. Bibliog.
A hostile view of F.D.R.'s and Secretary of State Hull's foreign policy. Contrasts the president's anti-war statements with his actions and shows how these change with the exigencies of the times. A factual and well-documented account of the programs and statements in foreign policy as the U.S. moved slowly into deeper involvement in the international arena.

325   Beard, Charles Austin. **President Roosevelt and the Coming of the War, 1941: A Study in Appearances and Realities.** New Haven, Yale University Press, 1948. 614p. Bibliog.
A very critical study of Roosevelt's conduct of U.S. foreign policy. Places the responsibility on F.D.R. for the U.S. entry into World War II by accusing him of policies which forced Japan to war with the U.S. This is a recognized biased study with the admittedly partial nature of the evidence used.

326   Bell, Leland V. **In Hitler's Shadow: The Anatomy of American Nazism.** Port Washington, N.Y., Kennikat Press, 1973. 135p. Bibliog.
The anatomy of the most publicized hate movement in the United States of the mid-1930s. It attempted to Nazify the German-American community through an expression of pan-Germanism and an espousal of Nazi ideals. It was but a shell of its old self by the time it was suppressed in December 1941.

327   Blum, John M. **From the Diaries of Henry Morgenthau, Jr.** Boston, Houghton Mifflin, 1959-64. 2v.

Volume one is entitled *Years of Crisis, 1928-1938* and volume two is called *Years of Urgency, 1938-1941.* Valuable narrative of the political and economic history of the New Deal period. The diaries of F.D.R.'s Secretary of the Treasury provide an excellent account of the financial center for U.S. domestic and foreign policies.

328   Burns, James MacGregor. **Roosevelt: The Lion and the Fox.** New York,
        Harcourt, Brace, 1956. 553p. Bibliog.
A frank analysis of the character and political career of FDR from 1933 through the election of 1940. A valuable objective contribution to an understanding of his strengths and weaknesses as president and a political leader.

329   Cole, Wayne S. **Senator Gerald P. Nye and American Foreign Relations.**
        Minneapolis, University of Minnesota Press, 1962. 293p. Bibliog.
The history of the development and decline of U.S. isolationism between the wars seen through the role of the senator from North Dakota (1925-1945). He was a key figure in the enactment of neutrality laws and a dominant political figure in the non-entanglement movement before the war. His agrarian isolationism strongly influenced his attitudes and courses of action during the interwar years.

330   Dallek, Robert. **Democrat and Diplomat: The Life of William E. Dodd.**
        New York, Oxford University Press, 1968. 415p. Bibliog.
Considered to be a definitive biography of the U.S. historian, democratic politician and Ambassador to Germany from 1933 to 1938. A perceptive study drawn from personal papers and U.S. State Department archives. He is seen to have been, after all, a shrewd observer of events in Germany in the years of Nazi consolidation of power.

331   Davis, Forrest, and Ernest K. Lindley. **How War Came: An American**
        White Paper, from the Fall of France to Pearl Harbor. New York, Simon
        and Schuster, 1942. 342p.
A clearly written journalists' account of how war came about. Defines the major events shaping U.S. foreign policy from the spring of 1940 to the attack on Pearl Harbor. Provides a well-informed understanding of the issues in which the U.S. was involved.

332   Davis, George Theron. **A Navy Second to None: The Development of**
        Modern American Naval Policy. New York, Harcourt, Brace, 1940. 508p.
        Map, Bibliog.
A well balanced and documented analysis of U.S. naval problems and policies from 1850. Provides a fundamental understanding of the development of U.S. foreign policy as affected by naval considerations of strengths and weaknesses.

333   Ellis, Lewis Ethan. **Frank B. Kellogg and American Foreign Relations,**
        1925-1929. New Brunswick, N.J., Rutgers University Press, 1961. 303p.
        Bibliog.
Using private papers and archival materials the author presents a full and detailed synthesis of Secretary of State Frank B. Kellogg's diplomacy. Centers on the problems and decisions regarding the operations of U.S. foreign policy in the four years preceding the great depression period of the 1930s.

334   Ellis, Lewis Ethan. **Republican Foreign Policy, 1921-1933.** New Bruns-
       wick, N.J., Rutgers University Press, 1968. 404p. Bibliog.
A survey of U.S. foreign relations under Presidents Harding, Coolidge and Hoover
and their Secretaries of State Hughes, Kellogg and Stimson. Deals with events from
the Washington Naval Conference to somewhat beyond the Manchurian incident.
Shows vividly the involvement of the United States in foreign affairs up to the point
of serious commitment to action as exemplified in the case of the Kellogg-Briand
Pact.

335   Faulkner, Harold Underwood. **From Versailles to the New Deal: A
       Chronicle of the Harding-Coolidge-Hoover Era.** New Haven, Yale Univer-
       sity Press, 1950. 388p. Bibliog.
Political and economic developments during this period are stressed with due
regard, however, to the social and cultural scene.

336   Fehrenbach, T. R. **F.D.R.'s Undeclared War, 1939-1941.** New York,
       D. McKay Co., 1967. 344p.
Reveals F.D.R.'s policy of leading the country step-by-step into a war he considered
to be unavoidable and yet could not support sooner due to a lack of public
support. Summarizes U.S. military preparation and describes the F.D.R. administration's conflict with the America First Committee. Notes the real start of the tradition breaking extension of the president's executive powers.

337   Ferrell, Robert H. **American Diplomacy in the Great Depression: Hoover-
       Stimson Foreign Policy, 1929-1933.** New Haven, Yale University Press,
       1957. 319p. Maps, Bibliog.
A well written narrative of U.S. foreign policy in the Hoover administration as
formulated and carried out by Secretary of State Henry L. Stimson.

338   Ferrell, Robert H. **Frank B. Kellogg. Henry L. Stimson.** New York,
       Cooper Square, 1963. 360p.
Volume eleven of the set edited by Bemis on *The American Secretaries of State
and Their Diplomacy.* This volume deals with the major problems of U.S. foreign
policy between 1925 and 1933.

339   Hull, Cordell. **The Memoirs of Cordell Hull.** New York, Macmillan, 1948.
       2v.
An exceedingly detailed account by the former U.S. Secretary of State under FDR
of his political career and theories, and his role in the realm of policy making. His
tenure in this office from March 1933 through November 1944 saw America's
course from isolationism to global war. Volume one covers the period 1871 to
1941 and volume two the war years.

340   Langer, William Leonard, and S. Everett Gleason. **The Undeclared War,
       1940-1941.** New York, Harper, 1953. 963p. Bibliog.
An outstanding scholarly work in diplomatic history analyzing the decisive events
which made the U.S. entry into World War II inevitable. Provides an understanding
and definitive analysis of the historical forces underlying world affairs. The work
begins with the Tripartite Act between Germany, Italy and Japan, and ends with

the attack on Pearl Harbor. This is the concluding volume in the study of
United States foreign policy begun with the author's *Challenge to Isolation.*

341   Nevins, Allan. **The New Deal and World Affairs: A Chronicle of International Affairs, 1933-1945**. New Haven, Yale University Press, 1950. 332p. Bibliog.
A concise diplomatic history of the period written from the standpoint of the
Roosevelt administration.

342   Nevins, Allan. **The United States in a Chaotic World: A Chronicle of International Affairs, 1918-1933**. New Haven, Yale University Press, 1950. 252p. Bibliog.
A description of the diplomatic moves resulting from the consequences of World
War I. The events and personalities are placed into their proper historical
perspectives.

343   Pratt, Julius W. **Cordell Hull, 1933-1944**. New York, Cooper Square, 1964. 2v.
Two volumes in the set edited by Bemis on *The American Secretaries of State and
Their Diplomacy*. A scholarly appraisal of the diplomatic role of the U.S. Secretary
of State during a very crucial period of U.S. and world history.

344   Rauch, Basil. **Roosevelt: From Munich to Pearl Harbor; A Study in the Creation of a Foreign Policy**. New York, Creative Age Press, 1950. 527p. Bibliog.
A counter-thesis to Charles A. Beard's implications of Roosevelt's maneuverings
of the U.S. into World War II. A history of the collective security policies of
Roosevelt with a detailed summary of the events leading to the attack on Pearl
Harbor. The author believes that F.D.R. was really an internationalist who was
forced to devote all his energies to the domestic scene before Munich.

345   Roosevelt, Franklin Delano. **Franklin D. Roosevelt and Foreign Affairs**.
Ed. by Edgar B. Nixon. Cambridge, Belknap Press of Harvard University
Press, 1969– . 3v. (to date).
An indispensable set for scholars of American history. The personal reports of
ambassadors, confidants, speeches and selections from news conferences are carefully annotated to convey a graphic impression of the policy making process and
world awareness of FDR. The three volumes published to date cover the period
from January 1933 to January 1937.

346   Russett, Bruce M. **No Clear and Present Danger: A Skeptical View of the United States Entry Into World War II**. New York, Harper and Row, 1972. 111p. Bibliog.
The author contends that Great Britain and the Soviet Union might well have been
able to hold out against Hitler without U.S. belligerency and that due compromise
with Japan might have averted war in that quarter.

347   Sanborn, Frederic Rockwell. **Design for War: A Study of Secret Power Politics, 1937-1941**. New York, Devin-Adair, 1951. 607p. Bibliog.

A strong plea that the executive branch ought to consult freely and publicly with Congress before making serious foreign entanglements. President Roosevelt is accused of designs for war in order to accomplish his own ends.

348   Schlesinger, Arthur Meier, Jr. **The Age of Roosevelt.** Boston, Houghton Mifflin, 1957-1963. 3v. (to date) Bibliog.
Superb narrative history in an excellent literary style, interpreting the political, economic, social and intellectual life of the United States. FDR is fitted into the time with great skill. The works are primarily concerned with domestic affairs but with considerable discussions of foreign affairs. Volume one is titled "The Crisis of the Old Order, 1919-1933," volume two "The Coming of the New Deal" covering 1933-1934, and the third volume is "The Politics of Upheaval" for the years 1935-1936.

349   Spykman, Nicholas John. **America's Strategy in World Politics: The United States and the Balance of Power.** New York, Harcourt, Brace and Company, 1942. 500p. Maps, Bibliog.
A geopolitical guide to power politics. A well-reasoned analysis of the position of the U. S. in terms of geography and power politics with contemporary assessment of the Axis alliance and U. S. foreign policy from a geopolitical viewpoint.

350   Tansil, Charles Callan. **Backdoor to War; The Roosevelt Foreign Policy, 1933-1941.**Chicago, H. Regnery Co., 1952. 690p. Bibliog.
A severe indictment of President Roosevelt's policies in which the author sees Germany as having been baited into a war with Great Britain and France, and Japan as having been drawn into attacking Pearl Harbor. F.D.R. is seen as deliberately plotting to get the U. S. into the European conflict in order to provide aid to Great Britain. This should be used with William Langer's *Challenge to Isolation* to provide some balance.

351   U. S. Department of State. **Peace and War; United States Foreign Policy, 1931-1941.** Washington, U. S. Government Printing Office, 1943. 874p.
The main events of the decade are set forth in chronological order using diplomatic dispatches, legislative acts, State Department communications and texts of public addresses. Shows the warnings from our ambassadors on the dangers of German and Japanese militarism.

352   Van Alstyne, Richard Warner. **American Crisis Diplomacy; The Quest for Collective Security, 1918-1952.** Stanford, Calif., Stanford University Press, 1952. 165p. Bibliog.
Primarily an informative account of the type of diplomacy affecting international affairs in Europe and the Far East since 1918 and U. S. involvement in the international search for collective security by one faction or another.

353   Welles, Sumner. **The Time for Decision.** New York, Harper and Bros., 1944. 431p. Map.
Stimulating comments on U. S. foreign policy in the inter-war years by the U. S. Undersecretary of State from 1937-1943. An important contribution to the

history of events leading to U. S. involvement in World War II and its European diplomacy to the North African invasion. His comprehensive and authoritative statements of world political situations and the changing reactions of the U. S. government lead into his elaborate prescriptions for future world organization and the need for establishing the main tenets of post-war settlement before the end of the war.

354   Wilson, Hugh Robert. **Diplomat Between Wars.** New York, Longmans, Green & Co., 1941. 344p.

An informed reflection dealing with twenty years of international affairs from 1917 to the summer of 1937. The author held posts in Tokyo, Washington, Paris, Geneva and Berlin. He was U. S. Minister to Switzerland from 1927-1937 and the U. S. Ambassador to Germany from 1937 into 1938.

Yugoslavia

355   Hoptner, Jacob B. **Yugoslavia in Crisis, 1934-1941.** New York, Columbia University Press, 1962. 328p. Bibliog.

A study of the foreign policy of Yugoslavia during the regency of Prince Paul in a period of mounting international crisis.

356   Lederer, Ivo J. **Yugoslavia at the Paris Peace Conference; A Study in Frontiermaking.** New Haven, Yale University Press, 1963. 351p. Maps, Bibliog.

An analysis of Yugoslav territorial issues which resulted from the Paris Peace Conference. These issues came to dominate Yugoslav foreign relations in the inter-war years and influenced its internal affairs in a political malaise that continued through World War II.

RELATIONS BETWEEN TWO OR MORE COUNTRIES

Baltic States

357   Tarulis, Albert N. **Soviet Policy Toward the Baltic States, 1918-1940.** Notre Dame, Ind., University of Notre Dame Press, 1959. 276p. Maps, Bibliog.

The work is concerned with the diplomatic and legal aspects of Baltic-Soviet relations including that between Germany and the Soviet Union over this area. Highlights their attendant objectives and maneuverings.

Central Europe

358   Gedye, George Eric Rowe. **Betrayal in Central Europe; Austria and Czechoslovakia: The Fallen Bastions.** New York, Harper and Brothers, 1939. 53lp.

A resume of the events leading to Hitler's successful diplomatic maneuvers of 1938 with a biting analysis of the incidents, situations, personalities, and morality of the participants.

Czechoslovakia and Germany

359   Luza, Radomir. **The Transfer of the Sudeten Germans; A Study of Czech-German Relations, 1933-1962**. New York, New York University Press, 1964. 365p. Maps, Bibliog

This is the Czech side of the Sudeten-German problem to the overall relations between the two countries.

Eastern Europe

360   Lukacs, John A. **The Great Powers and Eastern Europe**. New York, American Book Co., 1953, 879p. Maps. Bibliog.

For annotation, see item 1158.

361   Macartney, Carlile Aylmer, and A. W. Palmer. **Independent Eastern Europe: A History**. London, St. Martin's Press, 1962. 499p.

An analysis of the diplomatic intriguing of the independent states situated largely between the Soviet Union and Germany, covering the period 1914-1941. The countries extend from Finland down to Greece.

362   Seton-Watson, Hugh W. **Eastern Europe Between the Wars, 1918-1941**. 3rd ed. Hamden, Conn., Archon Books, 1962. 425p.

An analysis and description of the political, economic and social developments of Eastern Europe and the rivalries among themselves and the major powers.

Far East

363   Buss, Claude Albert. **War and Diplomacy in Eastern Asia**. New York, The Macmillan Company. 1941. 570p. Maps, Bibliog.

A review of the causes of the chaotic political and economic situation in the Far East from a contemporary point of view.

364   Iriye, Akira. **After Imperialism; The Search for a New Order in the Far East, 1921-1931**. Cambridge, Harvard University Press, 1965. 375p. Map, Bibliog.

A study of the foreign policies of individual governments in the Far East, incorporating the military and diplomatic activities of the states covered. There is a Japanese focus in the overall framework of the area's international relations.

365   Morin, Relman. **East Wind Rising; A Long View of the Pacific Crisis**. New York, Knopf, 1960. 359p.

The Chief of the Associated Press Bureau in Tokyo and Pulitzer Prize winner describes the scene in China and Japan from 1929 through 1941. A careful analysis of events leading to the war with Japan. Views Japanese actions and postwar Communist Chinese aggression as "manifestations of the law of retribution" due to revenge for insults and humiliations received at the hand of Americans and Europeans.

France and Germany

366   Francois-Poncet, Andre. **The Fateful Years; Memoirs of a French Ambas-
       sador in Berlin, 1931-1939**. Translated from the French by Jacques Le
       Clerge. New York, Harcourt, Brace, 1949. 295 p.
His vivid and incisive description of the events of the time and of the official French
and German positions thereon provide the basis of this narrative. An important
aspect are the biographical sketches of leading political figures of the time.

367   Micaud, C. A. **The French Right and Nazi Germany, 1933-1939: A Study
       of Public Opinion**. Durham, N. C., Duke University Press, 1943. 255p.
       Bibliog.
A study of French foreign policies and domestic affairs and the problems involved
that caused the eventual fall of France.

France and Russia

368   Scott, William Evans. **Alliance Against Hitler; The Origins of the Franco-
       Soviet Pact**. Durham, N. C., Duke University Press, 1962. 296p.
The Franco-Soviet rapprochement is seen to be a result of rising German power
set in the broad framework of European diplomacy.

Germany and Italy

369   Toscano, Mario. **The Origins of the Pact of Steel**. Baltimore, Johns Hop-
       kins Press, 1968, 417p. Bibliog.
A history and detailed narrative of the negotiations for the Treaty of Alliance,
concluded in the spring of 1939, between Germany and Italy in which the two
states agreed to provide each other aid in the event of war with another party.

370   Wiskemann, Elizabeth. **The Rome-Berlin Axis: A History of the Relations
       Between Hitler and Mussolini**. New and revised ed. London, Collins, 1966.
       446p. Bibliog.
A study of the pre-war diplomacy between Germany and Italy with a correlation
of the accounts of both sides showing the progressive dominance of Nazi Germany
over Fascist Italy.

Germany and Japan

371   Ikle, Frank William. **German-Japanese Relations, 1936-1940**. New York,
       Bookman Associates, c.1956. 243p. Bibliog.
A history of German-Japanese relations from the Anti-Comintern Pact to the
Tripartite Pact. Relates the differences of the various power groups in Japan and
their attitudes towards Germany, Great Britain and the United States.

372   Presseisen, Ernst Leopold. **Germany and Japan; A Study in Totalitarian
       Diplomacy, 1933-1941**. The Hague, Nijhoff, 1958. 365p. Bibliog.
The development of German-Japanese relations with a vivid picture of mutual
exploitations and betrayals as the situation suited each other's purposes. The
study is based on captured German and Japanese documents.

Germany and Poland (Including Danzig)

373   Kimmich, Christoph M. **The Free City: Danzig and German Foreign Policy, 1919-1934.** New Haven, Yale University Press, 1968. 196p. Map, Bibliog.
A concise, thorough study tracing the role of Danzig in German and Polish foreign policies in the interwar years. Traces German domination of the city's economic and political affairs and of the rise of the rival Polish port of Gdynia.

374   Leonhardt, Hans Leo. **Nazi Conquest of Danzig.** Chicago, University of Chicago Press, 1942. 363p. Map, Bibliog.
The author details the nine-year process of Danzig's Nazification from 1930 through 1939. The work is not only based on extensive documentation but also on the author's personal participation as a member of Danzig's opposition party.

375   Levine, Herbert S. **Hitler's Free City; A History of the Nazi Party in Danzig, 1925-39.** Chicago, University of Chicago Press, 1973. 223p. Bibliog.
A history of the Nazi conquest of this free city, a permanent ward of the League of Nations. Its unique place in the history of the inter-war period is attributed to the fact that the Nazis were forced to govern and hold elections under the League's watchful eyes. Open opposition to the Nazis did not disappear until 1937. The author seeks to view the structure of Hitler's world from the perspective of the political evaluations and decision making that Danzig's problems presented.

376   Lipski, Josef. **Diplomat in Berlin, 1933-1939: Papers and Memoirs of Josef Lipski, Ambassador of Poland.** New York, Columbia University Press, 1968. 679p. Bibliog.
A presentation of the Polish point of view of the failure of reconciliation between Poland and Germany. Papers on the negotiations for the Polish-German Non-Aggression Pact, the Danzig question, and other documents are included and chronologically arranged.

377   Mason, John Brown. **The Danzig Dilemma; A Study in Peacemaking by Compromise.** Stanford, Calif., Stanford University Press, 1946. 377p. Map, Bibliog.
A detailed documented study of the political, economic and administrative problems of Danzig and the resultant effects on international affairs while it was under the protection of the League of Nations.

378   Von Riekhoff, Herald. **German-Polish Relations, 1918-1933.** Baltimore, Johns Hopkins Press, 1971. 421p. Bibliog.
A penetrating study of the economic, military and diplomatic events in the years before the rise of Hitler to power with regard to the interplay of European diplomatic forces on German-Polish relations. Drawing heavily on German and Polish documents the book notes the inability of both parties to reconcile their differences.

Germany and Spain

379   Harper, Glenn T. **German Economic Policy in Spain During the Spanish Civil War, 1936-1939.** The Hague, Mouton & Co., 1967. 152p. Bibliog.

A reassessment of the relations between Germany and the Spanish Nationalist side of the conflict in the light of the practical motives of the Nazis and the independent nationalist interests of Franco.

Germany and Russia

380   Carr, Edward Hallett. **German-Soviet Relations Between the Two World Wars, 1919-1939**. Baltimore, Johns Hopkins Press, 1951. 146p.
A well-organized collection of six lectures on the fluctuating relations between Germany and the Soviet Union in the interwar period by former members of the British diplomatic service.

381   Dyck, Harvey Leonard. **Weimar Germany and Soviet Russia, 1926-1933: A Study in Diplomatic Instability**. New York, Columbia University Press, 1966. 279p. Bibliog.
A study focusing on the divisions between trade, foreign policy, domestic pressures in relation to the aims of the military general staffs of Germany and the Soviet Union. The main emphasis is placed on how policy matters and issues of foreign relations were framed in terms of the range and alternatives of choice.

382   Freund, Gerald. **Unholy Alliance; Russian-German Relations from the Treaty of Brest-Litovsk to the Treaty of Berlin**. London, Chatto and Windus, 1957. 283p. Bibliog.
An authoritative account of the relations between Germany and the Soviet Union during the period 1918-1926 with an emphasis on the secret arrangements for military cooperation between the Reichswehr and the Red Army.

383   Hilger, Gustav and Alfred G. Meyer. **The Incompatible Allies; A Memoir-History of German-Soviet Relations, 1918-1941**. New York, Macmillan, 1953. 350p.
An account from the German point of view, by an officer in the German embassy in Russia, of the extent of the German-Soviet military collaboration in the Weimar period and of the general relations between the two powers in the interwar period.

384   McSherry, James E. **Stalin, Hitler and Europe: The Origins of World War II, 1933-1939**. Cleveland, World Publishing Co., 1968. 308p. Bibliog.
The first volume in a two-part study of Nazi-Soviet relations. This volume analyzes Stalin's and Hitler's roles in the events leading to World War II, presenting the case against Stalin and the Soviet's popular front policy. Attention is given to Anglo-Franco-Soviet relations, Soviet-Japanese, and German-Japanese relations and the Soviet-German accommodation.

385   Rosenbaum, Kurt. **Community of Fate; German-Soviet Diplomatic Relations, 1922-1928**. Syracuse, N. Y., Syracuse University Press, 1965. 325p. Bibliog.
A compilation of the events and facts of the diplomatic negotiations and secret military cooperation between Germany and the Soviet Union during the Ambassadorship of Count Brockdorff-Rantzau to Moscow.

386   Weinberg, Gerhard L. **Germany and the Soviet Union, 1939-1941.** Leiden, E. J. Brill, 1954. 218p. Bibliog.
The period of the Soviet-German non-aggression pact is the subject of this chronological survey.

Great Britain and France

387   Jordan, W. M. **Great Britain, France and the German Problem: 1918-1939, A Study of Anglo-French Relations in the Making and Maintenance of the Versailles Settlement.** London, Oxford University Press, 1943. 235p. Bibliog.
An analysis of Anglo-French relations showing the solutions attempted under pressures of uninformed and emotional public opinion.

388   Selsam, John Paul. **The Attempts to Form an Anglo-French Alliance, 1919-1924.** Philadelphia, University of Pennsylvania Press, 1936. 85p. Bibliog.
The author details the negotiations that laid the basis for the Locarno treaties and the effects upon the diplomacy of the period of America's refusal to become involved in European affairs.

389   Wolfers, Arnold. **Britain and France Between Two Wars; Conflicting Strategies of Peace Since Versailles.** New York, Harcourt, Brace, 1940. 467p. Map, Bibliog.
A well-documented and lucid analysis based on material then available of the foreign policies of France and Great Britain and of the principal political events of the period.

Great Britain and Germany

390   Gilbert, Martin, ed. **Britain and Germany Between the Wars.** London, Longmans, 1964. 179p. Maps, Bibliog.
Uses short documents from many sources to help explain the main development of Anglo-German policies and opinions on the major issues confronting the two states.

391   Henderson, Sir Nevile Meyrick. **Failure of a Mission; Berlin 1937-1939.** New York, G. P. Putnam's Sons, 1940. 334p.
A shrewd analysis by the British Ambassador in Berlin of the developments of Hitler's policies and of events leading to World War II. The book presents a graphic record of the road of appeasement along with a vivid judgment of the personalities involved.

392   Middlemas, Robert Keith. **Diplomacy of Illusion; The British Government and Germany 1937-1939.** London, Weidenfeld and Nicolson, 1972. 510p. Bibliog.
A discussion of how the Chamberlain government understood the international situation in the light of the limits of its power due to military weaknesses, U. S. isolation, and Dominion and other foreign commitments. Compares British and German foreign policies in relation to Chamberlain's policies and his alternatives.

Great Britain and Japan

393   Kennedy, Malcolm Duncan. **The Estrangement of Great Britain and Japan, 1917-1935**. Berkeley, University of California Press, 1969. 363p. Maps, Bibliog.

A description of Japan's foreign policy of the period in relation to the Anglo-Japanese alliance of 1902-1922. Shows the influence of the geographical, economic and strategic implications on the interplay of their relations.

Great Britain and the Far East

394   Clifford, Nicholas Rowland. **Retreat from China; British Policy in the Far East, 1937-1941**. Seattle, University of Washington Press, 1967. 222p. Maps, Bibliog.

An examination of British responses to Japan's China policy in regards to the Sino-Japanese conflict and of the British position in relation to American policies and inaction in the area.

395   Lee, Bradford A. **Britain and the Sino-Japanese War, 1937-1939; A Study in the Dilemmas of British Decline**. Stanford, Calif., Stanford University Press, 1973. 319p. Bibliog.

An examination of Britain's response to the undeclared Sino-Japanese War through the use of the British Cabinet papers of the period. Emphasizes the interconnection of events in Asia and Europe with more specific detail on British evaluations of Japanese expansion, Chinese nationalism and communism. The author attempts to account for the contrasting policies of the British who pursued a firmer course of action in Asia than in Europe.

396   Louis, William Roger. **British Strategy in the Far East, 1919-1939**. Oxford, Clarendon Press, 1971. 284p. Map, Bibliog.

A scholarly survey using British archives of the official British perceptions of Far Eastern affairs. The problems of economic and diplomatic cooperation between Great Britain, Japan and the United States are detailed along with the ancillary matter of the race question and its "yellow peril" outgrowth.

Great Britain and the United States

397   Collier, Basil. **The Lion and the Eagle; British and Anglo-American Strategy, 1900-1950**. New York, Putnam, 1972. 499p. Maps, Bibliog.

A British military historian delves into the causes and effects of the ascendency of the United States over Britain as the leading global power. The study is concerned with the domestic politics, economic facts, military policies, strategies and tactics that brought this change about. He assesses the personalities of the key figures who helped shape their nation's policies.

Poland and France

398   Lukasiewicz, Juliusz. **Diplomat in Paris, 1936-1939; Papers and Memoirs of Juliusz Lukasiewicz, Ambassador of Poland.** New York, Columbia University Press, 1970. 408p. Bibliog.

The role played by the Polish Ambassador in Paris in a constantly worsening international situation. The major themes discussed are the frustrations of dealing with naive and uninformed allies, who refused to recognize the threat of the dictators, along with the necessity of continually requiring assurances of support from a reluctant French ally.

Poland and Russia

399   Budurowycz, Bohdan Basil. **Polish-Soviet Relations, 1932-1939.** New York, Columbia University Press, 1963. 229p. Bibliog.

An assessment of the relationship between Poland and the USSR and of Poland's policy of attempting to play off Germany against the USSR and to maintain a balance between the two.

400   Wandycz, Piotr Stefan. **Soviet-Polish Relations, 1917-1921.** Cambridge, Harvard University Press, 1969. 403p. Maps, Bibliog.

A well documented study dealing with the complex problems of Poland's shifting frontiers.

Russia and China

401   McLane, Charles B. **Soviet Policy and the Chinese Communists, 1931-1946.** New York, Columbia University Press, 1958. 310p. Bibliog.

For annotation, see item 963.

402   Whiting, Allen Suess. **Soviet Policies in China, 1917-1924.** Stanford, University Press, 1968, c.1953. 350p. Bibliog.

A record of the complex relations, stated from the Soviet side, of the period between the October Revolution and the establishment of Soviet-Chinese diplomatic relations.

Russia and the Far East

403   Moore, Harriet L. **Soviet Far Eastern Policy, 1931-1945.** Princeton, N. J., Princeton University Press, 1945. 284p. Bibliog.

A dispassionate and objective documentation, from Russian sources, of Soviet foreign policy in the Far East with some sidelights on European developments.

404   Tang, Peter Sheng-Hao. **Russian and Soviet Policy in Manchuria and Outer Mongolia, 1911-1931.** Durhan, N. C., Duke University Press, 1959. 494p. Maps, Bibliog.

Based on Chinese and Russian sources with, however, an anti-Russian bias, the author relates the negotiations, agreements and diplomatic and military conflicts in relation to Russian expansion and interests in the area.

United States and China

405   Buhite, Russell D. **Nelson T. Johnson and American Policy Toward China, 1925-1941**. East Lansing, Michigan State University Press, 1968. 163p. Bibliog.

Mr. Johnson was Chief of the Far Eastern Division of the U. S. State Department from 1925 into 1930, and advised Secretaries of State Kellogg and Stimson in this area. He was Minister to China from 1930 into 1941. He was thus an important figure in shaping American foreign policy for over fifteen years.

United States and France

406   Haight, John McVikar. **American Aid to France, 1938-1940**. New York, Atheneum, 1970. 278p. Bibliog.

Traces the efforts of the French government to purchase military aircraft from the U. S., the resultant positive effects on the American aircraft industry and F.D.R.'s realization of the benefits to future U. S. rearmament capabilities.

United States and Germany (and the Americas)

407   Compton, James V. **The Swastika and the Eagle; Hitler, the United States, and the Origins of World War II**. Boston, Houghton Mifflin, 1967. 297p. Bibliog.

An account of Nazi policies toward the U. S. during 1933-1941, the mistakes and failures which caused Hitler to declare war on the U. S. and an assessment of Hitler's influence on Japan.

408   Friedlander, Saul. **Prelude to Downfall; Hitler and the United States, 1939-1941**. Translated from the French by Aline B. and Alexander Werth. New York, Knopf, 1967. 328p. Bibliog.

Based on research in American, British and German archives, the author describes the impact of American policies on Hitler's decisions and of his dealings with President Roosevelt.

409   Frye, Alton. **Nazi Germany and the American Hemisphere, 1933-1941**. New Haven, Yale University Press, 1967. 229p. Bibliog.

Describes the methods, scope, and intent of German activities in Latin America, Hitler's views of the Americas, his underestimation of the power of the U. S., and German efforts to defeat F.D.R. in 1940. Develops a strong rationale for American entry in the war.

410   Trefousse, Hans Louis. **Germany and American Neutrality, 1939-1941**. New York, Bookman Associates, 1951. 247p. Bibliog.

A study of the development of Nazi attitudes, reactions and policies in relation to American policies and opinions during two crucial years.

United States and Japan (Including Events Leading
Up to the Attack on Pearl Harbor)

411   Baker, Leonard. **Roosevelt and Pearl Harbor**. New York, Macmillan,
       1970. 356p. Bibliog.
A journalist's study of President Roosevelt's involvement in the events of 1941
which led up to the Japanese attack on Pearl Harbor.

412   Borg, Dorothy and Shumpei Okamoto, eds. **Pearl Harbor as History**;
       Japanese-American Relations 1931-1941. New York, Columbia Univer-
       sity Press, 1973. 801p.
These papers presented at the Conference on Japanese-American Relations, 1931-
1941 are devoted to an examination of foreign policy decision making in the U. S.
and Japan during this period. Various levels of decision making in government and
in the private sector are investigated as to their influence and role in the complex
international issues of the time. A result of these excellent studies was the joint
belief that the causes of the war were far more difficult to discern than earlier
historians had supposed.

413   Feis, Herbert. **The Road to Pearl Harbor: The Coming of the War Between
       The United States and Japan**. Princeton, N. J., Princeton University
       Press, 1950. 350p. Bibliog.
A penetrating and objective diplomatic history of the events preceding the
Japanese attack on Pearl Harbor. A well documented study using the official
papers of the Roosevelt Administration, the papers and statements of Stimson,
Morgenthau, Hull and Grew as well as Japanese sources.

414   Grew, Joseph C. **Ten Years in Japan: A Contemporary Record Drawn
       from the Diaries and Private and Official Papers of Joseph C. Grew,
       United States Ambassador to Japan, 1932-1942**. New York, Simon and
       Schuster, 1944. 554p.
An invaluable interpretation and analysis of Japanese power politics, of the
Manchurian conflict, the German-Japanese alliance, Japan's war with China and
events pertaining to Japanese-American relations.

415   Hoehling, Adolph A. **The Week Before Pearl Harbor**. New York, Norton,
       1963. 238p.
An account of the petty inter-service quarreling that occurred in Washington, D. C.
the week prior to the Japanese attack on Pearl Harbor.

416   Johnstone, William Crane. **The U. S. and Japan's New Order**. London,
       Oxford University Press, 1941. 392p. Bibliog.
A review of U. S.-Japanese relations against a background of U. S. Far Eastern
policy. A scholarly analysis of the effects of Japan's activities on U. S. interests
and treaty rights of the period. Major attention is placed on the China concessions,
extraterritoriality and commerce. The author recommended a U.S. foreign policy
for peace through a genuine economic hard line against Japan and economic agreements and alliance with Great Britain.

417   Kimmel, Husband Edward. **Admiral Kimmel's Story**. Chicago, H. Regnery
       Co., 1955. 206p.
The personal story and explanation of the events of the Japanese attack on Pearl
Harbor. An important historical document by the commander of the Pacific
Fleet at the time. The Roosevelt administration is blamed for the disaster.

418   Koginos, Manny T. **The Panay Incident; Prelude to War**. Lafayette, Ind.,
       Purdue University Studies, 1967. 154p. Bibliog.
The author shows that the incident was a critical turning point in Japanese-
American relations. He analyzes the conflict between the diplomats and the
Roosevelt administration, world reaction to the attack on the gunboat, and the
impact of the event on U. S. naval policy.

419   Millis, Walter. **This is Pearl! The United States and Japan—1941**. New
       York, W. Morrow, 1947. 384p. Maps.
A concise review of Japanese-American relations in 1941, of the events, the
policies and the popular attitudes of the time. States that F.D.R. did not want
war with Japan nor did he precipitate it.

420   Morgenstern, George Edward. **Pearl Harbor: The Story of the Secret
       War**. New York, Devin-Adair, 1947. 425p. Maps, Bibliog.
A highly biased view, massively documented, indicting the Roosevelt Administration for misleading the public into thinking the U S. was supposedly seeking
peace when it was preparing for war.

421   Perry, Hamilton Darby. **The Panay Incident; Prelude to Pearl Harbor**.
       New York, Macmillan, 1969. 295p. Maps.
The events concerning the bombing and sinking of the U. S. Gunboat Panay by
Japanese aircraft. Discusses in minute detail what happened in this critical inter-
national incident in December 1937 from both Japanese and American viewpoints.

422   Rappaport, Armin. **Henry Stimson and Japan, 1931-1933**. Chicago, Uni-
       versity of Chicago Press, 1963. 238p. Bibliog.
An explanation of why the United States and Great Britain failed to act to stop
Japan's incursion in Manchuria between 1931 and 1933. The work is a very good
study of Stimson's doctrine of non-recognition and of the events leading to the
commission of inquiry (the subsequent Lytton Commission), its work and final
report.

423   Schroeder, Paul W. **The Axis Alliance and Japanese-American Relations,
       1941**. Ithaca, N. Y., Published for the American Historical Association by
       Cornell University Press, 1958. 246p. Bibliog.
Emphasizes the role of the Tripartite Alliance in Japanese relations with the U. S.
during the period prior to the outbreak of war between Japan and the U. S. The
author is very critical of U. S. policy under Cordell Hull for maintaining a rigidity
that prevented a possible settlement of Japanese-American differences.

424   Theobald, Robert Alfred. **The Final Secret of Pearl Harbor; The Washing-
       ton Contribution to the Japanese Attack**. New York, Devin-Adair, 1954.
       202p.
A sincere argument by an admiral serving at Pearl Harbor at the time of the attack,
that the responsibility for the eventual actions by the Japanese falls on President
Roosevelt due to his supposed desire to bring the U. S. into the war.

425   Trefousse, Hans Louis, ed. **What Happened to Pearl Harbor? Documents
       Pertaining to the Japanese Attack of December 7, 1941, and its Back-
       ground**. New York, Twayne Publishers, 1958. 324p.
A compilation of selected key and representational documents and testimony
covering the events leading to the Japanese attack on Pearl Harbor.

426   Wohlstetter, Roberta. **Pearl Harbor; Warning and Decision**. Stanford,
       Calif., Stanford University Press, 1962. 426p. Bibliog.
A lucidly written and fair presentation of the confusion and cross-purposes
inherent in the U. S. chain of command in relation to the Japanese attack on
Pearl Harbor. The author presents an accurate delineation of the intelligence
processes of the period.

United States and Russia

427   Davies, Joseph Edward. **Mission to Moscow**. New York, Simon and
       Schuster, 1941. 683p.
An outstanding source for the understanding of U. S. relations with Russia from
1936 to October 1941, of the state of Europe and the main international developments of the time. The work is a compilation of confidential dispatches to the
U. S. State Department, reports to the U. S. president, and personal correspondence by the American Ambassador in Moscow from 1936-1938.

United States and the Far East

428   Bisson, Thomas Arthur. **American Policy in the Far East, 1931-1941**.
       Rev. ed. New York, International Secretariat, Institute of Pacific
       Relations, 1941. 206p. Bibliog.
A contemporary study of official U. S. policy in the Far East from the Manchurian
conflict to three months before the attack on Pearl Harbor.

429   Borg, Dorothy. **The United States and the Far Eastern Crisis of 1933-
       1938; From the Manchurian Incident through the Initial Stage of the
       Undeclared Sino-Japanese War**. Cambridge, Harvard University Press,
       1964. 674p. Bibliog.
An important guide to the development of U. S. Far Eastern policy in the 1930s.
The author examines American attitudes on developments in China, U. S. naval
policy, and Roosevelt's approach to the international situation in the Far East.

430   Christopher, James William. **Conflict in the Far East; American
       Diplomacy in China from 1928-33**. Leiden, E. J. Brill, 1950. 335p.
       Maps, Bibliog.

The main emphasis is on the Mukden incident and the subsequent Manchurian take-over by Japan. The author tries to lay the responsibility for the U. S. timidity and inaction on President Hoover and ridicules the handling of U. S. policy by the Secretary of State, Mr. Stimson.

431   Griswold, Alfred Whitney. **Far Eastern Policy of the United States.**
           New York, Harcourt, Brace and Company, 1938. 530p. Map, Bibliog.
A thorough analytical treatment of the historical background of U. S. Far Eastern relations and policies in relation to its foreign policies as a whole since the annexation of the Philippines.

432   Stimson, Henry Lewis. **The Far Eastern Crisis: Recollections and**
           Observations. 3rd ed. New York, London, Harper & Brothers, 1938.
           293p. Maps.
A valuable analysis by the U. S. Secretary of State, from 1929-1933, of the special conditions and traditions that developed and gave U. S. policy in the Far East some very definite regional characteristics. The former Secretary of State describes the breakdown, due to a mutual lack of confidence, in Anglo-American cooperation over policies toward Japan and the failures of the attempts to bring moral pressure on the Japanese government.

433   Wheeler, Gerald E. **Prelude to Pearl Harbor: The United States Navy and**
           The Far East, 1921-1931. Columbia, University of Missouri Press, 1963.
           212p. Bibliog.
A careful analysis of the complex problems of the U. S. naval establishment in relation to U. S. foreign policy in the Far East, international developments, stringent military economics and a generally apathetic public and Congress.

CHAPTER 3—GENERAL INTRODUCTORY WORKS
ON THE WAR, 1939-1945,
AND WORKS ON STRATEGY

THE TOTAL WAR

434   Baldwin, Hanson Weightman. **Battles Lost and Won: Great Campaigns of World War II**. New York, Harper & Row, 1966. 532p. Maps, Bibliog.
An analysis of eleven major campaigns and battles considered most decisive or with long range importance. Each analysis offers an explanation of what happened, why it happened and the results. The campaigns and battles covered are: Poland, 1939, Battle of Britain, Crete, Corregidor, Stalingrad, Sicily, Tarawa, Normandy Invasion, Leyte Gulf, Battle of the Bulge and Okinawa. The author was military editor of the *New York Times*.

435   Buchanan, Albert Russell. **The United States and World War II**. New York, Harper & Row, 1964. 2v. Maps, Bibliog.
A general survey of the role of the United States in the war. Discusses the military aspects of the war and the political and economic impact of the war on the United States. Includes a good bibliographic essay although it is now somewhat dated.

436   Calvocoressi, Peter, and Guy Wint. **Total War: The Story of World War II**. New York, Pantheon, 1972. 959p. Maps, Bibliog.
One of the best comprehensive histories of the war. Covers the pre-war years and the military, political and social aspects of the war. Enhanced by numerous maps, illustrations and a bibliography. Gives almost equal coverage to the war in Europe and in the Far East. An excellent, well written introduction.

437   Churchill, Winston Leonard Spencer. **The Second World War**. Boston, Houghton Mifflin, 1948-53. 6v. Maps, Bibliog.
A combination of autobiography and general history. A literary and historical masterpiece by a great wartime leader. Churchill was Prime Minister and Minister of Defense from 1940-45. Especially good for coverage of grand strategy and the personalities of other political and military leaders. Although the work is a personal memoir it is included in this section because of its broad scope. The six volumes are: *The Gathering Storm, Their Finest Hour, The Grand Alliance, The Hinge of Fate, Closing the Ring,* and *Triumph and Tragedy*. [For an interesting essay on the publication history of this work see Frederick Woods, *A Bibliography of the Works of Sir Winston Churchill* (2nd rev. ed., Toronto, University of Toronto Press, 1969) p.351-356.]

438   Collier, Basil. **The Second World War: A Military History from Munich to Hiroshima**. New York, Morrow, 1967. 640p. Maps, Bibliog.
A well written history with emphasis on the military aspects of the war. Most of the work is devoted to Europe, but there is adequate coverage of the Far East. Useful appendices include materials on pre-war events and the organization and composition of the various land armed forces. Over 60 maps help amplify and clarify the text.

439   Congdon, Don, ed. **Combat**. New York, Dell, 1958-63. 4v.
These four volumes include well selected articles and excerpts from eyewitness
accounts of the war. Each selection is preceded by an introductory essay explaining the event and placing it in its proper context. The four volumes are: *Combat:
European Theater, World War II* (1958); *Combat: Pacific Theater, World War II*
(1958); *Combat: The War with Germany, World War II* (1963); and *Combat: The
War with Japan* (1962). One of the better anthologies.

440   Davis, Kenneth Sydney. **Experience of War: The United States in
        World War II**. Garden City, N. Y., Doubleday, 1965. 704p. Maps, Bibliog.
A general survey of the United States' participation in the war. Covers military,
political and social events that directly affected the United States. A good general
introduction enhanced by maps and a lengthy bibliographic survey of books on
all aspects of the United States at war.

441   Flower, Desmond and James Reeves, eds. **The Taste of Courage: The
        War, 1939-1945**. New York, Harper, 1960. 1120p. Maps, Bibliog.
An excellent anthology of eyewitness accounts from every theater of the war and
every period of the war. Includes narratives of American, British, German, Commonwealth, Italian and Japanese participants.

442   Fuller, John Frederick Charles. **The Second World War, 1939-45: A
        Strategical and Tactical History**. New York, Duell, Sloan and Pearce,
        1949. 431p. Maps, Bibliog.
Primarily a military history. Written shortly after the war, the author lacked
access to many then unpublished primary materials. However, this remains an
important analysis by one of the outstanding British military historians. The
book's great strength is its coverage of the development of strategical policy.
The reader should be aware of Fuller's anti-Churchill and anti-Roosevelt bias.

443   **History of the Second World War: United Kingdom Civil Series; United
        Kingdom Medical Series; United Kingdom Military Series**. London,
        H.M.S.O., 1952– . 79v. to date.
Nearly 80 volumes of this official history have been published. The works have
been well received and are generally well writeen and authoratative. Most works
in the military series were written by officers in the armed services and the works
in the civil series were written primarily by professional civilian historians. There
are two versions of the British official history. The version generally available to
the public excludes many references to official sources which were included in
the restricted edition. [Many individual volumes in the series will be cited throughout this bibliography.]

444   Liddell Hart, Basil Henry. **History of the Second World War**. New York,
        Putnam, 1970. 768p. Maps, Bibliog.
A well written comprehensive military history of the war. The author was one of
the leading British military theorists and historians. This history gives adequate
details about all military phases of the war and offers a penetrating analysis of
most of the important military engagements. Many of the author's judgments

regarding major strategic decisions are controversial. The reader should remember that Liddell Hart often disagreed with Churchill who was responsible for much of the war's grand strategy.

445   Pelling, Henry. **Britain and the Second World War**. Glasgow, Collins, 1970. 352p. Maps, Bibliog.
A general introduction to Britain's role in the war with emphasis on the war's domestic, social and political effects. The actions of British military forces are covered briefly. The author's analysis of Britain's role in the war is most useful. The annotated bibliography is useful particularly for studying Britain's wartime homefront. A good introduction.

446   **United States Army in World War II**. Washington, Office of the Chief of Military History, Dept. of the Army, 1947– . 71v. to date.
Over 70 volumes of a projected 99 have been published in this official history. When completed it will be the most comprehensive military history of any nation involved in the war. Although an official history, it is not an official interpretation of the U. S. Army's role in the war, but rather a critical and descriptive history. Most of the contributing authors are professional civilian historians. The sub-series in this set are: *The War Department*, *The Army Ground Forces*, *The Army Service Forces*, *The Western Hemisphere*, *The War in the Pacific*, *The Mediter-ranean Theater of Operations*, *The European Theater of Operations*, *The Middle East Theater*, *The China-Burma-India Theater*, *The Technical Services*, *Special Studies*, and *Pictorial Record*. A primary source and one of the most important works on the war. [Many individual volumes in the series will be cited through-out this bibliography.]

447   Young, Peter. **World War, 1939-1945: A Short History**. New York, Crowell, 1966. 447p. Maps, Bibliog.
A concise readable history with emphasis on the military aspects of the war. There is little discussion of economic, social or political activities. The coverage of all theaters is well balanced. This work is possibly the best short introduction to the war currently available.

THE WAR IN EUROPE–
THE MEDITERRANEAN–NORTH AFRICA

448   MacDonald, Charles Brown. **The Mighty Endeavor: American Armed Forces in the European Theater in World War II**. New York, Oxford University Press, 1969. 564p. Maps, Bibliog.
A general history of the European campaigns with emphasis on the role of the American army. There are good discussions of the major strategical decisions made in the campaigns, and enlightening biographical coverage of the major leaders of both the Americans and the Allies. Covers ground, air and naval aspects of the war. This volume refutes some of the assertions in Wilmot's pro-British *The Struggle for Europe*. The author served as a company commander in the U.S. Army and later as a historian in the Office of the Chief of Military History.

449   Wilmot, Chester. **The Struggle for Europe**. New York, Harper, 1952.
        766p. Maps, Bibliog.
Considered by many to be the finest one-volume history of the war in Europe.
Written from a pro-British point of view, many of the author's conclusions are
controversial. Primarily concerned with the military aspects of the war from the
Normandy Invasion in 1944 to the final defeat of Germany. Introductory chapters give the background of the German conquest of continental Europe in
1939-1940. Over 50 maps supplement the text.

450   Wright, Gordon. **The Ordeal of Total War, 1939-1945**. New York,
        Harper & Row, 1968. 315p. Maps, Bibliog.
A comprehensive study of Europe during the war years. Covers the military,
social, political, scientific and psychological aspects of the war. Discusses German
plans for the occupied countries and resistance movements in the occupied
countries. An excellent introductory work. Includes a lengthy annotated
bibliography.

THE WAR IN THE FAR EAST

451   Collier, Basil. **The War in the Far East, 1941-1945: A Military History**.
        New York, Morrow, 1969. 530p. Maps, Bibliog.
A well written one-volume introduction to the war in the Far East. Two sections
give the background of events leading to the start of the war and the remainder
of the book covers the military history of the war years. Numerous tables and
maps add to the value of the work.

452   Hayashi, Saburo and Alvin D. Coox. **Kogun: The Japanese Army in the
        Pacific War**. Quantico, Va., Marine Corps Association, 1959. 249p. Maps.
The best account of the war in the Far East from the Japanese view that has been
translated into English. Covers all military actions involving the Japanese. Discusses Japanese wartime strategy and the background of the modern Japanese
army. Over 90 biographical sketches of Japanese leaders are included in an appendix. The author was secretary to Japan's last Army Minister.

453   Hough, Frank Olney. **The Island War: The United States Marine Corps
        in the Pacific**. Philadelphia, Lippincott, 1947. 413p. Maps.
This volume remains one of the best works on the American campaigns in the
Pacific although it was written almost immediately after the end of the war. The
author gives a good analysis of both American and Japanese strategy and tactics.
Most major battles involving the U. S. Marines are covered including Guadalcanal,
Bougainville, Tarawa, Kwajalein, Saipan, Peleliu, Iwo Jima and Okinawa.

454   Toland, John. **The Rising Sun: The Decline and Fall of the Japanese
        Empire, 1936-1945**. New York, Random House, 1970. 954p. Maps, Bibliog.
A lengthy well researched narrative history of the Pacific war. Although written
by an American the story is told from the Japanese viewpoint. This is good popular history for the general reader, although it has been criticized by some historians. But, professional historians are almost always critical of popular history!
An easy painless way to get an overview of the war in the Pacific.

PICTORIAL HISTORIES

455   Churchill, Winston Leonard Spencer and Life (Chicago). **The Second World War: A History Combining New Selections from the Greatest Chronicles of the War and the Most Memorable Illustrations of the Men Who Took Part in It.** New York, Time Inc., 1959. 2v. Maps.
The narrative text is edited selections from Churchill's *The Second World War.* The selection of pictures is excellent and some are in color. Special captions have been written explaining the background of illustrations when needed.

456   Hatlem, John C. and Kenneth E. Hunter. **The War Against Germany and Italy: Mediterranean and Adjacent Areas.** Washington, Office of the Chief of Military History, Dept. of the Army, 1956. 465p. Maps.
Part of the official U. S. history of the war. Includes black and white photographs of the action in the Mediterranean area. Explanatory captions are given with the photographs. Includes photographs of weapons, terrain, living conditions and general human interest.

457   Hunter, Kenneth E. **The War Against Germany: Europe and Adjacent Areas.** Washington, Office of the Chief of Military History, Dept. of the Army, 1951. 448p.
One of the volumes in the official U. S. history series. A good selection of black and white photographs limited to the action of the American Army in Europe. Explanatory captions are given for the photographs. Shows equipment, terrain, weapons, living conditions.

458   Hunter, Kenneth E. and Margaret E. Tackley. **The War Against Japan.** Washington, Office of the Chief of Military History, Dept. of the Army, 1952. 471p. Maps
Another volume in the official U. S. history of the war. The photographs are limited to war action against Japan. The photographs are in black and white. Like other volumes in the series the emphasis is on weapons, living conditions, terrain and human interest.

459   Life (Chicago). **Picture History of World War II.** New York, Time Inc., 1950. 368p. Maps.
An excellent one-volume picture history of the war. There is a narrative text outlining the war, and explanatory paragraphs for the illustrations. Includes photographs, portraits and some paintings. Many of the pictures appeared originally in *Life* magazine.

460   Sulzberger, Cyrus Leo and others. **The American Heritage Picture History of World War II.** New York, American Heritage, 1966. 640p. Maps.
A carefully selected collection of over 700 photographs, drawings, art works and maps on the military, social and political aspects of the war. There is a concise narrative of the war and explanatory information with each picture. Photographs are in color and black and white.

STRATEGY

461   Addington, Larry H. **The Blitzkrieg Era and the German General Staff
       1865-1941**. New Brunswick, N. J., Rutgers University Press, 1971.
       285p. Maps, Bibliog.
Mostly concerned with the performance of the German army using the methods
of "blitzkrieg" from September 1939 to December 1941. The author maintains
that the motorized and mechanized units were a thin veneer which collapsed
because of lack of depth. Studies logistics as a major cause of the failure of
"blitzkrieg" strategy. Includes much information on the role of Franz Halder,
head of the German General Staff, 1938-1942.

462   Ansel, Walter. **Hitler and the Middle Sea**. Durham, N. C., Duke University
       Press, 1972. 514p. Maps, Bibliog.
An analytical and critical study of Hitler's Mediterranean strategy from 1940 to
the invasion of Russia in June 1941. The analysis is based on the author's personal
wartime experiences in North Africa and the Mediterranean and from correspondence and interviews with German commanders. Concerned primarily with the
use of naval forces in modern war and Hitler as a strategist. Useful too for an
insight into British strategy in the Mediterranean.

463   Bialer, Seweryn, ed. **Stalin and His Generals: Soviet Military Memoirs of
       World War II**. New York, Pegasus, 1969. 644p. Bibliog.
Autobiographical sketches of 45 major Soviet military leaders taken primarily
from their memoirs. There is a lengthy introduction to Soviet military leadership
under Stalin both before the war began for Russia in June 1941 and during the
war years. Useful for insights into the thinking of Soviet military leaders.

464   Baldwin, Hanson Weightman. **Great Mistakes of the War.** New York,
       Harper, 1950. 114p. Bibliog.
A compact work concerned with what Baldwin considers the major political
mistakes of the war. The mistakes led directly to the "cold war" and the generally
unsatisfactory conclusion of the war itself. The author was for years the military
editor of the *New York Times*.

465   Bryant, Arthur. **The Turn of the Tide; A History of the War Years Based
       on the Diaries of Field-Marshal Lord Alanbrooke, Chief of the Imperial
       General Staff**. Garden City, N. Y., Doubleday, 1957. 624p. Maps, Bibliog.

466   Bryant, Arthur. **Triumph in the West; A History of the War Years Based
       on the Diaries of Field-Marshal Lord Alanbrooke, Chief of the Imperial
       General Staff**. Garden City, N. Y., Doubleday, 1959. 438p. Maps,
       Bibliog.
An excellent memoir by the British Chief of the Imperial General Staff from
1941-45. Alanbrooke was responsible for the day to day conduct of the war and
formulation of strategy. A British view of the war at the highest levels of command.
Alanbrooke is anti-Churchill, Eisenhower and to some degree most U. S. commanders. A defense of British and Alanbrooke's war strategy. Indispensable, but should

be read with Alanbrooke's and the editor's prejudices in mind. These diaries cover the years 1939 to 1946.

467   Burdick, Charles Burton. **Germany's Military Strategy and Spain in World War II**. Syracuse, N. Y., Syracuse University Press, 1968. 228p. Bibliog.

An interesting well written analysis of German plans to capture Gibraltar and close the Mediterranean Sea to the Allies. Although the plans were never carried out, they remained a topic for German planners from 1940 to 1944. A valuable work even if the plans described were never attempted.

468   Butler, James Ramsay Montagu, ed. **Grand Strategy**. London, H. M. Stationery Office, 1956– . 6v. Maps, Bibliog.

The official British history of wartime strategy in all theaters of the war. A massive, but consistently high level account of grand strategy. Tends to be pro-British in its interpretations, but not to any extent that would detract from the overall value of the work. Specifically the volumes cover: v.l, 1933 to September 1939, N. H. Gibbs—not yet published; v.2, September 1939-June 1941, J. R. M. Butler—an account of strategy from the viewpoint of the Cabinet and the Chief of Staff from the outbreak of the war to the invasion of Russian in June 1941; v.3 (2 parts)–June 1941-August 1942, J. M. A. Gwyer and J. R. M. Butler—covers the period of final axis conquests from the invasion of Russia to early American victories in the Pacific. Describes the beginning of Anglo-American cooperation and a coordinated grand strategy; v.4, August 1941-August 1943, Michael Howard— begins the story at the high tide of axis success in all theaters to the almost complete reversal one year later when Japan and Germany were on the defensive and Italy had surrendered; v.5-6, August 1943-August 1945, John Ehrman—covers the final two years of the war including the Allied invasions of Italy and France and the great Russian offensives. Both volumes give extensive treatment to the Far East during this time period.

469   Cline, Ray S. **Washington Command Post: The Operations Division**. Washington, Office of the Chief of Military History, Dept. of the Army, 1951. 413p. Bibliog.

The official history of the Operations Division which was "charged with the responsibility . . . for the Army's part in the strategic planning direction of operations in World War II." Good on the development of coalition strategy between the United States and Great Britain.

470   Germany. Kriegsmarine. Oberkommando. **Fuehrer Conferences on Matters Dealing with the German Navy, 1939-1945**. Washington, U. S. Navy, 1947. 7v. in 9. Maps.

Translations of archival materials concerning Hitler's conferences on naval affairs. An excellent insight into planning at the highest levels. This material can also be found in Brassey's *Naval Annual*, 1948, pp. 25-496.

471   Germany. Wehrmacht. Oberkommando. **Blitzkrieg to Defeat: Hitler's War Directives, 1939-1945**. New York, Holt, Rinehart and Winston, 1965. 231p.

A selective collection of 74 of Hitler's major war directives. Each directive is preceded by a brief historical introduction putting it into the proper context. This is not a general strategical history, but it does give an insight into Hitler's military thinking. English title is *Hitler's War Directives, 1939-1945.*

472   Germany. Wehrmacht. Oberkommando. **Hitler Directs His War: The Secret Records of His Daily Military Conferences.** New York, Oxford University Press, 1950. 187p. Bibliog.
A carefully selected and edited set of documents on Hitler's military conferences. Unfortunately very little remains of the original stenographic records of the conferences. The editor's introduction and explanatory footnotes are helpful. Useful for both German strategy and as a psychological study of Hitler as a military leader from December 1942 to March 1945.

473   Greenfield, Kent Roberts. **American Strategy in World War II: A Reconsideration.** Baltimore, Johns Hopkins Press, 1963. 145p. Bibliog.
Although brief, this volume is one of the best scholarly works on American war strategy. The author presents his conclusions in four sections: "Elements of American Coalition Strategy," "American and British Strategy: How Much Did They Differ," "Franklin D. Roosevelt: Commander-in-Chief," and "Air Power and Strategy." A good analysis by the former Chief Historian of the Department of the Army.

474   Halder, Franz. **The Halder Diaries.** Washington, Infantry Journal, 1950. 7v.
The private diaries of the German Chief of the General Staff from 1938 to 1942. These diary entries actually cover the period from 14 August 1939 to 24 September 1942. Excellent for insights into the German campaigns in Poland, Norway, France, the Balkans and Russia which were all successfully completed before Halder's dismissal in 1942. Although not originally written for publication the diary still provides a valuable insight into German strategic planning.

475   Halder, Franz. **Hitler as Warlord.** London, Putnam, 1950. 70p.
A brief but important study of Hitler as a military planner and wartime military leader. Halder was Chief of the General Staff from 1938 to his dismissal by Hitler in 1942, and he was in a unique position to judge Hitler. Halder concludes that overall Hitler was a failure in the military sphere.

476   Higgins, Trumbull. **Soft Underbelly: The Anglo-American Controversy Over the Italian Campaign, 1939-1945.** New York, Macmillan, 1968. 275p. Bibliog.
Covers the background of the operations and planning of strategy in the African and Mediterranean campaigns. Describes Churchill's efforts to block a cross-channel attack and fight a limited war on the Italian peninsula. Fully covers the controversies over variant strategies of the Americans and their English allies.

477   Higgins, Trumbull. **Winston Churchill and the Second Front, 1940-1943.** New York, Oxford University Press, 1957. 281p. Bibliog.

A history of British and American strategy and their conflicts from the fall of France in 1940 to the Casablanca Conference in 1943. Special attention is given to Churchill's argument for a periphery attack on the European continent versus the Russian demand for a full scale second front. A good defense of U.S. policy.

478   Hinsley, Francis Harry. **Hitler's Strategy**. Cambridge, University Press, 1951. 254p. Bibliog.
A study concerned mainly with the formulation of grand strategy with little attention given to the actual battle operations. Emphasis is upon naval strategy. A good evaluation of Hitler as a maker of strategy and as a military leader.

479   Howard, Michael Eliot. **The Mediterranean Strategy in the Second World War**. New York, Praeger, 1968. 82p. Bibliog.
A scholarly study of the controversial Anglo-American Mediterranean strategy proposal to attack Germany through its "soft underbelly" instead of the northern Europe cross-channel attack. Analyzes the differences between British and American policy and their fluctuations throughout the war. The author contends that Anglo-American differences over Mediterranean strategy were not as serious as some historians have maintained.

480   Ismay, Hastings Lionel. **Memoirs**. New York, Viking Press, 1960. 488p.
While basically a "desk general" Ismay played an important role in wartime military policy while serving as Churchill's Chief of Staff Officer. As a liaison between Churchill and the generals—both Allies and British—he was often able to smooth the way for successful cooperation. Good insight into the British and Allied high command by a man who is not overly critical of others.

481   Kennedy, John. **The Business of War; The War Narrative of John Kennedy**. New York, Morrow, 1958. 370p. Maps.
One of the better memoirs by a British general at the General Staff level. An interesting British view of the development of the Anglo-American wartime relationship. Good for an intimate view of the personal relationships of top Allied leaders and especially Dill, Wavell, Churchill, Eisenhower and Marshall. Particularly good insights into Churchill.

482   Leach, Barry R. **German Strategy Against Russia, 1939-1941**. Oxford, Clarendon Press, 1973. 308p. Maps, Bibliog.
A comprehensive work on the strategic planning of the German invasion of Russia in June 1941—"Operation Barbarossa." Concentrates on Hitler's two major strategy policies—"Lebensraumpolitik" and "Blitzkrieg." Covers the military, political and economic problems of the campaigns in great detail.

483   Leighton, Richard M. and Robert W. Coakley. **Global Logistics and Strategy, 1940-1945**. Washington, Dept. of the Army, Office of the Chief of Military History, 1955-68. 2v. Maps, Bibliog.
A comprehensive study of American planning of strategy and logistics needed to fight a global war. A very detailed study showing the immense complexity of the planning operations behind the great campaigns and battles fought by American

armed forces. An official U. S. Army history. The first volume covers the years
1940-1943 and the second volume 1943-1945.

484   Liddell Hart, Basil Henry. **Strategy.** 2d rev. ed. New York, Praeger, 1967.
       Maps.
An expansion and revision of his *The Decisive Wars of History* first published in
1929. Of particular interest for the section on Hitler's strategy. Although some
conclusions are controversial, it remains a concise penetrating analysis. A special
appendix of a letter from Eric Dorman-Smith, Chief of the General Staff, Middle
East, discusses "The Strategy of Indirect Approach in the North African Campaign,
1940-42."

485   Marshall, George Catlett, Henry Harley Arnold and Ernest Joseph King.
       **The War Reports of General of the Army George C. Marshall, Chief of
       Staff, General of the Army, H. H. Arnold, Commanding General, Army
       Air Forces, and Fleet Admiral Ernest J. King, Commander-in-Chief,
       United States Fleet and Chief of Naval Operations.** Philadelphia,
       Lippincott, 1947. 801p. Maps.
A compilation of the reports of the heads of the Army, Navy and Air Force on
the progress of the war. The reports are those periodically made to the Secretaries of War and Navy. Although much could not be told because of wartime
restrictions, they remain a valuable source on war planning at the highest levels.

486   Matloff, Maurice and Edwin Marion Snell. **Strategic Planning for
       Coalition Warfare, 1941-1944.** Washington, Office of the Chief of
       Military History, Dept. of the Army, 1953-59. 2v. Maps, Bibliog.
A comprehensive study and evaluation of the evolution of American strategy
from the pre-war years to its development during the war. The first volume
covering 1941-42 is devoted to the development of defensive strategy; the
second volume covering 1943-44 is devoted to the development of offensive
strategy and coalitions with the Allies. These volumes are part of the official
U. S. Army history of the war.

487   Morison, Samuel Eliot. **Strategy and Compromise.** New York, Little
       Brown, 1958. 120p.
A concise study of the major strategic decisions made during the war by the
British and American Chiefs of Staff. The European and Far Eastern theaters
are both covered by the author. Good overview of coalition warfare.

488   Morton, Louis. **Strategy and Command: The First Two Years.**
       Washington, Office of the Chief of Military History, Dept. of the Army,
       1962. 761p. Maps, Bibliog.
An excellent overview of American and Japanese pre-war planning and wartime
strategy. Discussed in the context of global strategy and the complex diplomacy
which often decided the course of military actions. It is primarily a "history of
the council table," not the battlefield. Covers the place of the Army, Navy and
Air Force in planning combined operations. An official history of the U. S.
Army.

489   Pogue, Forrest C. **George C. Marshall**. New York, Viking Press, 1963— .
         3v. to date. Maps, Bibliog.
The definitive biography of the wartime U. S. Army's Chief of Staff. Marshall was
one of the most able strategists and administrators in the war. Pogue's work is
based on interviews and massive documentary evidence. Marshall wrote no
memoirs as he felt it was improper for a military leader to attempt such self-
serving devices. An excellent look at the war from the high command levels.
The three volumes published to date are: v.1, *Education of a General, 1880-1939*;
v.2, *Ordeal and Hope, 1939-1942*; and v.3, *Organizer of Victory, 1943-1945*.

490   Pogue, Forrest C. **The Supreme Command**. Washington, Office of the
         Chief of Military History, Dept. of the Army, 1954. 607p. Maps, Bibliog.
This volume is the official U. S. history of SHAFE—Supreme Headquarters,
Allied Expeditionary Force. Limited to the study of command of the ground
forces. Provides an introduction to the planning of the Normandy Invasion and
the subsequent Allied land operations leading to the defeat of Germany. Some
good material on the military-civilian relationships in liberated areas.

491   Romanus, Charles F. and Riley Sunderland. **Stilwell's Command
         Problems**. Washington, Office of the Chief of Military History, Dept. of
         the Army, 1956. 518p. Maps, Bibliog.
A study of General Stilwell's problems in the China-Burma-India theater. Written
at the level of the commandpost and is not a battlefield history. Concerned with
a theater commander who had to be as concerned with politics, diplomacy and
logistics as with battle strategy. An excellent history of a unique and difficult
battle command.

492   Steele, Richard W. **The First Offensive, 1942; Roosevelt, Marshall and
         the Making of American Strategy**. Bloomington, Indiana University
         Press, 1973. 239p. Bibliog.
A scholarly study of the complex political and military background of the decision
to invade North Africa in 1942. Good for an understanding of how strategy was
developed at the highest levels. The decision in favor of an offensive in North
Africa was not by any means unanimous.

493   Strawson, John. **Hitler's Battles for Europe**. New York, Scribner, 1971.
         256p. Maps, Bibliog.
This book is primarily "an analysis of strategic direction given to the war by
Hitler." Good insight into the personality of Hitler as a military leader and its
effect on German strategy. The story is told from the German view. The English
edition is titled *Hitler as Military Commander*.

494   U. S. Dept. of the Army. Office of Military History. **Command Decisions**.
         Washington, Government Printing Office, 1960. 565p. Maps, Bibliog.
A selection of twenty essays on ground operations with U. S. participation considered most important to the outcome of the war. Studies the far reaching consequences stemming from decisions of individual commanders responsible for a
particular military operation and for those commanders who made strategy
decisions. Some examples of the essays are: "Germany First: The Basic Concept

of Allied Strategy in World War II"; "MacArthur and the Admiralties"; and "The Decision to Use the Atomic Bomb." While this is not an official history, the selections are taken from various volumes in the official history of the U. S. Army. An excellent survey of some important wartime military decisions.

495   Watson, Mark Skinner. **Chief of Staff: Prewar Plans and Preparations.**
       Washington, Historical Division, Dept. of the Army, 1950. 551p. Bibliog.
A study of the U. S. Army in the years immediately preceding the war. An excellent historical survey of prewar rearmament, troop training, the development of war objectives and strategy, coordination with Great Britain and the development of outlying defenses. An overview of the state of the U. S. Army when war begins. One of the volumes in the official history of the U. S. Army.

496   Weigley, Russell Frank. **The American Way of War: A History of**
       United States Military Strategy and Policy. New York, Macmillan,
       1973. 584p. Bibliog.
A general history covering U. S. military strategy from its beginning to the present. The section of World War II is an excellent overview of American policy and grand strategy. Useful as a brief introductory survey.

CHAPTER 4 – THE WAR YEARS, 1939-1945:
MILITARY ASPECTS

GROUND WAR IN EUROPE

General Works

497   Ambrose, Stephen E. **The Supreme Commander; The War Years of General Dwight D. Eisenhower.** Garden City, N. Y., Doubleday, 1970. 732p. Maps, Bibliog.

A scholarly analysis of Eisenhower's military career from 1941-45 with emphasis on his "command decisions." Most of the "command decisions" related to North Africa, preparations for Overlord, the Normandy Invasion and the Ardennes. Studies Eisenhower's relationships with military and political leaders such as Roosevelt, Churchill, De Gaulle and Alanbrooke. Based primarily on *The Papers of Dwight David Eisenhower.* (See item 501).

498   Bradley, Omar Nelson. **A Soldier's Story.** New York, Holt, 1951. 618p. Maps.

The war memoirs of one of the most consistently successful Allied commanders. The memoirs are honest and in no way pretentious or overly critical of others. Bradley was involved in North Africa, Sicily, the preparation for the Normandy Invasion, the Normandy Invasion, the capture of Paris, the Battle of the Bulge, and the final defeat and surrender of Germany. Good insights into other leaders with whom Bradley worked—Patton, Eisenhower, Montgomery, Collins and Alexander.

499   De Guingand, Francis Wilfred. **Operation Victory.** New York, Scribner, 1947. 488p. Maps.

A memoir by Montgomery's Chief of Staff throughout most of the war. A headquarters view of the actions of the 8th Army in North Africa and the 21st Army in Northwest Europe—both commanded by Montgomery. De Guingand tells only of the experiences he knew of first hand. As expected the memoirs present a pro-Montgomery view.

500   Eisenhower, Dwight David. **Crusade in Europe.** Garden City, N. Y., Doubleday, 1948. 559p. Maps, Bibliog.

A memoir history by the Supreme Commander of the Allied Expeditionary Force in 1944-45. In 1942 Eisenhower commanded the U. S. troops during the invasion of North Africa. These memoirs tell the story of his command in North Africa and Europe. One of the best, most readable and most important memoirs of the war. Eisenhower, whose strength lay in his ability to get people to work together, has written a book which is fair to everyone and shows no bitterness or vindictiveness. Essential reading.

501   Eisenhower, Dwight David. **The Papers of Dwight David Eisenhower; The War Years.** Baltimore, Johns Hopkins Press, 1970. 5v. Maps, Bibliog.

A massive collection of carefully selected and edited wartime papers of General Eisenhower. The documents are only those that "he himself had written or dictated or which he had taken a direct part in preparing . . ." There are no "routine" documents and the arrangement makes use easy. The period covered is from December 1941 to May 1945. A primary research source, but not very easy reading—but it was not intended to be "light" reading.

502   Farago, Ladislas. **Patton; Ordeal and Triumph.** New York, Obolensky, 1964. 885p. Maps, Bibliog.

Patton is a difficult subject to capture on paper, but this study comes as close as any to that goal and overall is a better study than others published to date. Patton served in Morocco, with the 2nd Army Corps in Tunisia, the U. S. 7th Army in Sicily and led the U. S. 3rd Army in Northwest Europe fighting from France to Czechoslovakia. This account shows both Patton's weaknesses and strengths but on the whole is a favorable interpretation.

503   Freidin, Seymour, and William Richardson, eds. **The Fatal Decisions.** New York, Sloane, 1956. 302p. Maps.

A collection of essays by German officers on six decisive battles involving German armed forces. The battles are: Battle of Britain, Moscow, El Alamein, Stalingrad, France (1944), and the Ardennes. Hitler's strategy is blamed for each of these crucial defeats. Lack of troops and equipment are also considered important factors in the defeats. Good military analysis from the German viewpoint.

504   Gaulle, Charles de. **War Memoirs.** New York, Viking Press, 1955-60. 5v.

The memoirs of the wartime leader of the Free French. After distinguishing himself fighting the Germans in the invasion of France in 1940 De Gaulle fled to England where he was recognized as the leader of the Free French. The five volumes of these memoirs are: v.1, *The Call to Honor, 1940-1942*; v.2, *Unity, 1942-1944*; v.3, *Salvation, 1944-1946*; v.4, *Unity, 1942-1944. Documents*; and v.5, *Salvation, 1944-1946. Documents.*

505   Guderian, Heinz. **Panzer Leader.** New York, Dutton, 1952. 528p. Maps.

An autobiographical treatment of some of the major battles in Europe by a leading German general. Guderian is excellent on the military aspects of war, but says almost nothing about the morality of war. Good treatment of armor tactics. Mostly concerned with the Blitzkrieg battles of 1939-40 in Poland and the West and the Russian campaigns. The author also studies Hitler as a military leader and strategist.

506   Jacobsen, Hans Adolf, and Jurgen Rohwer, eds. **Decisive Battles of World War II: The German View.** New York, Putnam, 1965. 509p. Maps, Bibliog.

A collection of essays on ten decisive battles and campaigns which were turning points leading to the defeat of Germany. Emphasis is on German strategy and tactics and Hitler's role in their formulation. Generally the authors are critical of Hitler's influence. The various essays are devoted to the army, air force or

navy's role in a particular battle or campaign. The authors are all German historians or German generals who participated in the war.

507   Keitel, Wilhelm. **The Memoirs of Field Marshal Keitel**. New York, Stein
        & Day, 1966. 288p. Maps.
A memoir by Hitler's Chief of the High Command of the Armed Forces (O.K.W.).
Keitel was a "yes man" and seldom if ever questioned any of Hitler's military
decisions. Keitel was a poor excuse for a field marshal, and he says very little of
real interest in these memoirs. They are of value only because Keitel was in a
high position from 1938 to 1945. Keitel was convicted of war crimes at Nuremberg and hanged.

508   Kesselring, Albert. **Kesselring: A Soldier's Record**. New York, Morrow,
        1954. 381p.
An important memoir primarily because its author held high military positions
in nearly every European campaign. His most important assignments were as
Commander-in-Chief in Italy where he conducted a successful defensive action,
and in the final days of the war as Commander-in-Chief in the West. Kesselring's
only regret is apparently the fact that Germany was defeated. The English title
is *The Memoirs of Field Marshal Kesselring*.

509   Liddell Hart, Basil Henry. **The Other Side of the Hill: Germany's
        Generals, Their Rise and Fall, with Their Own Account of Military
        Events, 1939-1945**. London, Cassell, 1948. 320p. Maps.
This work is based on Liddell Hart's post-war interviews with a number of
German generals. Most of the generals were "essentially technicians, intent on
their profession, and with little idea of things outside it." Covers Hitler's pre-
war struggle to subordinate the German army to his will, and most of the important wartime campaigns. Excellent for insights into the personalities of German
military leadership. Emphasis is on Hitler's relations with his generals. The shorter
American edition is titled *The German Generals Talk*.

510   Manstein, Erich von. **Lost Victories**. Chicago, Regnery, 1958. 574p. Maps.
A memoir by the German Field Marshal who was called "the Allies' most formid-
able military opponent—a man who combined modern ideas of mobility with a
classical sense of manoeuvre, a mastery of technical detail and great driving
power." Valuable for insights into Hitler as a military leader although Manstein
is, perhaps, overly critical and places too much blame for the German defeat on
Hitler. Most of the book is on the campaigns in Russia. Good military history,
but no effort is made to condemn either the Nazis or their war aims.

511   Mellenthin, Friedrich Wilhelm von. **Panzer Battles: A Study of the
        Employment of Armor in the Second World War**. Norman, University
        of Oklahoma Press, 1956. 383p. Maps, Bibliog.
An excellent detailed study of the use of armor by the Germans. The book is
divided into four parts: "Poland, France, and the Balkans," "The Western
Desert," "Russia," and "Campaign in the West." The greatest attention is given
to the campaigns in Russia. A number of well done maps help the reader to

interpret the flow of battles. Good analysis of battles and the strategy of armored warfare. The author was a general and Chief of Staff of the 4th Panzer Army.

512   Montgomery, Bernard Law. **El Alamein to the River Sangro.** New York, Dutton, 1948. 192p. Maps.

An "operations report" rather than a memoir. An account of the military operations of the British 8th Army in North Africa, Sicily and Italy from 13 August 1942 to 31 December 1943. Montgomery avoids personal sentiment and gives a good account of high command planning. The narrative is aided by good maps.

513   Montgomery, Bernard Law. **Memoirs.** Cleveland, World Publishing, 1958. 508p.

The memoirs of one of the most controversial and successful British field commanders. Montgomery can claim never to have lost a battle. Discusses the differences in strategy between the U. S. and Britain which in many cases were differences between Montgomery and Eisenhower. His evaluation of Eisenhower as a military leader is less than complimentary. Good insight into understanding Montgomery's military leadership. Montgomery served in North Africa, Sicily, Italy and Northwest Europe.

514   Patton, George Smith. **War as I Knew It.** Boston, Houghton Mifflin, 1947. 425p. Maps.

The personal memoirs, diary entries and letters of the U. S. Army's most controversial and possibly most successful general. Patton held command positions in North Africa, Sicily, the recapture of France, the Battle of the Bulge and the final drive into Germany. One of the best Allied tacticians of armored warfare. Patton commanded the U. S. 7th Army in Sicily and the 3rd Army in Europe. Patton is often critical of those with whom he disagrees.

515   Ruppenthal, Roland G. **Logistical Support of the Armies.** Washington, Office of the Chief of Military History, Dept. of the Army, 1953-59. 2v. Maps, Bibliog.

Simply stated these two volumes are concerned with "how in the European Theater the tank got its gas, how the ammunition went forward, and how the food reached the troops." There is a good section on the effect of logistics on tactical planning. The first volume covers May 1941 to September 1944, and the second volume September 1944 to May 1945. Good chapters describing the buildup for Overlord.

516   Shirer, William Lawrence. **The Rise and Fall of the Third Reich: A History of Nazi Germany.** New York, Simon and Schuster, 1960. 1245p. Bibliog.

A popular history of the rise of National Socialism, its consolidation of power in Germany, its military conquests, and its ultimate defeat. A complex social, political and military history of Nazi Germany. The military history is primarily at the command level with little detail on individual battles. An encyclopedic treatment and one of the most widely read books on World War II. However, historians have generally been critical of the book and it should be read with some caution.

517   Sixsmith, Eric Keir Gilborne. **Eisenhower as Military Commander.**
       New York, Stein & Day, 1972. 248p. Maps, Bibliog.
A study of Eisenhower's military career from his West Point graduation through
World War II. Most of the book is concerned with the war years 1941-45. The
three areas given most consideration are the North African Campaigns, the invasions of Sicily and Italy, and the planning of "Operation Overlord." There is also
a discussion of Eisenhower's post-Normandy strategy for the conquest of Germany.
The author's generally favorable assessment concludes that Eisenhower's "special
genius was his skill at management." The author is a British general.

518   Stein, George H. **The Waffen SS; Hitler's Elite Guard at War, 1939-1945.**
       Ithaca, Cornell University Press, 1966. 330p. Maps, Bibliog.
A scholarly study of the military branch of the SS—the Waffenschutzstaffel.
Traces the evolution of the SS and its military arm and its relationship with the
Wehrmacht. Although at first limited to "pure" Aryans, by 1944-45 the Waffen
SS was mostly composed of foreigners. Based on German documents and Himm-
ler's papers.

519   Taylor, Telford. **The March of Conquest: The German Victories in
       Western Europe, 1940.** New York, Simon and Schuster, 1958. 460p.
       Maps, Bibliog.
The story of the German conquest in 1940 of Norway, Denmark, Belgium,
Netherlands and France. Told from the German viewpoint. Covers the coordi-
nation of the Army, Air Force and Navy in these "Blitzkriegs." Good coverage of
Hitler as a strategist and his relationship with the German generals. Discusses
both grand strategy and battle action.

520   Truscott, Lucian King. **Command Decisions: A Personal Story.** New
       York, Dutton, 1954. 570p. Maps.
One of the better memoirs by a senior U. S. commander who saw a great deal of
action at Dieppe, Tunisia, Sicily, and Italy. In Italy Truscott participated in
both the Anzio and Salerno landings. A good study of a commander making
decisions in fluid and often critical battle situations.

521   Warlimont, Walter. **Inside Hitler's Headquarters, 1939-1945.** New York,
       Praeger, 1964. 658p. Bibliog.
An "inside" view of Hitler's conduct of the war. The author was a high ranking
member of Hitler's military staff throughout the war. This appears to be an
honest view of events as seen by a high ranking German officer. Warlimont's
only complaint seems to be that Hitler was an amateur, and did not win the
war. Warlimont was convicted of war crimes at Nuremberg.

522   Ziemke, Earl Frederick. **The German Northern Theater of Operations,
       1940-1945.** Washington, Government Printing Office, 1960. 342p.
       Maps, Bibliog.
The story of the German military campaigns against Denmark and Norway and of
the collaboration with Finland in the campaign against Russia. Numerous maps
help the reader follow the narrative description of the major battles. The author's

brief but succinct concluding chapter places the whole German northern European campaigns in their proper perspective along with the reasons for their failure.

Germany-Poland, 1939

523   Bethell, Nicholas William. **The War Hitler Won: The Fall of Poland, September 1939.** New York, Holt, Rinehart and Winston, 1973. 472p. Maps, Bibliog.
A scholarly history of the German conquest of Poland in September-October 1939. This was the German's first full-scale "Blitzkrieg," and the rapidity of its success shocked the Western powers who expected the Poles to resist for at least six months. Critical of the Allies for their failure to act after their declaration of war on September 3, 1939. F.D.R.'s "neutrality," Russian complicity and the French and British inaction are all denounced by the author.

524   Kennedy, Robert M. **The German Campaign in Poland, 1939.** Washington, Dept. of the Army, 1956. 141p. Maps, Bibliog.
One of the official German Report Series published by the U. S. Army. Devoted to a detailed analysis of the military conquest of Poland. Studies the strategy and tactics used by the German offensive and the Polish defense.

Russia-Finland, 1940

525   Engle, Eloise Katherine and Lauri Paananen. **The Winter War: The Russo-Finnish Conflict, 1939-40.** New York, Scribner, 1973. 176p. Bibliog.
A historical survey of the Russo-Finnish War in 1939-40. Military aspects of the war and the related political issues are well covered. The viewpoints of both the Finns and the Russians are presented.

526   Lundin, Charles Leonard. **Finland in the Second World War.** Bloomington, Indiana University Press, 1957. 303p. Maps, Bibliog.
A well documented study of Finland in World War II with emphasis on the Russo-Finnish "Winter War" of 1939-1940. The book divides the Finnish involvement into three separate phases: "Winter War, 1939-40," "Continuation War, 1941-44," and "Lapland War, 1944-45." A good critical analysis of Finalnd's role in the war especially as an ally of Germany.

527   Mannerheim, Carl Gustaf Emil. **Memoirs.** New York, Dutton, 1954. 540p. Maps.
The memoirs of the distinguished Finnish statesman and wartime leader of Finland. While these memoirs cover his entire career they are especially useful for the war years. The strong character of the man comes through to his credit throughout the book. An insight into a leader's view of the Russo-Finnish Winter War and the later dealings with Nazi Germany.

528   Tanner, Vaino Alfred. **The Winter War: Finland Against Russia, 1939-1940.** Stanford, Calif., Stanford University Press, 1957. 274p.
Based on the personal diary of Tanner who was Finland's Foreign Minister during the Russo-Finnish War. Good description of the military and diplomatic phases of the war. Tanner gives both sides of the struggle and is critical of Finland's pre-war reluctance to come to terms with the Russians which might have avoided the war.

Germany-Norway, 1940

529   Andenaes, Johannes, Olav Riste, and Magne Skodvin. **Norway and the Second World War.** Oslo, Tanum, 1966. 167p. Maps, Bibliog.
A general history of Norway during the war. Some discussion of the pre-war position of Norway in German and Allied planning. Written from the Norwegian viewpoint and is primarily a condemnation of Bidkun Quisling.

530   Derry, Thomas Kingston. **The Campaign in Norway.** London, H. M. Stationery Office, 1952. 289p. Maps, Bibliog.
The official British history of this unsuccessful confrontation with the Germans. This was the first clash on land between British and German troops. Norway was the first British use of combined operations—coordination of land, naval and air forces. Good background on British and German strategy.

531   Macintyre, Donald G. F. W. **Narvik.** New York, Norton, 1960. 224p. Maps, Bibliog.
A critical study of the British failure at Narvik in 1940 during the Norwegian Campaign. A good examination of the first British use of combined operations—coordination of land, naval and air forces—to achieve a military objective. The author blames the failure on poor planning by the British at the highest levels.

532   Moulton, James Louis. **A Study of Warfare in Three Dimensions: The Norwegian Campaign of 1940.** Athens, Ohio University Press, 1967. 328p. Maps, Bibliog.
The history of the Norwegian Campaign is told from the view of all participants—German, British, Norwegian. The author has used sources from all sides and stresses that the importance of this peripheral campaign lies in the first British attempt at combined operations—the coordinated use of land, air and naval forces. The work is critical of both British and Norwegian strategical planning.

Germany-France, 1940

533   Bloch, Marc Leopold Benjamin. **The Strange Defeat: A Statement of Evidence Written in 1940.** New York, Oxford University Press, 1949. 178p.
A classic interpretation of the reasons for the French defeat in 1940. The work was written shortly after the final defeat by a leading medieval historian who was a soldier and member of the Resistance. Bloch maintained the two main

reasons for the defeat were the failure of military leaders to comprehend that the technological advances of warfare called for new strategy, and the fatal complacency of the bourgeoisie to the dangers of aggression.

534   Ellis, Lionel Frederic. **The War in France and Flanders, 1939-40.**
       London, H. M. Stationery Office, 1953. 425p. Maps.
The official British history of the German conquest of the Netherlands, Belgium and France in six weeks of May-June 1940. Concerned with the part played by the army, navy and air forces. Emphasis is, of course, given to the role of the British Expeditionary Force (BEF), and the Royal Navy at Dunkirk.

535   Horne, Alistair. **To Lose a Battle: France, 1940.** Boston, Little, Brown,
       1969. 647p. Maps, Bibliog.
This excellent history is an account of the military defeat of France in May-June 1940. It is particularly detailed for the crucial ten days from May 10th to May 20th. The early chapters cover the important political, social and economic background in France from 1919 to 1940 necessary to an understanding of the tragedy to come. Horne blames the fall of France in part on internal social decay, but ultimately as a military defeat. Probably the best book in English on the fall of France.

536   Shirer, William Lawrence. **The Collapse of the Third Republic: An**
       Inquiry into the Fall of France in 1940. New York, Simon and
       Schuster, 1969. 1082p. Maps, Bibliog.
A lengthy examination of political and social developments in nineteenth and twentieth century France which culminated in the military debacle of May-June 1940. The battles and campaigns are described in detail with emphasis on higher command and strategy. Good maps help clarify the narrative of the battles. A good introduction and overview written in an engaging style.

537   Weygand, Maxime. **Recalled to Service: The Memoirs of General**
       Maxime Weygand. Garden City, N. Y., Doubleday, 1952. 454p.
The memoirs of the French Supreme Commander from the time of his recall to active service in August 1939 to the Allied landing in North Africa in 1942. Of particular interest is the material on the French military defeat in May and June of 1940. Weygand served the Vichy government on several diplomatic missions until his forced retirement in late 1941. After the war Weygand was charged with collaboration with the Germans but acquitted.

Dunkirk—Battle of Britain, 1940—
Operation Sea Lion—Commando Raids

[Note: The "Battle of Britain" is included in this chapter to preserve some chronological sequence of events. Strictly speaking the "Battle of Britain" was an air battle, not a land battle. The evacuation at Dunkirk, the planned German invasion of England—"Operation Sealion"—and the Battle of Britain are treated together.]

538   Ansel, Walter. **Hitler Confronts England**. Durham, N. C., Duke University
        Press, 1960. 348p. Maps, Bibliog.
A study of Hitler's plan for the invasion of England—"Operation Sealion." Concerned with Hitler as a war leader and strategist particularly in the area of naval
operations. Examines the German command system and its failure in combined
operations—combined air, land and naval forces. Written primarily from the German viewpoint. The author was an admiral in the U. S. Navy.

539   Collier, Basil. **The Defense of the United Kingdom**. London, H. M.
        Stationery Office, 1957. 557p. Maps.
The official British history of the wartime measures taken to protect the United
Kingdom from land, naval and air attack. The greatest peril was considered to
be air attacks and amphibious invasion. There is particularly good coverage of
the "Battle of Britain" and the defenses against possible invasion. There are
good background chapters on the struggle for rearmament in the 1930s and the
general military situation on the eve of war. The last chapters discuss the threat
from the V-bombs. Excellent statistical tables in the appendix. The summary
chapter is an excellent overview.

540   Divine, Arthur Durham. **The Nine Days of Dunkirk**. New York, Norton,
        1959. 308p.
One of the best accounts of the evacuation of British and French soldiers from
the beaches at Dunkirk. The work presents a great number of details, yet it is
interesting and easy reading. The author shows that Dunkirk was no "miracle,"
bur rather the result of planning and hard work.

541   Fleming, Peter. **Operation Sea Lion; The Projected Invasion of England
        in 1940: An Account of the German Preparations and the British
        Countermeasures**. New York, Simon and Schuster, 1957. 322p. Maps,
        Bibliog.
An excellent history of the projected but never attempted invasion of England
by the Germans. There is full coverage given to the English defense measures.
The author argues that the "Battle of Britain" was a significant turning point
not only in the war, but in British history. The English edition is titled *Invasion,
1940*.

542   Great Britain. Combined Operations Command. **Combined Operations:
        The Official Story of the Commandos**. New York, Macmillan, 1943.
        155p.
A well written and exciting contemporary account of several important commando
operations. This official history was somewhat limited, of course, by wartime
security. The commando operations covered include the raid on Rommel's headquarters, Vaagso, St. Nazaire, Diego Suarez and Dieppe. The anonymous author
is Hilary St. George Saunders.

543   Middleton, Drew. **The Sky Suspended**. New York, Longmans, 1960.
        282p.
A personal view of the Battle of England by an American correspondent who
was in England during the "blitz." A well written exciting history of this

crucial battle told from the view of both civilian and military. One of the best of many books on the subject.

544   Robertson, Terence. **Dieppe: The Shame and the Glory**. Boston, Little, Brown, 1963. 432p. Maps.
The story of the unsuccessful Dieppe Raid in August 1942 by 5,000 Canadian soldiers. Because of poor planning over 3,000 were killed or made prisoners of war. Many valuable lessons were learned and used nearly 2 years later at the successful Normandy invasion.

545   Taylor, Telford. **The Breaking Wave: The Second World War in the Summer of 1940**. New York, Simon and Schuster, 1967. 378p. Maps, Bibliog.
A history of "Operation Sealion" and the "Battle of Britain" from the German perspective. The author is critical of German strategy at the most crucial time in the war. Good analysis of the important German military leaders. A scholarly lively book.

546   Wheatley, Ronald. **Operation Sea Lion: German Plans for the Invasion of England, 1939-1942**. Oxford, Clarendon Press, 1958. 201p. Maps, Bibliog.
This work is an official history although it is not part of the official British series. The origin and development of the German invasion plans are studied in detail. Of special interest is the evaluation of Hitler's role as a strategist and military leader.

547   Wood, Derek and Derek D. Demster. **The Narrow Margin: The Battle of Britain and the Rise of Air Power, 1930-1940**. New York, McGraw-Hill, 1961. 536p. Bibliog.
The authors have written an excellent history of the Battle of Britain which is especially valuable for its study of the background leading to the confrontation. The British victory was a victory of British science and technology—radar, the Hurricane and Spitfire fighters and the ability of the British to coordinate their aircraft and to modify tactics. The book is divided into three sections: 1) preparation and background, 2) the early phases of the battle, and 3) a detailed daily account of the battle from July 10th to October 31st. Appendices include valuable statistical tables.

548   Young, Peter. **Commando**. New York, Ballantine Books, 1969. 159p. Bibliog.
A well told story of the major commando raids on various German occupied territories. The five raids discussed are Lofoten, Spitzbergen, Vaagso, St. Nazaire and Dieppe. Although brief this volume is excellent and the illustrations add to the interest.

The Balkans, 1941

549   Buckley, Christopher. **Greece and Crete, 1941**. London, H. M. Stationery Office, 1952. 311p. Maps.

A popular history published originally pending the completion of the official British history. For a brief introduction, however, it has not been superseded by the official history. A good military history of the events involved in the fall of Greece and Crete during the spring of 1941. Offers an analysis and criticism of British and German military strategy.

550   Cervi, Mario. **The Hollow Legions: Mussolini's Blunder in Greece, 1940-1941**. Garden City, N. Y., Doubleday, 1971. 373p. Maps, Bibliog.
A history of the Italian Army's disastrous invasion of Greece. The Italian defeat is blamed on the incompetence of their leadership. The story of the Greek defense is not as well detailed as the Italian attack—if it can be called an attack! The struggle is shown at all levels from high command to troops in the field. The author served in the Italian Army in Greece.

551   **The German Campaigns in the Balkans, Spring, 1941**. Washington, Dept. of the Army, 1953. 161p. Maps, Bibliog.
"The purpose of this study is to describe the German campaigns in the Balkans and the seizure of Crete within the framework of Hitler's military policy during the second year of World War II." There are four sections devoted respectively to the Balkan military and political situation and the conquest of Yugoslavia, Greece and Crete. A final section discusses the relationship of the Balkan campaigns to the invasion of Russia in June 1941.

552   Heckstall-Smith, Anthony and Harold Tom Baillie-Grohman. **Greek Tragedy, 1941**. New York, Norton, 1961. 238p. Maps.
A history of the campaign in Greece from the invasion to the final evacuation of British troops to Crete. Equally good treatment is given to political and military events. Baillie-Grohman and Heckstall-Smith were commander and a craft commander, respectively, in Operation Demon, the British evacuation of some 40,000 troops to Crete. The story is told primarily from the British point of view.

553   Papagos, Alexandros. **The Battle of Greece, 1940-1941**. Athens, Scazikis, 1949. 406p.
A personal history of the Greek struggle against the Italian invasion in 1940 and the later German invasion. Papagos was the Commander-in-Chief of the Greek Armed Forces during the war. An honest well documented account of the Greek tragedy.

Germany-Russia, 1941-1945

554   Blau, George E. **The German Campaign in Russia: Planning and Operations, 1940-1942**. Washington, Dept. of the Army, 1955. 187p. Maps, Bibliog.
One of the better unbiased studies of the planning and early German military campaigns in Russia. There is good coverage of the strategy and tactics used in both the German offensive and Russian defense.

555   Chuikov, Vasilii Ivanovich. **The Battle for Stalingrad.** New York, Holt,
       Rinehart and Winston, 1964. 364p. Maps.
A personal memoir by the Russian military commander at Stalingrad. The story
of Stalingrad is obviously told from the Russian side. There is some distortion in
the political discussions and the reader should use some discretion. The account
of military action is more unbiased. The English edition is titled *The Beginning
of the Road.*

556   Clark, Alan. **Barbarossa: The Russian-German Conflict, 1941-45.** New
       York, Morrow, 1965. 522p. Maps, Bibliog.
A definitive military history of Operation Barbarossa—the German military plan
to conquer Russia. Clark skillfully shows the ferocity of war on the Eastern Front.
A critical analysis of German and Russian leadership although the history is told
primarily from the German viewpoint. Clark defends Hitler's military leadership
and disputes the claim that the war was lost solely because of Hitler's decisions.
There are five useful appendices including one giving biographical information
on German and Russian leaders.

557   Craig, William. **Enemy at the Gates: The Battle for Stalingrad.** New York,
       Reader's Digest Press, 1973. 457p. Bibliog.
A popularized account of the Battle of Stalingrad that began in the summer of
1942 and ended with the disastrous German defeat in the winter of 1943. The
work is based on research and numerous personal interviews of participants on
both sides. A good introduction to life in the besieged city, but not a definitive
account.

558   Goerlitz, Walter. **Paulus and Stalingrad: A Life of Field-Marshal Friedrich
       Paulus, with Notes, Correspondence and Documents from his Papers.**
       New York, Citadel, 1963. 301p. Maps, Bibliog.
A biography of Field-Marshal Paulus, the commander of the German Sixth Army,
which was surrounded and forced to surrender at Stalingrad. The biography is
short and factual stressing Paulus' background as it eventually related to the
crises at Stalingrad. The greater part of the book is devoted to documents and
correspondence relating to Stalingrad.

559   Goure, Leon, **The Siege of Leningrad.** Stanford, Calif., Stanford Univer-
       sity Press, 1962. 363p. Maps, Bibliog.
The 900-day siege of Leningrad lasting from August 1941 to January 1944 is
vividly described by the author. Equal attention is given to the military action,
civil life in the besieged city and the Russian civil and military leadership.
Scholarly, but sometimes difficult reading. Based on a PhD dissertation.

560   Howell, Edgar M. **The Soviet Partisan Movement, 1941-1944.** Washing-
       ton, Dept. of the Army, 1956. 217p. Maps, Bibliog.
A clearly written ". . . factual account of the organization and operations of the
Soviet Resistance movement behind the German lines on the Eastern Front
during World War II." There is background material on the operations of the
Wehrmacht and the Red Army. Based mostly on German sources.

561   Jukes, Geoffrey. **Kursk: The Clash of Armour**. New York, Ballantine
         Books, 1968. 160p. Maps, Bibliog.
The Battle of Kursk or "Fall Zitadelle" as it was called by the Germans, was the
greatest tank battle in history. This German defeat in July 1943 once and for
all demonstrated that the Russian Army now clearly outclassed the German Army.
The Germans put 900,000 troops, 10,000 pieces of artillery, 2,700 tanks and
2,500 aircraft into the offensive; the Russians countered with 1,300,000 troops,
20,000 pieces of artillery, 3,300 tanks and 2,000 aircraft. A short, well written
and well illustrated work.

562   Jukes, Geoffrey. **Stalingrad: The Turning Point**. New York, Ballantine
         Books, 1968. 160p. Maps, Bibliog.
A first rate popular military history of the Battle of Stalingrad and the final
annihilation of the German Sixth Army. The numerous maps and illustrations
help amplify and clarify the narrative and add to the book's value.

563   Pruller, Wilhelm. **Diary of a German Soldier**. New York, Coward-McCann,
         1963. 200p.
A memoir by a German (Austrian) soldier telling of his experiences in the Polish
Campaign, the Balkans and the Russian Campaign. Good detail of battle action
and of Pruller's political motivations. Pruller was a loyal Nazi and has little to
say about the morality of the war. His convictions as a Nazi are a frightening
tribute to the effectiveness of Nazi propaganda.

564   Ryan, Cornelius. **The Last Battle**. New York, Simon and Schuster,
         1966. 571p. Maps, Bibliog.
A popular readable history of the final three weeks of the war on the Eastern
front culminating in the Battle of Berlin and the fall of the German capital to
Russian soldiers. Ryan's analysis of military action is acceptable, but as a whole
the book should be read with caution.

565   Sajer, Guy. **The Forgotten Soldier**. New York, Harper & Row, 1971.
         465p. Map.
A moving autobiography of a German soldier's experience on the Eastern front.
Sajer served in three campaigns in Russia and eventually became a prisoner of
war. This is one of the best accounts of the fighting in Russia as seen by an
infantryman. Sajer vividly shows the desperate lot of the German soldier in
Russia after Stalingrad. Unfortunately Sajer ignores the question of the immorality of the Germans' presence in Russia in the first place.

566   Salisbury, Harrison Evans. **The 900 Days: The Siege of Leningrad**. New
         York, Harper & Row, 1969. 635p. Maps, Bibliog.
A detailed account of the siege of Leningrad which lasted from August 1941 to
January 1944. The general military situation is adequately covered, but the
stress is on the life of the Russians in the besieged city. Based primarily on
Russian sources and numerous personal interviews.

567   Schmidt, Paul Karl. **Hitler Moves East, 1941-1943**. Boston, Little,
       Brown, 1965. 640p. Maps, Bibliog.
The story of the Russo-German war from the beginning of Operation Barbarossa
to the collapse of the German Sixth Army at Stalingrad. Good details of front
line action. Both viewpoints are given, but emphasis is on the Germans. Schmidt,
the former press chief of the Nazi Foreign Office writes under the pseudonym
Paul Carell. Published in England under the title *Hitler's War on Russia.*

568   Schmidt, Paul Karl. **Scorched Earth: The Russian-German War, 1943-
       1944**. Boston, Little, Brown, 1970. 556p. Maps, Bibliog.
This sequel to *Hitler Moves East, 1941-1943* continues the story of the Russo-
German war from the Battle of Kursk to the Soviet offensive of 1944 in East
Prussia. The author used many German sources and interviews in researching
this volume. Like the author's previous volume the work is detailed and easy to
read.

569   Schroter, Heinz. **Stalingrad**. New York, Dutton, 1958. 263p.
A German version of the Battle of Stalingrad and the ensuing German defeat.
Schroter is critical because he does not accept Hitler's strategy as being correct.
There is no apology for the immorality of the German invasion, but only criti-
cism of German strategy for not winning the war.

570   Seaton, Albert. **The Battle for Moscow**. London, Hart-Davis, 1971.
       320p. Maps, Bibliog.
An account of the unsuccessful German attempt to capture Moscow in the fall
and winter of 1941. There is good coverage of military action at both the command
level and the front line. Includes informative sketches of the important generals
on both sides. The battle is told from both views with more emphasis on the
Germans.

571   Seaton, Albert. **The Russo-German War, 1941-45**. New York, Praeger,
       1971. 628p. Maps, Bibliog.
This encyclopedic work is basically an "analysis of the planning strategy and
tactics of the high command on each side." Seaton sees bad weather, poor
planning, geography and logistics as the main elements responsible for the German
defeat rather than the actions of the Russian Army. Detailed to the point that it
is somewhat difficult to read. Indispensable for reference.

572   **Small Unit Actions During the German Campaign in Russia**. Washington,
       Dept. of the Army, 1953. 289p. Maps.
A collection of selected narratives of German soldiers' personal experiences on
the Russian front. This official publication "provides lessons in tactics, logistics,
and techniques in the coordination of weapons, in the influence of terrain, climatic and weather conditions upon operations, and in the qualities of the officers
and men who fought on the Russian front."

573   Thorwald, Jurgen. **Flight in the Winter: Russia Conquers, January to
       May, 1945.** New York, Pantheon, 1951. 318p.
A day by day account of the final stages of the German defeat on the Eastern
front. Concerned with military actions and the plight of the German civilian
population. The evil of war is shown on both sides, but nothing is said about the
Germans having started the war. Another edition is titled *Defeat in the East.*

574   Werth, Alexander. **Moscow War Diary.** New York, Knopf, 1942. 297p.
An eye-witness account of the early months of the war in Russia. Written in diary
form, this volume gives a good insight of Russia at its darkest period in modern
history. The author who was raised in Russia gives a sympathetic portrait of the
Russian people.

575   Werth, Alexander. **Russia at War, 1941-1945.** New York, Dutton, 1964.
       1100p. Maps, Bibliog.
An interesting but by no means definitive account of the Russo-German war.
Werth, a correspondent for the London *Sunday Times* spent most of the war
years in Russia. Many personal vignettes based on personal interviews are included.
Covers the military, political and social developments during the war.

576   Werth, Alexander. **The Year of Stalingrad: A Historical Record and A
       Study of Russian Mentality, Methods and Policies.** New York, Knopf,
       1947. 475p. Maps.
Like the author's earlier work this is also an interpretation of the Russian mentality and Russian life during the war. This work is based on the author's diary and
is limited to his experiences in the summer of 1942.

577   Zhukov, Georgii Konstantinovich. **Marshal Zhukov's Greatest Battles.**
       New York, Harper & Row, 1969. 304p. Maps, Bibliog.
A somewhat biased poorly written Russian interpretation of four major battles.
Zhukov was a leading Russian military leader and served as Commander-in-Chief
on the Russian western front. The four battles described are the Defense of
Moscow in 1941, Stalingrad, Kursk-Orel and Berlin.

578   Ziemke, Earl Frederick. **Stalingrad to Berlin: The German Defeat in the
       East.** Washington, Office of the Chief of Military History, U. S. Army,
       1968. 549p. Maps, Bibliog.
A well researched history of the Russo-German war from the Battle of Stalingrad
to the fall of Berlin in May 1945. There is a good analysis of the failure of the
1941 blitzkrieg—Operation Barbarossa—and of the German and Russian strategy
after Stalingrad. Ziemke argues that Russian strategy and fighting performance
equaled the Germans by 1943. Although published by the government this is
not an official history.

Germany and Italy—Anglo-Americans and Allies

The Defeat of Italy, 1943-1945

579   Blumenson, Martin. **Anzio: The Gamble That Failed**. Philadelphia,
        Lippincott, 1963. 212p. Maps.
A history of the nearly disastrous Allied emphibious landing at Anzio in an
attempt to break a battlefield stalemate and capture Rome. The work focuses
on the major political and military leaders most responsible—Churchill, Generals
Harold Alexander, Mark Clark and John Lucas. Good details of the various misunderstandings that caused the Allied failure.

580   Blumenson, Martin. **Bloody River: The Real Tragedy of the Rapido**.
        New York, Houghton Mifflin, 1970. 150p. Maps, Bibliog.
A study of the command of Generals Mark Clark, Geoffrey Keyes and Fred
Walker, and the 36th Division, a Texas National Guard Division. The British
title is *Bloody River; Prelude to the Battle of Cassino*. The story is told at the
commander's level with little emphasis on the fighting in the battlefield. As a
result of the 1,600 casualties there were charges of poor leadership. This work
is based on the author's official history *Salerno to Cassino* but with slightly
altered conclusions.

581   Blumenson, Martin. **Salerno to Cassino**. Washington, Office of the Chief
        of Military History, U. S. Army, 1969. 491p. Maps, Bibliog.
The official U. S. history of the first eight months of the Italian campaign. The
time period covered is from September 1943 to May 1944. The author defends the
decision to attack the Germans through their "soft underbelly." The study
focuses on the U. S. 5th Army and their difficulties with terrain, weather and
logistics along with fighting the Italians and Germans. Some German views are
presented.

582   Clark, Mark Wayne. **Calculated Risk: A Personal Story of the Campaign
        in North Africa and Italy**. New York, Harper, 1950. 500p. Maps.
One of the better "top brass" memoirs. Clark gives an honest appraisal of his
part in the war which at times was as much in the political arena as on the battlefield. Most of the memoirs deal with the U. S. 5th Army and the British 8th Army
in the Italian campaign. There is some material on North Africa and Clark's later
role in Austria.

583   Garland, Albert N. and Howard McGaw Smyth. **Sicily and the Surrender
        of Italy**. Washington, Office of the Chief of Military History, Dept. of
        the Army, 1965. 609p. Maps, Bibliog.
The official U. S. history of the campaign in Sicily and the complex negotiations
for the Italian surrender. Emphasis is on the U. S. role in Sicily with good coverage of the amphibious operations and the use of airborne troops. The second
part of the study covers the extraordinarily complex negotiations for the surrender of Italy.

584   Jackson, William Godfrey Fothergill. **Alexander of Tunis as Military Commander.** New York, Dodd Mead, 1972. 344p. Maps, Bibliog.
A study of one of the most successful and respected British generals. Harold Alexander was a commanding general in Tunisia, Sicily and Italy. In 1944 he became the Supreme Allied Commander, Mediterranean Forces and was responsible for the successful Italian campaign. A fair study, but perhaps a bit too much praise and ignoring of minor faults.

585   Jackson, William Godfrey Fothergill. **The Battle for Italy.** New York, Harper & Row, 1967. 372p. Maps, Bibliog.
One of the best comprehensive works on the Italian campaign. There is a presentation of the background of the Allied and Axis strategies and their consequences. There is particular emphasis on the origins, differences and compromises of British and American strategy. The sections on various battles are clear and good maps enhance the narrative. Jackson is often critical of various policies and leaders—particularly Generals Mark Clark and Harold Alexander.

586   Jackson, William Godfrey Fothergill. **The Battle for Rome.** New York, Scribner, 1969. 224p. Maps, Bibliog.
A detailed account of "Operation Diadem," the Allied offensive to join the Anzio beachhead with the main front and capture Rome. Jackson has told the story accurately.

587   Linklater, Eric. **The Campaign in Italy.** London, H. M. Stationery Office, 1951. 480p. Maps.
A popular "official" British history of the Italian campaign from 1943 to May 1945. Although it was to superseded by the official history this remains a valuable study. A detailed account of the British 8th Army and the U. S. 5th Army from the first landings to the German surrender at Caserta in May 1945.

588   Majdalany, Fred. **The Battle of Cassino.** Boston, Houghton Mifflin, 1957. 309p. Maps, Bibliog.
A definitive study of the most lengthy and costly battle in the Italian campaign. This is the story of the four months from February to May 1944 when the Allies attempted to capture Monte Cassino and Break the Gustav Line, thus opening the road to Rome. There is a good assessment of the commanders and troop performance and of life in the monastery.

589   Murphy, Audie. **To Hell and Back.** New York, Holt, 1949. 274p.
One of the better personal narratives by a front line soldier. Murphy was the most decorated U. S. soldier in the war winning 21 medals including the Congressional Medal of Honor. Murphy fought at Salerno, Anzio, Southern France and the final drive into Germany.

590   Pond, Hugh. **Salerno.** Boston, Little, Brown, 1962. 269p. Maps.
A day by day chronological account of the first large scale Allied landing on the European continent in 1943. There is good detail of the landing operation and good accounts of the battle at the command and battlefield levels.

591   Shepperd, Gilbert Alan. **The Italian Campaign, 1943-45: A Political and Military Re-Assessment**. New York, Praeger, 1968. 450p. Maps, Bibliog.
Considered to be one of the finest overall histories of the war in Italy. The author discusses the political decisions behind the Italian campaign and the resulting military strategy. There is a good critical analysis of both and the analysis is particularly strong in military strategy and tactics. A well told history of the U. S. 5th Army and British 8th Army from the Sicily invasion to the final victory in northern Italy.

The Defeat of Germany, 1944-1945

General

592   Ellis, Lionel Frederic, and others. **Victory in the West**. London, H. M. Stationery Office, 1962-68. 2v. Maps, Bibliog.
A comprehensive history of the Allies' defeat of the German Army in the West. Accounts for the part played by the British and American naval, land and air forces. The two volumes are: v.l, *The Battle for Normandy*—surveys the background, planning and landings in Normandy on June 6, 1944 to the liberation of France in September 1944; v.2, *The Defeat of Germany*—covers the final German defeat from September 1944 to May 1945. This work is part of the official British history of the war.

593   Montgomery, Bernard Law. **Normandy to the Baltic**. Boston, Houghton Mifflin, 1948. 351p. Maps.
An "operations report" by the commander of the 21st Army Group. The report covers operations in Northwest Europe from June 1944 to March 1945. In spite of the intended nature of the "report" Montgomery allows some anti-U. S. sentiments to show. The not always clear narrative is supplemented with excellent maps of the battle action.

594   Supreme Headquarters Allied Expeditionary Force. **Report by the Supreme Commander to the Combined Chiefs of Staff on the Operations in Europe of the Allied Expeditionary Force, 6 June 1944 to 8 May 1945**. Washington, Government Printing Office, 1946. 123p. Maps.
The official report by General Eisenhower on the activities of the Allied Expeditionary Force from the Normandy invasion to the defeat of Germany. The report covers the preparation for Overlord, the Normandy invasion, breakthrough in France, Ardennes and the counteroffensive, occupation of Germany and junction with the Russians. A good unbiased summary of the European campaign.

Normandy Invasion, 1944

595   Belfield, Eversley Michael Gallimore and Hubert Essame. **The Battle for Normandy**. Philadelphia, Dufour, 1965. 239p. Maps, Bibliog.
This volume is primarily a study of the British in the Battle for Normandy. The story begins on June 7, 1944, D-Day plus 1, and ends on August 22nd when the Falaise Gap was secured. There is no coverage of the landings. There is some

coverage of American forces, but the primary emphasis is on the British contribution in the post-invasion fighting in northern France.   .

596   **D-Day: The Normandy Invasion in Retrospect.** Lawrence, University
          Press of Kansas, 1971. 254p. Bibliog.
An evaluation of all aspects of the Normandy invasion of June 6, 1944. Among
the factors considered are planning, logistics, weather, equipment and landings.
The work is a collection of essays by many scholars such as Omar Bradley and
Martin Blumenson and the essays are of uniformly high quality.

597   Harrison, Gordon A. **Cross-Channel Attack.** Washington, Office of the
          Chief of Military History, Dept. of the Army, 1951. 519p. Maps, Bibliog.
The official U. S. history of the development of strategy and planning for the invasion of Europe. The volume is concerned with the planning and preparation—
seven chapters—and the actual landing operations and combat activities of the
U. S. 1st Army from June 6 to July 1, 1944—three chapters. In the chapters on
strategy and planning both the U. S. and German sides are covered from 1941
to 1944. This work is concerned primarily with the role of American forces and
the Allies are discussed only as they relate to American participation. Possibly
the best study of Overlord.

598   Majdalany, Fred. **The Fall of Fortress Europe.** Garden City, N. Y.,
          Doubleday, 1968. 442p. Maps, Bibliog.
A summary of the German efforts to develop and hold "fortress Europe." The
time covered is from December 1941, to the Normandy invasion in June 1944.
There are many biographical sketches of the German generals most responsible
for defending continental Europe from invasion.

599   Marshall, Samuel Lyman Atwood. **Night Drop: The American Airborne
          Invasion of Normandy.** Boston, Little, Brown, 1962. 425p. Maps.
The story of the U. S. 82nd and 101st Airborne Divisions which were parachuted
behind the Normandy beaches just hours before the landings to help establish a
foothold. Good on small unit action. Based on personal interviews.

600   Morgan, Frederick Edgeworth. **Overture to Overlord.** Garden City,
          N. Y., Doubleday, 1950. 302p.
A personal memoir on the planning of Overlord rather than an account of
battle action. The author was Chief of Staff to the Supreme Allied Commander
and did much of the preliminary "brainwork" and planning for the invasion of
Europe. This is a fair account of the American and British contributions to
Overlord at the planning level. Most of Morgan's ideas were ultimately incorpor-
ated into the final invasion plans.

601   Ryan, Cornelius. **The Longest Day, June 6, 1944.** New York, Simon and
          Schuster, 1959. 350p. Maps, Bibliog.
A fascinating popular account of the Normandy landings. The book is based on
personal interviews and gives interesting stories of the participation of many individuals. Told how the invasion was seen personally by men on both sides. Not
definitive, but this work presents an interesting viewpoint and is worth reading.

602   Schmidt, Paul Karl. **Invasion—They're Coming! The German Account of the Allied Landings and the 80 Days' Battle for France.** New York, Dutton, 1963. 288p. Maps, Bibliog.

A German view of the Normandy invasion and the ensuing breakout into France. Based on personal interviews of many German soldiers. This is not the best book on this phase of the war, but it is interesting because it presents the German's side of the campaign.

603   Stagg, James Martin. **Forecast for Overlord, June 6, 1944.** New York, Norton, 1972. 128p.

A specialized account of weather and climatic conditions and their effect on the launching of Operation Overlord. The weather was one of the crucial factors which could have caused the failure of the Normandy invasion.

604   Stanford, Alfred Boller. **Force Mulberry: The Planning and Installation of the Artificial Harbor off U. S. Normandy Beaches in World War II.** New York, Morrow, 1951. 240p. Maps, Bibliog.

A specialized study of the planning and building of the artificial docks off Normandy by the Allies. Shows the importance of logistics and supplies to a military operations.

Liberation of France, 1944

605   Aron, Robert. **De Gaulle Before Paris: The Liberation of France, June-August, 1944.** London, Putnam, 1962. 312p.

606   Aron, Robert. **De Gaulle Triumphant: The Liberation of France, August 1944-May 1945.** London, Putnam, 1964. 360p.

A detailed scholarly account of the liberation of France. Includes many vignettes and humorous comments relating to the liberation's effects on a wide cross section of Frenchmen. The author is pro-De Gaulle, and these volumes are a defense of De Gaulle's policies while being generally critical of the Allies. The American edition is abridged and issued under the title *France Reborn: The History of the Liberation, June 1944-May 1945.*

607   Blumenson, Martin. **Breakout and Pursuit.** Washington, Office of the Chief of Military History, Dept. of the Army, 1961. 748p. Maps, Bibliog.

The official U. S. history of the U. S. Army in France and Northwest Europe from July to September 1944. This period saw the liberation of France from German control and the retreat of the German Army into Germany. Blumenson is critical of both German and Allied strategy and is particularly hostile to General Montgomery. Excellent maps help clarify the narrative account of various battles. The author has also written a popular history based on this official history—
The Duel for France, 1944 (New York, Houghton Mifflin, 1963). (See item 608).

608   Blumenson, Martin. **The Duel for France, 1944.** Boston, Houghton Mifflin, 1963. 432p. Maps, Bibliog.

A popular history based on the author's official history *Breakout and Pursuit.* (See previous entry).

609   Cole, Hugh Marshall. **The Lorraine Campaign.** Washington, Historical
           Division, Dept. of the Army, 1950. 657p. Maps, Bibliog.
The official U. S. history of the campaign fought by the U. S. 3rd Army under
General Patton in Lorraine from September 1st to December 18th 1944. This
work is primarily concerned with the tactical operations at the battlefield level
and it seldom discusses high command decisions. Excellent maps help the reader
through the sometimes complex narrative description of the battlefield action.

610   Collins, Larry and Dominique Lapierre. **Is Paris Burning?** New York,
           Simon and Schuster, 1965. 376p. Maps, Bibliog.
A popular account retelling the story of the liberation of Paris in August 1944.
There are many narratives of personal experiences. Emphasis is placed on Hitler's
order to burn Paris before the German evacuation and the German failure to
carry out the order.

611   Robichon, Jacques. **The Second D-Day.** New York, Walker, 1969. 314p.
           Maps.
The story of "Operation Dragoon," the Allied landings in Southern France in
August 1944. The author successfully covers the background and planning of
the campaign and the military activities of the Allies and Germans after the
landings. While not the best written book it does give adequate coverage to an
often overlooked campaign.

Final Defeat of Germany in the West, 1944-1945

612   Ambrose, Stephen E. **Eisenhower and Berlin, 1945: The Decision to
           Halt at the Elbe.** New York, Norton, 1967. 119p. Maps, Bibliog.
A scholarly defense of Eisenhower's decision to halt the Allies at the Elbe and
leave Berlin to the Russians. Ambrose points out that the Allies would have to
have withdrawn from Berlin anyway because of earlier political decisions.

613   Chuikov, Vasilii Ivanovich. **The Fall of Berlin.** New York, Holt,
           Rinehart and Winston, 1968. 261p. Maps.
A candid personal account of the last days of fighting on the Eastern front.
There is good detail on the battles and some criticism of strategy and tactics
on both sides. Chuikov plays down the contributions of the Allies and throws
in some propaganda, but this does not detract from the overall contribution of
the book. The English title is *The End of the Third Reich.*

614   Cole, Hugh Marshall. **The Ardennes: Battle of the Bulge.** Washington,
           Office of the Chief of Military History, Dept. of the Army, 1965.
           720p. Maps, Bibliog.
The official U. S. history of the Battle of the Bulge from December 16, 1944 to
January 3, 1945, which ended with the exhaustion of the German counteroffensive. There is also detailed coverage of battle action based on official
sources and numerous interviews of participants on all sides. As in other volumes
of this series there are excellent maps which help clarify the narrative.

615   Eisenhower, John S. D. **The Bitter Woods; The Dramatic Story, Told at all Echelons, from Supreme Command to Squad Leader, of the Crisis that Shook the Western Coalition: Hitler's Surprise Ardennes Offensive.** New York, Putnam, 1969. 506p. Maps, Bibliog.

The Battle of the Bulge, or the Ardennes, is studied in great detail by the son of the Supreme Allied Commander in Europe. The Ardennes counteroffensive was Hitler's last attempt to drive the Allies out of Europe. Based on numerous interviews there is excellent coverage of high level command and of small unit action on both sides. There are good maps that help amplify the text. The background material is, perhaps, overly long and the book would have been better if it were shorter.

616   Essame, Hubert. **The Battle for Germany.** New York, Scribner, 1969. 228p. Maps, Bibliog.

A British view of the conquest of northwest Europe and Germany in late 1944 and 1945. The narrative is confined to the campaigns of General Montgomery's 21st Army Group. The author praises Montgomery's leadership and gives little credit to American leaders.

617   MacDonald, Charles Brown. **The Battle of Huertgen Forest.** Philadelphia, Lippincott, 1963. 215p. Maps.

The story of the series of battles between September and December 1944 involving seventeen divisions of the Allied 1st Army. MacDonald maintains that the battles were unnecessary and could have been avoided. There is criticism of the responsible American commanders.

618   MacDonald, Charles Brown. **Company Commander.** Washington, Infantry Journal Press, 1947. 278p.

The war memoirs of a company commander in the U. S. 2nd Infantry Division. The author tells of his experiences in Northwest Europe from October 1944 to July 1945. A well told honest view of the trials and tribulations of a lower level commander and of daily life in combat.

619   MacDonald, Charles Brown. **The Siegfried Line Campaign.** Washington, Office of the Chief of Military History, Dept. of the Army, 1963. 670p. Maps, Bibliog.

The official history of the U. S. 1st and 9th Armies and the Allied 1st Airborne Army and some U. S. units under British command in northwest Europe from September to December 1944. There are good accounts of "Operation Market-Garden" and the battles of Huertgen Forest. While not as exciting as the Normandy landings and "blitzkrieg" through France, these slower paced battles also proved the excellence of the U. S. soldier. Good detailed account of battlefield action.

620   MacDonald, Charles Brown and Sidney T. Mathews. **Three Battles: Arnaville, Altuzzo, and Schmidt.** Washington, Office of the Chief of Military History, Dept. of the Army, 1952. 443p. Maps, Bibliog.

This official U. S. history discusses three separate small unit actions to show "the difficulties of small unit commanders and soldiers in executing missions assigned by higher headquarters." Based on official records and many personal interviews. Arnaville was fought in France; Altuzzo in Italy; and Schmidt in Germany.

621   Marshall, Samuel Lyman Atwood, and others. **Bastogne: The Story of the First Eight Days in Which the 101st Airborne Division was Closed Within the Ring of German Forces.** Washington, Infantry Journal Press, 1946. 261p. Maps.
The siege of Bastogne during the Battle of the Bulge is told in the words of the men on the front lines. The book is based on Marshall's interviews with American soldiers. Describes how soldiers from infantry, artillery and armour units formed a successful defense.

622   Merriam, Robert E. **Dark December: The Full Account of the Battle of the Bulge.** New York, Ziff-Davis, 1947. 234p. Maps.
A now classic book on the Battle of the Bulge although it has in part been superseded by later official histories. Both the German and American sides are told. The author wrote from official records and extensive personal interviews with most of the American and German commanders.

623   Minott, Rodney G. **The Fortress that Never Was: The Myth of Hitler's Bavarian Stronghold.** New York, Holt, Rinehart and Winston, 1964. 208p. Map, Bibliog.
The importance of the alleged Nazi redoubt on Allied strategy and planning is the subject of this book. As late as the early spring of 1945 U. S. planners believed the rumors of strong Nazi troop and material concentrations in Germany's mountainous forest regions. Although the rumors proved false they did affect Allied thinking and caused great concern.

624   Stacey, Charles Perry. **The Victory Campaign : The Operations in North-West Europe, 1944-1945.** Ottawa, Queen's Printer, 1960. 770p. Maps, Bibliog.
This excellent and unbiased history is a volume in the official history of the Canadian Army in World War II. The often overlooked role of Canadian forces in the struggle against Germany is told in great detail against the total background of the fighting. There is an unemotional analysis of both British and American leadership with many fair criticisms of both sides.

625   Strawson, John. **The Battle for the Ardennes.** New York, Scribner, 1972. 212p. Maps, Bibliog.
A well written revisionist account of the Battle of the Bulge. The author points out the strategic value of the Ardennes and the errors made by both sides during the battles. Good coverage at both the high command level and the company level.

626   Thompson, Reginald William. **Montgomery, The Field Marshal: The Campaign in North-West Europe, 1944/45.** New York, Scribner, 1970. 344p. Maps, Bibliog.
This is in effect the history of the British armed forces in northwest Europe from the Normandy invasion to the German surrender. Although told from the British

view, the author is critical of Montgomery. A good work on this most important campaign in the European theater. One of the better studies of Montgomery as a military leader.

627   Toland, John. **Battle, The Story of the Bulge**. New York, Random House, 1959. 400p. Maps.

While somewhat weak in interpretation of strategy this work remains valuable for its insight into the feelings and reactions of men on the front line. The story of the Battle of the Bulge is told in an exciting narrative style which places the reader in the action. This, however, is not a definitive study nor does it claim to be one.

628   Toland, John. **The Last 100 Days**. New York, Random House, 1966. 622p. Maps, Bibliog.

A popular account of the final three months of the war in Europe. Based on research and a great number of personal interviews. Mostly concerned with the war on the Eastern front. Exciting reading, but it is not definitive and should be used with some caution.

THE WAR IN NORTH AFRICA AND THE MEDITERRANEAN

629   Agar-Hamilton, John Augustus Ion and Leonard Charles Frederick Turner. **Crisis in the Desert, May-July 1942**. New York, Oxford University Press, 1952. 368p. Maps.

A well written unbiased account of the battles of Tobruk in 1942 and the action just prior to the Battle of El Alamein in 1942. This is a volume in the official history of the Union of South Africa forces in the war. Considers the North African war from a slightly different perspective.

630   Agar-Hamilton, John Augustus Ion and Leonard Charles Frederick Turner. **The Sidi Rezeg Battles, 1941**. New York, Oxford University Press, 1957. 505p. Maps, Bibliog.

A volume in the official history of the Union of South Africa in World War II. A skillfully told history of the British Eighth Army offensive in November-December 1941 against German forces under Rommel. The strategy and tactics of both sides are described in great detail although the story is centered around the South African contribution. Good too for a study of desert armoured warfare tactics.

631   Barnett, Correlli. **The Desert Generals**. New York, Viking, 1961. 320p. Maps, Bibliog.

A history of the North African campaigns. The emphasis is on the role of five British generals—Auckinleck, O'Connor, Montgomery, Cunningham and Ritchie. There is good material on the personalities of the generals and some emphasis on strategy. The author does not agree with many of the decisions of Churchill or Montgomery.

632   Blumenson, Martin. **Kasserine Pass**. Boston, Houghton Mifflin, 1967. 341p. Maps, Bibliog.

The first major direct clash between German and American soldiers in February 1943 at Kasserine Pass in Tunisia is described in this book. The American defeat led directly to important reforms and new commanders and demonstrated convincingly the toughness of German soldiers. The English edition is titled *Rommel's Last Victory: The Battle of Kasserine Pass.*

633   Buckley, Christopher. **Five Ventures: Iraq, Syria, Persia, Madagascar, Dodecanese.** London, H. M. Stationery Office, 1954. 257p. Maps.
An "official" popular history of some important but little known military actions. Each action took place between 1941 and 1943 and was relatively small in scale. The author gives the reasons for undertaking each venture, the action involved and the results.

634   Carver, Michael. **El Alamein.** New York, Macmillan, 1962. 216p. Maps.
General Carver, who fought at El Alamein in 1942, has written a detailed story of the battles. The views of both sides are given with emphasis on the British. El Alamein is shown as a battle of great confusion. He concludes that Montgomery beat Rommel because he had a better grasp of the tactical situation.

635   Carver, Michael. **Tobruk.** Philadelphia, Dufour, 1964. 271p. Maps.
The author, a British general, has written a very detailed scholarly account of the seven-month siege of Tobruk in 1941-42. The first part covers operation "Crusader"—a British victory—and the final part operation "Aida"—a German victory and the retreat of the British Eighth Army to Egypt. These are also called the Sidi Rezeg Battles.

636   Heckstall-Smith, Anthony. **Tobruk: The Story of a Siege.** New York, Norton, 1960. 255p. Maps, Bibliog.
A well written account of the seven-month siege of Tobruk and the importance of this seaport on the North African campaigns. There is good use made of diaries and other first hand sources.

637   Howe, George Frederick. **Northwest Africa: Seizing the Initiative in the West.** Washington, Office of the Chief of Military History, Dept. of the Army, 1957. 748p. Maps, Bibliog.
The history of the Allied struggle to free North Africa from the first invasions of Operation Torch to the final German surrender in Tunisia. The final struggle pitted American, British and French forces against German and Italian forces. Includes background material on the Mediterranean strategy of the Allies and Axis. The battles are described in detail and analyzed from the views of both the Allies and Axis.

638   Kippenberger, Howard. **Infantry Brigadier.** New York, Oxford University Press, 1949. 371p. Maps.
A memoir by an outstanding New Zealand general. Associated with the British Eighth Army Kippenberger saw action in Greece, Crete, Libya, Syria, North Africa and Italy. Good view of the war as seen by one of the Commonwealth participants.

639   Lewin, Ronald. **Rommel as Military Commander.** Princeton, N. J.,
        Van Nostrand, 1968. 262p. Maps, Bibliog.
A useful and fair assessment of Rommel's military commands. Discusses in
detail the operations in which Rommel participated and his influence on their
outcome. Especially useful for the North African campaigns and the building of
the Atlantic Wall against Allied invasion. The final chapter offers a concise
evaluation of Rommel's generalship.

640   Liddell-Hart, Basil Henry. **The Tanks: The History of the Royal Tank
        Regiment and its Predecessors.** New York, Praeger, 1959. 2v. Maps.
An official history of the Royal Tank Regiment from 1914 to 1945. There is good
coverage of tank warfare in the North African campaigns. An excellent survey of
the development of the tank and tank strategy and tactics particularly as practiced
by the British. Also includes excellent discussion of British pre-war military policy.
Volume 2 includes the material on World War II.

641   Macksey, Kenneth John. **Crucible of Power: The Fight for Tunisia,
        1942-1943.** London, Hutchinson, 1969. 325p. Maps, Bibliog.
The story of the crucial early years of the war in North Africa. There is coverage
of the incredibly complex desert campaigns which eventually resulted in the
Allied victory. Tunisia was especially important to the Allies because of its
strategic location for any invasion of Sicily and Italy. There is some material
on the interaction of military and political goals and their effect on the campaign.

642   Maughan, Barton. **Tobruk and El Alamein.** Canberra, Australian War
        Memorial, 1966. 854p. Maps, Bibliog.
An official Australian history which "chronicles the participation of Australian
military forces in the North African campaigns from March 1941 to December
1942." Primarily the story of the 9th Australian Division with other units
covered only as they are related. Very detailed. Good military history, but
not easy reading.

643   Moorehead, Alan. **The March to Tunis: The North African War, 1940-
        1943.** New York, Harper & Row, 1965. 592p. Maps.
A personal narrative of the desert war which the author views "as a colonial
extension of the war in Europe." This volume is a trilogy comprising three works
first published in 1942-1943: *Mediterranean Front, Don't Blame the Generals,*
and *The End in Africa.* Moorehead gives an unbiased journalistic account and
offers a good insight into contemporary views of this important and frustrating
campaign.

644   Murphy, Walter Edward. **The Relief of Tobruk.** Wellington, N. Z., War
        History Branch, Dept. of Internal Affairs, 1961. 566p. Maps, Bibliog.
The official history of New Zealand forces in North Africa under General Frey-
berg in 1941-42. A major part of the book is concerned with "Operation
Crusader" to relieve the siege of Tobruk, Libya, in late 1941 and early 1942.
The story of these extremely complex battles is well told. Although Crusader
was not a total success it possibly helped save Malta and Egypt.

645   Perowne, Stewart. **The Siege Within the Walls: Malta, 1940-1943.**
        London, Hodder & Stoughton, 1970. 192p. Maps, Bibliog.
The story of the siege of Malta from 1940 to 1943 as seen by the island's inhabitants. Told from the Maltese point of view. Based on the author's personal
experiences, interviews and documentary sources.

646   Phillips, Cecil Ernest Lucas. **Alamein.** Boston, Little, Brown, 1963.
        434p. Maps. Bibliog.
An account of the battle of El Alamein told from the view of both the British
and Germans. Philips is pro-Montgomery and offers little serious criticism of
his strategy. There is good coverage of the complex and confusing series of
battles which irreversibly changed the course of the war in North Africa against
the Germans.

647   Playfair, Ian Stanley Ord and others. **The Mediterranean and the Middle
        East.** London, H. M. Stationery Office, 1954– . 6v. (5v. published)
        Maps, Bibliog.
A comprehensive treatment of the Mediterranean and Middle East theaters.
There is coverage of land, air and naval operations. The volumes are part of
British official history series. The five volumes published to date are: v.l, *Early
Successes Against Italy (To May 1941)*; v.2, *The Germans Come to the Help
of Their Ally*—the fighting in Greece, German intervention and the evacuation
to Crete; v.3, *British Fortunes Reach Their Lowest Ebb*—the story of Malta and
the fighting in the western deserts of North Africa; v.4, *The Destruction of the
Axis Forces in Africa*-the defeat of the Italians and Germans by Allied forces.
El Alamein, North African landings to the surrender in Tunisia in 1943; v.5,
*The Campaign in Sicily 1943 and the Campaign in Italy 3rd September 1943
to 31st March 1944*—these two Allied campaigns are covered in detail with
emphasis on the British view. V.6, not yet published. Each of these volumes is
a highly detailed and scholarly treatment of complex military operations.

648   Robertson, John Henry. **Auchinleck: A Biography of Field Marshal
        Sir Claude Auchinleck.** 2nd ed. London, Cassell, 1959. 975p.
An excellent biography of one of the more underrated British military leaders.
He was probably unfairly made a scapegoat for the early British defeats in North
Africa. Auchinleck was the British Commander-in-Chief in India in 1941 and
after 1943, and Commander-in-Chief in the Middle East from July 1941 to
August 1942. The "Crusader" campaign to relieve Tobruk was carried out under
Auchinleck's leadership.

649   Robertson, John Henry. **Wavell, Scholar and Soldier.** New York, Har-
        court, Brace & World, 1964. 573p. Maps, Bibliog.
A valuable scholarly biography of Field Marshal Wavell. The work unfortunately
covers only up to mid-1941 when Wavell was in command of the Middle Eastern
Theater. Although unsuccessful in the field, Wavell always faced difficult situa-
tions in the early and bleak years of the war. Wavell later became the Supreme
Commander, Southwest Pacific and in 1943 the Viceroy of India.

650   Rommel, Erwin. **The Rommel Papers**. New York, Harcourt Brace,
       1953. 545p. Maps.
A selected collection of Rommel's memoranda, letters, diaries and personal
narrative. Especially helpful for studying Rommel's role in North Africa and in
the defense of the Atlantic Wall. Although an early supporter of Hitler, Rommel
later became involved in anti-Hitler plots which eventually ended in his death.
One of the more important German generals who became a living legend even
among the Allies.

651   Schmidt, Paul Karl. **The Foxes of the Desert**. New York, Dutton, 1961.
       370p. Maps.
An easy to read popular account of the Afrika Corps in the 1941-42 campaigns
in North Africa. The story is told from the German view. The major battles
covered are Agedabia, Baria, Sollum, El Alamein, the landing of the Americans
and the final battle for Tunisia. Unlike some other general works there is good
coverage on the espionage aspects of the military actions. During the war Schmidt
was the press chief of the Nazi Foreign Office and writes under the pseudonym
Paul Carell.

652   Stewart, Ian McDougall Guthrie. **The Struggle for Crete, 20 May—1 June
       1941: A Study of Lost Opportunity**. London, Oxford University Press,
       1966. 518p. Maps, Bibliog.
The author, a British medical officer on Crete, has written an interesting first
hand account of the military action in Crete. Stewart is critical of leadership at
all levels for this British defeat. There is good detail of the fighting. Although
the battle is covered from both views the book is balanced toward the British
view.

653   Strawson, John. **The Battle for North Africa**. New York, Scribner,
       1969. 226p. Maps, Bibliog.
A brief account of the North African campaigns. The materials on strategy
offer a cogent explanation of why the North African campaigns took place.
There are good battle descriptions with a strong emphasis on the "ordinary"
fighting man rather than at the command levels.

654   Thomas, David Arthur. **Nazi Victory: Crete, 1941**. New York, Stein
       and Day, 1973. 224p. Maps, Bibliog.
The story of the evacuation of British troops from Greece to Crete and the
ensuing battle for Crete. There is good coverage of all aspects of the fighting,
and special attention is given to the role of the Luftwaffe and the use of airborne
troops. There is also some analysis of the effect of the delay of the German invasion of Russia because of the Balkan invasion and battle for Crete. The English
ediction is titled *Crete 1941, The Battle at Sea*.

655   Thompson, Reginald William. **Churchill and the Montgomery Myth**.
       New York, M. Evans, 1968. 276p. Maps, Bibliog.
The author builds a case against the "Montgomery legend." The claim is made
that Churchill created the aura of heroism around Montgomery at a time in the
war when a hero and good news were badly needed. The time covered in the

book is August 1942 to October 1943. According to other British generals—Auchinleck for one—the North African campaign was under control and the battle at El Alamein was unnecessary. The author is not always convincing, but he does present a different view. The English edition is titled *The Montgomery Legend*.

656   Wilson, Henry Maitland. **Eight Years Overseas, 1939-1947.** London, Hutchinson, 1950. 285p. Maps.

The memoirs of the man considered by many to have had one of the best military minds of the war. Wilson conducted the British campaign in Greece in 1941 and later served in North Africa, Palestine, Syria, Lebanon, Persia and Iraq. In 1943 he became Commander-in-Chief in the Middle East and in 1944 Supreme Allied Commander in the Mediterranean.

657   Woollcombe, Robert. **The Campaigns of Wavell, 1939-1943.** London, Cassell, 1959. 227p. Maps.

A scholarly study of one of the better British generals who, unfortunately, was often placed in commands where victory was improbably or impossible. Wavell was assigned first to North Africa when British power was at a low and later to the Far East when Japanese power was at its greatest. Wavell directed or was involved in fourteen campaigns including North Africa, Somaliland, Abyssinia, Crete, Iraq, Malaya, Dutch East Indies, Burma and others. A good overview of a commander with uniquely varied assignments.

THE WAR IN THE FAR EAST

General

658   Eichelberger, Robert L. **Our Jungle Road to Tokyo.** New York, Viking, 1950. 306p. Maps.

A personal memoir and history by one of the most successful yet unheralded American generals in the struggle atainst Japan. A well told personal view of the fighting in New Guinea, Hollandia, Biak, and the Philippines. A reminder that the Army played a significant role in the Pacific in spite of the belief that it was only the Marines' war. In 1944 Eichelberger commanded the U. S. 8th Army during the invasion and capture of the Philippines.

659   Isely, Jeter Allen and Phillip A. Crowl. **The U. S. Marines and Amphibious War: Its Theory and Practice in the Pacific.** Princeton, N. J., Princeton University Press, 1951. 636p. Maps, Bibliog.

One of the most competent analyses of the development and practice of amphibious warfare. The parts played by air, naval and land forces are covered. Five amphibious campaigns are discussed in detail: Guadalcanal, Tarawa, Marshalls, Iwo Jima and Okinawa.

660   Kirby, Stanley Woodburn, and others. **The War Against Japan.** London, H. M. Stationery Office, 1957-69. 5v. Maps, Bibliog.

The official British history of the war in the Far East. There is coverage of the American role in the Pacific but emphasis is on the British involvement. The volumes are: v.l, *The Loss of Singapore*—covers causes of the war, Pearl Harbor, and Japanese conquest of the Philippines, Malaya and Singapore; v.2, *India's Most Dangerous Hour*—covers the loss of Europe, Japanese threat to India, Coral Sea, Midway and the Chindits in Burma; v.3, *The Decisive Battles*—covers the reconquest of the Indian Ocean, the Royal Air Force in the Far East, Imphal and Kohima, Wingate's Chindits, and the U. S. offensive up to the Philippine invasion; v.4, *The Reconquest of Burma*—primarily the story of Slim's 19th Army versus the Japanese 15th Army from August 1944 to May 1945; v.5, *The Surrender of Japan*—covers the military action from the capture of Rangoon in May 1945 to the dissolution of the South East Asia Command.

661   Krueger, Walter. **From Down Under to Nippon: The Story of the Sixth Army in World War II**. Washington, Combat Forces Press, 1953. 393p. Maps.

A personal account by a commanding general of the U. S. Sixth Army who served in the Pacific from Australia to the conquest of Japan. Based on the author's personal experiences and recollections and his official reports.

662   Long, Gavin Merrick. **MacArthur as Military Commander**. Princeton, N. J., Van Nostrand, 1969. 243p. Maps, Bibliog.

Perhaps not the definitive biography of MacArthur, but the most objective published to date. Long covers MacArthur's military career from his graduation from West Point through the Korean War with emphasis on his activities from 1941-1945. While critical of MacArthur's defense of the Philippines and some island battles the overall evaluation of MacArthur's command is positive. Coverage is given to his conflicts with civilian political leaders. The author is an Australian journalist which may account for the objectivity of the study.

663   MacArthur, Douglas. **Reminiscences**. New York, McGraw-Hill, 1964. 438p. Maps.

These are the somewhat disappointing memoirs of one of the most successful generals of the war. At any rate the memoirs do not match the man. MacArthur was appointed commanding general of the U. S. Army in the Far East in 1941 and later Allied Supreme Commander in the Pacific. In this book he tells his view of the war against Japan. MacArthur was considered by one military analyst, Liddell-Hart, to be in "a class above Allied commands in any theatre."

664   Smith, Stanley E., ed. **The United States Marine Corps in World War II**. New York, Random House, 1969. 965p. Maps.

An anthology of over 100 selections covering all phases of the war in the Pacific which involved the Marine Corps. Most of the selections are accounts of battle action by people who took part in the war. There are introductory sections which meaningfully piece the selections together in chronological order.

665   U. S. Marine Corps. **History of U. S. Marine Corps Operations in World War II**. Washington, Historical Division, Headquarters, U. S. Marine Corps, 1958-1971. 5v. Maps, Bibliog.

This set is the official history of the U. S. Marine Corps. It supersedes most of the pamphlets published earlier by Marine Corps Historical Division. The five volumes are: v.1, *Pearl Harbor to Guadalcanal*; v.2, *Isolation of Rabul*; v.3, *Central Pacific Drive*; v.4, *Western Pacific Operations*; v.5, *Victory and Occupation*. There is coverage of both strategic planning and battlefield action. The volumes are well documented and attempt to show both the Japanese and American views. The role of the Army and Navy are discussed, but the main emphasis is, of course, on the part played by the Marine Corps.

666   Wigmore, Lionel. **The Japanese Thrust**. Canberra, Australian War
        Memorial, 1957. Maps, Bibliog.
The story of the Japanese advance into the south Pacific and South-East Asia in 1941-42 and their encounters with the Australian Army. Although the forces of other countries are covered this official Australian history is concerned with Australia's role in the context of the overall action. Among the campaigns covered are Malaya, Singapore, Java, Timor, Borneo and New Britain. There is a section on Australian prisoners and their treatment.

667   Willoughby, Charles Andrew and John Chamberlain. **MacArthur, 1941-**
        1951. New York, McGraw-Hill, 1954. 441p. Maps.
A subjective study of MacArthur's military command by his former Chief of Intelligence. An apology for MacArthur, but there is almost nothing written about him that is strictly objective. A headquarters history of the Pacific war and of the general whose name is most often associated with the U. S. victory.

Pearl Harbor

668   Barker, A. J. **Pearl Harbor**. New York, Ballantine Books, 1969. 160p.
        Bibliog.
A short popular history of the Japanese attack on Pearl Harbor and the diplomatic background leading to the attack. Pearl Harbor signaled the entry of Japan into a war with the United States and drastically crippled the United States' Pacific naval defenses. Numerous maps, diagrams and pictures make the book more useful and interesting.

669   Lord, Walter, **Day of Infamy**. New York, Holt, 1957. 243p.
A popular account of the events leading to Pearl Harbor and the actual Japanese attack on Pearl Harbor. The Pearl Harbor attack is presented as an hour by hour record of the events. Good accounts of individual experiences based on official records and personal interviews.

670   U. S. Congress. Joint Committee on the Investigation of the Pearl
        Harbor Attack. **Pearl Harbor Attack: Hearings Before the Joint Com-**
        mittee on the Investigation of the Pearl Harbor Attack. Washington,
        Government Printing Office, 1946. 39 parts.
A massive compilation of testimony and documents relating to the Japanese attack on Pearl Harbor. Besides the post-war testimony these volumes also include the war-time investigations of the Roberts Commission, the Hart Inquiry, Proceeding of Navy Board of Inquiry, Clarke Investigation, Clausen Investigation and the Hewitt Inquiry. A primary source.

671   U. S. Congress. Joint Committee on the Investigation of the Pearl
       Harbor Attack. **Report**. Washington, Government Printing Office,
       1946. 580p. Maps.
A summary report of the 39 volumes of testimony taken at the Congressional
hearings cited in the previous entry. An unbiased work with the conclusions of
all sides presented.

Japanese Advance and Allied Victory

[Note: See also the section on the Naval Warfare in the Far Eastern
Theater, pp. 130-33, 138-41.]

672   Appleman, Roy Edgar, and others. **Okinawa: The Last Battle**. Washing-
       ton, Historical Division, Dept. of the Army, 1948. 529p. Maps, Bibliog.
The official history of "Operation Iceberg," the American campaign to seize the
Ryukyu Islands. Okinawa is the most important of these islands. The role of the
Marine Corps is covered, but greater emphasis is placed on the Army's role. The
authors all participated in the campaign and were witnesses to much of the action.
There is good detail of the battle action.

673   Barber, Noel. **A Sinister Twilight: The Fall of Singapore, 1942**. Boston,
       Houghton Mifflin, 1968. 364p. Maps, Bibliog.
The story of the Japanese victory over the British seen through the eyes of
people trapped in the city. Vividly portrays the atmosphere in Singapore caused
by the shocking British defeat.

674   Barker, A. J. **The March on Delhi**. London, Faber and Faber, 1963.
       302p. Maps, Bibliog.
The important battles leading to the defeat of the Japanese attempt to capture
India in 1944 are often forgotten because of the important events taking place
in Europe. The volume, however, emphasizes the important struggle between
the British 14th Army and the Japanese 15th Army in the Japanese drive on
India. The story of the Japanese defeat is treated fairly with good coverage given
both sides.

675   Belden, Jack. **Retreat with Stilwell**. New York, Knopf, 1943. 368p.
       Maps.
A first hand journalistic account of the fighting in Burma and the Japanese
victory over Allied troops. Primarily about Stilwell's retreat from Burma to
India with a ragged group of soldiers and civilians. One of the better personal
accounts of this action.

676   Belote, James H. and William M. Belote. **Corregidor: The Saga of a
       Fortress**. New York, Harper & Row, 1967. 272p. Maps, Bibliog.
A well written and well illustrated story of Corregidor during the war years.
The main segments of this work cover the fall of Corregidor to the Japanese in
1942 to its recapture in early 1945. Includes a wealth of interesting facts and
figures.

677   Belote, James H. and William M. Belote. **Typhoon of Steel: The Battle
       for Okinawa.** New York, Harper & Row, 1970. 368p. Maps, Bibliog.
Okinawa was the final military campaign of World War II. This is the story of
both sides in this last epic battle. There is material on the planning of the operation and the coordinated use of land, naval and air forces. Good for battle details
at the command level and for the individual soldier.

678   Cannon, M. Hamlin. **Leyte: The Return to the Philippines.** Washington,
       Office of the Chief of Military History, Dept. of the Army, 1954. 420p.
       Maps, Bibliog.
The official U. S. history of the invasion of Leyte on October 20, 1944 and the
ensuing capture of the island. While Leyte was not the largest island it was strategically located and divided the Japanese forces in the Philippines. The invasion
of Leyte represented the return of U. S. forces to the Philippines. There is
coverage of the part played by air, land, naval and guerrilla forces. There are
detailed accounts of the military action during the campaign.

679   Carew, John Mohun. **The Longest Retreat: The Burma Campaign,
       1942.** London, Hamilton, 1969. 276p. Maps, Bibliog.
The story of the defeat of the British in Burma by an underrated Japanese army.
Carew places the defeat on a poorly trained British army facing a well trained
Japanese force. There is good detail on the British retreat into India, where
unlike the troops returning from Dunkirk, there was no hero's welcome.

680   Coggins, Jack. **The Campaign for Guadalcanal: A Battle that Made
       History.** Garden City, N. Y., Doubleday, 1972. 208p. Maps, Bibliog.
A good popular account of the six month battle for Guadalcanal. The author shows
that Guadalcanal was not merely a land campaign, but equally a naval and air struggle. An especially strong feature of the book are the maps and special feature drawings. Some examples of the drawings are weapons of all kinds, and special subjects
such as "Naval Gunnery Fire Control," and"Mine Laying."

681   Craig, William. **The Fall of Japan.** New York, Dial Press, 1967. 368p.
       Maps, Bibliog.
The history of the final few weeks of the campaign to defeat Japan. Covers the
two atomic bombings, the final intervention by the Emperor, the prisoner
release, resistance to the Emperor's surrender order and the final surrender and
Allied occupation. Strong on personalities, especially Japanese, and for presenting
the Japanese view. Good popular history.

682   Crowl, Philip Axtell. **Campaign in the Marianas.** Washington, Office of
       the Chief of Military History, Dept. of the Army, 1960. 505p. Maps,
       Bibliog.
This volume is concerned with the battles to capture Saipan, Tinian and Guam.
There is background material on the military planning of the campaign. The
objective of the campaign was "to secure control of sea communications through
the Central Pacific . . . and by establishment of sea and air bases for operations
against Japanese sea routes and long-range air attacks against the Japanese home

land." In this campaign the Army played a subordinate but important role to the Marine Corps.

683 Crowl, Philip Axtell and Edmund G. Love. **Seizure of the Gilberts and Marshalls.** Washington, Office of the Chief of Military History, Dept. of the Army, 1955. 414p. Maps, Bibliog.

This is the story of the American campaigns in 1943-44 to recapture the Central Pacific. The recapture of five atolls—Makin, Tarawa, Kwajalein, Majuro, Eniwetok—was the first real test of the American theory of amphibious operations. While the recapture of the Central Pacific was primarily a Marine Corps operation this volume concentrates on the lesser although important contribution of the Army. This volume is one of the official histories of the U. S. Army.

684 Cunningham, Winfield Scott. **Wake Island Command.** Boston, Little, Brown, 1961. 300p.

A personal account of the battle for Wake Island and the author's subsequent years as a prisoner of war. There is good detail of the fierce fighting between Japanese and Americans. The author, the ranking naval commander on Wake Island, contends that the major battle decisions were his and not Major Devereux's. For another account see Major Devereux's book cited below.

685 Devereux, James Patrick Scott. **The Story of Wake Island.** Philadelphia, Lippincott, 1947. 252p. Maps.

This is a well told story of the brief but heroic struggle of the Americans on Wake Island in December 1941. The author was the Marine officer in command of the island's 500 man defense force.

686 Dexter, David. **The New Guinea Offensives.** Canberra, Australian War Memorial, 1961. 851p. Maps.

A volume in the official Australian history of World War II. Tells the story of Australian ground forces in their struggle to recapture New Guinea from April 1943 to mid-1944. An excellent study of war at the lower levels—individuals, squads, companies—with very little material on the higher command or higher strategy. A good account of some of the war's toughest fighting in the most unpleasant physical conditions of the Pacific war.

687 Evans, Geoffrey Charles. **Slim as Military Commander.** Princeton, Van Nostrand, 1969. 239p. Maps, Bibliog.

A biography of one of the outstanding British generals of the war. After brief service in the Africa and the Middle East Slim was transferred to Southeast Asia where he became the most successful British general in the land war against Japan. Slim led his troops to victories at Imphal, Kohima, Arakan, Mandalay and Rangoon culminating in the military defeat of the Japanese in Southeast Asia.

688 Fellowes-Gordon, Ian. **The Magic War: The Battle for North Burma.** New York, Scribner, 1971. 180p.

A special study of a little known arena of the war in Burma. Tells the story of a company of Kachin tribesmen fighting as irregulars behind Japanese lines in cooperation with the regular troops. Sympathetic to Stilwell and the problems he faced.

689   Garfield, Brian Wynne. **The Thousand Mile War: World War II in Alaska and the Aleutians.** Garden City, N. Y., Doubleday, 1969. 351p. Maps, Bibliog.

A definitive account of the little publicized military actions in Alaska and the Aleutians. Primarily the story of the fifteen month campaign in 1942-43 of the Japanese to capture the Aleutians and the victorious American counterattack. This was the only fighting on the North American soil in World War II. A first rate book.

690   Griffith, Samuel B. **The Battle for Guadalcanal.** Philadelphia, Lippincott, 1963. 282p. Maps, Bibliog.

A good study of the military action on Guadalcanal. Written from the view of high command, but there is some coverage of individual fighting men. Describes both the Japanese and American points of view.

691   Johnston, George Henry. **The Toughest Fighting in the World.** New York, Duell, Sloan and Pearce, 1943. 240p.

One of the better journalistic eyewitness accounts of the struggle in New Guinea. Emphasis is on the personal involvement of the "common soldier." The author is an Australian journalist.

692   Kirby, Stanley Woodburn. **Singapore: The Chain of Disaster.** New York, Macmillan, 1971. 270p. Maps, Bibliog.

This is possibly the best work in English on the Japanese campaign which resulted in the capture of Malaya and the British disaster at Singapore. The author covers the background of the war in Malaya including British preparations, the military campaign leading to the Japanese victory and an evaluation of the responsibility for the defeat which resulted in the post-war collapse of British colonialism in the Far East.

693   Marshall, Samuel Lyman Atwood. **Island Victory: The Battle of Kwajalein Atoll.** Washington, Infantry Journal, 1945. 117p. Maps.

This work is a collection of combat narratives based on "official interviews with all the men who fought." The stories of many individuals and units of the U. S. Army's 7th Infantry Division are told in great detail based on their own words describing the battle. The operation resulted in the capture of twenty-six Japanese-held islands between January 31 and February 5, 1944.

694   Miller, John. **Cartwheel: The Reduction of Rabaul.** Washington, Office of the Chief of Military History, Dept. of the Army, 1959. 418p. Maps, Bibliog.

The official history of the U. S. and allied operations in the South and Southwest Pacific to neutralize the Japanese forces in Rabaul and New Britain. The campaign began on June 30, 1943 with landings in the Solomons, Trobriands and New Guinea and ended on March 20, 1944 with the capture of Emirau Island in the

Bismarks. The success of these battles opened the way for the invasion of the Philippines.

695   Miller, John. **Guadalcanal: The First Offensive**. Washington, Historical
        Division, Dept. of the Army, 1949. 413p. Maps, Bibliog.
The campaign for Guadalcanal in 1942-43 was the start of the American offensive leading to the military defeat of Japan. The contribution of land, air and naval forces are all discussed. Emphasis is placed on the value of the "fighting team" rather than crediting victory to any one service. There is detailed description of the fighting at all levels, including some individuals. This is the official U. S. Army history.

696   Milner, Samuel. **Victory in Papua**. Washington, Office of the Chief of
        Military History, Dept. of the Army, 1957. 409p. Maps, Bibliog.
The story of one of the lesser known but strategically important Allied victories in the Southwest Pacific. This history is primarily concerned with the Army's 32nd Division's battle for Papua and the American adjustment to warfare in tropical conditions. The role of the Australian forces is well covered. This battle was important too for helping blunt the Japanese offensive which endangered Australia. There is good detail of the military operations. This is an official U. S. Army history.

697   Morton, Louis. **The Fall of the Philippines**. Washington, Office of the
        Chief of Military History, Dept. of the Army, 1953. 626p. Maps, Bibliog.
This official U. S. Army history covers the prewar plans and preparations for the defense of the Philippines and their fall to the Japanese in 1941-42. The five parts of the work are self-descriptive: Prewar Plans and Preparations, The Isolation of the Philippines and the Japanese Landings, The Withdrawal to Bataan, The Siege of Bataan and Corregidor and the Southern Islands. Both the American-Philippine and Japanese sides of the military events are discussed.

698   Ogburn, Charlton. **The Marauders**. New York, Harper, 1959. 307p. Maps.
A good account of Frank Merrill's "Marauders" and their part in the reconquest of Burma. There is detailed coverage of the physical difficulties of the land and of battle tactics. Strong on the personal involvement of individual soldiers.

699   Percival, Arthur Ernest. **The War in Malaya**. London, Eyre & Spottis-
        woode, 1949. 336p. Maps.
A sober and defensive account of the British defeat in 1942 culminating in the surrender of the British garrison at Singapore. Percival was the British commander who surrendered in spite of Churchill's orders to fight. Percival spent the war as a prisoner of Japan. Not a definitive account, but valuable because of Percival's position.

700   Romanus, Charles F. and Riley Sunderland. **Stilwell's Mission to China**.
        Washington, Office of the Chief of Military History, Dept. of the Army,
        1953. 441p. Maps, Bibliog.

This is the official U. S. history of the American military and political involvement in China from 1941 to 1946. The story is told at the theater command level and is therefore primarily the story of General Stilwell. The greater part of the book is concerned with the Japanese blockade of China and the Allied efforts to break the blockade. An excellent history of one of the most politically sensitive and militarily complicated theaters of the war.

701   Romanus, Charles F. and Riley Sunderland. **Time Runs Out in CBI.**
        Washington, Office of the Chief of Military History, Dept. of the Army,
        1959. 428p. Maps, Bibliog.
This official U. S. Army history tells the story of the China Theater from October 1944 when General Stilwell was recalled to August 1945 and the final defeat of Japan. With General Wedemeyer as the U. S. commander the story centers on the complex military and political problems he faced and the U. S. effort to build the Chinese Nationalists' army into an effective fighting force.

702   Romulo, Carlos Pena. **I Saw the Fall of the Philippines.** Garden City,
        N. Y., Doubleday, Doran, 1942. 323p.
Romulo, a colonel in the Philippine Army, served as an aide de camp to General MacArthur early in the war. He served at both Bataan and Corregidor during the Japanese conquest of the Philippines. Romulo escaped to Australia shortly before the fall of Corregidor. This book is one of the best eyewitness accounts of the struggle on the Bataan peninsula and the retreat and final resistance on Corregidor.

703   Sherrod, Robert Lee. **Tarawa: The Story of a Battle.** New York, Duell,
        Sloan and Pearce, 1944. 183p. Maps.
An eyewitness journalistic account of one of the toughest island battles fought by the U. S. Marines against the Japanese. The story of the 2nd Marine Division is told from the view of the front line soldier.

704   Slim, William. **Defeat into Victory.** 2nd ed. London, Cassell, 1956.
        576p. Maps.
A personal account of the Burma campaigns from 1942 to 1945 by the British commanding general. The story begins with the long retreat into India in 1942 and tells of the buildup in 1943-44 leading to the Japanese defeat at Imphal and the final defeat of all Japanese forces in 1945. While this is not a complete history of the war in Burma it is an important and fascinating version. Many consider Slim's memoirs to be the best of any wartime field commander.

705   Smith, Robert Ross. **The Approach to the Philippines.** Washington,
        Office of the Chief of Military History, Dept. of the Army, 1953.
        623p. Maps, Bibliog.
The official history of U. S. Army's amphibious and ground operations in Southwest Pacific and Central Pacific from April to October 1944. Among the major campaigns discussed are Hollandia, Biak, Morotai and Peleliu. There are detailed accounts of the battlefield action on both sides. The contributions of the Air Corps, Navy and Marine Corps are discussed as they related to the role of the Army, but the main emphasis is on the Army's role.

706   Smith, Robert Ross. **Triumph in the Philippines.** Washington, Office
        of the Chief of Military History, Dept. of the Army, 1963. 756p. Maps,
        Bibliog.
This official U. S. Army history tells of the recapture of the Philippines in the
seven months from January to August 1945. This campaign was the largest joint
operation in the Pacific war. This volume is "devoted principally to the accomplishments of U. S. Army ground combat forces and to the operations of major organized Philippine guerrilla units that contributed notably to the success of the
campaign . . . "

707   Smyth, John George. **Percival and the Tragedy of Singapore.**
        London, Macdonald, 1971. 304p. Maps, Bibliog.
A sympathetic defense of General Percival and his conduct of the British defensive actions in the Malayan campaign in 1941 and early 1942. The author contends that many of the criticisms of Percival are unjustified. Of the actions of
Gort at Dunkirk, Wainwright in the Philippines and Percival in Singapore, only
the last was considered "unheroic."

708   Stilwell, Joseph Warren. **The Stilwell Papers.** New York, Sloane, 1948.
        357p. Maps.
The personal views of the American general in command of American and Chinese
troops in the China-Burma-India Theater from 1942 to 1944. Stilwell also served
as Chief of Staff to Chiang Kai-shek. These papers are based on private diaries,
letters to his wife and parts of his "black notebook" which give some insight
into "Vinegar Joe." Honestly written with not always flattering views of other
military leaders. The British and Chiang Kai-shek are harshly criticized. Stilwell
was a relatively successful commander in a most difficult and important, but
secondary, theater of the war.

709   Swinson, Arthur. **The Battle of Kohima.** New York, Stein and Day,
        1967. 275p. Maps, Bibliog.
An account of the series of battles that ended the Japanese "march to Delhi"
and their attempt to conquer India. At the battles of Kohima and Imphal, British
and Indian troops decisively defeated the Japanese. Covers the battles from both
sides. These important battles are usually overshadowed by events in the European
theater and the U. S. Pacific campaigns.

710   Swinson, Arthur. **Four Samurai: A Quartet of Japanese Army Com-
        manders in the Second World War.** London, Hutchinson, 1968. 266p.
        Maps, Bibliog.
An interesting study of four leading Japanese generals, their generalship and
their campaigns. The four are Masaharu Homma, Masaki Honda, Renya Mutoguchi
and Tomoyuki Yamashita. Swinton says only Yamashita was a front rank general. He accepts Slim's analysis that "the fundamental fault of their generalship
was lack of moral, as distinct from physical courage. They were not prepared to
admit they had made a mistake . . . " This inflexibility was due mostly to the
Samurai tradition.

711   Toland, John. **But Not in Shame: The Six Months After Pearl Harbor.**
       New York, Random House, 1961. 427p. Maps.
A popular account of the U. S. reaction from Pearl Harbor on December 7, 1941
through June 1942. Based on documentary research and numerous personal
interviews. Some of the major military actions in this six months were Pearl
Harbor, Wake Island, the fall of the Philippines, Java Sea and Midway. This
period was the time of the great Japanese offensive and ended with the U.S.
victory at Midway.

712   Tregaskis, Richard William. **Guadalcanal Diary.** New York, Random
       House, 1943. 263p.
A now classic day by day account of the struggle for Guadalcanal from July to
September 1942. The author was a war correspondent in the thick of the battle.
Not a very pretty story, but accurate in its detail. The story is told at the foxhole
level not the command level.

713   Tsuji, Masanobu. **Singapore: The Japanese Version.** New York, St.
       Martin's Press, 1960. 358p.
The former Chief of Operations and Planning Staff for the 25th Japanese Army
tells the Japanese version of the British defeat at Singapore. While good for an
insight into the Japanese side, it should be read with care as the author's interpretations are often chauvinistic. Tsuji was an ardent nationalist.

714   Wainwright, Jonathan Mayhew. **General Wainwright's Story: The
       Account of Four Years of Humiliating Defeat, Surrender, and Captiv-
       ity, by General Jonathan M. Wainwright, Who Paid the Price of his
       Country's Unpreparedness.** Garden City, N. Y., Doubleday, 1946.
       314p. Maps.
The personal story of Wainwright's participation in the Philippines campaign,
the fighting on Bataan and Corregidor, and his four years as a prisoner of the
Japanese. There is considerable material on life as a prisoner and the Japanese
brutalities inflicted on Americans. In spite of Wainwright's experience, he avoids
becoming vindictive in his memoirs, and they remain a valuable insight into a
tragic American military defeat.

715   Whitson, William W. and Chen-Hsia Huang. **The Chinese High Command:
       A History of Communist Military Politics, 1927-41.** New York, Praeger,
       1973. 638p. Bibliog.
A study of top Chinese military leaders. Part of the book covers the Communists
during World War II. Includes material on army organization, and tactical and
strategic doctrines.

THE WAR IN THE AIR

General

716   Arnold, Henry Harley. **Global Mission.** New York, Harper, 1949. 626p.
A memoir by the wartime commander of the U. S. Army Air Force. Tells of
the pre-war development of U. S. air power and the role of air power in the war.

Good insights into strategy and high command. Arnold was a member of the Joint Chiefs of Staff and the Allied Combined Joint Chiefs of Staff.

717   Brereton, Louis Hyde. **The Brereton Diaries: The War in the Air in the Pacific, Middle East and Europe, 3 October 1941-8 May 1945**. New York, Morrow, 1946. 450p. Maps.
A general account of the war in the air by an American general who served in high command positions in almost every theater. The value of the work lies in the positions held by the author and much of what is said is not new or told in an exciting style.

718 ʹ   Huston, James Alvin. **Out of the Blue: U. S. Army Airborne Operations in World War II**. West Lafayette, Ind., Purdue University Studies, 1972. 327p. Maps, Bibliog.
The story of the development and strategic use of U. S. airborne forces during the war. There is coverage of the development of specialized transport aircraft and equipment, and the training of troops. There are detailed accounts of airborne troops in many major campaigns and battles in both the European and Pacific theaters.

719   Jablonski, Edward. **Airwar**. Garden City, N. Y., Doubleday, 1971. 2v. Maps, Bibliog.
A popular general history of aerial warfare in World War II. All theaters of the war are covered. The two volumes are divided into four "books": "Terror from the Sky"—the beginning of the war in Poland and western Europe with some emphasis on the Battle of Britain; "Tragic Victories"—the beginnings of the Pacific war and the start of the strategic bombing of Europe; "Outraged Skies"—this book is devoted entirely to the Pacific theater; and "Wings of Fire"—covers the conclusion of the airwar in the Pacific and European theaters. These volumes are enhanced by numerous well selected photographs.

720   LeMay, Curtis E. **Mission with LeMay: My Story**. Garden City, N. Y., Doubleday, 1965. 581p.
An autobiography of LeMay from boyhood through his military career. Most of the story, of course, is concerned with the years 1939-1945. LeMay played a large part in the development of the Army Air Force. During the war he served in both Europe and the Pacific. LeMay was responsible for many new techniques and tactics including pattern bombing, new combat formations and low level bombing.

721   Richards, Denis and Hilary Aidan St. George Saunders. **Royal Air Force, 1939-1945**. London, H. M. Stationery Office, 1953-54. 3v. Maps.
An excellent popular history of the RAF in World War II. While not an official history, it was "officially commissioned" and was intended to be superseded by the official history. The volumes and some of their subjects include: v.1, *The Fight at Odds, 1939-41*—rearmament, preparation for war, "Battle of Britain," the "Blitz" and Africa and the Mediterranean; v.2, *The Fight Avails, 1941-43*—Far East, Western Desert, Malta, Sicily and the Invasion of Italy; v.3, *The Fight is*

Won, 1943-45—the strategic bombing offensive, Normandy Invasion, victory in
Europe, Burma, the Far East and a general summary.

722   Sims, Edward H. **The Fighter Pilots: A Comparative Study of the Royal
       Air Force, The Luftwaffe, and the United States Army Air Force in
       Europe and North Africa, 1939-45.** London, Cassell, 1967. 294p.
       Maps, Bibliog.
An interesting study of eight selected fighter pilots and their role in several
major campaigns. For each pilot there is a detailed account of their "biggest"
sorte and an attempt to show the reader how it felt to be in the cockpit of a
fighter in combat. There is some introductory material on the role of fighter
in air warfare.

723   U. S. Air Force. USAF Historical Division. **The Army Air Forces in
       World War II.** Chicago, University of Chicago Press, 1948-58. 7v.
       Maps, Bibliog.
This set is the official history of the U. S. Army Air Forces. All theaters involving
the Army Air Forces are covered. The volumes are well written and attempt to
present an unbiased factual account of the air war. The volumes are: v.l, *Plans
and Early Operations, January 1939 to August 1942*; v.2, *Europe: Torch to
Pointblank, August 1942 to December 1943*; v.3, *Europe: Argument to V-E
Day, January 1944 to May 1945*; v.4, *The Pacific: Guadalcanal to Saipan,
August 1942 to July 1944*; v.5, *The Pacific: Matterhorn to Nagasaki, June
1944 to August 1945*; v.6, *Men and Planes*; v.7, *Services Around the World*.
The two final volumes are concerned with technological developments, aircraft
production, troop training and a variety of special services necessary to support
air combat forces.

724   United States Strategic Bombing Survey. **Reports.** Washington, Govern-
       ment Printing Office, 1945-47. 319 parts.
A series of 319 reports on the effects of strategic bombing on Germany and
Japan. The Stretegic Bombing Survey was established in November 1944 to
make "an impartial and expert study of the effects of our aerial attacks on
Germany." In late 1945 the survey was expanded to cover Japan. The entire
set of reports is seldom found in most libraries, but good summaries can be
found in two volumes—*Summary Report (Pacific War)* (1946) and *Over-all
Report (European Report)* (1945).

725   Wedemeyer, Albert Coady. **Wedemeyer Reports!** New York, Holt,
       1958. 497p. Maps, Bibliog.
Wedemeyer's memoirs present the view of a conservative who is generally critical
of U. S. grand strategy. During most of the war Wedemeyer served in the War
Plans Division of the General Staff and later as Mountbatten's Deputy Chief of
Staff in Southeast Asia. He succeeded Stilwell in China after the latter's departure.
Wedemeyer expresses the view that Roosevelt could have avoided war if he had
desired. A different and controversial view of wartime strategy.

Europe, North Africa, and the Mediterranean

726   Andrews, Allen. **The Air Marshals: The Air War in Western Europe.**
        New York, Morrow, 1970. 299p.
The role of air power in western Europe and the men who led it are the subject
of the book. Tells the role of Arnold, Dowding, Harris, Portal, Tedder and
Goering. Studies the technical developments in the interwar years, strategy and
tactics of use of bombers and fighters, air support of ground troops, strategic
bombing and effect of bombing on civilian morale.

727   Baumbach, Werner. **The Life and Death of the Luftwaffe.** New York,
        Coward-McCann, 1960. 224p.
A somewhat biased account of the Luftwaffe by the former head of the Luftwaffe
Bomber Command. Includes reliable technical data, but many other "facts" are
open to question.The English edition is titled *Broken Swastika: The Defeat of
the Luftwaffe.*

728   Berenbrok, Hans Dieter. **The Luftwaffe War Diaries.** Garden City,
        N. Y., Doubleday, 1968. 399p. Maps, Bibliog.
An interesting German version of the Luftwaffe's part in the war. Based on
official Luftwaffe war diaries, personal papers of officers, and personal interviews. Covers the battles for Poland, the low countries, France, Crete, the Mediterranean area, Russia and to a lesser extent other areas in the European war.

729   Brickhill, Paul. **The Dam Busters.** New York, Norton, 1966. 190p.
A popular account of the 617 Squadron of the R.A.F. The squadron became
famous because of the special assignments they carried out, two of which were
the bombing of the Moehne and Elder Dams and the capsizing of the battleship
Tirpitz. Later in the war they were assigned to attack V-weapon launching sites.
There is some good material on the British inventor Barnes Wallis and the development of the special bombs used on some of 617 Squadron's missions. A fascinating
study.

730   Caidin, Martin. **Black Thursday.** New York, Dutton, 1960. 320p.
A popular and accurate account of the American raid on the ball bearing plants
at Schweinfurt on October 14, 1943. The bombing of this key German industry
cost the Americans over 600 men and created a great controversy. This book is
a vivid description of that tragic raid.

731   Collier, Basil. **The Battle of the V-Weapons, 1944-45.** New York,
        Morrow, 1965. 191p. Maps, Bibliog.
A popular account of the measures taken by the British to defeat the German's
V-weapons. The author concludes that there were really no effective solutions
except to attack the launching sites.

732   Constable, Trevor J. and Raymond F. Toliver. **Horrido! Fighter Aces
        of the Luftwaffe.** New York, Macmillan, 1968. 348p.

A collection of biographical sketches of Luftwaffe fighter aces. There are good descriptions of the air battles and of the contributions of individual pilots. Good supplemental reading.

733   Douglas, Sholto. **Combat and Command: The Story of an Airman in Two World Wars.** New York, Simon and Schuster, 1966. 806p.

The memoirs of a British air marshal who held a number of responsible commands during the war. Among Douglas' more important posts were Deputy Chief of Air Staff, Chief of Fighter Command (succeeding Dowding), Middle East Commander of the R.A.F., Chief of Costal Command, and Commander of the British Expeditionary Air Forces during the Normandy Invasion. Well written and honest memoirs which give a good view of the war at the command level. The English edition was published in two volumes: *Years of Combat* and *Years of Command*.

734   Dugan, James and Carroll Stewart. **Ploesti, The Great Ground-Air Battle of 1 August 1943.** New York, Random House, 1962. 407p. Maps, Bibliog.

An interesting special study of the raid of August 1, 1943, on the great Rumanian oil refineries at Ploesti. Called by the code name *"Tidalwave"* this was one of the greatest air battles of the war. Based on documentary research and over 160 interviews with participants of the Ploesti mission. Very detailed, yet easy reading.

735   Galland, Adolf. **The First and the Last: The Rise and Fall of the German Fighter Forces, 1938-1945.** New York, Holt, 1954. 368p.

An exciting and scholarly history of the Luftwaffe fighter forces. The author, a high ranking Luftwaffe officer, presents a strong case against German leadership and their use of air power. One of the best works presenting the German version of the air war. The book is autobiographical.

736   Guedalla, Philip. **Middle East, 1940-1942: A Study in Air Power.** London, Hodder and Stoughton, 1944. 237p. Maps.

An interesting contemporary account of the strategy and influence of air power in the Middle East. In this book Middle East extends from Gibraltar to India and includes the use of airpower in North Africa, Greece, Crete, Iraq, Syria, Persia and Malta. Superseded in parts this remains an important work.

737   Harris, Arthur Travers. **Bomber Offensive.** New York, Macmillan, 1947. 288p. Maps.

A memoir by the British wartime Commander-in-Chief of the Bomber Command of the RAF. Harris, a strong advocate of strategic bombing, offers an evaluation of the effects of strategic bombing on Germany, especially its effect on V-weapons and synthetic oil production. Good coverage of the Bomber Command's training program, supply problems, technical developments and tactics.

738   Infield, Glenn B. **The Poltava Affair: A Russian Warning: An American Tragedy.** New York, Macmillan 1973. 265p. Bibliog.

The little known story of the establishment of three U. S. air bases in western Russia and their destruction by German air raids. The author suggests the success of the raids was due to Russian-German cooperation and may have been one of the first acts of the "cold war." The use of Russian bases was called "Operation Frantic."

739   Irving, David John Cawdell. **The Destruction of Dresden.** Rev. and up-
         dated ed. London, Transworld, 1966. 287p. Maps, Bibliog.
The horror of saturation bombing is accurately and realistically portrayed in this book. The subject is the series of bombings of Dresden in February 1945, which resulted in 135,000 deaths. The author makes the work an effective anti-war statement.

740   Lee, Asher. **The German Air Force.** New York, Harper, 1946. 310p.
Although written shortly after the war this book remains a good general account of the Luftwaffe's role in the war. The author maintains that Hitler's and Goering's policies were mainly responsible for the defeat of German air power.

741   Lukas, Richard C. **Eagles East: The Army Air Forces and the Soviet
         Union, 1941-1945.** Tallahassee, Florida State University Press, 1970.
         256p. Bibliog.
Tells the little known story of the disappointing collaboration between the U. S. Air Force and the Russians. The failure was due to the difficulty of getting planes to Russia and keeping them supplied and even more to the suspicious attitude of the Russians towards the Americans.

742   Pile, Frederick Arthur. **Ack-Ack: Britain's Defense Against Air Attack
         During the Second World War.** London, Harrap, 1949. 410p.
A personal memoir by the Commander-in-Chief of the Anti-Aircraft Command from 1939-45. Tells of the application of science to anti-aircraft defense. Particularly good coverage of the Battle of Britain, the "Blitz" and the defenses against the German V-l and V-2 weapons.

743   Rudel, Hans Ulrich. **Stuka Pilot.** New York, Ballantine Books, 1958.
         239p.
An autobiographical account of the airwar on the Russian front by one of Germany's leading fighter pilots. Good description of the battles from the view of the individual pilot. Rudel shows little concern for German actions on the Eastern front, but only regrets that Germany lost the war and even goes so far as claiming the German soldier was not defeated—just overwhelmed!

744   Rumpf, Hans. **The Bombing of Germany.** New York, Holt, Rinehart
         and Winston, 1963. 256p. Bibliog.
A general study of the strategic bombing of Germany and bombing as a strategy. There is a good analysis of the effects of bombing on industrial production and human morale. A presentation of the German view.

745   Shores, Christopher F. and Clive Williams. **Aces High: The Fighter Aces of
         the British and Commonwealth Air Forces in World War II.** London,
         Spearman, 1966. 335p. Maps, Bibliog.

A series of sketches of the exploits of fighter aces. Good for first hand accounts of fighter operations.

746   Slessor, John Cotesworth. **The Central Blue: Autobiography**. New York,
       Praeger, 1957. 709. Maps.
A personal memoir by a British Air Marshal who held many responsible positions including that of Commander-in-Chief of the R.A.F. in the Mediterranean. Good insights into the development of air strategy and the operation of the high command. Slessor gives background on the development of the R.A.F. and pre-war planning. These memoirs are fair but critical when necessary.

747   **The Soviet Air Force in World War II: The Official History Originally
       Published by the Ministry of Defense of the USSR**. Garden City, N. Y.,
       Doubleday, 1973. 440p. Bibliog.
A translation of an official Russian history of the Soviet air force in World War II. Limited to the operations where the air force played the major role. There is no coverage of combined land-air operations nor is any mention made of the Allies. Includes operations in Asia and Europe from June 22, 1941 to the end of the war.

748   Tantum, William H., and E. J. Hoffschmidt. **The Rise and Fall of the
       German Air Force, 1933-1945**. Old Greenwich, Conn., WE Press,
       1969. 422p. Maps.
A detailed but non-technical operational history of the Luftwaffe from 1939 to 1945. This work is based primarily on German sources considered to be reasonably accurate and unbiased. There are two brief introductory chapters on the pre-war development of the Luftwaffe.

749   Tedder, Arthur William. **With Prejudice: The War Memoirs of Marshal
       of the Royal Air Force, Lord Tedder**. Boston, Little, Brown, 1967.
       692p. Maps, Bibliog.
An honest memoir by a British Marshal of the R.A.F. Tedder held many important commands during the war including Allied Air Commander in the Mediterranean and Deputy Supreme Commander under Eisenhower. Very good for insights into the high command. Critical of other military and political leaders when necessary—especially Montgomery.

750   **USAF Historical Studies**. Maxwell Air Force Base, Ala., USAF Histor-
       ical Division, Research Studies Institute, Air University, 195–.
A series with currently over 30 studies on the air war, mostly by former German officers. All the studies are available from the Air University, but otherwise their availability is limited. Recently, however, a subseries, "The German Air Force in World War II" has been reprinted. The twelve volumes now generally available are: Deichmann, Paul, *German Air Force Operations in Support of the Army* (New York, Arno Press, 1968); Drum, Karl, *Airpower and Russian Partisan Warfare* (New York, Arno Press, 1968); Morzik, Fritz, *German Air Force Airlift Operations* (New York, Arno Press, 1968); Nielsen, Andreas, *The German Air Force General Staff* (New York, Arno Press, 1968); Plocher, Hermann, *The German Air Force Versus Russia, 1941-1943* (New York, Arno Press, 1968,

3v.); Suchenwirth, Richard, *Command and Leadership in the German Air Force* (New York, Arno Press, 1970); Suchenwirth, Richard, *The Development of the German Air Force, 1919-1939* (New York, Arno Press, 1970); Suchenwirth, Richard, *Historical Turning Points in the German Air Force War Effort* (New York, Arno Press, 1968); Schwabedissen, Walter, *The Russian Air Force in the Eyes of German Commanders* (New York, Arno Press, 1968); Uebe, Klaus, *Russian Reactions to German Airpower in World War II* (New York, Arno Press, 1968).

751   Webster, Charles Kingsley and Noble Frankland. **The Strategic Air Offensive Against Germany.** London, H. M. Stationery Office, 1961. 4v. Maps, Bibliog.

The official British history of the airwar. The four volumes are: v.1, *Preparation*—covers 1939-1942, development of air strategy, results of bombing in Germany and the first thousand bomber raids; v.2, *Endeavor, 1943-44*—details of the action involved in bombing Germany—Ruhr, Hamburg, Berlin, etc.; v.3, *Victory, 1944-45*—study of the final air assault, precision bombing, and some emphasis on the destruction of German oil production; v.4, *Annexes and Appendices*—includes technical information, documents, statistics of all kinds including casualties and the effects of bombing.

752   Wright, Robert. **The Man Who Won the Battle of Britain.** New York, Scribner, 1970. 291p.

A study of Hugh Dowding, the commander of the RAF Fighter Command during the Battle of Britain in 1940. Although Dowding was relieved of his command just after his successful defense of England, the succeeding years have shown his strategy to have been correct. This study is critical of the Air Ministry and a successful defense of Dowding and his policies. The author was Dowding's personal assistant during the Battle of Britain. The English edition is titled *Dowding and the Battle of Britain.*

Far East

753   Caidin, Martin. **The Ragged, Rugged Warriors.** New York, Dutton, 1966. 384p. Maps, Bibliog.

An accurate popular account of the air war against Japan from 1937 to the Battle of Midway in June 1942. Covers the contributions of the U. S. Army Air Force, the Australian Air Force, the American Volunteer Group (Flying Tigers) and other air forces involved in the Pacific.

754   Chennault, Claire Lee. **Way of a Fighter.** New York, Putnam, 1949. 374p. Maps.

An autobiography by the leader of the American Volunteer Group contingent of the Chinese Air Force. The group was better known as the Flying Tigers. A biased self-aggrandizing story which unfortunately distorts many facts. Very pro-Chiang and anti-U. S. policy view of the war in China. Of interest only because of Chennault's position.

755   Glines, Carroll V. **Doolittle's Tokyo Raiders.** Princeton, N. J., D. Van Nostrand, 1964. 447p. Maps, Bibliog.

A fascinating factual story of the 80 men and 16 planes launched from the carrier Hornet is 1942 to carry out a surprise raid against Tokyo. The Japanese, in fact, discovered only after the war that the planes were launched from a carrier. The book tells the background and planning of the raid, the consequences of the raid, the escape of the crews in China and the fate of two captured crews who were eventually court martialed by the Japanese.

756   Inoguchi, Rikihei and Tadashi Nakajima. **The Divine Wind: Japan's Kamikaze Force in World War II**. Annapolis, United States Naval Institute, 1958. 240p.
A fully documented accurate account of the Japanese suicide Kamikaze force. Over 4,000 Kamikaze pilots were lost in the defense of the Philippines, Okinawa and Japan. There is material on the strategic and tactical justification—both pro and con—for the Kamikaze force.

757   Kenney, George Churchill. **General Kenney Reports: A Personal History of the Pacific War**. New York, Duell, Sloan and Pearce, 1949. 594p. Maps.
This memoir is "the history of the [U.S.] Fifth Air Force in the Pacific from 1942 when General Kenney took command up to the day the Japanese surrendered." Based on diaries this is one of the better memoirs by a high level commander. While perhaps overly long Kenney gives detailed descriptions of day to day fighting seen from the command level.

758   Mikesh, Robert C. **Japan's World War II Balloon Bomb Attacks on North America**. Washington, Smithsonian Institution Press, 1973. 85p. Maps, Bibliog.
A special study of the Japanese use of balloon attacks against the United States. Tells of the origins of the balloon bombs and the countermeasures used to neutralize their effect. There is a wealth of information on the development of balloons and technical details. Admittedly not a terribly important aspect of the war, but interesting nonetheless.

759   Okumiya, Masatake, Jiro Horikoshi and Martin Caidin. **Zero!** New York, Dutton, 1956. 424p. Maps.
The Japanese version of the Japanese-American air war in the Pacific. Battle action is described in many accounts of individual action on both sides. A critical and fair history.

760   Sakai, Saburo. **Samurai!** New York, Dutton, 1957. 382p.
An autobiographical account of the airwar in the Pacific by one of Japan's most successful fighter pilots. Sakai saw action in the South Pacific and Central Pacific including Guadalcanal, Rabul and the Philippines. There are exciting descriptions of aerial combat. One of the better works in English giving the Japanese view of the war.

761   Sherrod, Robert Lee. **History of Marine Corps Aviation in World War II**. Washington, Combat Forces Press, 1952. 496p. Maps, Bibliog.

A reliable history of Marine Corps aviation in the Pacific. Introductory material on the development of Marine aviation prior to the war is valuable. Includes battle descriptions and discussions of strategy and tactics for all the major encounters where the Marine Corps aviation was involved.

THE WAR ON THE SEAS

General

762   Ballantine, Duncan Smith. **U. S. Naval Logistics in the Second World War.** Princeton, N. J., Princeton University Press, 1947. 308p. Bibliog.
This scholarly work ". . . deals . . . with that limbo between the factory and the beachhead in which economic and military considerations are inextricably woven together." An interesting insight into the complexities of developing sources of military supplies and delivering them where and when needed.

763   Connery, Robert Hough. **The Navy and the Industrial Mobilization in World War II.** Princeton, Princeton University Press, 1951. 527p. Bibliog.
For annotation, see item 1248.

764   Creswell, John. **Sea Warfare, 1939-1945.** Rev. and augm. ed. Berkeley, University of California Press, 1967. 343p. Maps, Bibliog.
A general history with some emphasis on the development of naval doctrine during the war and the years between the wars. Covers the naval strategy and tactics of the six major navies—American, British, French, German, Italian and Japanese. A good interpretation of new and unique naval battle experiences.

765   Kemp, Peter Kemp. **Key to Victory: The Triumph of British Sea Power in World War II.** Boston, Little, Brown, 1957. 382p. Bibliog.
An excellent comprehensive study of the Royal Navy's participation in all theaters of the war. Although the author gives few personal opinions he does offer adequate criticism when necessary. There is good coverage of pre-war naval problems. The author was head of the Admiralty's Historical Section. The English title is *Victory at Sea, 1939-1945*.

766   King, Ernest Joseph and Walter Muir Whitehill. **Fleet Admiral King, A Naval Record.** New York, Norton, 1952. 674p. Maps.
An autobiographical memoir by the Unites States' wartime Commander-in-Chief of the U. S. Fleet and the Chief of Naval Operations. An inside view of the war at the highest levels of command—King was a member of the Joint Chiefs of Staff. Under King's leadership the U. S. Navy conducted one of the most decisive campaigns in naval history. King's development of fleet logistics was particularly important to the conduct of naval action in the vast Pacific area. Although

unpopular because of his almost single minded effort to make the Pacific rather than Europe first priority, King remains one of the war's most successful naval leaders.

767   Lane, Frederic Chapin, and others. **Ships for Victory: A History of Shipbuilding Under the U. S. Maritime Commission in World War II.** Baltimore, Johns Hopkins Press, 1951. 881p. Maps, Bibliog.
While not exactly a "military history" this study of shipbuilding is closely tied to all aspects of naval operations. This is the definitive study of the U. S. shipbuilding program which built 5,777 ships during the war. Covers the organization and administration of the program and many of the technical problems which had to be solved.

768   Morison, Samuel Eliot. **History of United States Naval Operations in World War II.** Boston, Little, Brown, 1947-1962. 15v. Maps, Bibliog.
This work is the unofficial "official history" of the U. S. Navy in World War II. The volumes are uniformly outstanding and should be consulted as one of the first sources on any question involving the U. S. Navy. Each volume has helpful statistical appendices. The volumes in the set are: v.1, *The Battle of the Atlantic, September 1939-May 1943*; v.2, *Operations in North African Waters, October 1942-June 1943*; v.3, *The Rising Sun in the Pacific, 1931-April 1942*; v.4, *Coral Sea, Midway, and Submarine Actions, May 1942-August 1942*; v.5, *The Struggle for Guadalcanal, August 1942-February 1943*; v.6, *Breaking the Bismarcks Barrier, 22 July 1942-1 May 1944*; v.7, *Aleutians, Gilberts and Marshalls, June 1942-April 1944*; v.8, *New Guinea and the Marianas, March 1944-August 1944*; v.9, *Sicily–Salerno–Anzio, January 1943-June 1944*; v.10, *The Atlantic Battle Won, May 1943-May 1945*; v.11, *The Invasion of France and Germany, 1944-1945*; v.12, *Leyte, June 1944-January 1945*; v.13, *The Liberation of the Philippines, Luzon, Mindanao, the Visayas, 1944-1945*; v.14, *Victory in the Pacific, 1945*; v.15, *Supplement and General Index*.

769   Morison, Samuel Eliot. **The Two-Ocean War: A Short History of the United States Navy in the Second World War.** Boston, Little, Brown, 1963. 611p. Maps, Bibliog.
A highly readable popular history by the "official" historian of the U. S. Navy. Although an independent work it is based on the author's fifteen volume *History of United States Naval Operations in World War II*. There is adequate treatment of the most important battles and campaigns of the U. S. Navy.

770   Potter, Elmer Belmont and Chester William Nimitz, eds. **The Great Sea War: The Story of Naval Action in World War II.** Englewood Cliffs, N. J., Prentice-Hall, 1960. 468p. Maps.
A popular "general history of World War II with emphasis on the sea power aspect." The work is adapted from *Sea Power* (New York, Prentice-Hall, 1960), a comprehensive history covering 2,500 years of naval warfare. The emphasis of the book is on the role of the U. S. Navy, but the navies of all participants in all theaters are covered.

771   Roscoe, Theodore. **United States Destroyer Operations in World War II.**
        Annapolis, United States Naval Institute, 1953. 581p. Maps.
A general history of the role of the destroyer in every major naval campaign and
sea battle fought by the U. S. Navy. An introductory chapter gives the background
of the development and a detailed technical description of the destroyer. Good
maps and other illustrations add to the value of the book.

772   Roscoe, Theodore. **United States Submarine Operations in World War II.**
        Annapolis, United States Naval Institute, 1949. 577p. Maps.
The definitive story of U. S. submarine operations in World War II. While not an
official history, this volume is based on the official navy operational histories.
The greater part of this volume is devoted to the Pacific theater. Statistical
appendices, maps and other illustrations add to the value of the volume.

773   Roskill, Stephen Wentworth. **The War at Sea, 1939-1945.** London, H. M.
        Stationery Office, 1954-61. 3v. in 4. Maps.
A comprehensive official history of the Royal Navy in World War II. There is
adequate coverage for the Pacific, but the emphasis is on action in the Atlantic,
Arctic and Mediterranean. Very good on strategy and high command. The volumes
are: v.l, *The Defensive*—covers the years 1939-1941; v.2, *The Period of Balance*—
covers January 1942 to May 1943; v.3, (2 parts), *The Offensive*—covers June
1943 to August 1945.

774   Roskill, Stephen Wentworth. **White Ensign: The British Navy at War,**
        1939-1945. Annapolis, United States Naval Institute, 1960. 480p. Maps.
This excellent study of the British Navy is based on the author's official history,
The War at Sea, 1939-1945. Probably the best one volume introduction available
on the role of the British Navy in all theaters of the war. The British edition has
the title *The Navy at War, 1939-1945*.

775   Smith, Stanley E., ed. **The United States Navy in World War II: The**
        One-Volume History, from Pearl Harbor to Tokyo Bay. New York,
        Morrow, 1966. 1049p. Maps.
An anthology of selected articles and excerpts giving personal insights into various
actions of the U. S. Navy. Emphasis is on the action in the Atlantic and Pacific
oceans. The editor's introductory sections bring the selections together in a
unified volume.

776   Thomas, David Arthur. **Submarine Victory: The Story of British Sub-**
        marines in World War II. London, Kimber, 1961. 224p. Maps.
A general popular history of the role played by British Submarine Service during
the war. Emphasis is on submarine action in the Atlantic, Arctic and Mediterranean with several concluding chapters on the Pacific.

777   Thomas, David Arthur. **With Ensigns Flying: The Story of H. M. Destroyers**
        at War, 1939-1945. London, Kimber, 1958. 216p.
One of the better popular histories of the contribution of the Royal Navy's destroyer forces during the war. Emphasis is on the sea battles to protect the Atlantic
and Arctic convoys and the action in the Mediterranean.

778   Willoughby, Malcolm Francis. **The U. S. Coast Guard in World War II.**
        Annapolis, United States Naval Institute, 1957. 347p. Maps.
This is a history of the U. S. Coast Guard's role in the war and is not a general
history of the naval war. For the duration of the war the Coast Guard was under
the control of the Navy and did not function independently. The Coast Guard's
domestic and combat area duties are thoroughly discussed.

779   Woodward, David. **The Secret Raiders: The Story of the German Armed
        Merchant Raiders in the Second World War.** New York, Norton, 1955.
        288p.
The story of German merchant raiders is told based on the diaries of the ships'
captains. While these raiders played no decisive role at sea, they did serve to dis-
rupt shipping all over the world.

The Atlantic, Arctic, and Mediterranean

780   Auphan, Gabriel Adrien Joseph Paul and Jacques Mordal. **The French
        Navy in World War II.** Annapolis, United States Naval Institute, 1950.
        413p. Maps.
One of the few works on the French Navy that has appeared in English. Covers
the active role of the French Navy in the early months of the war until the fall
of France; the tragic fate of the French fleet; and the reactivated fleet under the
Free French. A good treatment of a highly controversial chapter in the naval
action of World War II.

781   Belot, Raymond de. **The Struggle for the Mediterranean, 1939-1945.**
        Princeton, N.J., Princeton University Press, 1951. 287p. Maps. Bibliog.
A general history of the naval and air forces in the Mediterranean with emphasis
on the naval forces. The author, a navy admiral, discusses Mediterranean strategy
in the context of the whole war effort. A good history of the Mediterranean struggle
from the French viewpoint.

782   Bragadin, Marć Antonio and Guiseppe Fioranvanzo. **The Italian
        Navy in World War II.** Annapolis, United States Naval Institute,
        1957. 380p.
A history of the Italian Navy and the naval struggle in the Mediterranean Sea from
the Italian point of view. The failure of the Italian Navy is placed primarily on the
lack of proper air support. A valuable study of an often overshadowed navy.

783   Carse, Robert. **A Cold Corner of Hell: The Story of the Murmansk
        Convoys, 1941-45.** Garden City, N. Y., Doubleday, 1969. 268p. Bibliog.
The struggle of men and ships to take vital war supplies to Russia through the
Arctic Ocean is well told in this volume. Attention is centered on the convoys in
1941-1942 with special attention given to the tragic voyage of convoy PQ17.

784   Carter, Worrall Reed, and Elmer Ellsworth Duvall. **Ships, Salvage, and
        Sinews of War: The Story of Fleet Logistics Afloat in Atlantic and
        Mediterranean Waters During World War II.** Washington, Dept. of the
        Navy, 1954. 533p. Maps.

The official U. S. history of naval logistics in the Atlantic and Mediterranean. The authors show the absolute importance of logistics in modern naval warfare. Without adequate supplies victory was not possible in what was essentially a war of production. For a study of logistics in the Pacific see Carter R. Worrall, *Beans, Bullets and Black Oil*. (Item 812).

785   Chalmers, William Scott. **Max Horton and the Western Approaches: A Biography of Admiral Sir Max Kennedy Horton**. London, Hodder and Stoughton, 1954. 301p.
A definitive biography of the British admiral in charge of the campaign against German submarines from 1942-45. In 1942 Horton was appointed Commander-in-Chief, Western Approaches, with responsibilities to protect Allied ships from German submarine attacks. Horton's earlier assignments had been to command the Reserve Fleet and later as a ranking submarine officer.

786   Cocchia, Aldo. **The Hunters and the Hunted: Adventures of Italian Naval Forces**. Annapolis, U. S. Naval Institute, 1958. 179p. Maps.
A personalized history of Italian submarine operations. Emphasis is, of course, on action in the Mediterranean. There is some coverage of surface action and the "human torpedoes." Published in England as *Submarine Attacking*.

787   Cunningham, Andrew Browne. **A Sailor's Odyssey: The Autobiography of Admiral of the Fleet, Viscount Cunningham of Hyndhope**. New York, Dutton, 1951. 715p. Maps.
An autobiography by the man considered to be the outstanding British admiral of the war. There are good descriptions of combat action and insights into battle tactics. Cunningham was known as a man of action. He served as Commander-in-Chief of the Mediterranean in 1940-41, British representative to the Joint Chiefs of Staff in 1942, Allied Naval Commander-in-Chief in North Africa under Eisenhower in 1942 and as First Sea Lord from 1943 to 1945.

788   Donitz, Karl. **Memoirs: Ten Years and Twenty Days**. Cleveland, World Publishing, 1959. 500p. Maps.
Primarily a history of the German navy with emphasis on the role of the submarine. Donitz comes across in these memoirs as an unrepentant military leader whose only regret is that Germany lost the war. For example, he claims ignorance of concentration camps. Covers the development of German naval strategy from 1939-45. Donitz served as Commander-in-Chief of the German Navy and as Head of the Reich during the last 10 days of its existence. A frank memoir valuable for the German viewpoint. Donitz was convicted at Nuremberg and sentenced to a prison term.

789   Farago, Ladislas. **The Tenth Fleet**. New York, Obolensky, 1962. 366p.
The story of the U. S. effort to coordinate naval operations against German submarine action. The Tenth Fleet had no ships, but was comprised solely of officers engaged in locating German submarines. A great part of the book is devoted to descriptions of submarine hunting operations at sea. Not well organized, but the author seldom loses the reader's interest.

790   Frank, Wolfgang. **The Sea Wolves: The Story of German U-Boats at War.**
        New York, Rinehart, 1955. 340p.
A chronological account of German U-boat operations in World War II with emphasis on the Atlantic theater. Includes materials on the development of the U-
boat—both the technical, scientific and political aspects. Told from the German view.

791   Golovko, Arsenii Grigor'evich. **With the Red Fleet: The War Memoirs of
        the Late Admiral Arseni G. Golovko.** London, Putnam, 1965. 247p. Maps.
One of the few items from Russian sources on naval operations. Concerned with
Russian destroyer and submarine operations in the Arctic and the supply convoys.
The work is generally critical of the Allies, inaccurate at times and offers few
statistics. This is the memoir of the Russian Commander-in-Chief of the Northern
Fleet.

792   Gretton, Peter. **Convoy Escort Commander.** London, Cassell, 1964.
        223p. Maps, Bibliog.
A memoir by a British naval officer who served as a convoy commander in the
Atlantic and Mediterranean. Good insights into convoys. There is a good section
on convoy management and defense.

793   Heckstall-Smith, Anthony. **The Fleet That Faced Both Ways.** London,
        Blond, 1963. 232p. Bibliog.
The story of the destruction of the French fleet at Mers-el-Kebir by the British.
The author has written a readable accurate version of what was probably an
unnecessary military action which at the time caused much hard feelings.

794   Herrick, Robert Waring. **Soviet Naval Strategy: Fifty Years of Theory
        and Practice.** Annapolis, United States Naval Institute, 1968. 197p.
        Map, Bibliog.
This is a general work on Soviet naval strategy with one chapter devoted to World
War II. Although brief the coverage of the war is enlightening and tells what the
author conceived Soviet naval strategy to be.

795   Irving, David John Cawdell. **The Destruction of Convoy PQ17.** New
        York, Simon and Schuster, 1969. 337p. Maps, Bibliog.
The story of the tragic convoy of July 1942, in which 23 of 37 merchant ships
and 153 seamen were lost. PQ17 was sent in response to a Russian request and
was planned hastily and poorly. A story of men and their reaction to a disaster
which saw crews mutiny, deliberate attempts to run aground and nine seaworthy
ships deserted by their crews.

796   Isakov, Ivan Stepanovich. **The Red Fleet in the Second World War.**
        London, Hutchinson, 1947. 124p. Maps.
A general history of the Russian navy by the Admiral of the Fleet. There is little
mention of the Allies. The story of the larger fleets in the Arctic, Baltic and Black
Sea and the flotillas on Lake Ladoga, Lake Onega, the Danube, the Dnieper, Sea
of Azov, the Volga and the Caspian Sea is briefly told.

797   Macintyre, Donald G. F. W. **The Battle for the Mediterranean.** New
       York, Norton, 1965. 216p. Maps, Bibliog.
This study is an "account of the struggle from June 1940-May 1943 for control
of the supply routes to the opposing armies in North Africa." Strong on strategic
analysis and higher command with lesser coverage of battle details. Also offers
an analysis of air power and its relation to control of the seas.

798   Macintyre, Donald G. F. W. **The Battle of the Atlantic.** New York,
       Macmillan 1961. 208p. Maps, Bibliog.
Basically the book covers the struggle to control the North Atlantic from 1939
to May 1943. In May 1943 over 40 German submarines were lost ending the major
threat to Allied shipping. Some of the more important topics discussed are coordination of air and naval forces, the convoy system and submarine strategy.

799   Macintyre, Donald G. F. W. **The Naval War Against Hitler.** New York,
       Scribner, 1971. 376p. Maps.
An interesting well written history of the Allied naval struggle against Germany.
There is good discussion of both Allied and German naval strategy. Among the more
important topics covered are the Graf Spee, Norway, the Mediterranean, Taranto,
Dunkirk, the Normandy Invasion, North Africa, Sicily and submarine tactics.
The narrative is enhanced by maps, diagrams and photographs.

800   Payne, Donald Gordon. **Red Duster, White Ensign: The Story of Malta
       and the Malta Convoys.** Garden City, N. Y., Doubleday, 1960. 260p.
       Maps.
A judicious critical work on the two year siege of Malta and the naval convoys
which enabled the island to withstand the German assault. There is some discussion of the strategy and tactics of defense which allowed Malta to hold off
long term sustained air and sea attacks. Emphasis is placed on the important
convoys of June-August 1942.

801   Pope, Dudley, **Graf Spee: The Life and Death of a Raider.** Philadelphia,
       Lippincott, 1957. 256p. Maps.
One of the best of many books about the destruction of the German battleship
Graf Spee by three British cruisers off the South American coast in December
1939. The title of the English edition is *The Battle of the River Plate.*

802   Pope, Dudley. **73 North: The Defeat of Hitler's Navy.** Philadelphia,
       Lippincott, 1958. 288p.
The story of an Allied convoy's struggle to break through defending German
naval surface ships to Russia. The convoy's success led to Hitler's decision to
limit future German naval action to submarines. That decision had far reaching
consequences. Based on official records of the Allies and Germans. The English
edition is titled: *73 North: The Battle of the Barents Sea.*

803   Raeder, Erich. **My Life.** Annapolis, United States Naval Institute, 1960.
       430p.

A memoir by the Grand Admiral and Commander-in-Chief of the German Navy for over 10 years until his resignation in 1943 when he broke with Hitler. Raeder tells about the pre-war navy and the development of wartime strategy. Analyzes his own decisions and the influence of Hitler on naval strategy. An interesting German view. Raeder was convicted of war crimes at Nuremberg.

804   Rogge, Bernhard and Wolfgang Frank. **The German Raider Atlantis.** New
       York, Ballantine Books, 1956. 154p.
The story of the German armed merchant raider Atlantis which sunk 22 ships in 622 days at sea while cruising over 100,000 miles. The Atlantis was finally sunk in November 1941. The author, Rogge, was captain of the Atlantis for two years.

805   Ruge, Friedrich. **Der Seekrieg: The German Navy's Story, 1939-1945.**
       Annapolis, United States Naval Institute, 1957. 440p. Maps.
A dispassionate history of the German navy by a former German admiral. The emphasis is on the German and Italian navies in the North Atalntic and Mediterranean. Shows the influence of naval power on land campaigns. The English edition is titled *Sea Warfare, 1939-1945: A German Viewpoint.*

806   Schofield, Brian Betham. **The Russian Convoys.** Philadelphia, Dufour
       Editions, 1964. 224p. Maps, Bibliog.
A history of the successful Allied efforts to supply Russia by convoys to Murmansk. Tells of the four year fight to control the Arctic route and the Allied development of protective strategy. Good details of action in one of the most geographically and climatically inhospitable theaters of the war.

807   Seth, Ronald. **The Fiercest Battle: The Story of North Atlantic Convoy
       ONS5, 22nd April-7th May, 1943.** New York, Norton, 1962. 208p. Maps.
The story of the successful passage of North Atlantic convoy ONS5. This successful passage was considered to be the final turning point in the Allied struggle against German U-boats. The story is an exciting one and is told in an engaging narrative that is easy to follow.

808   Smith, Peter Charles. **Pedestal: The Malta Convoy of August 1942.**
       London, Kimber, 1970. 208p. Maps, Bibliog.
The story of the successful convoy WS.5.21.S—"Pedestal"—undertaken in August 1942 to resupply Malta. The success of this convoy getting to Malta enabled the RAF and Royal Navy to regain their dominant position in the central Mediterranean. There are good chapters on the strategic importance of Malta and the British Mediterranean strategy.

809   Tute, Warren. **The Deadly Stroke: The Tragic Little Known Story of the
       British Destruction of the French Fleet in Oran in July 1940, After the
       Armistice with Germany.** London, Collins, 1973. 221p. Map, Bibliog.
A well researched account of the destruction of a major portion of the French fleet by the British in July 1940. The tragedy that struck the French at Oran—or Mers-el-Kebir—was possibly unnecessary, but the situation in 1940 after the fall of France forced the British to be sure that the French fleet stayed out of German hands.

The Pacific

810   Barbey, Daniel E. **MacArthur's Amphibious Navy: Seventh Amphibious Force Operations, 1943-1945.** Annapolis, United States Naval Institute, 1969. 375p. Maps.

The author, one of the least known but most successful admirals in the Pacific, expertly tells the story of the naval force that provided the means for MacArthur's amphibious operations. Besides the details of landing operations in the Southwest Pacific there is good background material on ship design, staff development and training. The author was the commanding admiral of the Seventh Amphibious Force.

811   Barker, A. J. **Midway: The Turning Point.** New York, Ballantine Books, 1971. 160p. Maps, Bibliog.

A brief popular history of the great air and naval battle of June 1942 that proved to be the beginning of the end for Japanese naval power. Numerous pictures, diagrams and maps make the book even more valuable and enjoyable.

812   Carter, Worrall Reed. **Beans, Bullets and Black Oil: The Story of Fleet Logistics Afloat in the Pacific During World War II.** Washington, Dept. of the Navy, 1953. 483p. Maps.

The official U. S. history of naval logistics in the Pacific. While logistics is not the "exciting" part of the war, Carter ably demonstrates its absolute importance in modern naval warfare. Without adequate supplies victory was not possible in what was essentially a war of production. For a study of logistics in the Atlantic and Mediterranean, see Carter's *Ships, Salvage, and Sinews of War.* (Item 784)

813   Dyer, George Carroll. **The Amphibians Came to Conquer: The Story of Admiral Richmond Kelly Turner.** Washington, U. S. Dept. of the Navy, 1972. 2v. Maps, Bibliog.

An outstanding study of Admiral Turner and his role in the Pacific theater. As much a general history of the Pacific campaign as a biography. Dyer has written a scholarly revisionist history which questions many former conclusions about the war. Turner fought in most major actions including Guadalcanal, Savo Island, Tarawa, Makin, Marshalls, Saipan, Guam, Tinian, Iwo Jima and Okinawa.

814   Forrestel, Emmet P. **Admiral Raymond A. Spruance, USN: A Study in Command.** Washington, Government Printing Office, 1966. 275p. Maps.

A detailed study of the command of the man many consider to be the U. S. Navy's most successful admiral in the Pacific theater. There is some introductory material on Spruance's pre-war career with the rest of the book concerned with his war-time activities. Spruance was involved in naval and air action at Midway, Philippine Sea, Tarawa, Gilbert Islands, Truk and Iwo Jima. More than any other commander he was responsible for the U. S. victory at Midway. Although Spruance did not receive much publicity during the war, he nonetheless will probably go down in history as one of the U. S. Navy's greatest wartime commanders.

815   Fuchida, Mitsuo and Masatake Okumiya. **Midway, The Battle That Doomed Japan: The Japanese Navy's Story.** Annapolis, United States Naval Institute, 1955. 266p. Maps.
The story of the Battle of Midway is told from the Japanese viewpoint. There is background material on the conception and strategic planning for Midway. The details of the battle are well told and it is enlightening to get the Japanese reaction to the battle. The final chapter analyzes the causes for the Japanese defeat.

816   Grenfell, Russell. **Main Fleet to Singapore.** New York, Macmillan, 1952. 238p. Bibliog.
Tells of the rise of Japanese seapower and the events leading to the Japanese capture of Singapore. Discusses the importance of Singapore to the British defenses. Critical of Churchill's and Roosevelt's policy in the Far East.

817   Halsey, William Frederick and Joseph Bryan. **Admiral Halsey's Story.** New York, Whittlesey House, 1947. 310p. Maps.
The story of one of the U. S. Navy's most successful and flamboyant admirals. The work is autobiographical and covers Halsey's life from his graduation from the Naval Academy through 1945. There are vivid battle accounts, especially for Guadalcanal and Leyte Gulf. Halsey was an "air admiral" and saw naval aviation as the key to control of the seas. An interesting story of an exciting man.

818   Hara, Tameichi. **Japanese Destroyer Captain.** New York, Ballantine Books, 1961. 311p.
An eyewitness account of some of the most important naval battles in the Pacific by a Japanese destroyer captain. Hara, called the "unsinkable captain" in Japan, participated in or was associated with naval action at Pearl Harbor, Java Sea, Coral Sea, Midway, Guadalcanal, Leyte Gulf and Okinawa. Good for the Japanese view of the important battles.

819   Hashimoto, Mochitsura. **Sunk: The Story of the Japanese Submarine Fleet, 1941-1945.** New York, Holt, 1954. 276p. Maps.
An important Japanese version of submarine activities in the Pacific. The work, however, is mostly undocumented and should be read with caution. The introduction, by an American, gives an interesting summary of the causes for Japanese failure—inflexible command, dated technology and underestimation of American submarines.

820   Holmes, Wilfred Jay. **Undersea Victory: The Influence of Submarine Operations on the War in the Pacific.** Garden City, N. Y., Doubleday, 1966. 505p. Maps, Bibliog.
A chronologically arranged history of American, Japanese, German, Dutch and Australian submarine operations in the Pacific. Most coverage, of course, is given to American and Japanese operations. Analyzes submarine strategy and tactics and the role of submarine operations in modern warfare.

821   Hough, Richard Alexander. **Death of the Battleship.** New York, Macmillan,
       1963. 216p. Maps, Bibliog.
The story of the Japanese sinking of the British battleships Prince of Wales and
Repulse in December 1941. Showed the decisive influence of air power against
unprotected battleships. Title of the English edition is *The Hunting of Force Z.*

822   Hoyt, Edwin Palmer. **How They Won the War in the Pacific: Nimitz and
       His Admirals.** New York, Weybright and Talley, 1970. 554p. Maps,
       Bibliog.
A biographical account of Admiral Nimitz and his Central Pacific Command.
There is good material on Admirals King, Halsey, Spruance, Fletcher and Turner.
A picture of the Pacific war from the level of high command.

823   Ito, Masanori. **The End of the Imperial Japanese Navy.** New York,
       Norton, 1962. 240p. Maps.
A Japanese version of the Japanese Navy's role in the Pacific. All major naval
actions are covered. The author blames the lack of air power after Midway for the
ultimate defeat of the Japanese Navy. The appendices have some useful data on
Japanese warships and general statistical information.

824   **The Japanese Navy in World War II: An Antology of Articles.** Annapolis,
       United States Naval Institute, 1969. 147p. Maps.
An anthology of articles by former Japanese navy and air defense officers. A
good Japanese view of naval warfare from Pearl Harbor to the final battles at
Okinawa.

825   Johnston, Stanley. **Queen of the Flat-Tops: The U.S.S. Lexington and
       the Coral Sea Battle.** New York, Dutton, 1942. 280p. Maps.
A now classic account of the aircraft carrier Lexington in the Battle of the Coral
Sea by a war correspondent aboard the carrier.

826   Lockwood, Charles A. **Sink 'Em All: Submarine Warfare in the Pacific.**
       New York, Dutton, 1951. 416p. Map.
The exciting story of the "silent service" in the war against Japan is told by the
wartime commander of U. S. submarine operations in the Pacific. There are many
details and statistics of submarine operations and an analysis of the submarine's
role in support of major operations. Told from the author's personal experience.

827   Lord, Walter. **Incredible Victory.** New York, Harper & Row, 1967.
       331p. Maps, Bibliog.
A lively popular history of the Battle of Midway based mostly on personal interviews. This battle in June 1942 was the first major Japanese defeat of the war.
Both the American and Japanese views are given. While interesting this work is
not a final authority--and does not presume to be.

828   Reynolds, Clark G. **The Fast Carriers: The Forging of an Air Navy.**
       New York, McGraw-Hill, 1968. 498p. Maps, Bibliog.
An engaging scholarly study of the development of the fast carrier and naval
aviation in the U. S. Navy. All of the major engagements against the Japanese

involving carrier action are discussed. Good coverage of the "battleship admirals" versus the "air admirals." Reynolds is pro "air admiral" in his critical evaluations of naval air power. Includes a lengthy annotated bibliography.

829   Taylor, Theodore. **The Magnificent Mitscher.** New York, Norton, 1954. 364p.

A fair biography of one of the American "air admirals." Mitscher was one of the first naval officers to go into aviation, and he fought for the development of naval aviation. He was one of the most successful admirals in the Pacific and participated in the Doolittle raid, Midway, Philippine Sea, the Solomons and Okinawa. Mitscher wrote no memoirs and there is little documentary material except for the major actions in which he participated.

830   Thomas, David Arthur. **The Battle of the Java Sea.** New York, Stein and Day, 1969. 259p. Maps, Bibliog.

A terse account of the Pacific war from the American disaster at Pearl Harbor to the Allied disaster in the Java Sea in the Southeast Pacific on February 27-28, 1942. The emphasis is on the Battle of the Java Sea with adequate background to place the battle in perspective.

831   Winton, John. **The Forgotten Fleet: The British Navy in the Pacific, 1944-1945.** New York, Coward-McCann, 1970. 433p. Maps, Bibliog.

The story of the British East Indies and British Pacific fleets. There is coverage of the political background behind British military policy in the Pacific. There is adequate detail of the various military operations. A good account of a secondary theater of the war.

CHAPTER 5—WEAPONS

GENERAL WORKS

832   Blore, Trevor. **Commissioned Barges: The Story of the Landing Craft.**
London, Hutchinson, 1946. 216p.

A chronicle of the men and the landing crafts that made possible Allied amphibious
operations in the European and South Asian theaters of the war. The author describes the use of these crafts in the Mediterranean, Normandy, the Low Countries,
and in Burma. He enthusiastically records the achievements of this specialized
service.

833   Chamberlain, Peter and Chris Ellis. **British and American Tanks of World
War II. The Complete Illustrated History of British, American and Commonwealth Tanks, Gun Motor Carriages and Special Purpose Vehicles,
1939-1945.** New York, Arco, 1969. 222p. Bibliog.

Arranged by country of origin and then by chronological development this is a
well-written technical and illustrated history of the design, evolution and development of the armored fighting vehicle. The pictorial and textual coverage includes
more than 2,000 models and their variants with more than 500 photographs.
The work includes a section on half tracks that were developed for use in armored
units. An appendix provides material on interior layout, guns, engines and diagrams
of the tanks. The index is arranged by country and function and by class within
this function. Another title of interest is Brian T. White's *British Tanks and Fighting Vehicles, 1914-1945*. (London, Allan, 1970.)

834   Coggins, Jack. **The Campaign for Guadalcanal.** (See Item 680 for review of
the text.)

The multiplicity of the excellent drawings of arms and equipment complement
the text and serve to provide a very interesting picture of the variety of weapons
employed by the combatants during this campaign.

835   Ellis, Chris. **Military Transport of World War II: Including Post War
Vehicles.** New York, Macmillan, 1971. 177p.

A representative cross-section of the types of transport vehicles used by the major
combatant nations. Each vehicle selected is illustrated in color and is accompanied
by detailed technical and historical information, official descriptions and des-
ignations.

836   Green, William. **War Planes of the Second World War.** Garden City,
N. Y., Doubleday, 1960— . 10v. (to date).

An excellent comprehensive illustrated series of handbooks (5-1/4" x 4-3/4") of
all the aircraft of the combatant countries. The volumes include aircraft built
during this period but which never saw service. Three view line drawings supplement the photographs and descriptions of the basic models and their major variants.
The concise text covers the history of the aircraft's development and a brief listing
of its basic specifications. Volumes one to four cover fighter aircraft, five covers

flying boats, six covers float planes, and seven to ten cover bombers and reconnaissance aircraft.

837   Green, William. **Famous Bombers of the Second World War**. Garden City, N. Y., Doubleday, 1959-1960. 2v.

The author continues the series of famous aircraft of the war with these two supportive volumes. The stories of the more famous bombers of the United States, Britain, Germany, Italy and Japan are presented with numerous clear photographs, excellent tone drawings and comparative line drawings of variant designs. The commentary provides a detailed history of each aircraft's production, combat service and specifications.

838   Green, William. **Famous Fighters of the Second World War**. New York, Hanover House, 1957 (v.1), Garden City, N. Y., Doubleday, 1962 (v.2). 2v.

Excellent detailed histories of twenty-nine of the most famous fighter planes of the war. The clear and excellent photographs are complemented by highly detailed full page tone drawings and comparative side views of variant designs. A wealth of detail is included in the description of the development of each aircraft. This is one of the finest books of its kind by a recognized authority in the field.

839   Hartley, Arthur Bamford. **Unexploded Bomb: A History of Bomb Disposal**. New York, Norton, 1959. 272p.

An account of the experiences and methods of the Bomb Disposal Sections of the Royal Engineers and of the Germans and Japanese in defusing unexploded bombs. The descriptions include pictures and diagrams of the various types of bombs and mines dropped by the combatants. This is also a record of physical courage and intellectual ingenuity as new types of fuses and exploding devices had to be coped with throughout the war.

840   Hoffschmidt, E. J. and W. J. Tantum, eds. **Second World War Combat Weapons**. Old Greenwich, Conn., WE, Inc., 1968–. (2v. to date).

The first two volumes of this series are titled *German Combat Weapons* (212p.) and *Japanese Combat Weapons* (228p.). The weapons covered include those for the infantry, artillery, combat vehicles and various miscellaneous other weapons. The illustrations are accompanied by several paragraphs of text and the weapon's specifications.

841   Hogg, Ian V. **The Guns, 1939-45**. New York, Ballantine Books, 1970. 160p. Bibliog.

An inexpensive paperback series, well illustrated with photographs, tone drawings, maps (where applicable) and diagrams. This particular title, well-written by an authority in the field, covers the major large guns of the combatant nations. The topics covered include the larger infantry guns, field guns, medium sized artillery, anti-tank guns, anti-aircraft guns, the big guns (such as the railway guns and large howitzers) and recoilless weapons. Some of the other titles in the series are *ME109* by Martin Caidin, *German Secret Weapons* by Brian Ford, *Spitfire* by John Vader, *Zero* by Martin Caidin, *U-Boat* by David Mason and *PT Boats* by Bryan Cooper.

842   Irving, David John Cawdell, **The Mare's Nest.** Boston, Little Brown,
            1965. 320p. Maps.
The story of the efforts of the British and the Germans to destroy or preserve
respectively the V-1 and V-2 rocket programs. The author recounts the internal
struggles among the Germans to decide what weapons to develop and of the British
in discerning what the Germans were up to and what needed to be done to counter
this threat.

843   **Jane's All the World's Aircraft, 1945-46.** New York, Arco, 1970. 724p.
This is the reprint of a basic reference work of the aircraft of the world's air
forces. The brief documentation, with basic specifications for the major types
and notations of the variant models, is accompanied by over 700 illustrations.
This volume includes data of aircraft to the end of the war, corrected to September
1, 1945 and with an addenda to the beginning of 1946. The war-time silhouettes
are still included in this volume. The historical sections for each country cover
also a review of operations, service commands and national markings. A separate
section on the world's aircraft engines is included.

844   **Jane's Fighting Ships, 1942.** New York, Macmillan, 1943. (The 1944-45
            edition with 784 pages has been reprinted by Arco Publ.)
This important reference work (the 1942 edition was issued in June 1943) covers
the wide variety and types of the world's warships. The several hundred photographs are complemented with silhouettes of ship types, top views in line drawings,
and side views in also line drawings showing location and thicknesses of the ships'
armor belts. The specifications include available data on armament, size, tonnage,
speed and date built. National ensigns and insignias of rank are noted. A special
section on war losses gives the type of ship, an illustration (where available), its
name, size and the date and how it was sunk. Earlier volumes need to be referenced
in order to find fuller information on ships sunk.

845   Kirk, John and Robert Young, Jr. **Great Weapons of World War II.**
            New York, Walker, 1961. 347p.
Divided into sections on aircraft, ships, tanks and tank destroyers, artillery, small
arms and miscellaneous weapons, the author provides a general book on the major
weapons of World War II. Brief information and technical notations accompany
each illustration of the world's lethal weapons.

846   Munson, Kenneth G. **Aircraft of World War II.** 2nd ed. New York, Double-
            day, 1972. 272p.
An excellent handy one-volume guide, with color plates and over three hundred
photos, giving basic data of the principal aircraft of the period. Minor types are
also well illustrated but are given somewhat briefer notations. Experimental and
less important aircraft are listed with very brief notations. Good textual background
history is provided for each of the belligerents with also a section on their aircraft
nomenclature.

847   White, Brian Terence. **Tanks and Other A. F. V.'s of the Blitzkrieg Era,
            1939 to 1941.** New York, Macmillan, 1972. 161p.

The armored fighting vehicles of the period 1939-1941 participated in the crucial initial campaigns of the war, from the German invasion of Poland to the start of Operation Barbarossa against the U.S.S.R. Each selected representative vehicle is illustrated in color with factual descriptive texts including technical and developmental data. An appendix includes further detail on camouflage, markings, comparative data and cross-sectional drawings. This excellent general illustrated series by this publisher also includes titles by Kenneth Munson, *Fighters and Bombers Between the Wars, 1919-39* (2v.); and *Fighters and Bombers, 1939-45* (2v.); also a title on the A.F.V. is E. J. Hoffschmidt's and W. A. Tantum's *German Tank and Antitank in World War II* published by WE, Inc.

848   Windrow, Martin C., ed. **Aircraft in Profile**. Garden City, N. Y., Doubleday, 1968-70. Vols. 108. Cain, Charles W., ed. **Aircraft in Profile**. Garden City, N.Y., Doubleday, 1971, v.9-10.
A comprehensive and excellent series featuring individual profiles of the world's aircraft from the First World War into the post Second World War period. Somewhat over half of the aircraft described and illustrated cover the period of World War II. Profile illustrations in color complement the clear photographs, performance data, specifications and the detailed historical text on each aircraft's development, production and operations. Similar series are also produced by this publisher titled *Armoured Fighting Vehicles*, ed. by Duncan Crow; and *Warships in Profile*, ed. by John Wingate.

INDIVIDUAL COUNTRIES

Canada

849   Eggleston, Wilfred. **Scientists at War**. New York, Oxford University Press, 1950. 291p.
A concise reporting of the work of Canadian scientists during the Second World War. A record of their achievements in the research on radar, wood-pulp, atomic energy and the amazing investigation of aircraft carriers to be made from huge icebergs.

Germany

850   Davis, Brian L. **German Army Uniforms and Insignia, 1933-1945**. New York, World Pub., 1972. 244p. Bibliog.
A basic reference work containing photographs of every aspect of German regular army uniforms of the period of the Third Reich. Many of the illustrations are shown set against a background of service conditions.

851   Dornberger, Walter. **V-2**. New York, Viking, 1954. 281p.
The German pioneer in the long range military rocket recounts his role in the development of German rocket research from 1930 to 1945. Scientist, general in the army and director of the experimental station at Peenemunde, he describes his work in full detail and relates the political and administrative difficulties encountered. Interwoven in the technical account are his experiences with the Gestapo, Hitler, Himmler and Goering.

852   Green, William. **Augsburg Eagle: The Story of the Messerschmitt 109.**
       Garden City, N. Y., Doubleday, 1972. 128p.
Lots of color detail make this history of the development and operations of the
ME.109 an excellent book. Very clear photographs complement the story of the
technical evolution from its inception in 1933 to its final phase out in Spain in
1967. An ironic fact is that this aircraft was used in combat for the last time
by Israel during its war for independence. Specifications are given for each
major model change.

853   Green, William. **The Warplanes of the Third Reich.** Garden City, N. Y.,
       Doubleday, 1970. 672p.
A definitive and monumental study of German warplanes from 1933 to 1945 by
an outstanding authority in the field of aircraft history. The profusely illustrated
work traces the development and service career of these German aircraft. The
historical and military reasons for the aircraft's development, the role of the
persons involved in the design, and the story of the rise and fall of the Luftwaffe
are well covered in the text. Other illustrations include profile and plan views
and a color section on aircraft markings

854   Hogg, Ian V. **German Secret Weapons of World War II.** New York, Arco,
       1970. 80p.
An interesting book by a British expert in weapons, of the so-called German
secret weapons. All sources are authoritative and were gathered from Allied
investigations or from the project developers themselves. The entries, complemented by photographs and line drawings, are listed in broad classification by
type (e.g., rockets, artillery) and within these groups alphabetically by their
German code name. Another title of interest on this subject is Leslie E. Simon's
Secret Weapons of the Third Reich, published by WE, Inc.

855   Huzel, Dieter. **Peenemunde to Canaveral.** Englewood Cliffs, N. J.,
       Prentice-Hall, 1962. 247p.
An authoritative account in diary form of the anxiety and elation experienced
by the German scientists in their work on the V-2 rocket project. The author was
involved in all phases of this work and relates the complications encountered in
the development and test-firing of this weapon. Appendices contain historical
notes on German rocket development, the rockets of this series and information on the test facilities.

856   Klee, Ernst and Otto Merk. **The Birth of the Missile: The Secrets of
       Peenemunde.** New York, Dutton, 1965. 126p. Maps.
A photographic and documentary record of the development of the V-2. This
popular historical record also includes copies of the official orders and correspondence regarding various phases of the V-2 project.

857   Senger und Etterlin, Ferdinand Marie von. **German Tanks of World
       War II: The Complete Illustrated History of German Armoured Fight-
       ing Vehicles, 1926-1945.** Harrisburg, Pa., Stackpole Books, 1969.
       214p. Bibliog.

This is a useful overall survey and guide to German tanks, half-tracks and armored cars. Each type and major variant is provided with detailed illustrations. Textual descriptions also concentrate on the details of the various types.

858   Simon, Leslie Earl. **German Research in World War II: An Analysis of the Conduct of Research.** New York, Wiley, 1947. 218p.
A critical review of the organization, the successes and failures of German weapons research. This background study reviews the methods, problems and functioning of Nazi war science research. A source of information on German secret weapons development and research in ballistics, tanks, rockets, jet engines and aerodynamics.

859   Smith, Peter Charles. **Stuka at War.** New York, Arco, 1971. 192p. Bibliog.
An excellent history of one of the most famous aircraft of the Second World War. This German dive bomber, whose name was a contraction for the general term Sturzkampfflugzeug (dive bomber), was successful both as a tank destroyer and against shipping. The book describes the development of the aircraft and its use throughout Germany's combat zones. It is extensively illustrated with over 150 photographs.

860   Wagner, Ray and Heinz Nowarra. **German Combat Planes.** Garden City, N. Y., Doubleday, 1971. 400p. Bibliog.
The entire scope of German military aircraft development from 1914 to 1945 is presented in this comprehensive history explaining each plane's role in the Luftwaffe. Brief specifications are given for each major type along with an extensive collection of photographs.

861   Windrow, Martin C. **German Air Force Fighters of World War Two.** Garden City, N. Y., Doubleday, 1969. 64p.
This series also includes works on the aircrafts of the other combatant nations. The text also includes brief specifications, colored plates and photographs. The series is similar to the "Profile" series but with less detail.

Great Britain

862   Cowie, J. S. **Mines, Minelayers and Minelaying.** New York, Oxford University Press, 1949. 216p. Maps, Bibliog.
Tracing the development of the sea mine from the 16th century, the work discusses the legal aspects of mine warfare and the contributions to the field of scientists and engineers. The book emphasizes the work of the British Royal Navy and a detailed consideration of British minelaying efforts in both world wars.

863   Hartcup, Guy. **The Challenge of War: Britain's Scientific and Engineering Contributions to World War Two.** New York, Taplinger, 1970. 295p. Bibliog.
The extent of Britain's scientific contributions during the period from 1930 to the end of the war are described against the background of the war effort. The development of such contributions as radar, proximity fuses and amphibious craft are seen in relation to the human factors involved and the urgent timetable

brought on by the exigencies of the war. Another related title is R. Stuart Macrae's *Winston Chruchill's Toy Shop* published by Walker (1972).

864   Kemp, Norman. **The Devices of War.** London, Laurie, 1956. 232p.
An adventurous narrative of how some of the war-time special equipment came to be developed. Describes such projects as the famed Mulberry Harbor, the trans-channel fuel pipe-line and smaller ones but also far reaching such as the bonded plywood battery containers, which remained unbroken under great stress, for use in submarines.

865   Pawle, Gerald. **The Secret War, 1939-45.** New York, Sloan Associates, 1957. 297p.
An accurate non-technical account of weapon and counter weapon developments by the British Admiralty's Department of Miscellaneous Weapon Development. The author was in charge of this department and eventually the whole research and development program of the British Navy. He recounts with some humor the activities of this area. Anti-submarine and anti-aircraft devices as well as involvement in the development of the Mulberry Harbor were among the areas of research.

866   Postan, Meisei Mikhail, D. Day and J. D. Scott. **Design and Development of Weapons: Studies on Government and Industrial Organization.** London, Longmans, Green, 1964. 579p.
The coverage is limited to an account of the development of British aircraft and army weapons. The work is divided into chapter narratives, each dealing with individual subjects or problems and the military administrative and private forces behind the design and development of the weapons. The subjects cover aircraft, aircraft engines and armament, artillery and small arms development, anti-aircraft defense, armored fighting vehicles and radar and its various applciations. Some detail is provided on the status of the British research establishment.

867   Price, Alfred. **Aircraft Versus Submarine: The Evolution of the Anti-Submarine Aircraft, 1912-1972.** London, Kimber, 1973. 268p. Maps, Bibliog.
An excellent book on the use of the aircraft against primarily the German U-boats. Almost three fourths of the book covers the period of the Second World War. Vividly written, the author describes the techniques and tactics of the anti-submarine activities of the British and how the science of electronics greatly helped influence the outcome.

868   Price, Alfred. **Instruments of Darkness.** London, Kimber, 1967. 254p.
An explanation in precise terms of the operational development of radar. Presents the reasons why the British who were behind the Germans in this area overtook and kept ahead of them in most of the subsequent applications. The author notes the German success later in the war of detecting the emissions of the topographical identification system (H2S) thus being able to intercept Allied aircraft using this radar. He also takes note of the electronic jamming counter-measures undertaken by the Allies and the war end development by the Germans of a jam proof radar system.

869   Robertson, Bruce. **Spitfire—The Story of a Famous Fighter.** Fallbrook,
         Calif., Aero Pub., 1961. 216p.
Featuring great detail this comprehensive work covers every possible aspect of
the history and development of the Spitfire and the Seafire. Color schemes complement the extensive scope of the text.

870   Rowe, Albert Percival. **One Story of Radar.** Cambridge, Eng., Cambridge
         University Press, 1948. 207p.
Covering the period from June 1934 to September 1945, this is the story of
telecommunications research in Britain and its work on radar. This succinct
account of the development of radar relates the disappointments and triumphs
of the scientists working on this project.

871   Saward, Dudley. **Bomber's Eye.** London, Cassell, 1959. 264p.
An account of the operational side of radar describing its uses for aircraft naviga-
tion, aids to pin-point bombing release and providing a map-like screen picture
of the area beneath the aircraft and thirty miles ahead. The author shows how the
various variant developments of radar increased the effectiveness of the bombers
and notes the cooperation between the military and the scientists in solving the
medium's difficulties and the enemy's attempts to reduce its effectiveness.

872   Thetford, Owen Gordon. **Aircraft of the Royal Air Force Since 1918.**
         4th rev. ed. New York, Funk and Wagnalls, 1968. 611p.
An encyclopedia of British aircraft giving technical data for each type, design
origins, technical, manufacturing and operational history and squadron allocations.
Shows the interrelationships of the various design elements. The work is well
illustrated including three view line drawings. A companion work is *British Naval
Aircraft Since 1912* by the same author and publisher (1968, c.1962).

873   Watson-Watt, Sir Robert Alexander. **Pulse of Radar: The Autobiography
         of Sir Robert Alexander Watson-Watt.** New York, Dial Press, 1959.
         438p.
A vigorous and detailed personal account of the development of radar and radio-
direction finding by the leading pioneer in the field. An exciting story of the historical, developmental and technological aspects of radar.

Japan

874   Francillon, Rene J. **Japanese Aircraft of the Pacific War.** London, Putnam,
         1970. 570p.
An exhaustive and detailed survey of Japanese aircraft design, production and
operational service from the early 1930s to the end of the Second World War.
The author takes note of the surprise of the Allies at the high quality of Japanese
military aviation which in many cases was a situation of too little and too late
to affect Japan's role in the war. Extensive illustrations and technical detail aid
in providing a comprehensive picture of this period of Japanese aircraft development.

875   Watts, Anthony John. **Japanese Warships of World War II.** Garden City,
         N. Y., Doubleday, 1967. 400p.

An overall view of Japanese warships of this period. Technical and historical data is provided for each type from battleship to submarine. Photographs illustrate each class with profile and deck plan drawings for most of the major classes.

Russia

876   Barker, A. J. and John Walter. **Russian Infantry Weapons of World War II.** New York, Arco, 1971. 80p.

A well illustrated history of the development of the basic infantry weapons in use by the Soviet Army in World War II. General introductory information precedes each of the specialized sections on pistols and revolvers, rifles, mortars, grenades and ammunition. An appendix of comparative performance data is included. Other titles in this series by the same author are *German Infantry Weapons of World War II* and *British and American Infantry Weapons of World War II.* In similar format by the same publisher is J. Anthony Carter's *Allied Bayonets of World War II.*

877   Meister, Jurg. **The Soviet Navy.** Garden City, N. Y., Doubleday, 1972. 4v.

One of the most interesting of the various series on World War II is the Navies of the Second World War of which these volumes are a part. Volume one provides an introductory description of the Soviet Navy's role in the war. These handbooks (6 x 4) on the war fleets of the combatant nations include photographs illustrating the various types and classes, brief histories of the type of ship (cruiser) and the class (Kirov), specifications on displacement, dimensions, armament, complement, the ship's builder, date built and its fate. The following titles edited by H. T. Lenton are also a part of this series. *American Battleships, Carriers and Cruisers*; *American Fleet and Escort Destroyers*, 2v.; *American Submarines*; *British Battleships and Aircraft Carriers*; *British Cruisers*; *British Fleet and Escort Destroyers*, 2v.; *British Submarines*; *French Navy*, 2v.; *German Submarines*, 2v.; *German Surface Vessels*, 2v.; *Japanese Battleships and Cruisers*; *Japanese Aircraft Carriers and Destroyers*; and *Royal Netherlands Navy*.

878   Perrett, Bryan. **Fighting Vehicles of the Red. Army.** New York, Arco, 1969. 104p.

An officer in the British Royal Tank Regiment presents an excellent well illustrated reference work on the armored fighting vehicles of the Soviet Army from the First World War to 1968. This guide to the development of Russian armor analyzes the strengths and weaknesses of Soviet design and tactics. Most of the vehicles discussed were in use during the Second World War.

United States

879   Barnes, Gladeon Marcus. **Weapons of World War II.** New York, Van Nostrand, 1947. 317p.

The Chief of the U. S. Research and Development Service relates the part played by the United States in the design, development, standardization and mass production of one thousand major weapons. Detailed information on the characteristics and uses is given on small arms, machine guns, artillery, aircraft, bombs, tanks and other various weapons.

880   Baxter, James Phinney. **Scientists Against Time.** Boston, Little Brown, 1952. 473p.

This reprint of the 1946 edition covers the story of the major scientific accomplishments of the U.S. Office of Scientific Research and Development. This historical record describes the stages of organization, the obstacles encountered (including U.S. and Allied military leaders), the weapons developed and their successes in combat. A clear dramatic description of the inside story of scientific war research.

881   Birdsall, Steve. **Famous Aircraft: The B-17 Flying Fortress.** New York Arco, 1965. 56p.

A brief history of the development of the B-17. Less emphasis is given to specifications and more on photographs and tone drawings. Also included is a reprint of the main body of the B-l7's flight handbook. Other titles in this series include Birdsall's *The B-24 Liberator*; James Craig's *The Messerschmitt Bf.109*; Gene Gurney's *The P-38 Lightning*; Ernest R. McDowell's *The P-40 Kitty Hawk*; and Len Morgan's *The Douglas DC-3, The P-47 Thunderbolt*, and *The P-51 Mustang*.

882   Boyce, Joseph Canon, ed. **New Weapons for Air Warfare: Fire-Control Equipment, Proximity Fuses, and Guided Missiles.** Boston, Little, Brown, 1947. 292p.

A description of the work of the special divisions of the National Defense Research Committee on devices to control behavior of bombs, shells, rockets and missiles through some elaborate and important scientific developments of the war.

883   Bunker, John Gorley. **Liberty Ships: The Ugly Ducklings of World War II.** Annapolis, Naval Institute Press, 1972. 287p.

A history of the origins, design, development, building program and combat experiences of these famous ships of the Second World War. Besides numerous photographs, the book includes drawings of hull lines and deck plans. Appendices include a list of the names, numbers and fate of twenty-six hundred liberty ships. Another title of interest is Frederic C. Lane's *Ships for Victory: A History of Ship-Building Under the U. S. Maritime Commission in World War II*. Johns Hopkins Press, 1951. (Item 767.)

884   Burchard, John Ely. **Rockets, Guns and Targets: Rockets, Target Information, Erosion Information and Hypervelocity Guns Developed During World War II by the Office of Scientific Research and Development.** Boston, Little, Brown, 1948. 482p.

Describes the development of such weapons as flame throwers, hypervelocity guns, train destroying aircraft gunnery weapons, and how the science of rocketry developed into the tank destroying bazooka.

885   Chamberlain, Peter and Chris Ellis. **The Sherman.** New York, Arco, 1969. 80p.

A detailed illustrated history of the design and development of the U. S. Army's Sherman tank. The book describes its variant models, its special purpose uses such as mine exploders, dozers, and rocket launchers, armament used and series specifications. Also by the same authors are *The Churchill Tank: The Story of Britain's Most Famous Tank, 1939-1965* and *Soviet Combat Tanks, 1939-1945*.

886   Freeman, Roger Anthony. **The Mighty Eighth: Units, Men and Machines: A History of the U. S. 8th Army Air Force.** Rev. ed. Garden City, N. Y., Doubleday, 1972. 311p.
A detailed illustrated history of this group from its inception in January 1942 to its departure from Britain after World War II. Details its operations, emphasizing its combat units and the roles they played in the war. Over four hundred photographs and full color illustrations depicting aircraft markings accompany the text.

887   Gruenhagen, Robert W. **Mustang: The Story of the P-51 Fighter.** New York, Arco, 1969. 240p.
The very comprehensive and definitive history and service record of one of the best fighter planes of the Second World War. Lavishly illustrated, this excellent book relates the story of the British supported initial development of this aircraft, its Axis adversaries, and its service accomplishments in the European and Pacific theaters. Extensive information is provided on its performance, production data, specifications and modifications with information also on the aircraft's units of assignment. Another book on this aircraft is William N. Hess's *Fighting Mustang: The Chronicle of the P-51* (Doubleday, 1970).

888   Jablonski, Edward. **Flying Fortress: The Illustrated Biography of the B-17s and the Men Who Flew Them.** Garden City, N. Y., Doubleday, 1965. 362p. Bibliog.
The development and contribution of the B-17 is seen through the stories of the units they were assigned to and the men who flew them. Primarily describes its European combat history but also includes actions in the Pacific until they were virtually replaced there by B-24s and B-29s. Some interesting notes are included of life in a German prisoner-of-war camp. Supplementary data is provided on the aircraft's design from inception through its evolutionary modifications. Excerpts from the pilot's training manual are appended.

889   Shores, Christopher F. **Curtiss P-40D-N Warhawk in USSAF—French and Foreign Service.** New York, Arco, 1969. 46p.
Each title in the publisher's Arco-AirCam Aviation Series illustrates a type or major sub-type of a noted aircraft. The text provides concise historical information on developmental data and combat operations. Numerous photographs depict the aircraft from many views, its variant models and in combat action. A feature is a color section showing various unit insignias and national markings. Other titles include the *North American P-51D Mustang, Republic P-47 Thunderbolt, North American Mustang MKI-IV, Supermarine Spitfire MKI-IV, Curtiss Kitty Hawk MKI-V, Lockheed P-38 Lightning, Avro Lancaster, Consolidated B-24D-M Liberator, Nakajima Ki. 43, Hayabusha I-III, Boeing B-l7 Flying Fortress, Mitsubishi Abm-Zero-Sen, Nakajima Ki.27, Grumman F6F3/5 Hellcat, Kawasaki Ki.61-I/III Hien/Ki.100, Vought F4U-1/7 Corsair, North American B-25 A/J Mitchell,* and *Hawker Hurricane MKI-IV*. Undoubtedly many more titles will be forthcoming. A similar series with generally briefer text, and less color

illustrations but showing some areas of the aircraft in closer detail is one published by Aero Publishers, Inc. Its *Curtiss P-40* published in 1965 can be used for comparison with the primary title reviewed.

890   Silverstone, Paul H. **U. S. Warships of World War II**. Garden City, N. Y., Doubleday, 1965. 444p. Bibliog.

This excellent comprehensive handbook presents a well illustrated survey of the major ships and support vessels of the U. S. Navy and Coast Guard. The illustrations were selected from official Navy sources accounting for their excellent clarity. An introduction is provided for each type and each class is described with specification details including armaments, complement, displacement, dimensions, name, number, builder, launch date and fate. Individual war histories of important ships are given in additional brief notes. A special section lists U. S. war losses by name and cause. Another title by this publisher is John Charles Taylor's *German Warships of World War II*. Also of interest is Alan Ravan's and John Roberts' *British Warships of the Second World War* published by Arco. (This title includes twelve triple fold-out scale drawings.)

891   Stewart, Irvin. **Organizing Scientific Research for War: The Administrative History of the Office of Scientific Research and Development**. Boston, Little, Brown, 1948. 358p.

A sober and detailed account of how Dr. Vannevar Bush set up this organization to mobilize the scientific resources of the U. S. Describes the administrative framework of the organization, its workings and principal activities in the development and improvement of weapons and the aspects of liaison with the various U. S. Armed Service units and those of the Allies in such matters as the exchange of information on radar.

892   U. S. Naval History Division. **Dictionary of American Naval Fighting Ships**. Washington, Government Printing Office, 1959– . 5v. (to date)

An alphabetical arrangement of the ships of the U. S. Navy from the Continental Navy to modern times. Historical sketches are provided for each ship giving the origin of the given name and also information on its service and combat history and statistical data. Volume five includes a substantial section on naval aircraft. Excellent photographs are provided for many of the ships and aircraft listed.

893   Wagner, Ray. **American Combat Planes**. Rev. ed. Garden City, N. Y., Doubleday, 1968. 442p. Bibliog.

A comprehensive well illustrated study of the development of military aircraft of the United States from 1915. The fully detailed descriptions are complemented with specifications for every significant aircraft.

ATOMIC BOMB

894   Amrine, Michael. **The Great Decision: The Secret History of the Atomic Bomb**. New York, Putnam's Sons, 1959. 251p.

This is the story of the hundred days between the death of FDR and the dropping of the first atomic bomb. The events and policy decisions leading up to the decision to use the bomb are presented against a background of the roles of the scientists, politicians and military men involved and of the military events of the period.

895   Clark, Ronald William. **The Birth of the Bomb: The Untold Story of Britain's Part in the Weapon that Changed the World**. New York, Horizon Press, 1961. 209p.

A thorough account of British research towards making a nuclear weapon in the early months of World War II. Based on interviews with participants, the book describes Britain's decision to proceed with this project which essentially made it the first nation in the world to set about making a nuclear explosive.

896   Groves, Leslie R. **Now it Can Be Told: The Story of the Manhattan Project**. New York, Harper, 1962. 464p.

A candid account of the policy decisions, the magnitude of the job and the complexities of the construction of an atomic weapon and the facilities to manufacture it. This record of the bomb project by its chief executive provides an account of the relations between the scientists and the military and the reasons why the Manhattan Project (Sept. 1942-Dec. 1946) was successful.

897   Irving, David John Cawdell. **The German Atomic Bomb: The History of Nuclear Research in Nazi Germany**. New York, Simon and Schuster, 1968. 329p. Bibliog.

Fascinating reading of how the Germans fell hopelessly behind the United States and Great Britain in nuclear research and development due to Allied bombing and disputes among German scientists and administrators. The scientific aspects and the complex problems involved are related in detail as well as the story of the Allied commando raids on the heavy water plants in Norway. The British edition is titled *Virus House*.

898   Jungk, Robert. **Brighter Than a Thousand Suns: A Personal History of the Atomic Scientists**. New York, Harcourt Brace, 1958. 369p.

A history of atomic research from 1920 to 1955 that provides a moral and political side based on conversations with world-wide participants in atomic research. A portrayal of the conflicting emotions of the scientists involved. The work is somewhat pro-German and anti-U. S. in bias.

899   Lamont, Lansing. **Day of Trinity**. New York, Antheneum, 1965. 333p. Maps, Bibliog.

The author provides the background of the test of the atomic bomb and relates the experiences of the participants in its creation. Through interviews and correspondence the author, a Washington correspondent for *Time* magazine, notes the tensions and physical stress of the people directly involved. A moving account is presented of the first atomic explosion at Alamogordo, New Mexico.

900   Laurence, William Leonard. **Dawn Over Zero: The Story of the Atomic Bomb**. 2nd ed. New York, Knopf, 1947. 289p.

A most interesting report of the *New York Times* writer who was assigned to cover all aspects of the inception, development, trial and final use of the atomic bomb. He supplies an easily understood explanation of nuclear theory. This excellent factual account traces clearly the evolution of nuclear physics in human as well as technical terms and also provides a review of the project's organization and the research achievements between the United States and Great Britain.

CHAPTER 6—THE WAR YEARS, 1939-1945:
POLITICAL ASPECTS

COMPREHENSIVE WORKS

901   **Canada in World Affairs.** Toronto, Oxford University Press, 1935/39– .
Primarily a triennial summary of events concerning the Canadian people and government in contemporary world affairs. A reliable record and discussion of the purposes and conduct of Canadian foreign policy.

902   **Documents on American Foreign Relations.** Boston, World Peace
         Foundation, 1939– .
A compilation of the most important documents bearing on U. S. diplomacy, providing a concise documentary record of the key speeches, reports, communiques, agreements and treaties. They are presented in an orderly sequence, topically arranged, from general to more specific matters. The series was published by the World Peace Foundation from 1939 to 1951 after which the Council on Foreign Relations took over publication.

903   **Documents on International Affairs.** London, Oxford University
         Press, 1929– .
This major continuing work accompanies and supplements the *Survey of International Affairs*. It lists the more important speeches, treaties and documents of the year for which the background will be found in the *Survey* volumes. From 1960 on the *Documents* are being produced in conjunction with the *Survey* volumes by the latter's editing team.

904   **Survey of International Affairs.** London, Oxford University Press,
         1925– . Maps, Bibliog.
Published under the auspices of the Royal Institute of International Affairs this series is a factual summary of international events. A well annotated and documented objective interpretation of world affairs. Some volumes have distinctive titles covering a particular subject, others cover a time period of one to several years, in a general chronological sequence.

905   U. S. Department of State. **Papers Relating to the Foreign Relations**
         of the United States. Washington, Government Printing Office,
         1862– .
The official record of the foreign policy of the United States. It provides a comprehensive record of the major foreign policy decisions along with appropriate materials which contributed to the formulation of these policies. The volumes are individually titled for the subject, country or area covered, providing a general chronological sequence of events. Some volumes cover long periods of time for a particular subject such as the volumes covering U. S. relations with Japan from 1931 to 1941. Also of interest are individual volumes covering the major wartime conferences.

906   **United States in World Affairs: An Account of American Foreign
       Relations**. New York, Harper, 1932– . Maps, Bibliog.
A running narrative account of American foreign relations published for the
Council on Foreign Relations, written almost contemporaneously with the events
recorded. This excellent survey of U. S. foreign policy, as it develops from year to
year, includes comprehensive analyses of events, relating each to the preceding one
so as to provide a better understanding through setting them in historical contexts
and order.

GENERAL WORKS

General Accounts

907   Clark, Douglas. **Three Days to Catastrophe**. London, Hammond, 1966.
       288p. Map, Bibliog.
An interesting account of how in the winter of 1939-40 Britain and France very
nearly got involved in the war between Finland and the Soviet Union. The author
provides a devastating story of the dream world of the West in regards to the
phoney war. Indicative of this mentality is the talk by French and British officials
of the desirability of fighting both Germany and the Soviet Union, thus killing
two birds with one stone.

908   Fleming, Denna Frank. **While America Slept: A Contemporary Analysis
       of World Events from the Fall of France to Pearl Harbor**. New York,
       Abingdon-Cokesbury Press, 1944. 269p.
A reportorial survey and analysis of the events of the war up to Pearl Harbor.
Factual statements of the events precede each of his weekly broadcasts as a
news commentator.

909   Gardner, Brian. **The Year that Changed the World: 1945**. New York,
       Coward-McCann, 1964. 356p. Maps, Bibliog.
A journalistic approach with some useful insights to the events of 1945. A year
which included the surrender of Germany and Japan, the use of the atom in warfare, the formation of the United Nations and the loss of two major war leaders,
one by death and the other at the polls.

910   Middleton, Drew. **Our Share of Night: A Personal Narrative of the War
       Years**. New York, Viking Press, 1946. 380p.
The impressions of six years of war by a noted Associated Press foreign correspondent. A chronicle of people under stress, with commentary and observations
of the significant events, done with insight and sensitivity. Covers France, Great
Britain, North Africa, the subsequent return to France and the drive into Germany.

911   **Public Opinion: 1935-1946**. Princeton, N. J., Princeton University
       Press, 1951. 1191p.
The results of nationwide public opinion polls conducted in sixteen countries
within the British Empire and Europe and including the United States. Classified

by subject matter, the areas cover foreign relations, politics, finance, industry, agriculture, entertainment and every major aspect of the events of World War II.

912   Weiss, John, ed. **Nazis and Fascists in Europe, 1918-1945**. Chicago, Quadrangle Books, 1969. 241p. Bibliog.
An introductory survey for general reading on the history of fascism. Describes the political situations that allowed the Nazis and Fascists to gain power in Germany and Italy and discussed the development of fascism elsewhere in Europe. The selections also provide an analysis of the political and social policies of totalitarianism in practice.

General Diplomacy

913   Alperovitz, Gar. **Atomic Diplomacy; Hiroshima and Potsdam: The Use of the Atomic Bomb and the American Confrontation with Soviet Power.** New York, Simon and Schuster, 1965. 317p. Bibliog.
A study of the four-month period to September 1945 that seeks to show that the atomic bombs were used on Japan for diplomatic or political purposes to improve the bargaining power of the U.S. in its relations with the Soviet Union rather than for military purposes.

914   Feis, Herbert. **The Atomic Bomb and the End of World War II**. Rev. ed. Princeton, N.J., Princeton University Press, 1966. 213p. Bibliog.
Originally published under the title *Japan Subdued* in 1961, this is the last of the author's series on the diplomatic history of World War II. He evaluates and interprets the plans and acts of the Allies and Japan leading to the end of the war with objectivity and perception. In this later edition, the author maintains that the atomic bomb was used by the U.S. as a way to impress the Soviets and that its diplomatic effect was an important factor in this decision.

915   Feis, Herbert. **Between War and Peace: The Potsdam Conference.** Princeton, N.J., Princeton University Press, 1960. 367p. Maps. Bibliog.
Continuing his narrative of the diplomatic history of World War II from the *Churchill–Roosevelt–Stalin* volume, the author discusses the period between May 1945 (the defeat of Germany) and July 1945 (The Conference). With meticulous attention to detail, this scholarly presentation discusses the deliberations preceding the meetings as well as the conferences themselves and notes the beginnings of the breakup of the Wartime Alliance.

916   Fireside, Harvey. **Icon and the Swastika: The Russian Orthodox Church Under Nazi and Soviet Control.** Cambridge, Harvard University Press, 1971. 242p. Bibliog.
The complex pattern of the nature of Nazi relations with the Russian Orthodox Church and the efforts of both the Nazis and the Soviets to manipulate the religious aspirations of the Russian population provide the basis for this study. The major influences on the making of German policy are seen against a background of conflicting military and civilian institutional and personal interests.

917   Fox, Annette Baker. **The Power of Small States: Diplomacy in World War II**. Chicago, University of Chicago Press, 1959. 211p. Bibliog.

The diplomacy of Turkey, Finland, Norway, Sweden and Spain during the prewar and war years. The intertwining of ideology and power politics, in the efforts to resist the pressure of the great powers of these smaller states, provides the main theme.

918   Snell, John Leslie. **Illusion and Necessity: The Diplomacy of Global War, 1939-1945**. Boston, Houghton Mifflin, 1963. 229p. Maps, Bibliog.
A comparison of the policies of the major powers revealing the mixture of realism and illusion in their wartime diplomacy. The main thesis of this excellent contribution is that the tie holding the Allied powers together was temporarily held together due to the unrealistic policies of the Axis states.

919   Snell, John Leslie. **Wartime Origins of the East-West Dilemma over Germany**. New Orleans, Hauser Press, 1959. 268p. Bibliog.
A clear compilation of documentation of wartime Allied planning for the occupation of Germany which shows the different approaches to the problem of the U. S., Great Britain and the Soviet Union.

920   Toynbee, Arnold and Veronica M. Toynbee, eds. **The War and the Neutrals**. London, Oxford University Press, 1956. 378p. Maps, Bibliog.
This volume in the *Survey of International Affairs* series consists of a group of topics covering the British and American efforts at economic warfare, the blockading of shipments to the Axis and the political repercussions involved in relations with Sweden, Switzerland, Eire, Spain, Portugal and Turkey. Both the Allied and Axis activities in these countries are discussed.

Peace

921   Carr, Edward Hallett. **Conditions of Peace**. New York, The Macmillan Co., 1942. 282p. Bibliog.
Written before Pearl Harbor this provocative study is concerned with the conditions required for a durable peace. Argues that the problem is fundamentally moral necessitating moral and not only political and economic solutions. A scholarly treatment of the problems facing the world and of the part of Great Britain and the United States in dealing with these problems.

922   Dunn, Frederick Sherwood. **Peace-Making and the Settlement with Japan**. Princeton, N. J., Princeton University Press, 1963. 210p.
A case study of the decision making process and the international environment which conditioned the policies of the Allied powers in the making of the Japanese peace treaty.

923   Junger, Ernst. **Peace**. Hinsdale, Ill., Regnery, 1948. 77p.
Written between 1941 and 1943 by a German author it is a plea for peace based on the renunciation of nationalism and for a federation of Europe. German in outlook, the author sees the Versailles Treaty as the sole cause of the Second World War.

924   Leiss, Amelia Catherine, ed. **European Peace Treaties After World War II**: **Negotiations and Text of Treaties with Italy, Bulgaria, Hungary, Rumania, and Finland**. Boston, World Peace Foundation, 1954. 341p. Map, Bibliog.
The text of the peace treaties with a general narrative of the diplomatic setting and the chief issues involved.

925   Lippmann, Walter. **U.S. War Aims**. Boston, Little, Brown, 1944. 235p. Bibliog.
An analysis of the situation from a geopolitical aspect. The author proposes a peace plan in a system of world organization. Discusses mankind's behavior and duties and attempts to answer the question of why the U.S. is at war and how the method used to wage the war will affect the shaping of the peace.

926   MacIver, Robert Morrison. **Towards an Abiding Peace**. New York, Mac-Millan, 1943.
A quietly reasoned study that states the broad general principles for a lasting peace. The well-known sociologist and political philosopher points out the necessary changes in attitudes which must take place and sets up a specific framework for world reconstruction and order.

927   MacNeil, Neil. **An American Peace**. New York, Scribners, 1944. 276p.
A blueprint for a pax Americana in, first, providing a statement of the problems to be faced and the role of the U.S. in solving them and, secondly, advocating that the U.S. only help those nations that are willing to help the U.S. attain an American peace and security.

928   Morganthau, Henry. **Germany Is Our Problem**. New York, Harper, 1945. 239p. Maps.
This is the famous Morganthau plan for the maintenance of peace in Europe by directing the German economy away from heavy industry to agriculture and service trades. This was to, in effect, serve to control Germany's war potential and yet support the general European economy.

929   Moulton, Harold Glenn, and Louis Marlio. **The Control of Germany and Japan**. Washington, The Brookings Institution, 1944. 116p. Maps, Bibliog.
A lucid and clear analysis over the future of Germany and Japan in practical terms of what can be accomplished to prevent the regrowth of their war power.

930   Neumann, William Louis. **Making the Peace, 1941-45: The Diplomacy of the Wartime Conferences**. Washington, Foundation for Foreign Affairs, 1950. 101p. Bibliog.
Through the use of documentary materials and the memoirs of leading political figures the author reconstructs the course of negotiations between the big three, the United States, Great Britain, and the Soviet Union—during the period from the Atlantic through the Yalta Conferences—towards a future world peace.

931   Sadler, William Samuel. **Prescription for Permanent Peace**. Chicago, Wilcox and Follett, 1944. 202p.
A psychiatrist diagnoses the war and traces it to an inherent paranoia in German

and Japanese policies over the last century which came about due to the delusions of grandeur, persecution complex, egotism and desire to dominate. The author feels that it is up to the United States to exert leadership and bear responsibility for world peace.

932   Spykman, Nicholas John. **The Geography of the Peace.** New York, Harcourt, Brace and Co., 1944. 66p. Maps.
Geopolitical analysis is used as a guide to show that the realities of national existence from the standpoint of geography require the cooperation of the U.S., Great Britain and the Soviet Union in order to maintain world peace.

933   United Nations. **Surrender of Italy, Germany and Japan, World War II: Instruments of Surrender, Public Papers and Addresses of the President and of the Supreme Commander.** Washington, U.S. Government Printing Office, 1946. 111p.
The texts of the instruments of surrender of the three major Axis powers along with related documents and speeches.

934   U.S. Department of State. **Making the Peace Treaties, 1941-1947: A History in the Making of Peace Beginning with the Atlantic Charter, the Yalta and Potsdam Conferences, and Culminating in the Drafting of Peace Treaties with Italy, Bulgaria, Hungary, Rumania, and Finland.** Washington, Department of State, 1947. 150p. Maps, Bibliog.
A brief succinct history with supporting documentation of the provisions of the surrenders, the draft treaties, the declared aims of Yalta and Potsdam, and the substance of the various major meetings of the Council of Foreign Ministers of the major Allied powers. Excellent detailed maps reflect the pre-war and post-war situations and settlements.

935   Vansittart, Robert Gilbert V. **Bones of Contention.** New York, Knopf, 1945. 157p.
A collection of articles and speeches calling for a drastic and relentless watch and control of Germany against future war-like preparations. His advocacy of a harsh peace results from his viewing the Germans only in an unfavorable light. He calls for complete and permanent demobilization, abolition of military training, reparations, re-education of the German people, supervision of the press and radio, war crimes prosecution and strict control of Germany's war potential.

936   Wheeler-Bennett, John Wheeler, and Anthony J. Nicholls. **The Semblance of Peace: The Political Settlement After the Second World War.** London, Macmillan, 1972. 878p. Bibliog.
Important for the comparison of the five peace treaties with the initial policies adopted in the various war-time declarations from the Atlantic Charter to Yalta. Shows the gradual shift of policy positions under changing aims and the results of inter-Allied negotiations.

937   Wriston, Henry Merritt. **Strategy of Peace.** Boston, World Peace Foundation, 1944. 159p.
Discusses the problem of making peace with the defeated powers and the position

of the U.S. in terms of its interests and commitments. Considers what broad
strategy the U.S. should follow.

938   Ziff, William Bernard. **The Gentlemen Talk of Peace.** New York, Mac-
       millan, 1944. 530p. Bibliog.
An argument for a more realistic approach to peace, according to the author,
through complete rearrangement of global forces into a more logical world.
Discusses the barriers to world federation and government and the need for radical
action to avoid post-war chaos. The author proposes a five-part world configura-
tion loosely joined together with each area to be a self-sustaining unit, thus
eliminating the old causes of conflict.

Propaganda

939   Boelcke, Willi A., comp. **The Secret Conferences of Dr. Goebbels: The
       Nazi Propaganda War, 1939-1943.** New York, Dutton, 1970. 364p.
       Bibliog.
An inside view of the methods used by the Nazis to manipulate public opinion.
Through the minutes of his staff conferences one sees the distortions, slanted
simplifications and outright untruths that were used as the basis for Nazi
propaganda.

940   Briggs, Asa. **A History of Broadcasting in the United Kingdom: Volume
       3, The War of Words.** London, Oxford University Press, 1971.
The role of the BBC within the general history of the war. This documented and
critical account describes its work in propaganda, intelligence operations by spreading information and giving instructions to resistance groups, counteraction of
German propaganda broadcasts to the occupied European nations, its battles
with the Ministry of Information for free and truthful broadcasts and its overseas
broadcasting services.

941   Carroll, Wallace. **Persuade or Perish.** Boston, Houghton Mifflin, 1948.
       392p.
An account of the use of psychological warfare and U.S. wartime propaganda from
the North African landing to the end of the war.

942   Cole, John Alfred. **Lord Haw-Haw—and William Joyce: The Full Story.**
       New York, Farrar, Strauss and Giroux, 1965. 316p. Bibliog.
The career of the British traitor, William Joyce, to his execution for treason following World War II. Throws some light on wartime conditions in Germany. His
activities in the British speaking German radio service centered on beaming
demoralizing comments and news to Great Britain.

943   Delmer, Sefton. **Black Boomerang.** New York, Viking Press, 1962.
       303p.
The director of the British wartime black radio propaganda operations against
Germany describes the techniques and defends the use of psychological warfare.
They broadcast messages to the troops and civilians of Germany, purporting
to come from underground stations in Germany, creating the myth of the good

anti-Nazi Wehrmacht and civilian population through their loyal German, anti-British and anti-war broadcasts.

944   George, Alexander L. **Propaganda Analysis: A Study of Inferences Made from Nazi Propaganda in World War II.** Evanston, Ill., Row Peterson, 1959. 287p. Bibliog.
The development of content analysis through a detailed breakdown of monitored German propaganda broadcasts. The attempt to sort out useful information by the U.S. Federal Communications Commission for U.S. political and military leaders was shown to be 80 percent effective. Case studies are included to illustrate each function to which the results of the analysis were put to use.

945   Kris, Ernest, and Hans Speier. **German Radio Propaganda: Report on Home Broadcasts During the War.** London, Oxford University Press, 1944. 529p. Bibliog.
A comprehensive account of what the Germans were told about the war by Goebbels. A picture of the Nazi mind and the changing German morale. Divided into three parts, the first explains the methods of the propaganda broadcasts within Germany, the second analyzes the general features of this internal propaganda and the third part traces the changing treatment of selected events as the fortunes of war changed and adjustments in emphasis and content was called for.

946   Lerner, Daniel, ed. **Propaganda in War and Crisis: Materials for American Policy.** New York, G. W. Stewart, 1951. 500p. Bibliog.
Twenty-seven essays on the theory, practice, effects and role of psychological warfare.

947   Lerner, Daniel. **Sykewar: Psychological Warfare Against Germany, D-Day to VE-Day.** New York, G. W. Stewart, 1949. 463p. Bibliog.
An account of the Psychological Warfare Division of SHAEF. Makes a good case for propaganda as an instrument of international policy.

948   Linebarger, Paul Myron Anthony. **Psychological Warfare.** 2nd ed. Washington, Combat Forces Press, 1954. 318p. Bibliog.
A description of how psychological warfare was organized and functioned during the Second World War, its aims, media, techniques and effectiveness. Notes how populations react to their own and enemy propaganda through a study of national characteristics.

949   Meo, Lucy D. **Japan's Radio War on Australia, 1941-1945.** London, Cambridge University Press, 1968. 300p. Bibliog.
Based on transcripts of Japanese radio broadcasts, this analysis of the chief characteristics of the propaganda concludes that it essentially was a resounding failure. To be relevant propaganda must contain more than a grain of truth. These broadcasts had neither going for it as well as the problems associated with the medium of shortwave broadcasting. The author feels that somewhat early in the war the Japanese began to abandon attempts at intimidation and instead began laying down a basis for post-war trade.

950   White, John Baker. **The Big Lie**. New York, Crowell, 1955. 235p.
A review of international propaganda and psychological warfare. An interesting
account also of the deceptions the British used to confuse and mislead the Germans concerning Great Britain's defenses.

951   Zeman, Zbynek A. B. **Nazi Propaganda**. 2nd ed. London, Oxford
       University Press, 1973. 260p. Bibliog.
Considered to be a definitive work, it recaptures the atmosphere of the period
and offers a clear account of the vital manipulation and control of public opinion
by Hitler and the Nazis. Also notes the manner in which the German government
used propaganda to further its policies abroad.

Unconditional Surrender

952   Armstrong, Anne. **Unconditional Surrender: The Impact of the Casa-
       blanca Policy Upon World War II**. New Brunswick, N.J., Rutgers
       University Press, 1961. 304p. Bibliog.
A detailed analysis of the unconditional surrender policy as applied to the
European aspect of the war. The author tries to discern the methods by which this
policy was adopted by the U.S. and the aims and motives behind it. The German
reaction is seen to back up the thesis that this policy served to prolong the war
with Germany.

953   Dulles, Allen Welsh. **The Secret Surrender**. New York, Harper and Row,
       1966. 268p. Maps, Bibliog.
An account of the negotiations for Operation Sunrise, the surrender of German
troops in Italy in 1945. The author took a leading role in Sunrise and recounts
the attempts of the SS Command to speed up the surrender and the unexpected
factors on the German side which contributed to the surrender.

954   Kecskemeti, Paul. **Strategic Surrender: The Politics of Victory and
       Defeat**. Stanford, Calif., Stanford University Press, 1958. 287p.
       Bibliog.
A critical analysis of the unconditional surrender policy of the Allies. Presents four
case studies in judging the effectiveness of this doctrine in the context of strategic
constraints and political necessities.

955   O'Connor, Raymond Gish. **Diplomacy for Victory: FDR and Uncondi-
       tional Surrender**. New York, Norton, 1971. 143p. Maps, Bibliog.
A concise study of FDR's policy of unconditional surrender proclaimed at the
Casablanca Conference. Traces the origin, development and execution of the
policy and concludes it to be a thoughtful and intelligent strategy move to enable
the Allies to concentrate on defeating the Axis powers instead of becoming
involved in divisive differing surrender policies.

INDIVIDUAL COUNTRIES

Australia

956   Hasluck, Paul. **The Government and the People**. Canberra, Australian
War Memorial, 1952– . 2v.
A two-volume study of the political and social history of Australia during World
War II. Emphasizes the decisions, and their significance, of the Australian Cabinet,
Parliament and the electorate and the circumstances in which these decisions were
taken. The social aspects depict the effects of the war on the lives and habits of
the Australians.

Burma

957   Collis, Maurice Stewart. **Last and First in Burma (1941-48)**. London,
Faber and Faber, 1956. 303p. Map.
An account of the political events and social developments in Burma with the
invasion of the Japanese, the development of inherent nationalism, and the
return of the British. Much of the work deals with Sir Reginald Dorman-Smith,
Governor of Burma.

China

958   Chiang, Kai-shek. **Resistance and Reconstruction: Messages During
China's Six Years of War, 1937-1943**. New York, Harper, 1943. 322p.
A collection of sixty speeches and messages to the Chinese people. A picture of
the personality of Chiang and of some of the internal and external problems of
maintaining the nation's morale through the years of conflict and occupation.

959   Johnson, Chalmers A. **Peasant Nationalism and Communist Power: The
Emergence of Revolutionary China, 1937-1945**. Stanford, Calif.,
Stanford University Press, 1962. 256p. Maps, Bibliog.
An excellent study of Chinese politics that incorporates a great deal of historical
material concerning the development of the Chinese Communist movement. The
author's main thesis is that the basis for the success of the Communists is their
effectiveness in gaining peasant support during the wartime resistance to Japan,
in the name of nationalism. Also provides a detailed description of guerrilla warfare and its use in the expansion of Mao's power.

960   Liang, Chin-Tung. **General Stilwell in China, 1942-1944: The Full Story**.
Jamaica, N.Y., St. John's University Press, 1972. 321p. Bibliog.
A highly biased apologia from the Nationalist point of view of why Chiang
dumped Stilwell.

961   Lin Yutang. **The Vigil of a Nation**. New York, John Day Co., 1945.
262p. Map.
An analysis of China at war and of her main problem, that of disunity. An
account of his journey through seven provinces with an eye for human detail.

A defense of the Nationalist regime though he does repeat and accept many of the criticisms directed at it.

962   Mao, Tse-Tung. **Selected Works.** New York, International Publishers, 1954-62. 5v.
Four of five volumes cover the years 1926-1945. The first volume covers the period from 1926 to 1936, the time of the first and second revolutionary civil wars. It includes comments on the peasant movement in Hunan, problems of party organization and strategic problems of the revolution. The next three volumes continue into the period of the war of resistance against Japanese aggression and include policies, measures and perspectives of combatting the Japanese strategic problems, the role of the Chinese Communist Party in the national war and on matters regarding the Kuomintang.

963   McLane, Charles B. **Soviet Policy and the Chinese Communists, 1931-1946.** New York, Columbia University Press, 1958. 310p. Bibliog.
Based on Russian sources, this is a stimulating account and sound analysis of Soviet foreign relations with the Chinese Communists. The author attempts to discern what political and ideological links were extant between the two parties. The primary findings were that after January 1931 Moscow made no further efforts to intervene in internal affairs of the Chinese Communist Party (CCP) on one side or another. There also was no evidence that the CCP used their independence to evade international Soviet policies or programs, or to refute any Marxist-Leninist dogmas, regardless of any adverse affects, but that they kept to a fundamental Marxist path. There was also no occasion after January 1931 when the Soviet Union expressed disapproval of CCP policies.

964   Rosinger, Lawrence Kaelter. **China's Crisis.** New York, Knopf, 1945. 259p. Map, Bibliog.
Clear statements of the events and issues concerning China's military, political and economic position and its relations with the major powers along with penetrating comments on the political cross-currents, economic crises and arms and politics on the fighting fronts.

965   Rosinger, Lawrence Kaelter. **China's Wartime Politics, 1937-1944.** Princeton, N.J., Princeton University Press, 1944. 133p.
An objective and documented study of the complicated political forces and tensions at work in China. Included are documents ranging from Sun Yat-sen's will to declarations of the Nationalist government regarding the Communist problem.

966   Snow, Edgar. **Red Star Over China.** Rev. and enl. ed. New York, Random House, 1968. 543p. Maps, Bibliog.
One of the most perceptive accounts of the rise of communism in China. Shows continued relevance of China's problems from when these statements were first made thirty-two years back. His main conclusions have stood the test of time. The significance is not that Red China is red, but that it is Chinese. This is a valuable guide to a comprehension of the tremendous forces then in motion, of China's war tactics and objectives in the war against Japan. Good biographical notes on China's leaders.

967   Thornton, Richard C. **China: The Struggle for Power 1917-1972.**
       Bloomington, Indiana University Press, 1973. 403p. Map, Bibliog.
Two principal themes are discussed in this history of the origin and development
of the Chinese communist movement. The first is concerned with the great impact
of foreign powers such as the Soviet Union, the United States, and Japan on the
decisions of the Chinese Communist Party. The second details the constant conflict within the Party and between them and the Soviet Union. This major work is
divided into three parts: the growth and development of the Chinese Communist
Party and Mao Tse-tung's rise to power (1917-1941); the struggle between the
Nationalists and the Communists for control of the state (1941-1949); and the
post-1949 period of Sino-Soviet relations (1949-1972).

968   White, Theodore Harold, and Annalee Jacoby. **Thunder Out of China.**
       New York, William Sloane Associates, 1946. 331p. Maps.
A factual account of what went on in China in the war years and immediately
after. Records the tragedy of a China caught between revolution and war. An
overall interpretation of China's complexities whose only solution is political
unity.

Czechoslovakia

969   Benes, Edvard. **Memoirs: From Munich to New War and New Victory.**
       Boston, Houghton Mifflin, 1954. 346p.
A sincere account, candid within limits, of the policies he pursued in the interests
of his country. The revocation of Munich is considered by him to have been the
whole point of the war. Important for a better understanding of Czechoslovakian
history.

970   Korbel, Josef. **The Communist Subversion of Czechoslovakia, 1938-
       1948: The Failure of Coexistence.** Princeton, N.J., Princeton University
       Press, 1959. 258p. Bibliog.
The author, formerly in the Czech Ministry of Foreign Affairs, traces the process
of communist subversion from the pre-war years, World War II, and its subsequent
rise to power. Shows how coexistence was used as a weapon of conquest through
a combination of infiltration in and increasing pressures on the state.

971   Mamatey, Victor S., and Radomir Luza. **A History of the Czechoslovak
       Republic, 1918-1948.** Princeton, N.J., Princeton University Press, 1973.
       534p. Maps, Bibliog.
A comprehensive history comprising fourteen critical essays which examine all
aspects of the establishment, development and problems of the Czechoslovak state.
The first section covers the years 1918 to 1938. The years of the development
of Czech democracy, the German minority problem, Benes' foreign policy, and
the tragic results of the Munich Agreement. The second part covers the occupation, war and liberation years of 1938 to 1945, and includes the Nazi break-up of
the Czech state, exile politics and the Czech and Slovak resistance movements.
The third part comprises the period 1945 to 1948 and the conflict between
democracy and communism.

Finland

972   **Finland and World War II, 1939-1944.** Ed. by John H. Wuorinen. New
       York, Ronald Press, 1948. 228p. Maps.
An important work, using exclusively Finnish source materials, of the origins of
Finland's involvement in the war and her role in it.

973   Gripenberg, Georg A. **Finland and the Great Powers: Memoirs of a**
       Diplomat. Lincoln, University of Nebraska Press, 1965. 380p. Bibliog.
Illumination of Finland's basic foreign policies by one of her leading diplomats.
Describes, interprets, and evaluates Finnish thinking from his experience as
Minister in London, 1933-1941, envoy to the Vatican, 1942, and in Stockholm,
1943-1944. He helped to arrange the negotiations ending Finland's participation
in the war.

974   Krosby, H. Peter. **Finland, Germany and the Soviet Union, 1940-1941:**
       The Petsamo Dispute. Madison, University of Wisconsin Press, 1968.
       276p. Bibliog.
Centering around the important nickel ore deposits of Petsamo, the work des-
cribes the rivalry among the great powers to keep Finland out of the political and
economic sphere of their competitors during the first year and a half of World
War II. Discusses the complex events leading up to Finland's alliance with
Germany.

975   Upton, Anthony F. **Finland in Crisis, 1940-1941: A Study in Small-Power**
       Politics. Ithaca, N.Y., Cornell University Press, 1965. 318p. Maps,
       Bibliog.
A well balanced critical study of Finland's diplomatic relations with Russia and
Germany. Analyzes the events and the policies of Finland's leaders which
brought about the country's decision to join Germany in the attack on the Soviet
Union. Describes Finnish-German military relations.

France

976   Anglin, Douglas George. **The St. Pierre and Miquelon Affaire of 1941:**
       A Study in Diplomacy in the North Atlantic Quadrangle. Toronto,
       Canada, University of Toronto Press, 1966. 219p. Maps, Bibliog.
The story of the Free French liberation of these Vichy held islands. The author
describes the developments leading to their seizure and the relevance of this act
to subsequent relations among the Allies. He feels that one consequence was a
legacy of suspicion and misunderstanding of the Allies toward the Free French.

977   Aron, Robert. **The Vichy Regime, 1940-44.** Boston, Beacon Press, 1969.
       536p. Bibliog.
A reprint of a study originally published in 1958. Slightly anti-British, it traces
the roles played by Laval, Darlan and Petain in this time of deep national crisis.

978   DePorte, Anton W. **De Gaulle's Foreign Policy, 1944-1946.** Cambridge,
       Harvard University Press, 1968. 327p. Bibliog.

A study of the foreign policy of De Gaulle during his Presidency of the Provisional Government of the French Republic. He relentlessly pursued the recognition and resumption of France's great power status, sought a Franco-Soviet pact and attempted to organize and be the spokesman of the smaller west European states. An assessment of his motives and the measures he took to accomplish his aims.

979   Farmer, Paul. **Vichy: Political Dilemma.** New York, Columbia University Press, 1955. 376p. Bibliog.
A comprehensive analysis of the controversial period from July 10, 1940, through August 20, 1944, in French history. Traces the trends, thoughts and events leading up to Vichy, analyzes the positions of the men who participated in this government and discusses their problems, ideas and actions.

980   Funk, Arthur Layton. **Charles De Gaulle: The Crucial Years, 1943-1944.** Norman, University of Oklahoma Press, 1959. 336p. Bibliog.
De Gaulle's emergence as a political figure is depicted in this study of his relations with Great Britain, the United States, and the Soviet Union. His efforts to place France and the Free French foremost in the thoughts of Roosevelt and Churchill and to become the acknowledged leader of France becomes a study in human obstinacy and perseverance. This clear study of wartime diplomacy includes an analysis of the Casablanca Conference.

981   Geraud, Andre (Pertinax, pseud.). **The Gravediggers of France: Gamelin, Daladier, Reynaud, Petain, and Laval; Military Defeat, Armistice, Counterrevolution.** Garden City, N.Y., Doubleday, Doran, 1944. 612p. Maps, Bibliog.
A meticulously documented analysis of the French military and political collapse and the establishment of the Vichy government. A good history by a French journalist of the political problems that undermined the Third Republic, the war years and of the men and forces involved in this complex story.

982   Griffiths, Richard M. **Petain: A Biography of Marshall Philippe Petain of Vichy.** Garden City, N.Y., Doubleday, 1972. 379p. Bibliog.
An account of how the hero of Verdun in World War I became the leader of Vichy, convicted of treason to France. A thoroughly researched and balanced life of the French leader whose role in Vichy, France, was considered to be an extension of his views and actions of prior years. His earlier prominent role in the military and political circles of the interwar years is also examined.

983   Huddleston, Sisley. **France; The Tragic Years, 1939-1947: An Eyewitness Account of War, Occupation and Liberation.** New York, Devin-Adair, 1955. 360p.
In an argument in defense of the Vichy regime, an Englishman who adopted France and stayed after 1940 observes French life in those years. He surveys the legality of Vichy, the real and false resistance, the shattering of French unity, French opposition to Churchill, the roles of Laval, Darlan, Petain and De Gaulle, and general military and diplomatic events.

984   Hytier, Adrienne Doris. **Two Years of French Foreign Policy: Vichy,**
       1940-1942. Geneva, E. Droz, 1958. 402p. Bibliog.
       402p. Bibliog.
The author feels that the period between June 1940 and November 1942 was
the only one in which Vichy had a real foreign policy. This was the period before
the resurgence of the Free French and the landings in North Africa. This study
notes the motives, significance and resultant consequences of Vichy's foreign
policy and the reasons behind its progressive lessening of initiative.

985   Mengin, Robert. **No Laurels for De Gaulle.** New York, Farrar, Straus
       and Giroux, 1966. 402p.
A Frenchman's indictment of De Gaulle's maneuverings for personal power. The
author worked for the Free French and broke from De Gaulle's leadership.
A personal account describing the period from September 1939 to the summer of
1943. He considers De Gaulle to be courageous, ambitious, vain, and devious with
a certain amount of duplicity and faithlessness thrown in.

986   Paxton, Robert O. **Parades and Politics at Vichy: The French Officer**
       Corps Under Marshal Petain. Princeton, N.J., Princeton University
       Press, 1966. 472p. Bibliog.
The active role played by the French professional officer corps in the Vichy
regime is seen as the result of its attempts to focus national pride upon itself
partly as a reaction to its burden of defeat and in response to the U.S. landings
in North Africa.

987   Paxton, Robert O. **Vichy France: Old Guard and New Order, 1940-1944.**
       New York, Knopf, 1972. 399p. Bibliog.
A discussion of the government and people of Vichy France, the power struggles
between Petain, Laval and Darlan, and the domestic programs and foreign policy
of a state the author feels was treated no better than the fully occupied nations.
A fully documented summary of what happened in France during the war years,
why it happened, the Franco-German relationship and the nuances of French life
and politics.

988   Roy, Jules. **The Trial of Marshal Petain.** New York, Harper and Row,
       1967. 263p.
Based on official records and newspaper accounts, this is a day-by-day account
of the trial of Petain for treason. Excellent character sketches support the
narrative of the trial and the circumstances of 1940 and the Vichy years
following.

989   Spears, Edward Louis. **Assignment to Catastrophe.** London, Heinemann,
       1954. 2v.
A pointed, candid, and moving testimony to the collapse of France. It captures
the mood and disintegration of a government and its final collapse, besides being
an indictment of the democracies in the way they acted at a critical time. Volume
one covers the period from July 1939 through May 1940, and volume two is
concerned with the final collapse the following month.

990   Warner, Geoffrey. **Pierre Laval and the Eclipse of France**. New York,
       Macmillan, 1969. 461p. Maps, Bibliog.
This British account is mainly concerned with French international relations and
Franco-German diplomacy besides also being a political biography of Laval. The
latter half of the work is devoted to the five Vichy years and the former half to
Ethiopian affairs and the Hoare-Laval deal.

991   Werth, Alexander. **France 1940-1955**. New York, Holt, 1956. 764p.
       Bibliog.
An excellent book covering the complex currents of French history from the
German invasion to the disintegration of the French colonial empire. A sound
description of Vichy and the resistance movement with a penetrating insight and
authentic flavor of French politics and events.

992   White, Dorothy Shipley. **Seeds of Discord: De Gaulle, Free France, and
       the Allies**. Syracuse, N.Y., Syracuse University Press, 1964. 471p.
       Bibliog.
An in-depth exploration of the relations between De Gaulle, the Free French,
Great Britain and the United States for the years 1940-1942. Discusses the
Allied quandry as to who represented the real France, the Free French or the
Vichy French, the development of the Free French movement and its initial
success in French Central Africa.

Germany

993   Bracher, Karl Dietrich. **The German Dictatorship: The Origins, Structure
       and Effects of National Socialism**. New York, Praeger, 1970. 553p. Bibliog.
An analysis of the Third Reich, of Hitler, and the men around him. Explores the
psychological and sociological causes of Hitler's rise to power, the role of Hitler
as a war leader, and his foreign policy. Provides an insight into the Nazi
experience.

994   Bramsted, Ernest Kohn. **Goebbels and National Socialist Propaganda,
       1925-1945**. East Lansing, Michigan State University Press, 1965.
       488p. Bibliog.
Analyzes the characteristic attitudes and methods employed by Goebbels in the
development of Nazi propaganda as well as its themes and functions.

995   Broszat, Martin. **German National Socialism, 1919-1945**. Santa Barbara,
       Calif., ABC-Clio Press, 1966. 154p. Bibliog.
A concise work on the antecedents of Nazism during the Weimar Republic, the
motives of the early conservative and nationalist supporters of Hitler, and how he
took advantage of the divisions of the various political parties to achieve control
of the state. Shows how a people attuned to German traditions acquiesced to an
eventual dictatorship.

996   Bullock, Alan Louis Charles. **Hitler: A Study in Tyranny**. New York,
       Harper, 1952. 776p. Bibliog.

An excellent heavily documented study of the character and policy of the German dictator. The author, a British historian, makes use of the extensive records of the Nuremberg trials in tracing the career and influence on the history of the period of Adolf Hitler.

997   Cecil, Robert. **The Myth of the Master Race: Alfred Rosenberg and Nazi Ideology**. New York, Dodd, Mead, 1972. 266p. Bibliog.
An evaluation of Rosenberg's influence in the National Socialist movement as the originator of much of its official ideology. Discusses his general ideological role in the Nazi seizure of power as well as his overall career and thought.

998   Conway, John S. **Nazi Persecution of the Churches, 1933-1945**. New York, Basic Books, 1968. 474p. Bibliog.
An account of the differing persecutions of the Catholic, Evangelical and Confessing churches. Deals with the methods used to impose a repressive control of these churches such as depriving them of most of their property, defamation and imprisonment of their ministers, dissolving of youth and trade organizations and suppression of the denominational press.

999   Crankshaw, Edward. **Gestapo, Instrument of Tyranny**. New York, Viking Press, 1956. 275p. Bibliog.
The organization and activities of the Gestapo, the men who ran it, and the part it played in the Third Reich. Ample evidence of the dangers to any nation of a police organization which is above the law.

1000   Delarue, Jacques. **The Gestapo: A History of Horror**. New York, Morrow, 1964. 384p. Bibliog.
A profile of the organization and its leaders. Notes its role in supplying cheap slave labor to German industrialists. Special emphasis is given to its activities in France and its relations with the French police.

1001   Fest, Joachim C. **The Face of the Third Reich: Portraits of the Nazi Leadership**. New York, Pantheon Books, 1970. 402p. Bibliog.
Brief biographical and character sketches of the principal Nazi leaders. Each portrait is filled out with background material of the period as seen by the person. Discusses their relationships to each other, to Hitler, the party, and with the government bureaucracy.

1002   Fredbord, Arvid. **Behind the Steel Wall: A Swedish Journalist in Berlin, 1941-1943**. New York, Viking Press, 1944. 305p. Maps.
A running report on wartime Germany. Realistic, penetrating descriptions of the conditions in the conquered countries, the activities of the partisans, and the position of Germany's allies and satellites.

1003   Goebbels, Joseph. **The Goebbels Diaries, 1942-1943**. Garden City, N.Y., Doubleday, 1948. 566p.
A revealing story of the transition of Germany from victory to the road to defeat by the Reich Minister for Public Enlightenment and Propaganda. Pictures the

steady disintegration of the Nazi leadership and shows Goebbels to be a major force behind the vicious Nazi campaign against the Jews.

1004   Hale, Oron James. **The Captive Press in the Third Reich**. Princeton, N.J., Princeton University Press, 1964. 353p. Bibliog.
Drawing on interviews and unpublished documentary materials, this is a study of the Nazi Party press with an emphasis on the Volkischer Beobachter and its role in the Third Reich.

1005   Hildebrand, Klaus. **The Foreign Policy of the Third Reich**. Berkeley, University of California Press, 1973. 209p. Bibliog.
This translation of a 1970 assessment of the foreign policy of Nazi Germany from 1933 to 1945 focuses on the central political issues and personalities of the Third Reich. The author analyzes the interrelationship between the Reich's domestic and foreign policies and the actions of Hitler and the major Reich political and military leadership. This is a very good outline of the main points in the planning, realization and failures of Nazi foreign policy.

1006   Hitler, Adolf. **Secret Conversations, 1941-1944**. New York, Farrar, Straus and Young, 1953. 597p.
The notes of Martin Bormann on the wide range of subjects covered by Hitler's monologues. An important revelation of Hitler's thoughts, his interpretations of fact, theories, savage prejudices and distortions, all disguised in the aura of patriotism and idealism.

1007   Hohne, Heinz. **The Order of the Death's Head: The Story of Hitler's S.S.** New York, Coward-McCann, 1970. 670p. Bibliog.
Based on the records of the Nuremberg trials and on Himmler's files and that of the Nazi Party, the study shows the development of the Schutzstaffel, its role in Hitler's rise, and its use in crushing opposition to the party and state.

1008   Institute fur Zeitgeschichte, Munich. **Anatomy of the SS State**. New York, Walker, 1968. 614p. Bibliog.
A valuable set of scholarly essays prepared for war crimes trials in Frankfurt, a.M. Provides an analysis of the S.S. system stressing the organization and administration of the state and its role in the domination of the German people and the occupied territories. A major contribution to the understanding of Nazism and its moral, political, and organizational background. Includes a valuable glossary of Nazi terms and ranks, a list of the main personalities of the Reich, and a chronology of leading events.

1009   Jarman, Thomas Leckie. **The Rise and Fall of Nazi Germany**. New York, New York University Press, 1956. 388p. Bibliog.
A compact general history of the Third Reich written with common sense and impartiality. Notes the influence of German history on the national character and its effects on the rise of the Nazi state.

1010   Kersten, Felix. **The Kersten Memoirs, 1940-1945**. New York, Macmillan, 1957. 314p.

Accounts of the political and social life of the Nazi leaders especially in relation to Himmler. The author was Himmler's masseur and describes how he used his influence to save the lives of thousands of Jews and defying the policies and ideology of Himmler.

1011   Koehl, Robert Lewis. **RKFDV: German Resettlement and Population Policy, 1939-1945: A History of the Reich Commission for the Strengthening of Germandom.** Cambridge, Harvard University Press, 1957. 263p. Bibliog.
Covers the aspects of the Nazi population policy and the attempts at German resettlement in areas under state control. An insight into the complex personal feuds of the Nazi elite and the clash between long range objectives and wartime needs.

1012   Manvell, Roger, and Heinrich Fraenkel. **Dr. Goebbels: His Life and Death.** New York, Simon and Schuster, 1960. 306p. Bibliog.
A reconstruction of the mental climate of Germany and the career and character of Goebbels. Covers the period from 1925 to 1945. Analyzes his rise to power and his relations with Hitler and the Nazi elite.

1013   Manvell, Roger, and Heinrich Fraenkel. **Goering.** New York, Simon and Schuster, 1962. 442p. Bibliog.
A penetrating biography covering the full range of his contradictory character and career as a leader of the Nazi Party and Hitler's official deputy. The story of how he came to power and behaved on achieving it, revealing a lust for power, arrogance, vanity, and passion for the pleasures of life. His lack of moral courage is underscored by his complete subservience to Hitler.

1014   Manvell, Roger, and Heinrich Fraenkel. **Himmler.** New York, Putnam, 1965. 285p. Bibliog.
A biography of the would-be soldier who rose to success in the Nazi hierarchy as Hitler's police chief. An examination of his character and behavior, noting his initial successes in accumulating immense power as head of the S.S. and the Gestapo and the reasons for his ultimate failure.

1015   Meinecke, Friedrich. **The German Catastrophe: Reflections and Recollections.** Cambridge, Harvard University Press, 1950. 121p.
Reflections on the development of German thought and character and the causes which led to two disastrous wars. Provides an analysis of the moral defects and failures of the governing class. The author feels that Hitler owed his success more to chance than anything else.

1016   Meyer, Henry Cord, ed. **The Long Generation: Germany from Empire to Ruin, 1913-1945.** New York, Walker, 1973. 359p. Bibliog.
A volume in the Documentary History of Western Civilization series. This book is a compilation of extracts from books, articles and documents providing a continuous flavor of society, politics and life in Germany for the period covered.

1017 Neumann, Franz Leopold. **Behemoth: The Structure and Practice of National Socialism, 1933-1944.** 2nd ed. New York, Oxford University Press, 1944. 649p. Bibliog.
A pioneer study of the origins of National Socialism and its interrelation with the politics and economics of the state. Through an appraisal of its causes and motives, the author concludes that it was a mass middle class movement.

1018 Orlow, Dietrich. **The History of the Nazi Party.** Pittsburgh, University of Pittsburgh Press, 1969-73. 2v. Bibliog.
An indispensable history of the growth of the organizational apparatus of the Nazi Party. With a lucid narration the author emphasizes Hitler's magnetic personality in the development of the party and in gaining support of the middle class. Notes the central ideological importance of the Fuhrerprinzip. Volume one covers 1919-1933 and volume two continues to 1945.

1019 Orlow, Dietrich. **The Nazis in the Balkans: A Case Study of Totalitarian Politics.** Pittsburgh, University of Pittsburgh Press, 1968. 235p. Bibliog.
A case study in Nazi intra-system politics using the power struggles of a microcosm of the system—the Southeast Europe Society. This analysis of the bureaucratic functioning of Nazi Germany within the Balkan setting illustrates the nature of decision-making in the Third Reich. The conflicts of issues, personalities of the various Nazi institutions provide an insight into the overall system.

1020 Papen, Franz von. **Memoirs.** New York, Dutton, 1953. 634p.
One of the most readable of the apologias of the Nazi regime. Tries to show that he was misunderstood and that the blame for Hitler and the war was really due to the Versailles Treaty. Vivid self-portrait and interpretation of German domestic and foreign policies since World War I.

1021 Payne, Pierre Stephen Robert. **Life and Death of Adolf Hitler.** New York, Praeger, 1973. 623p. Bibliog.
An engrossing biography that details the character of Hitler and how he became the dictator over millions of people. A rounded portrait through a good compilation of what has been written to date.

1022 Peterson, Edward Norman. **Hjalmar Schacht: For and Against Hitler; A Political-Economic Study of Germany, 1923-1945.** Boston, Christopher House, 1954. 416p. Bibliog.
An examination of the record of Schacht in the context of the economic and political problems of Europe and specifically Germany. Discusses his role in the mainstream of German political and economic history in the problems encountered with the Dawes Plan, reparations, Young Plan, his gravitation to the Nazis, rearmament, foreign trade policy and his activities in the anti-Hitler underground.

1023 Peterson, Edward Norman. **The Limits of Hitler's Power.** Princeton, N.J., Princeton University Press, 1969. 472p. Bibliog.
Through an analysis of the Interior Ministry of Bavaria, the cities of Nuremberg, Augsburg and several smaller communities, the author shows how the civil servants of the Reich pursued many of their own purposes in the control of the

operations of their government entities. Presents a sharper definition of the Reich governments in actual practice.

1024   Reitlinger, Gerald Roberts. **The S.S.: Alibi of a Nation, 1922-1945**. New
        York, Viking Press, 1957. 502p. Maps, Bibliog.
A scholarly study by a British historian of the history of the SS from its inception as a police guard to a military force of half a million. Analyzes its conflicts and manipulations with the party hierarchy and government bureaucracy and the reasons for the tacit tolerance of the German people.

1025   Rich, Norman. **Hitler's War Aims: Ideology, the Nazi State, and the Course
        of Expansion.** New York, Norton, 1973. 352p. Maps, Bibliog.
The first volume of a two-volume work on Hitler's war aims and his policies towards the pople and territories under his control. This first volume describes Hitler's statements, actions and the development of his policies within Germany and in regard to the occupied areas. The author analyzes the political system of the Nazi state, the machinery of German expansion and the motives and timing of Hitler's diplomatic and military moves.

1026   Schmidt, Paul. **Hitler's Interpreter**. New York, Macmillan, 1951. 286p.
The memoirs of the Chief Interpreter of the German Foreign Office from1943-1945. He was present as the interpreter at almost all major diplomatic moments of Ribbentrop or Hitler. The work throws some additional light on German foreign policy during the war years.

1027   Seabury, Paul. **The Wilhelmstrasse: A Study of German Diplomats under
        the Nazi Regime**. Berkeley, University of California Press, 1954.
        217p. Bibliog.
Excellent portraits of the bureaucrats of the Nazi Foreign Office in action. This study of the careers and activities of the German diplomats exemplifies the behavior and morality of the German bureaucrat and of the machinery of government in action.

1028   Smith, Howard Kingsbury. **Last Train from Berlin**. New York, Knopf,
        1942. 359p.
A narrative of the author's tour as a CBS correspondent in Berlin from 1939-1941. His account of the political and economic situation in Germany during the initial period of the war and just prior to U. S. entry provides a good picture of the psychological conditions in Nazi Germany.

1029   Speer, Albert. **Inside the Third Reich: Memoirs**. New York, Macmillan,
        1970. 596p. Bibliog.
These memoirs of Hitler's minister in charge of armaments and munitions, who was in the Nazi leader's circle for almost twelve years, provide a vivid portrait of Hitler's personality and working methods and the problems of wartime production.

1030   Steinert, Marlis G. **23 Days: The Final Collapse of Nazi Germany.**
        New York, Walker, 1969. 326p. Bibliog.

A scholarly study of the final collapse of the Third Reich centering around the person of Admiral Karl Donitz. The work is divided into four main parts: the personalities of Donitz, Speer, Keitel and Jodl; the activities of the twenty-three day Donitz interim government; internal politics and foreign affairs; and the arrest of the interim government.

1031 Taylor, Telford. **Sword and Swastika: Generals and Nazis in the Third Reich**. New York, Simon and Schuster, 1952. 431p. Maps, Bibliog.
The Chief Counsel for the prosecution at Nuremberg traces the activities of the military in the Third Reich, their alliance with the Nazis, their intrigues with the Junkers and the industrialists and their role in Hitler's rise to power. The author contends that without this alliance between the military leadership and the Nazis there would have not been German aggression and a world war.

1032 Trevor-Roper, Hugh Redwald. **The Last Days of Hitler**. 3rd ed. New York, St. Martin's Press, 1956. 283p.
A first hand study into the character of Hitler and the Nazi leadership. The author carried out an official inquiry into Hitler's death. This has produced a great deal of documentary material and eye witness evidence of the last days of the Nazi regime.

1033 Vogt, Hannah. **The Burden of Guilt: A Short History of Germany, 1914-1945**. New York, Oxford University Press, 1964. 318p. Maps, Bibliog.
An excellent German account of the complex history of Germany. Written with candor, the author is concerned with individual responsibility in describing what went wrong in the past and in a more accurate review of the legends and actual causes of the World Wars.

1034 Zahn, Gordon C. **German Catholics and Hitler's Wars: A Study in Social Control**. New York, Sheed and Ward, 1962. 232p. Bibliog.
The author attempts to verify the generalization that the Catholic Church has not condemned a specific aggressive war in modern history and the resulting effects of this policy on the German Catholics. Shows that Hitler received the enthusiastic patriotic support of laity in general through exhortations to conform to the general support of the war effort. The work indicates that the Church was not a pillar of resistance to the regime. One of the author's main theses is that the Church justified its lack of opposition in its need to maintain its freedom to administer sacraments vital for salvation.

Great Britain

1035 Agar, Herbert. **The Darkest Year: Britain Alone, June 1940-June 1941**. Garden City, N. Y., Doubleday, 1973. 228p. Map, Bibliog.
The significance of Britain's achievement in her heroic resistance to Nazi aggression is explained against the background of Britain's predicament. Focuses on British attempts to bring the United States into the war and analyzes the problems facing FDR in this regard. Records the roles of the RAF and radar in the struggle and the influence of the war upon the British civilian.

1036   Bullock, Alan Louis Charles. **The Life and Times of Ernest Bevin: Volume 2, Minister of Labour, 1940-1945**. London, Heinemann, 1967. 407p. Bibliog.

This second of three volumes covers Bevin's service in Churchill's wartime cabinet. It describes his labor policies and the influence he extended over the whole range of social, economic and even foreign policy. He enjoyed Churchill's confidence and was a member of the inner circle of the war government. This political biography discusses in part Bevin's handling of the problems with the unions, manpower, strikes, coal production and post-war plans.

1037   Cadogan, Alexander. **Diaries of Sir Alexander Cadogan, O. M., 1938-1945**. New York, Putnams, 1972. 881p. Bibliog.

British Permanent Under Secretary of State from 1938 to 1946, he accompanied Churchill on summit conferences during World War II. A very detailed and important contribution to the understanding of British diplomatic negotiations of the period. At the center of British foreign policy making from Munich to the defeat of the Axis he comments upon the matters affecting wartime diplomacy. The diary entries are accompanied by extensive explanatory notes by the editor setting the historical tone of events covered.

1038   Churchill, Winston Leonard Spencer. **War Speeches**. London, Cassell, 1941-1946. 6v. (U. S. edition publ. by Putnam v.1 and Little Brown v.2-6)

An invaluable documentation of the tempo and development of the world crisis and the Second World War. The dynamic eloquence of the speeches reflect the depth of his emotion in their fine descriptive passages and provide an insight into the quality of mind and leadership of this great world figure. The editor has provided short chronological notes of the war's events. The volumes are individually titled as follows: *Into Battle* (U.S. ed.–*Blood, Sweat and Tears*–Putnam), covers May 1938-Nov. 1940; *Unrelenting Struggle*, covers Nov. 12, 1940-Dec. 30, 1941; *The End of the Beginning,* covers 1942; *Onwards to Victory*, covers 1943 from the opening of the Casablanca Conference to the end of the Conference at Teheran; *Dawn of Liberation*, covers Feb.-Dec. 31, 1944; and *Victory* covers Jan. 1, 1945-Aug. 16, 1945–the day after Japan's surrender. Also of interest is a shorter three volume set with the same title published by Houghton Mifflin in 1953.

1039   Cooper, Duff. **Old Men Forget: The Autobiography of Duff Cooper, 1st Viscount Norwich**. New York, Dutton, 1954. 309p.

Covering primarily his career with the British Foreign Office the autobiography provides insights into British politics and foreign affairs over twenty years of tumult. The work is good on descriptions of the relations between De Gaulle and Churchill. Among other positions he was a Member of Parliament from 1924-1926, Secretary of State for War from 1935-1937, First Lord of the Admiralty, 1937-1938, Minister of Information during the period 1940-1941 and Ambassador to Franch during 1944-1947.

1040   Dalton, Hugh, **The Fateful Years: Memoirs, 1931-1945**. London, Muller, 1957. 493p.

Frank observations about colleagues and opponents from one of the leaders of the British Labor Party. Consistently opposed the policies of Chamberlain and attempted to convince his party of the actual realities and the dangers of foreign aggression and to support British rearmament. He urged support for the Czechs and for an Anglo-French-Soviet Pact.

1041   Eden, Anthony. **Freedom and Order: Selected Speeches, 1939-1946.**
        Boston, Houghton Mifflin, 1948. 436p.
A collection of speeches delivered in the House of Commons and elsewhere record-ing the official Conservative government viewpoint. The speeches are useful in appraising the man and the various crises he was involved with.

1042   Eden, Anthony. **The Reckoning: The Memoirs of Anthony Eden,**
        Earl of Avon. Boston, Houghton Mifflin, 1965. 716p. Maps, Bibliog.
Carries the memoirs of the British Secretary of State for Foreign Affairs (1940-1945) from 1938 through the middle of 1945. A valuable contribution of Great Britain's foreign policy during the war years with an assessment of FDR's wartime foreign policies.

1043   Macmillan, Harold. **The Blast of War, 1939-1945.** New York, Harper and
        Row, 1968. 623p. Maps, Bibliog.
An illumination of British and American military and political policies and objec-tives. Concentrates on the Mediterranean Theater as Churchill's wartime political representative at Allied Force Headquarters there for two and a half years. Describes the pitfalls and achievements in pursuing national political considerations and relating them to military objectives.

1044   Nicolson, Harold George. **Diaries and Letters, Vol. II: The War Years,**
        1939-1945. New York, Atheneum, 1967. 511p.
Excellent portraits of Churchill and other British leaders by the Governor of the BBC from July 1941-1946 and Member of Parliament from 1935-1945. Describes his work in reconciling British opinion toward the Free French. Covers all the major turning points of the war with a good sense of proportion and judgment of the events.

1045   Schoenfeld, Maxwell Philip. **The War Ministry of Winston Churchill.**
        Ames, Iowa State University Press, 1972. 283p. Bibliog.
A favorable assessment of Churchill and his development as a manager of men and his ability to carry out a complex war. This administrative history sees Churchill as placing political values above military ones and as a catalyst in the formation of the Allied front. The book gives a synthesis of Churchill's war aims and reveals the controversial issues and opinions of the time in his direction of British policy.

1046   Taylor, Alan John Percivale. **Beaverbrook.** New York, Simon and Schuster,
        1972. 712p. Bibliog.
A well balanced portrait of an important figure in British political and journalistic circles covering all aspects of his life and career. He is considered to be one of the heroes of the Battle of Britain for his role as the head of British aircraft production.

The book provides an excellent account of Beaverbrook's relationship with two British Prime Ministers, Bonar Law (1922) and Winston Churchill (1940) in widely separated but important periods of British history.

1047   Thompson, Lawrence Victor. **1940.** New York, Morrow, 1966. 256p. Bibliog.

A study of Britain's struggle during a crucial year of the war. A first rate popular history of the policical, diplomatic and military struggles of the time. Covers the home front, fall of France, Dunkirk and Battle of Britain. Describes the war in human terms such as the characters of men like Chamberlain and Churchill under pressure.

1048   Woodward, Ernest Llewelyn. **British Foreign Policy in the Second World War.** London, H. M. Stationery Office, 1970– . (3v. to date)

A comprehensive semi-official history of the formulation and execution of British foreign policy. Primarily from British sources and the archives of the Foreign Office. Somewhat of a general chronological arrangement within large subject breakdowns which are in turn divided into smaller chapters for in depth analysis. Essential, still unfinished work, to the study of British foreign policy of the period. See also the author's one volume edition with the same title.

Greece

1049   Kousoulas, Dimitrios George. **The Price of Freedom: Greece in World Affairs, 1939-1953.** Syracuse, N. Y., Syracuse University Press, 1953. 210p.

The story of the struggle against the Nazis in Crete and Greece and the conflicts with the communists in their attempts to dominate the country between 1941 and 1948.

1050   Woodhouse, Christopher Montague. **Apple of Discord: A Survey of Recent Greek Politics in Their International Setting.** London, Hutchinson, 1948. 320p.

A standard work on the subject of Greek affairs and resistance activities during World War II by the former Commander of the Allied Military Mission to the Greek guerrillas. Describes the influences on Greek politics from 1941-1944 of four major groups: the puppet government in Athens; the emigres and exiles in Egypt and the headquarters of the free Greek armed forces; the king and part of his government in London; and the armed resistance movements in the mountains. The latter consisted mainly of the popular communist directed ELAS and their political aspects KKE and EAM; the anticommunist republican EDES; and the EKKA who stood for social liberation. Includes a description of the period after December 3, 1944, the start of Greek civil war.

Hungary

1051   Horthy, Miklos. **Memoirs.** New York, R. Speller, 1957. 268p.
The former Regent of Hungary records the situation faced by his country prior
to and during World War II as it was overrun in turn by Germany and the Soviet
Union. Discusses the influence of small power politics on world affairs and his
friction with Hitler.

1052   Kallay, Miklos (Nicholas). **Hungarian Premier: A Personal Account of
        a Nation's Struggle in the Second World War.** New York, Columbia
        University Press, 1954. 518p.
The Premier of Hungary from 1942-1944 describes his pro-western, anti-Russian
policy that brought it into the wartime Nazi sphere. An important historical
document portraying Hungary's struggles and its statesmanship.

1053   Kertesz, Istvan. **Diplomacy in a Whirlpool: Hungary Between Nazi
        Germany and Soviet Russia.** Notre Dame, Ind., University of Notre
        Dame Press, 1953. 273p. Maps, Bibliog.
A short well documented study of Hungary's struggle for political survival from
1938-1946. This work, part history and part memoir of Hungary's international
position in this period, is by a former official of the Hungarian Foreign Ministry.

1054   Macartney, Carlile Aylmer. **October Fifteenth: A History of Modern
        Hungary, 1929-1945.** Edinburgh, University Press, 1956-57. 2v.
        Maps, Bibliog.
An in-depth reconstruction of the history of the period. Comprehensive and
intensively reasearched, the author was with the British Foreign Office during
World War II. The treatment is somewhat biased towards the old line political
ruling class.

Iran

1055   Hamzavi, Abdol Hossain. **Persia and the Powers: An Account of Diplo-
        matic Relations, 1941-1946.** London, Hutchinson, 1946. 125p. Maps.
A general review of Persian (now Iranian) affairs from the time of the entry of
British and Russian forces into the country in 1941 to Soviet withdrawal in 1946.
Moderate in tone the author describes the treaty of January 1942 whereby Great
Britain and the Soviet Union jointly guaranteed the independence, sovereignty
and territorial integrity of Persia. He lists the principal contributions of his
country to the Allied cause. Ascribing Persia's problems with the Soviets to his
country's refusal to grant the Russians oil concessions, he describes the resulting
Soviet attempts at interference in Persian internal affairs.

Italy

1056   Badoglio, Pietro. **Italy in the Second World War: Memories and Docu-
        ments.** London, Oxford University Press, 1948. 234p. Bibliog.
The head of the Italian government which surrendered to the Allies recounts
his role and Italy's participation in World War II. Describes the entry of Italy

into the war, Italian reversals, the eventual coup d'etat and establishment of a civil administration under Badoglio.

1057   Cassels, Alan. **Fascist Italy.** New York, Crowell, 1968. 136p. Maps, Bibliog.
An introductory essay on Fascist Italy. The author attempts to tread a middle road between the proponents who equate Italian Fascism with Mussolini and those viewing this movement as an outgrowth of Italian history and society.

1058   Ciano, Galeazzo. **The Ciano Diaries, 1939-1943: The Complete Unabridged
        Diaries of Count Galeazzo Ciano, Italian Minister for Foreign Affairs,
        1936-1943.** Garden City, N. Y., Doubleday, 1946. 584p. Map.
Mussolini's son-in-law and Foreign Minister records his impressions of the main events in Italy's diplomacy of the period. An indictment of Mussolini and the Nazis, he pictures Mussolini as piling on one blunder after another. Feels that the Italian people never wanted war, were anti-German and were also weary of Mussolini's Fascism.

1059   Collier, Richard. **Duce! The Rise and Fall of Benito Mussolini.** London,
        Collins, 1971. 447p. Bibliog.
The life and political career of a perplexing personality who craved to dominate and impress. Illuminates the highlights of the dictator's rise to power, the system he created, his ambitions, successes, reversals and pathetic end.

1060   Davis, Melton S. **Who Defends Rome? The Forty-Five Days, July 25-
        September 8, 1943.** New York, Dial Press, 1972. 560p. Maps, Bibliog.
The book covers the period from Mussolini's dismissal from office to the Bodoglio Government's armistice with the Allies and the German occupation of Rome. Through eyewitness interviews and the extensive use of primary and secondary sources, the author presents a human story of teachery, lies and betrayals compounded by blunders, indecision and misjudgments.

1061   Gallo, Max. **Mussolini's Italy: Twenty Years of the Fascist Era.** Tr. by
        Charles Lam Markmann. New York, Macmillan, 1973. 452p. Bibliog.
The story of how Mussolini's Fascist system created a political, psychological and social climate that allowed him to keep control of the state and its people without a great deal of violence. The Second World War and the Italian people's basic opposition to it became the turning point of his regime and ended in Italy's occupation by friend and enemy alike and subsequent defeat.

1062   Germino, Dante L. **The Italian Fascist Party in Power: A Study in
        Totalitarian Rule.** Minneapolis, University of Minnesota Press, 1959.
        181p. Bibliog.
The functions and organization of the Party and its conflicts with the other centers of power in the Italian dictatorship provide a serious study of the Italian Fascist Party in action. The role of the Party in the totalitarian character of the state is analyzed within the context of its complex organizational system.

1063   Kirkpatrick, Ivone. **Mussolini: A Study in Power.** New York, Hawthorne
        Books, 1964. 726p. Maps, Bibliog.

A biographical and political study by the former Permanent Under-Secretary of State at the British Foreign Office. A clearly written work of a complex personality incorporating much of the important work done on the subject. The author concentrates on foreign and military policies and the men and motives behind these decisions.

1064   Kogan, Norman. **Italy and the Allies.** Cambridge, Mass., Harvard University Press, 1956. 246p. Bibliog.
The course of Italian politics and foreign relations between the Italian surrender of September 1943 and the peace treaty with the   Allies. Discusses the negotiations for the armistice, the influence of the monarchy in these events and the gradual reformation of an Italian government under Allied supervision. Notes the attitudes of the Big Three to the various Italian political parties of the period.

1065   Mussolini, Benito. **The Fall of Mussolini: His Own Story.** New York, Farrar, Strauss, 1948. 212p. Map.
Nineteen articles by Mussolini from the period of October 1942 to September 1943 provide an insight to a confused inefficient leadership.

1066   Packard, Reynolds and Eleanor Packard. **Balcony Empire: Fascist Italy at War.** New York, Oxford University Press, 1942. 380p.
A contemporary narrative of Italy at war to June 1942, with comments on the Italian character in wartime, by the United Press's correspondent team in Rome.

1067   Rusinow, Dennison I. **Italy's Austrian Heritage, 1919-46.** Oxford, Clarendon Press, 1969. 423p. Maps, Bibliog.
The historical background of the matter of the German minority in the border area with Austria precedes an account of Italian Fascist policies to assimilate these German minorities (and the Slavic areas of Trieste). Describes the incorporation of these German areas into the Reich in 1943 and their restoration to Italy in 1946.

1068   Tompkins, Peter. **Italy Betrayed.** New York, Simon and Schuster, 1966. 352p. Map, Bibliog.
The story of the Allied failure to capitalize on Mussolini's downfall in 1943 and of the decisions that led to the occupation of Italy by the Germans and the subsequent costly Allied advance to drive them out. The author was close to many of the events described. There is a good account of the role of the Italian partisans.

Japan

1069   Brooks, Lester. **Behind Japan's Surrender: The Secret Struggle that Ended an Empire.** New York, McGraw-Hill Book Co., 1967. 428p. Bibliog.
Using interviews of surviving Japanese leaders the author describes the deliberations in Tokyo resulting from the dropping of the atomic bombs and their effect in bringing about the decision to surrender.

1070   Browne, Courtney. **Tojo: The Last Banzai.** New York, Holt, Rinehart and Winston, 1967. 260p. Bibliog.

The author, a former member of the British Commonwealth Occupation Force in Japan, presents a revealing picture of the rise of Japanese militarism and its actions during the war through this biography of its primary symbol. Much of the material was garnered through interviews with Tojo's wife. This is also a study in the methods by which extremist elements from political and military factions can ally and take control of the destiny of a country.

1071   Butow, Robert Joseph Charles. **Japan's Decision to Surrender.** Stanford, Stanford University Press, 1954. 259p. Bibliog.
A carefully documented study of the effects upon the Japanese leadership of the unconditional surrender policy of the Allies, and Japanese wartime international diplomacy and internal politics in relation to their decision to surrender.

1072   Coffey, Thomas M. **Imperial Tragedy: Japan in World War II, The First Days and the Last.** New York, World Pub. Co., 1970. 531p. Bibliog.
Deals with the events of only two months, December 1941 and August 1945. A popular historical reconstruction of the crucial events of these two months on a day to day basis. The first part begins with Ambassador Grew's visit to the Japanese Foreign Minister on December 8, 1941 (Tokyo time) and the second part with the bombing of Hiroshima on August 6, 1945.

1073   Elsbree, Willard H. **Japan's Role in Southeast Asian Nationalist Movements, 1940-1945.** Cambridge, Harvard University Press, 1953. 182p. Bibliog.
Based on material presented at the Tokyo War Crimes Trials the work tells of the role of Japan in fostering Southeast Asian nationalism. Studies the nationalist movements of Burma, Indo-China, Indonesia, Malaya, Philippines and Thailand and assesses their strengths and influence. Notes the conflicts between the Japanese Foreign Office and the Navy in the economic and political development of the Greater East Asia Co-Prosperity Sphere.

1074   Jones, Francis Clifford. **Japan's New Order in East Asia: Its Rise and Fall, 1937-1945.** London, Oxford University Press, 1954. 498p. Bibliog.
An exhaustive examination of Japanese relations in Asia based on western sources. Presents a detailed diplomatic history of the events leading to Japan's move into war and to her eventual surrender. Discusses the position of the army and the samurai mentality of its officer class.

1075   Kase, Toshikazu. **Journey to the Missouri.** Hamden, Conn., Archon Books, 1969. 282p. Bibliog.
For annotation, see item 303.

1076   Mosley, Leonard Oswald. **Hirohito: Emperor of Japan.** Englewood Cliffs, N. J., Prentice-Hall, 1966. 371p. Bibliog.
A history of modern Japan and its people from samurai to democracy through the life of Hirohito. The author feels that the Emperor could have prevented the war and did not act with firm resolution at critical moments.

1077   Shigemitsu, Mamoru. **Japan and Her Destiny: My Struggle for Peace.** New
         York, Dutton, 1958. 392p.
The Japanese point of view on Japan's foreign policy from 1931-1945 by a distinguished diplomat. This historical document by one of the makers of Japanese
policy discusses the role of the military extremists who brought Japan to war in
1941. Notes the part played by the Navy on national policy and appraises the
wartime leadership.

1078   Togo, Shigenori. **The Cause of Japan.** New York, Simon and Schuster,
         1956. 372p.
The Japanese Minister of Foreign Affairs at the beginning and end of the war (Oct.
1941-Aug. 1942 and Apr.-Aug. 1945) as well as Ambassador to Moscow from
1938 to August 1940 describes the events leading up to the war, the power alignments within Japan and the decision making process. He discusses the subsequent
wartime historical events as he saw them and the part he played in shaping Japanese
policy and of his struggles against the military factions.

Lithuania

1079   Sabaliunas, Leonas. **Lithuania in Crisis: Nationalism to Communism,**
         1939-1940. Bloomington, Indiana University Press, 1972. 293p. Bibliog.
A history of how the proximity of Germany and Russia constantly affected the
Lithuanian government's domestic and foreign policies and threatened its existence.
The author examines the country's political, social and economic conditions
against a background of internal domestic turmoil and international crisis. Analyzes
the effects of three major crises: the loss of Memel to Germany in 1939, the impact of the outbreak of World War II and the Soviet Union's annexation of Lithuania in 1940.

New Zealand

1080   Wood, Frederick Lloyd Whitfield, **The New Zealand People at War:**
         Political and External Affairs. Wellington, N. Z., War History Branch,
         Department of Internal Affairs, 1958. 395p. Maps, Bibliog.
The consequences of World War II on the external affairs of the country and of
the war's domestic impact. Shows how these external affairs parallel Australia's
except for the differences in the character of New Zealand's people and of its
economic structure.

Norway

1081   Hayes, Paul M. **Quisling: The Career and Political Ideas of Vidkun**
         Quisling, 1887-1945. Bloomington, Indiana University Press, 1972.
         368p. Bibliog.
A thorough and objective scholarly survey of the life and political development
of Quisling. Presents a comprehensive picture of his personality and his political
philosophy in action. Much about his relations with Germany and wartime administration and activities. The author allows Quisling's words and actions to speak for
themselves in leaving no doubt about the man's treasonable acts.

1082   Hewins, Ralph. **Quisling: Profile Without Honor.** New York, John Day, 1966. 384p.
A forceful attempt to rehabilitate the reputation of the Norwegian whose name became synonymous with being a traitor to one's country. The author maintains that Quisling was not a fascist and tries to make a case against the story that Quisling invited Hitler to occupy Norway and conspired to bring this about.

Philippines

1083   Friend, Theodore. **Between Two Empires: The Ordeal of the Philippines, 1929-1946.** New Haven, Yale University Press, 1965. 312p. Maps, Biliog.
A political study and historical analysis of U. S.–Philippine relations. Discusses Philippine politics and its bearing on Philippine–U. S. policy and the men behind the events. Emphasizes the independence acts of 1933-1934. The author also discusses the conduct and policies of the people and government during World War II.

Poland

1084   Ciechanowski, Jan. **Defeat in Victory.** Garden City, N. Y., Doubleday, 1947. 397p.
Wartime negotiations with the U. S. and other Allied governments on behalf of the Polish government in exile by its ambassador to the United States. Written with restraint the narrative describes the evasions, and hypocrisy of diplomacy in the transcripts of secret talks with the leaders of the Big Three. The author was a participant in many of the events described.

1085   Raczynski, Edward. **In Allied London.** London, Weidenfeld and Nicolson, 1962. 381p.
The World War II memoirs of the Polish Ambassador to London and the subsequent Polish Minister for Foreign Affairs. A narrative of events as seen through Polish eyes of the fortunes of Poland at war. Describes the political situation during its invasion, Poland's combat role from Britain, the political problems of dealing with the Big Three with their divergent viewpoints and policies to the final Allied withdrawal of recognition from the Polish government-in-exile.

1086   Rozek, Edward J. **Allied Wartime Diplomacy: A Pattern in Poland.** New York, Wiley, 1958. 481p. Maps, Bibliog.
A study of the diplomacy, relating to Poland, of the Western powers, the Soviet Union and the Polish government in exile. Discusses the composition and role of the Polish government in the years of the war. The work is supplemented by full texts of relevant diplomatic reports, confidential letters and official records.

1087   Stern, Harold Peter. **The Struggle for Poland, 1941-1947.** Washington, Public Affairs Press, 1953. 79p. Map, Bibliog.
The principal events concerning Poland's history and international relations from Hitler to Stalin. The Soviet-Polish relationship is described in the overall context of east-west relations.

Romania

1088   Cretzianu, Alexandre. **The Lost Opportunity**. London, Cape, 1957. 188p.
        Bibliog.
The Secretary General of the Romanian Ministry of Foreign Affairs from 1939-
1941 and Minister to Turkey from 1943-1945 describes Romania's wartime diplomacy and strategy in its dealings with Germany and the Soviet Union. The author
contends that the west made a political and strategic error in not deploying a
minimum military force in south-eastern Europe.

Russia

1089   Cassidy, Henry Clarence. **Moscow Dateline, 1941-1943**. Boston, Houghton
        Mifflin, 1943. 374p. Maps.
The Chief of the Associated Press Bureau in Moscow reports on the principal
events in Russian during this period. Good contemporary account of the government, people and the war. Includes his correspondence with Stalin on the Russian
leader's views on the formation of a second Allied front.

1090   Dallin, David. **Soviet Russia's Foreign Policy 1939-1942**. New Haven,
        Yale University Press, 1943. 452p. Maps, Bibliog.
A balanced account of Soviet diplomacy's objectives and methods. The author, a
member of the opposition in the Moscow Soviet until 1921 presents a good job of
historical analysis and interpretation.

1091   Ehrenburg, Il'ia Grigor'evich. **The War: 1941-1945**. Cleveland, World
        Publishing Co., 1965. 198p.
A vivid picture of the war in Russia. His outspoken comments on men and events,
his reflections on Stalin and the Soviet bureaucracy accompany a sincere exposi-
tion of the courage, hope and endurance of the Russian people. This work is
volume five of Ehrenburg's *Men, Years—Life*.

1092   Fischer, Louis. **The Road to Yalta: Soviet Foreign Relations, 1941-1945**.
        New York, Harper and Row, 1972. 238p. Bibliog.
A survey of the wartime relations between the Soviet Union and its allies based on
Russian and western sources. Clarifies Soviet expansionist policies and sees Poland
as the key to Stalin's control of Europe. The author feels that Roosevelt and
Churchill should have opposed the decision to partition Germany.

1093   Maisky, Ivan Mikhailovich. **Memoirs of a Soviet Ambassador: The War
        1939-43**. New York, Scribner's, 1968. 408p. Bibliog.
Soviet assessments of major historical events relating to Soviet-Allied diplomatic
relations. These insights from the Russian point of view are by the Soviet Ambassador to Great Britain from 1932 to 1943 and portray the policy dilemmas with the
various East European governments in exile in London as well as Soviet descriptions of western leaders.

1094   Rothstein, Andrew. **Soviet Foreign Policy during the Patriotic War**: **Documents and Materials**. London, Hutchinson, 1946– .
Documents illustrating the foreign policy of the Soviet Union. The first volume covers June 22, 1941 to December 31, 1943 and the second from January 1, 1944 to December 31, 1944. The volumes are divided into three parts. The first part reprints Stalin's statements and orders of the day, the second part covers documents and materials reflecting the foreign policy of the state, and the third part includes official TASS statements and other more minor documents.

1095   Seton-Watson, Hugh. **From Lenin to Khrushchev: The History of World Communism**. New York, Praeger, 1960. 432p. Bibliog.
A well documented analysis of communist behavior, strategy and tactics. Examines the realities of power, the growth of Soviet totalitarianism, and Soviet foreign policy in relation to regional and national communist movements around the world.

1096   Snow, Edgar. **The Pattern of Soviet Power**. New York, Random House, 1945. 219p. Map.
An informed report on Russia in 1944 under Stalin. Describes Soviet life and psychology, the laws, governmental structure, and Soviet foreign policy. Portrays the Russian leadership and outlines Soviet aspirations and attitudes on the problems of Germany and Poland and Sino-Soviet relations.

1097   Stalin, Iosif. **War Speeches, Orders of the Day, and Answers to Foreign Press Correspondents During the Great Patriotic War, July 3rd 1941-June 22nd 1945**. London, Hutchinson, 1946. 140p.
A compilation of Stalin's speeches and pronouncements for May Day, Red Army Day, the Anniversary of the October Revolution and including his major speech after the German invasion. They portray official Soviet accounts of the progress of the war.

1098   Steenberg, Sven. **Vlasov**. New York, Knopf, 1970. 230p. Bibliog.
For annotation, see item 1427.

1099   Ulam, Adam Bruno. **Stalin: The Man and His Era**. New York, Viking Press, 1973. 760p.
A comprehensive biography of the Soviet dictator, the most absolute and ruthless ruler in modern world history. How his life was affected and how he affected the Russian human existence and the politics of the time. A prime example of an oppressive social system. The study seeks to answer what caused one man to impose so much terror and suffering on a people and yet what enabled him to evoke such heroism from the Russian people when the need arose.

Spain

1100   Feis, Herbert. **Spanish Story: Franco and the Nations at War.** New York, Knopf, 1948. 282p.
An interpretive account of the diplomatic relations between Franco and the Axis and Allies from 1939 to 1945. Describes the Allied efforts to keep Spain neutral, Hitler's attempts to bring it into the war and Franco's conduct throughout it all. Explains why Germany did not carry out its expected invasion of Spain to neutralize the British base at Gibraltar.

1101   Payne, Stanley G. **Falange: A History of Spanish Fascism.** Stanford, Calif., Stanford University Press, 1961. 316p. Bibliog.
The origins of the Falange and its relations to the political, economic and ideological aspects of its peculiarly Spanish setting. Focuses on the years 1936-1943 and the basic structure and its internal political development in Franco Spain.

Switzerland

1102   Hartmann, Frederick H. **The Swiss Press and Foreign Affairs in World War II.** Gainesville, University of Florida Press, 1960. 87p. Bibliog.
The means by which the Swiss government directly or indirectly regulated the content of the press in the face of Nazi pressures. Though quite elastic for the most part, the Swiss tried to work out an equitable balance between the democratic right of the press to report and comment on foreign affairs and the very real dangers to the state from Nazi Germany.

Turkey

1103   Weisband, Edward. **Turkish Foreign Policy, 1943-1945: Small State Diplomacy and Great Power Politics.** Princeton, N. J., Princeton University Press, 1973. 390p. Bibliog.
How Turkish policy makers resolved the dilemmas of the creation of a balance of policy between the Allies and the Axis. Two major principles guided the Turks, that of peace, sovereignty and national development and that of concern for the threat of the Soviet Union. The first part of the book analyzes domestic policy making and the Turkish leadership and the second part discusses Turkish diplomacy and its responses to the various fortunes of the warring powers.

United States

1104   Acheson, Dean Gooderham. **Present at the Creation: My Years in the State Department.** New York, Norton, 1969. 798p. Bibliog.
The record of the involvement in government and diplomacy of the U. S. Assistant Secretary from February 1941 to August 1945, and subsequently Under Secretary and then Secretary of State. A leading proponent and mover in the shift of U. S. policy from isolationism to collective security between 1941 and 1953, this work also serves as a defense of his policies.

1105   Allen, Gwenfread Elaine. **Hawaii's War Years, 1941-1945.** Honolulu,
          University of Hawaii Press, 1950. 418p. Maps, Bibliog.
The impact of the war on Hawaii and its people is presented in a straightforward
detailed account. Based on material collected by the Hawaii War Records Department, the work includes a clear and fair discussion of the question of the military
government.

1106   Bohlen, Charles Eustis. **Witness to History, 1929-1969.** New York, Norton,
          1973. 562p.
An absorbing account reflecting on most of the major developments in international
relations between east and west. The former Ambassador to Russia attended the
conferences at Teheran, Yalta and Potsdam and gives a detailed study of the relations between the wartime Allies. He was an important influence on F.D.R.

1107   Buchanan, Albert Russell, comp. **The United States and World War II:**
          Military and Diplomatic Documents. Columbia, University of South
          Carolina Press, 1972. 303p. Bibliog.
A sampling of documents to illustrate the military and diplomatic phases of the
war. Each section is preceded by an introduction describing generally the events
of the period covered such as the pre-war period, Pearl Harbor, wartime diplomacy,
and war against Japan.

1108   Burns, James MacGregor. **Roosevelt: The Soldier of Freedom.** New York,
          Harcourt Brace Jovanovich, 1970. 722p. Bibliog.
The sequel to the author's *Roosevelt: The Lion and the Fox*, this work continues
FDR's presidency from his third term in 1940 until his death. Presents an excellent assessment of the diplomatic and political aspects of the war. A study of a
complex and divided leader and the transformation of the Presidency and American
society.

1109   Byrnes, James Francis. **Speaking Frankly.** New York, Harper and Bros.,
          1947. 324p. Map.
Covering the period from February 1945 to October 1946 the author details his
experiences as an observer at the Yalta Conference and as Secretary of State
(starting June 30, 1945) in the closing months of the war and in the postwar
settlements. Recounts his experiences in dealing with the Russian leaders. Provides
a better understanding for the foreign policies and international role of the United
States.

1110   Campbell, Thomas M. **Masquerade Peace: America's UN Policy, 1944-**
          1945. Tallahassee, Florida State University Press, 1973. 226p. Bibliog.
The work describes the efforts of the leaders of the U.S. to use the political conditions of World War II to bring about a new international order to provide the
vehicle for an enduring peace. Thus, this policy to bring about the United Nations
and U.S. active participation in it became a central one in U.S. diplomacy. The
planning for peace contributed greatly in determining U.S. actions during the war,
especially from Yalta to the San Francisco Conference.

1111   Catton, Bruce. **The War Lords of Washington.** New York, Harcourt, Brace, 1948. 313p.

A general history of the governmental war agencies and their internecine struggles. The wartime Director of Information for the War Production Board charges that U.S. industry determinedly continued a business as usual attitude during the war.

1112   Chadwin, Mark Lincoln. **The Hawks of World War II.** Chapel Hill, University of North Carolina Press, 1968. 310p. Bibliog.

For annotation, see item 177.

1113   Chamberlain, William Henry. **America's Second Crusade.** Chicago, Regnery, 1950. 372p. Bibliog.

A description of the reasons the United States went into World War II. Basically an attack on the foreign policy of FDR and his advisors. A consideration of the professed war aims and the ultimate results.

1114   Cohen, Bernard Cecil. **The Political Process and Foreign Policy: The Making of the Japanese Peace Settlement.** Princeton, N.J., Princeton University Press, 1957. 293p. Bibliog.

A case analysis of the complex domestic processes of the formation of foreign policy which affected the final peace settlement. Pictures the issues involved, public opinion, and the interaction of the Executive Branch and Congress in this excellent study of policy making.

1115   Corwin, Edward Samuel. **Total War and the Constitution.** New York, Knopf, 1947. 182p. Bibliog.

A documented analysis of the impact of total war upon the constitutional separation of powers. Discusses the broadened presidential powers to meet war emergencies and the replacement of judicial process by administrative actions. Portrays the course of events of the war and the relevant interpretations of the Supreme Court concerning war measures and acts.

1116   Current, Richard Nelson. **Secretary Stimson: A Study in Statecraft.** New Brunswick, N.J., Rutgers University Press, 1954. 272p. Bibliog.

A critical well-written study of FDR's Secretary of War and his role in the making of U.S. policy. A carefully documented assessment of which much deals with World War II.

1117   Dallek, Robert, comp. **The Roosevelt Diplomacy and World War II.** New York, Holt, Rinehart and Winston, 1970. 125p. Maps, Bibliog.

An excellent concise work of selections from well known writings of Beard, Langer and Gleason, Feis and Schlesinger. A good introduction to the major political aspects of American involvement prior to and during World War II.

1118   Divine, Robert A. **Roosevelt and World War II**. Baltimore, Johns Hopkins
        Press, 1969. 107p. Bibliog.
Four essays dealing with aspects of FDR's foreign policy before 1941, the
development of the United Nations and U.S.-Russian relations during the war.

1119   Divine, Robert A. **Second Chance: The Triumph of Internationalism
        in America During World War II**. New York, Atheneum, 1967. 371p.
        Bibliog.
A history of the international organization movement in the U.S. Analyzes the
shift in public thought from isolationism and non-involvement to the enthusiasm
toward U.S. participation in the United Nations. Concentrates on the role of
pressure groups, political leaders, writers and journalists that made U.S. sponsor-
ship and entry possible.

1120   Drury, Allen. **A Senate Journal, 1943-1945**. New York, McGraw-Hill,
        1963. 503p.
A daily account of events in the U.S. Senate from November 1943 to July 1945.
Recaptures much of the mood and tone of the legislative deliberations and conflicts with the executive branch. Sees the executive as grasping power seekers
at odds with legislative delays. Contains characterizations of individual senators of
the period.

1121   Duroselle, Jean-Baptiste. **From Wilson to Roosevelt: Foreign Policy of
        the United States**. Cambridge, Harvard University Press, 1963. 499p.
        Bibliog.
The course of U.S. diplomacy is analyzed by a French professor and longtime
friend of the United States. He points out the inadequacies and weaknesses and
explains the various moods of U.S. foreign policy. A penetrating, objective
assessment of men and events which on the whole is favorable to the United
States.

1122   Giovannitti, Len, and Fred Freed. **The Decision to Drop the Bomb**.
        New York, Coward-McCann, 1965. 348p. Bibliog.
A political history of how and why the decision was made, who made it, and who
opposed it. Traces the interplay of personalities, their attitudes and convictions
and the tensions and conflicts involved in the final decision.

1123   Grew, Joseph C. **Turbulent Era: A Diplomatic Record of Forty Years,
        1904-1945**. Boston, Houghton Mifflin, 1952. 2v.
A full account of the experiences of a devoted public servant and his role as a
professional diplomat. An impressive contribution to the history of American
diplomacy by the U.S. Ambassador to Japan at the start of hostilities between
them. He notes the limitations and achievements of his service. The work is
supplemented by the inclusion of official dispatches.

1124   Grodzins, Morton. **Americans Betrayed: Politics and the Japanese
        Evacuation**. Chicago, University of Chicago Press, 1949. 444p. Bibliog.
The author's main thesis is that the move was totally a political and economic one
and not for their or the country's protection. An important work dealing with a

wave of hysteria which set aside the constitutional rights of a group of United States citizens and residents.

1125   Hinshaw, David. **The Home Front.** New York, Putnam's Sons, 1943. 352p.

A contemporary account of the home front by a highly articulate conservative advisor to U.S. presidents. He analyzes the accomplishments and failures of various aspects of the United States in the winning of the war. His belief in the self-cleansing nature of democracy is emphasized against a background of the problems and efforts of the people, their administrative leaders, Congress, labor, and the farmers.

1126   Huzar, Elias. **The Purse and the Sword: Control of the Army by Congress through Military Appropriations, 1933-50.** Ithaca, N.Y., Cornell University Press, 1950. 417p. Bibliog.

Bearing on the question of civilian control of the military, this theme of congressional control describes how the military budget influences military appropriations and how they, in turn, influence military policy and administration. Shows the operation of the separation of powers in providing money for the military.

1127   Jonas, Manfred. **Isolationism in America, 1939-1945.** Ithaca, N.Y., Cornell University Press, 1966. 315p. Bibliog.

An intellectual history using the private papers and published sources of leading isolationists and isolationist groups to present the bases and varieties of isolationist thought. The twin dynamics of isolationism are seen to be unilateralism and a fear of war. Portraits of the major and minor isolationists are a strong feature.

1128   Kennan, George Frost. **Memoirs 1925-1950.** Boston, Little, Brown, 1967. 2v.

A perceptive and often frank evaluation of his years in the U.S. Foreign Service. Reveals the gap between diplomatic theory and practice and the perils of policy making in the U.S. government. Important for his comments and impressions of world leaders and the great events of the times. Presents a cry for morality in foreign policy.

1129   Kolko, Gabriel. **Politics of War: The World and United States Foreign Policy, 1943-1945.** New York, Random House, 1968. 685p. Bibliog.

A study of World War II from a revisionist standpoint. Sees a related nature between the broad objectives of U.S. capitalism and political policy. The author contends that the premises guiding the leaders of the U.S. through wartime diplomatic crises were based on a world domination by U.S. capitalism.

1130   Leahy, William Daniel. **I Was There: The Personal Story of the Chief of Staff to Presidents Roosevelt and Truman, Based on His Notes and Diaries Made at the Time.** New York, Whittlesey House, 1950. 527p.

The political and diplomatic memoirs of also the Ambassador to Vichy from 1940 to 1942. Highly personal day-to-day views and reactions to events in which he played a part. Revealing personal judgments of his colleagues and U.S. allies. He throws light on U.S. military planning and organization and relations between the U.S. and the Soviet Union.

1131   Long, Breckinridge. **The War Diary of Breckinridge Long: Selections from the Years 1939-1944.** Lincoln, University of Nebraska Press, 1966. 410p.

The U.S. Assistant Secretary of State from 1940 to 1944 gives a frank expression of his views of the period's diplomatic activities. Presents many portraits of personalities along with comments on the inner workings of the State Department during World War II.

1132   McIntyre, Stuart Hull. **Legal Effect of World War II on Treaties of the United States.** The Hague, M. Nijhoff, 1958. 392p. Bibliog.

Examines the effects of war on prewar political, economic and humanitarian treaties between the U.S. and one or more of the Axis. The principle of the sanctity of treaties is discussed in relation to the provisions of the peace treaties and the revival of prewar agreements.

1133   Marshall, George Catlett. **Selected Speeches and Statements of General of the Army George C. Marshall.** Washington, Infantry Journal, 1945. 263p.

Covering the period from October 1938 to June 16, 1945, the book illustrates the character and thinking of a man meeting great crises and responsibilities during a period of world crises. Presents some detailed expositions of the military needs and policies required for global warfare.

1134   Morse, Arthur D. **While Six Million Died: A Chronicle of American Apathy.** New York, Random House, 1968. 420p. Bibliog.

A reportorial account of the inaction of U.S. and British bureaucracy in dealing with the so-called Jewish problem. A sharp indictment of governments who could not be but aware of Nazi plans.

1135   Murphy, Robert Daniel. **Diplomat Among Warriers.** Garden City, New York, Doubleday, 1964. 470p.

The memoirs of the life and career of a major U.S. diplomat. Presents graphic descriptions of the situation at Vichy. He coordinated U.S. diplomacy with Allied military operations for the invasions of Italy and Germany. This account of the events in which he participated provides an indispensable personal history of U.S. wartime diplomacy.

1136   Range, Willard. **Franklin D. Roosevelt's World Order.** Athens, University of Georgia Press, 1959. 219p. Bibliog.

This study attempts to determine FDR's views on the reasons for the breakdown of world order, its implications for the United States, and what was to replace the old order. The primary reason of the breakdown is seen by FDR as a failure of democratic governments in meeting the modern needs and aspirations of their people. His proposals for a new world order consist of replacing power politics with a good neighbor policy; the eradication of the evil forces of Italian fascism, German Nazism and Japanese militarism; world disarmament; abolition of imperialism; worldwide democracy; a global economic and social New Deal; and a collective security system under the guardianship of the five major powers.

1137   Reston, James Barrett. **Prelude to Victory**. London, W. Heinemann, 1942. 151p.
Contemporary articles on the position of the United States during the early period of the war. He expounds the belief that victory is possible if the U.S. turns its war efforts into a national crusade and its people cease to emphasize personal aims and material benefits.

1138   Robinson, Edgar Eugene. **The Roosevelt Leadership, 1933-1945**. Philadelphia, Lippincott, 1955. 491p. Bibliog.
An analysis of the influence of FDR on U.S. politics and government. Underscores his innovations and shortcomings in relation to his handling of the country's basic problems of livelihood, cohesiveness and defense.

1139   Roosevelt, Franklin Delano. **For the President, Personal and Secret: Correspondence Between Franklin D. Roosevelt and William C. Bullitt**. Boston, Houghton Mifflin, 1972. 655p. Bibliog.
Letters relating the reflections and observations of FDR's Ambassador to the Soviet Union and subsequently to France from 1933 to 1940. A personal and intimate description of the unfolding events in Europe and Bullitt's relations with and opinions of foreign and domestic leadership.

1140   Roosevelt, Franklin Delano. **The Public Papers and Addresses of Franklin D. Roosevelt**. New York, 1938-1950. (Random House, vols. 1-5; Macmillan, vols. 6-9; Harper, vols. 10-13). 13v.
An indispensable and comprehensive documentary history of the Roosevelt era. The speeches are amplified by annotations by FDR for the earlier volumes and by the editor for the subsequent ones. The volumes are entitled as follows: *The Genesis of the New Deal, 1928-1932*; *The Year of Crisis, 1933*; *The Advance of Recovery and Reform, 1934*; *The Court Disapproves, 1935*; *The People Approve, 1936*; *The Constitution Prevails, 1937*; *The Continuing Struggle for Liberalism, 1938*; *War—and Neutrality, 1939*; *War—and Aid to Democracy, 1940*; *The Call to Battle Stations, 1941*; *Humanity on the Defense, 1942*; *The Tide Turns, 1943*; *Victory and the Threshold of Peace, 1944-45*.

1141   Ross, Davis R. B. **Preparing for Ulysses: Politics and Veterans During World War II**. New York, Columbia University Press, 1969. 315p. Bibliog.
A contribution to a better understanding of the politics of the New Deal administration and Congress during the years from 1940 to 1946. A history of the origin, enactment and implementation of legislation to benefit returning World War II veterans.

1142   Russell, Ruth, and Jeannette Muther. **A History of the United Nations Charter: The Role of the United States, 1940-1945**. Washington, Brookings Institution, 1958. 1140p. Bibliog.
The development of the U.N. Charter in the context of the foreign policy of the United States. Describes the plans, purposes, deliberations of each step from the Atlantic Charter through the San Francisco Conference. Basic diplomatic and historical background on the role of the United States.

1143   Sherwood, Robert Emmet. **Roosevelt and Hopkins: An Intimate History**. Rev. ed. New York, Harper, 1950. 1002p. Map, Bibliog.
A basic work on the age of Roosevelt describing the development of the New Deal, the operation of the U.S. political system, the history of the formation of the Allied coalition, the conduct and political strategy of the war, wartime diplomacy and intimate portraits of the leadership of the time. The author, a friend of both men, discusses the relationship between the two and especially the part played by Hopkins in some of the crucial decisions of the war.

1144   Smith, Gaddis. **American Diplomacy During the Second World War, 1941-1945**. New York, Wiley, 1965. 194p. Maps, Bibliog.
The problems, policies and events of U.S. wartime diplomacy. Notes that the primary task was the coordination of the wartime efforts of the Big Three, the United States, Great Britain and the Soviet Union, and that the style and results of these efforts were influenced a great deal by the personality of FDR.

1145   Spykman, N. J. **America's Strategy in World Politics: The United States and the Balance of Power**. New York, Harcourt, Brace 1943. 500p. Maps, Bibliog.
A study and analysis of the position of the United States in terms of the effects of geopolitics on U.S. foreign policy. Examines the workings of the system of power politics from political, geographic, economic and diplomatic aspects.

1146   Stimson, Henry Lewis, and McGeorge Bundy. **On Active Service in Peace and War**. New York, Harper, 1948. 698p.
An absorbing and revealing personal chronicle, a central document of the time. Stimson held public office from Theodore Roosevelt's into Truman's administration (with the exception of Harding's tenure). He served as Under Secretary of State for Hoover and Secretary of War for FDR. This authoritative record, based on his diaries, correspondence, speeches and papers, presents the key ideas of the period with portraits of salient personalities. The work is especially interesting from the point of view of the pre-war Far Eastern crisis.

1147   Truman, Harry S. **Memoirs: Volume 1, Year of Decisions**. Garden City, N.Y., Doubleday, 1955.
The first volume, *Year of Decisions*, covers the period from Truman's ascendancy to the presidency through the fall of 1946. An absorbing and candid story of the immense events with which he was concerned and the reasons for his actions. The freshness and clearness with which he illuminates the great military and diplimatic undertakings make this a volume of distinction.

1148   Van Valkenburg, Samuel, ed. **America at War: A Geographical Analysis**. New York, Prentice-Hall, 1942. 296p. Maps.
A consideration of the most critical war problems of the United States from a geographical point of view. This contemporary analysis covers such areas as coastal defense, the effect of climate on the timing of campaigns, the quality of one's people, terrain considerations on war strategy, food for defense, the importance of a raw material supply, and the relation of geography to strategy.

1149   Welles, Sumner. **Seven Decisions that Shaped History**. New York, Harper, 1951. 236p.

A personal account by FDR's Under Secretary of State of the crucial events and the decisions made concerning them in U.S. foreign policy during the war. A clear and concise explanation of FDR's thoughts regarding these decisions which the author also participated in. An appraisal of the men involved as well as a defense of FDR's handling of U.S. foreign policy.

1150   Young, Roland. **Congressional Politics in the Second World War**. New York, Columbia University Press, 1956. 281p. Bibliog.

A lucid and objective account of the course and development of congressional politics in the conversion of U.S. thought and efforts from peace to war. Discusses the functioning and performance of the U.S. Congress for this period.

Vatican

1151   Falconi, Carlo. **The Silence of Pius XII**. Boston, Little, Brown, 1970. 430p. Bibliog.

An assessment of Pope Pius XII's motives in choosing to say nothing regarding the predicament of the Jews. The author contends that this was due to a basic reluctance to provoke Nazi retaliation against the Catholic Church. He feels that the Pope's piety and religious fervor were beyond question but that a blind trust in diplomacy and an ecclesiastically fixed mentality determined Vatican diplomacy.

1152   Gonella, Guido. **The Papacy and World Peace: A Study of the Christmas Messages of Pope Pius XII**. London, Hollis and Carter, 1945. 214p. Bibliog.

A comprehensive commentary on the famous five points of the Pope's Christmas messages of 1939, 1940, and 1941, including extracts from the three subsequent messages as they expanded his basic thoughts. The five points of international reconstruction are national independence, reduction of armaments, an international tribunal, the protection of minorities and application of moral law to political activity as well as to one's individual actions. Also stressed is the need for charity to permeate international relationships.

1153   **Records and Documents of the Holy See Relating to the Second World War**. Washington, Corpus Books, 1968– . Multi-vol. Bibliog.

A collection of official papers dealing primarily with the correspondence between the Vatican and its representatives to world governments. Includes speeches, encyclicals and messages to world leaders of Pope Pius XII. Volume one is titled *The Holy See and the War in Europe, March 1939-August 1940*.

1154   Rhodes, Anthony. **The Vatican in the Age of the Dictators, 1922-1945**. London, Hodder and Stoughton, 1973. 383p. Bibliog.

A comprehensive in-depth examination of the various criticisms and charges that have been made against the Vatican in its relations with the world powers. The author contends that the diplomatic policies of the Vatican were shaped by its fears of the spread of communism and its desire to maintain the rights, prerogatives and aims of the Church within whatever type of government would seem to best protect, support or countenance the Church's activities.

Yugoslavia

1155   Fotitch, Constantin. **The War We Lost: Yugoslavia's Tragedy and the Failure of the West.** New York, Viking Press, 1948. 344p.
An anti-Tito defense of Mihailovic by the Ambassador in Washington of the Royal Yugoslav government-in-exile from 1942 to 1945. A review of the British and U.S. attitude toward Yugoslavia and how their inconsistent support finally shifted from Mihailovic to Tito.

RELATIONS BETWEEN TWO OR MORE COUNTRIES

China and Japan

1156   Boyle, John Hunter. **China and Japan at War, 1937-1945: The Politics of Collaboration.** Stanford, Calif., Stanford University Press, 1972. 430p. Bibliog.
A description of the wartime collaboration between the Chinese puppet government in Nanking under Wang Ching-wei and the Japanese occupying force. This Japanese attempt to win the allegiance of the Chinese away from the Nationalists and the communists failed due in part to the anti-Japanese sentiment of the emerging popular nationalism.

Czechoslovakia and Poland

1157   Wandycz, Piotr Stefan. **Czechoslovak-Polish Confederation and the Great Powers, 1940-1943.** Bloomington, Indiana University, 1956. 152p. Bibliog.
A fascinating study of the proposed post-war confederation between the two countries as discussed by their governments in exile in London. The goal was to come to a common policy with regard to foreign affairs, defense, and economic, financial, and social matters. The abandonment of the negotiations were due in large part to Soviet pressures and the desire of the two nations to maintain friendly relations with the Soviet Union.

Eastern Europe

1158   Lukacs, John A. **The Great Powers and Eastern Europe.** New York, American Book Co., 1953. 878p. Maps, Bibliog.
The diplomatic history of thirteen small central and eastern European states, all neighbors of the Soviet Union. Their activities and fortunes are told in detail and related to the actions of the major powers and especially the Soviet Union. Included are statistical tables and maps noting shifting state boundaries.

Finland and Russia

1159   Jakobson, Max. **The Diplomacy of the Winter War: An Account of the Russo-Finnish War, 1939-1940.** Cambridge, Harvard University Press, 1961. 281p. Map, Bibliog.

The course of Soviet-Finnish relations leading up to and including the Winter War is set against a background of great power politics in the developing world crisis. This work of high literary quality presents explicit and implicit criticisms of Finnish foreign policy by an official of Finland's Foreign Service. Anglo-French-Soviet negotiations in 1939 and Allied hopes of aiding Finland to open another front against Germany are discussed.

Germany and Great Britain

1160   Douglas-Hamilton, James. **Motive for a Mission: The Story Behind Hess's Flight to Britain.** London, Macmillan, 1971. 290p. Bibliog.
An authoritative and detailed account of the real story behind the flight of Rudolf Hess. The author contends that this attempt to bring about a peace between Great Britain and Germany, thus leaving Hitler a free reign to invade the Soviet Union, was a gross misjudgment and an impulsive action without official sanction. A good representation of the atmosphere of the political circles in both countries.

Germany and Japan

1161   Meskill, Johanna Margarete Menzel. **Hitler and Japan: The Hollow Alliance.** New York, Atherton Press, 1966. 245p. Bibliog.
The main thesis is that the two powers failed to coordinate their efforts on the diplomatic, economic, and military levels because of mutual distrust and incompatible goals in their basic foreign policy, such as with the Soviet Union. A detailed account of the disappointing workings and ultimate failure of the military partnership of the Tripartite Pact.

Germany and Russia

1162   Germany. Auswartiges Amt. **Nazi-Soviet Relations, 1939-1941: Documents from the Archives of the German Foreign Office as Released by the Department of State.** New York, Didier, 1948. 362p.
Vitally important and informative documents essential to an understanding of the development of the political relations of the German-Soviet Alliance.

1163   McSherry, James E. **Stalin, Hitler and Europe: The Imbalance of Power, 1939-1941.** Cleveland, World Publishing Co., 1970. 357p. Bibliog.
Covers the months from the German invasion of Poland to that of the Soviet Union. The main theme is the interaction between Hitler and Stalin against a background of the squeezing of the smaller powers such as Poland and Romania between the two giants. A good diplomatic history of the eve of the Russo-German war in which the author criticizes both leaders for a lack of understanding of each other's motives.

1164   Tasca, Angelo (Rossi). **The Russo-German Alliance, August 1939-June 1941.** London, Chapman and Hall, 1950. 218p. Bibliog.
A concise dispassionate study of German-Soviet relations during the crucial period when Hitler initially needed a non-hostile situation in the east to the

time when his Lebensraum policy was actively carried out with the invasion of
Russia.

Germany and the Arabs

1165   Hirszowicz, Lukasz. **The Third Reich and the Arab East**. London,
         Routledge and Kegan Paul, 1966. 403p. Maps, Bibliog.
Based on German archival material, the author relates German efforts to utilize
and exploit the Arab National movement. The German role in the Iraqi revolt in
1941, in Vichy Syria, and its Arab policies in the North African area are described
in detail.

1166   Schechtman, Joseph B. **The Mufti and the Fuehrer: The Rise and Fall of
         Haj Amin El-Husseine**. New York, T. Yoseloff, 1965. 336p. Bibliog.
A study of the political career of the former Mufti of Jerusalem who was a
dominant and influential figure in Palestine. He was the gray eminence behind the
pro-Axis Iraqi rebellion, openly joining the Axis side, broadcasting anti-Allied
propaganda and organizing Arab and Moslem military units for the Axis.

Great Britain and Poland

1167   Jedrzejewicz, Waclow, ed. **Poland in the British Parliament, 1939-1945**.
         New York, Jozef Pilsudski Institute of America, 1946-1962. 3v. Maps,
         Bibliog.
Stenographic reports of Parliamentary debates on Anglo-Polish relations from
March 3, 1939, to July 1945. Explanatory notes precede the documents. Volumes
two and three include material relating to Poland gathered from other sources
as well, but on the general topic.

Great Britain and Spain

1168   Templewood, Samuel John Gurney Hoare. **Complacent Dictator**. New
         York, Knopf, 1947. 318p.
The World War II memoirs of Great Britain's Ambassador to Spain (1940-1944).
The author recounts his struggle to keep Franco from openly joining the Axis. He
presents vivid portraits of the Spanish leadership and discusses Franco and Spanish
policy, the Falange, and British policy toward Spain.

Hungary and Germany

1169   Fenyo, Mario D. **Hitler, Horthy and Hungary: German-Hungarian Rela-
         tions, 1941-1944**. New Haven, Yale University Press, 1972. 279p. Bibliog.
Using German and Hungarian documents not available to C. A. Macartney (*October
Fifteenth*). this is a balanced and thorough treatment of Hungary's role in World
War II. The author describes Horthy's relations with Hitler and the reasons for
Hungary's collaboration on the side of the Axis.

Italy and Germany

1170   Alfieri, Dino. **Dictators Face to Face.** New York, New York University
        Press, 1955. 307p.
The memoirs of a senior Fascist who was the Italian Minister of Propaganda,
Ambassador to the Vatican, and Ambassador to Berlin, describe the relations
between Italy and Germany before and during World War II. Excellent analysis
of the disintegration of Fascist morale in the face of military defeats and economic
failures. Presents a good picture of Mussolini along with Italian observations on
Hitler.

1171   Deakin, Frederick William. **The Brutal Friendship: Mussolini, Hitler and
        the Fall of Italian Fascism.** New York, Harper and Row, 1962. 896p.
        Bibliog.
Considered to be a definitive scholarly work based extensively on German and
Italian sources. Deals with Mussolini's power in Italy, his relations with Germany
and its decline, and his ruin under the relentless pressures of a disastrous war. The
three parts cover the crisis that developed in the Fascist system due to military
defeats, the imprisonment of Mussolini under the Badoglio government, and
thirdly his rescue and the establishment of the puppet regime at Salo.

1172   Plehwe, Friedrich-Karl von. **The End of an Alliance: Rome's Defection
        from the Axis in 1943.** London, Oxford University Press, 1971. 161p.
        Bibliog.
The author, a member of the German military representative in Rome, assesses the
consequences of Mussolini's overthrow. He describes the breakdown of the Italo-
German alliance, the attempts of the Germans to smooth the growing rift, the
confusion in Rome, the decision of the Badoglio government to seek an armistice
with the Allies and the German reaction.

Japan and Russia

1173   Lensen, George Alexander. **The Strange Neutrality: Soviet-Japanese Rela-
        tions During the Second World War, 1941-1945.** Tallahassee, Fla.,
        Diplomatic Press, 1972. 332p. Bibliog.
A first-rate analysis of the motives behind the April 1941 neutrality pact between
Russia and Japan, Japan's decision not to attack the Soviet Union despite their
anti-Comintern Pact with Germany, and of the Soviet Union's decision not to
attack Japan during almost all of the war in spite of pressures to do so from the
United States.

Middle East

1174   Hurewitz, Jacob Coleman, ed. **Diplomacy in the Near and Middle East:
        A Documentary Record. Vol. II: 1914-1956.** Princeton, N.J., Van
        Nostrand, 1956. 427p.
An excellent collection of documents regarding European diplomacy in and
concerning the Near and Middle East. Explanatory notes and biographical
references preface the documents which underline the development of the relationships between the nations of Europe and the Near and Middle East.

1175   Kirk, George Edward. **The Middle East in the War.** 2nd ed. New York,
        Oxford University Press, 1953. 511p. Maps, Bibliog.
This, the second volume of the wartime series of the *Survey of International
Affairs*, deals with the political and economic events of the Middle East in their
wartime perspective. Indispensable for its detail and balanced evaluation, the
author states that Great Britain's recognition and approval of the forces of Arab
Nationalism would have provided a stabilizing influence in the area. The work
describes the efforts of the Allies to deal with the problems created by the war and
the Anglo-American differences thereon.

1176   Sachar, Howard Morley. **Europe Leaves the Middle East, 1936-1954.** New
        York, Knopf, 1972. 725p. Maps, Bibliog.
An account of eighteen years of British, French, and German influence. Traces the
Anglo-French contest for influence and Nazi attempts at penetration into the area.
Focuses on the negotiations and calculated gambles of the Allies, the Axis and
also of the Soviet strategists and on the nationalist exertions of Arab, Jewish,
Turkish and Iranian leaders.

Poland and Russia

1177   **The Dark Side of the Moon.** New York, Scribners, 1947. 299p.
An account of Polish-Soviet relations from 1939 to 1945 from the standpoint of
Soviet actions as a result of the 1939 pact between Germany and the Soviet Union
and the subsequent Soviet occupation of the Eastern part of Poland. Describes
the imposition of the Soviet pattern of life upon the Poles and the resultant
consequences.

1178   General Sikorski Historical Institute. **Documents on Polish-Soviet Rela-
        tions, 1939-1945.** London, Heinemann, 1961-67. 2v. Bibliog.
A comprehensive compilation of documentary materials relating to the policies
of the two governments and the influence of the western powers on these policies.
The volumes are divided into the major section on the documents themselves,
appendices supporting these materials, and a section of extensive notes regarding
the documents covered.

Russia and China

1179   Schwartz, Harry. **Tsars, Mandarins and Commissars: A History of
        Chinese-Russian Relations.** Philadelphia, Lippincott, 1964. 252p.
        Maps, Bibliog.
An analytical survey of Sino-Soviet disputes through October 1963. Traces the
long history of conflict and equivocal relations between the Russians and the
Chinese.

United States and China

1180   Feis, Herbert. **The China Tangle: The American Effort in China from
        Pearl Harbor to the Marshall Mission.** Princeton, N.J., Princeton Univer-
        sity Press, 1953. 445p. Maps, Bibliog.

An excellent study of U.S. policy toward China from late 1941 to early 1946. A thorough review of U.S. efforts on behalf of China with insight into the complexities and intricacies of U.S. policy-making for this area. Heavily documented facts drawn from published sources, official records, and papers of major U.S. officials.

1181   Kubek, Anthony. **How the Far East Was Lost: American Policy and the Creation of Communist China, 1941-1949.** Chicago, Regnery, 1963. 480p. Bibliog.

A revisionist study of U.S. foreign policy toward China. The author notes the errors he feels were made by the Roosevelt and Truman administrations and attributes many of these actions to malice by the U.S. officials involved.

1182   Tsou, Tang. **America's Failure in China, 1940-1950.** Chicago, University of Chicago Press, 1963. 614p.

A balanced and scholarly first-rate analysis of both U.S. and Chinese policy. Focuses on the failure of U.S. officials to comprehend the nature of the communist movement thus precipitating a long series of blunders in the making of U.S. foreign policy toward China. The fact that the U.S. was not prepared to use its power to intervene, according to the author, allowed the Nationalist leadership to place loyalty above efficiency, integrity and corruption, and thus contributed to the failure of U.S. efforts in China.

1183   Tuchman, Barbara. **Stilwell and the American Experience in China, 1911-45.** New York, Macmillan, 1970. 621p. Maps, Bibliog.

A very interesting and informative book on the complex story of the relations between the U.S. and China. Essentially limited to wartime events, it relates the role of this important figure in Sino-American relations. The events of his controversial command personify the strongest endeavors of the U.S. experience in China. The opposition of Chiang to having this man of high performance and integrity as the commander of China's armed forces stemmed from Chiang's realization that this would result in a loss of his close control of the army.

1184   Varg, Paul A. **The Closing of the Door: Sino-American Relations, 1936-1946.** East Lansing, Michigan State University Press, 1973. 300p. Map, Bibliog.

An analysis of the developments of United States policy toward China during and immediately after World War II. An examination of the differences in national interests and ambitions which contributed to the deep political, economic, and social divisions in China. An excellent analysis as well of the effects of the domestic policy of the United States and of the communists and nationalists on U.S. efforts to seek a coalition government in China.

1185   Young, Arthur Nichols. **China and the Helping Hand, 1937-1945.** Cambridge, Harvard University Press, 1963. 502p. Map, Bibliog.

The author was financial advisor to the Nationalist government from 1929 to 1947 and thus is uniquely qualified to provide an understanding of the complex and controversial role of U.S. foreign aid to China. This carefully written penetrating analysis depicts the serious deterioration of the Chinese regime and the difficulties that beset attempts to stabilize China's wartime economy and finances.

United States and France

1186   Langer, William Leonard. **Our Vichy Gamble**. Hamden, Conn., Archon
        Books, 1965. 412p. Bibliog.
A history of American relations with France from June 1940 to December 1942
for the period of the United States Vichy policy. Based on the records of the
U. S. State Department this factual scholarly record discusses why the United
States chose to recognize Petain and Vichy for so long instead of De Gaulle and
his Free French.

1187   Viorst, Milton. **Hostile Allies: F.D.R. and Charles De Gaulle**. New York,
        Macmillan, 1965. 280p. Bibliog.
A focus on the wartime relations between the two leaders describing the episodes
that separated them and even ran counter to each other. De Gaulle's rise to moral
and actual leadership of the Free French and of the anti-Nazi elements in France
is discussed in relation to United States reluctance to recognize De Gaulle and
its policies toward Petain and Vichy France.

United States and Great Britain

1188   Wilson, Theodore A. **The First Summit: Roosevelt and Churchill at
        Placentia Bay 1941**. Boston, Houghton Mifflin, 1969. 344p. Bibliog.
A comprehensive account of the Atlantic Conference and the origins of the
Atlantic Charter that gave the Allies their war aims. The style of the Conference,
the image presented and how differences were reconciled are fully discussed.

United States and India

1189   Hess, Gary R. **America Encounters India, 1941-1947**. Baltimore, Johns
        Hopkins Press, 1971. 211p. Bibliog.
Focusing on popular and official attitudes toward Indian political developments,
the author chronicles U. S. response and defines U. S. policy toward this South
Asian nationalist movement. The Atlantic Charter had seemingly committed
the United States toward a policy of supporting the self-determination of peoples.
Indian nationalism challenged the idealism and diplomatic skill of the United
States in the choice between supporting a prime ally in World War II and aiding
a nationalist movement demanding independence from that ally.

United States and Russia

1190   Crocker, George N. **Roosevelt's Road to Russia**. Chicago, Regnery, 1959.
        312p. Bibliog.
A revisionist critique of FDR's wartime diplomacy with the Soviet Union. The
author contends that the policies of FDR were designed to aid the rise of Soviet
communism and that the Yalta Conference culminated policies filled with blunders
and resulting in betrayals of European democracy in the peace that later followed.

1191   Dawson, Raymond H. **The Decision to Aid Russia, 1941: Foreign Policy and Domestic Politics.** Chapel Hill, University of North Carolina Press, 1959. 315p. Bibliog.
An examination of the developments that led to Roosevelt's determination to aid the Russians. These were seen to fully justify aid under the existing military situation. The description of how the administration prepared the public and Congress for this move is seen in the context of U. S. foreign and domestic considerations.

1192   Deane, John Russell. **The Strange Alliance: The Story of Our Efforts at Wartime Cooperation with Russia.** New York, Viking Press, 1947. 344p.
The head of the American military mission to Moscow from 1943 to 1945 describes the strains in U. S.-Soviet wartime collaboration. He provides some valuable information about the meetings at Teheran, Yalta and Potsdam in which he took part. An advocate of a policy of positive and firm action with the Russians he recounts his experiences with Soviet suspicions and bureaucracy in the face of a U. S. desire to help.

1193   Dennett, Raymond and Joseph E. Johnson, eds. **Negotiating with the Russians.** Boston, World Peace Foundation, 1951. 310p.
An examination of representative samples of East-West negotiations in meetings for the period 1940-1947. A study of the effectiveness of various negotiation techniques using the experiences of U. S. participants. Shows that Soviet conduct is related directly to its structure and dominant ideology and requires favorable political conditions to be successful.

1194   Gaddis, John Lewis. **The United States and the Origins of the Cold War, 1941-1947.** New York, Columbia University Press, 1972. 396p. Bibliog.
This counterattack on revisionist historiography presents a carefully researched analysis of U. S. policy toward the Soviet Union during and right after World War II. The work considers the impact on relations between the two nations of the issues of economic assistance, the atomic bomb, Germany, Eastern Europe and international communism and concludes that the U. S. was less responsible than Russia for the growing differences between the two.

1195   Herring, George C., Jr. **Aid to Russia, 1941-1946: Strategy, Diplomacy and the Origins of the Cold War.** New York, Columbia University Press, 1973. 265p. Bibliog.
Two main themes are presented in this overall evaluation of the evolution of the relations between the United States and the Soviet Union. The impact of economic aid in primarily military materials and the development and degeneration of their relations.

1196   Jones, Robert Huhn. **Roads to Russia: United States Lend-Lease to the Soviet Union.** Norman, University of Oklahoma Press, 1969. 326p. Maps, Bibliog.
An account of the maneuvering of Roosevelt and Harry Hopkins to establish a workable agreement with Stalin on lend-lease. The work describes the arrangements and terms of the aid, the way it was used and the attitudes of the recipients.

The personal, political, military and economic difficulties encountered are pictured in detail along with an evaluation of the impact of this aid on the Soviet war effort.

1197   Kuklick, Bruce. **American Policy and the Division of Germany: The Clash with Russia Over Reparations.** Ithaca, Cornell University Press, 1972. 286p. Bibliog.
A discussion of the basis, derivation and the historical context for U. S. policy towards the question of German reparations. The author reinterprets the Morganthau Plan for the postwar control of Germany, the U. S. commitment to a world politico-economic system and the effects of this global commitment on U. S. attitudes at the Yalta discussions of German reparations. The Russians felt a need for equipment and industrial plants to replace their war ravaged economy while the United States basically felt that the German industrial plant was vital to German economic regrowth and reparations should in the main be mostly in goods.

1198   Motter, Thomas Hubbard Vail. **The Persian Corridor and Aid to Russia.** Washington, Office of the Chief of Military History, Dept. of the Army, 1952. 545p. Maps, Bibliog.
The story of the development of a major pipe-line to Russia for lend-lease during the period covering 1941-1945. This description of an experiment in international cooperation betwen the Allies is seen within the framework of political, economic and social factors.

1199   Standley, William H. and Arthur A. Ageton. **Admiral Ambassador to Russia.** Chicago, H. Regnery, 1955. 533p.
The account of the U.S. Ambassador to Russia, from February 1942 to October 1943, of his experiences in Moscow. He describes the chaotic handling of U. S. relations and the realities of dealing with the Soviet leadership as they maneuvered diplomatically with a view toward post-war settlements. The Ambassador provides a picture of wartime life in Russia with sidelights on the Soviet leadership.

1200   Stettinius, Edward Reilly. **Roosevelt and the Russians: The Yalta Conference.** Garden City, N. Y., Doubleday, 1949. 367p. Map.
A daily account by the then U. S. Secretary of State of the Yalta Conference. He discusses in detail each decision taken at the Conference, characterizing it on the whole as a diplomatic triumph for the U. S. and Great Britain in that the Soviet Union conceded more than the West. He feels that the criticism of the West's actions at Yalta was not a case of FDR's concessions to the Russians but should be directed to the Soviet Union's failure to honor their agreements.

United States and Spain

1201   Hayes, Carlton Joseph Huntley. **Wartime Mission in Spain, 1942-1945.** New York, Macmillan, 1945. 313p. Bibliog.
The central concern of this candid narrative of the author's U.S. Ambassadorship to Spain is U.S. policy towards Spain and Spain's response. It discusses the efforts of Germany to bring Spain into the Axis Alliance and Franco's reasons

for not allowing her to be drawn into the conflict. The author felt at that time that until the Allies should win some decisive military victory Spain would continue her policy of non-belligerency. He describes the efforts of the Allies to force Spain to embargo the shipment of Wolfram ore (tungsten) to Germany.

United States and Switzerland

1202   Meier, Heinz K. **Friendship Under Stress: U. S.-Swiss Relations, 1900-1950.** Bern, Herbert Lang & Co., 1970. 423p. Bibliog.
The book is concerned with U. S.-Swiss relations under the impact and stress of major international tensions. The author feels that U. S.-Swiss relations were more determined by history than determining it. Interesting descriptions of Nazi wartime pressures on Switzerland and subsequent U. S. pressures during the latter part of the Second World War to restrict Swiss trade with Germany.

United States and the Vatican

1203   Roosevelt, Franklin Delano. **Wartime Correspondence Between President Roosevelt and Pope Pius XII.** New York, Macmillan, 1947. 127p.
A compilation of letters sent between 1940 and 1945 between the two leaders. Their declared purposes was to look into the possibility of joint action between political and religious authorities to help relieve the suffering of a world-wide war torn populace and to seek the eventual return of peace.

United States, Great Britain and Russia

1204   Beitzell, Robert Egner. **The Uneasy Alliance: America, Britain and Russia, 1941-1943.** New York, Knopf, 1972. 404p. Bibliog.
A study of the relationship of the main powers as they waged the war and planned for the peace. The work focuses on the conferences of Quebec, Moscow, Cairo and Tehran and deals with the official versions of the major negotiations regarding the problem of grand strategy.

1205   Dallin, David. **The Big Three: The United States, Britain, Russia.** New Haven, Yale University Press, 1945. 292p. Maps.
A discussion of the aspirations and patterns of behavior of the big three in terms of the effects of internal policies on their foreign policy and diplomatic stands. Each country is appraised as to its war-making capabilities and its relationship to national security.

1206   Feis, Herbert. **Churchill, Roosevelt, Stalin: The War They Waged and the Peace They Sought.** Princeton, N. J., Princeton University Press, 1957. 692p. Maps, Bibliog.
A brilliant account of the stresses and strains to which the Grand Alliance was exposed. Using the chronological method this lucid and balanced account of wartime policies pursues the complex story of the agreements, conferences, diplomatic moves and strategy of the big three from 1940 to 1945.

1207   McNeill, William H. **America, Britain and Russia: Their Cooperation and Conflict, 1941-1946**. New York, Johnson Reprint, 1970. 819p. Maps, Bibliog.

A good presentation of the complex problems of inter-allied cooperation against the Axis. The breakdown of this cooperation amid plans for post-war peace settlements is discussed against the background of the course of events that determined the war's conduct. Notes also the political, military and economic aspects of the Alliance. This is volume three of the wartime series of the *Survey of International Affairs*.

1208   Neumann, William Louis. **After Victory: Churchill, Roosevelt, Stalin and the Making of Peace**. New York, Harper and Row, 1967. 212p. Maps, Bibliog.

A succinct history of the efforts of the big three to create a peace within the framework of their national interests. The successes and failures of their efforts are also seen in the context of the international and national systems in which they worked.

1209   Snell, John L. **The Meaning of Yalta: Big Three Diplomacy and the New Balance of Power**. Baton Rouge, Louisiana State University Press, 1956. 239p. Maps, Bibliog.

A carefully documented appraisal of the problems and decisions concerning the Yalta Conference. This important study places these decisions in their proper context with the essential accompanying details.

1210   Stalin, Iosif. **Stalin's Correspondence with Churchill, Attlee, Roosevelt and Truman, 1941-1945**. New York, Dutton, 1958. 2v.

Originally published in Russia the letters range on subjects from the opening of the second front, British aid to Russia, preparations for international conferences and the progress of the war. The compilation is valuable for the general impression of the character of an edgy and uneasy alliance.

Vatican and Germany

1211   Friedlander, Saul. **Pius XII and the Third Reich: A Documentation**. New York, Knopf, 1966. 238. Bibliog.

Using documentation from the German archives and British and U. S. diplomatic papers, the author contends that the Pope was not anxious to weaken Germany by criticizing its wartime policies and thus possibly lay it and Europe open to Bolshevization. He also feels that the Pope exhibited a decidedly pro-German partiality in his actions.

1212   Lewy, Guenther. **The Catholic Church and Nazi Germany**. New York, McGraw-Hill, 1964. 416p. Map, Bibliog.

The role of the Catholic hierarchy in Nazi Germany is traced in detail. The tragic failure of the Church to live up to its moral canons is blamed on its political ideology to preserve and enhance the strength of the Church. Thus the stand of the Vatican and the Pope's silence in regards to Hitler's solution to the Jewish question is seen to be in harmony with Church policies of long standing.

Yugoslavia and Russia

1213   Dilas, Milovan. **Conversations with Stalin.** New York, Harcourt, Brace
         and World, 1962. 211p.
The account of three periods—1944, 1945 and 1948—in which the author met
with Stalin and other Soviet leaders, as a high Yugoslav communist official, to
discuss the situation in Yugoslavia and the needs of Tito. Describes the background
and results of these contacts with the Soviet leadership.

CHAPTER 7–THE WAR YEARS, 1939-1945:
ECONOMIC ASPECTS

GENERAL WORKS

1214   Gordon, David Livingston and Royden Dangerfield. **The Hidden Weapon:**
        The Story of Economic Warfare. New York, Harper, 1947. 238p.
A lucid analysis by two former chiefs of the Blockade Division of the U. S. Foreign
Economic Administration of the economic warfare aspects of World War II. Topics covered include the efforts of the Allies in establishing economic blockades
against hesitating neutrals, blacklisting of supplies which could aid the enemy
and the preclusive purchase of materials to deny them to the enemy's war efforts.

1215   Prest, Alan Richmond. **War Economics of Primary Producing Countries.**
        Cambridge, University Press, 1948. 308p.
An interesting study of several countries whose production and exports consist
of primary raw materials. The countries and areas studied include India, the
Middle East, Nigeria and Trinidad. Their wartime economic contributions form
the basis of this factual analysis.

1216   Roll, Erich. **The Combined Food Board: A Study in Wartime International**
        Planning. Stanford, Calif., Stanford University Press, 1956. 385p.
The story of the development and effective work of the Combined Food Board
whose members consisted of the United States, Great Britain and Canada. Their
work in meeting the pressing problems of the international distribution of foodstuffs was an important achievement in international cooperation during World
War II.

1217   Rosen, S. McKee. **The Combined Boards of the Second World War: An**
        Experiment in International Administration. New York, Columbia Uni-
        versity Press, 1951. 288p. Bibliog.
A study of the functions, activities and procedures of the various Allied combined
boards which mobilized and coordinated the economic resources of the Allies in
shipping, production and distribution of raw materials.

1218   Zagorov, Slavcho D., and others. **The Agricultural Economy of the Danubian**
        Countries, 1935-1945. Stanford, Calif., Stanford University Press, 1955.
        478p. Maps, Bibliog.
Statistical and descriptive essays on food and agriculture in Hungary,
Romania, Yugoslavia and Bulgaria before and during World War II. The studies
seek to analyze the area's wartime economy and system of land tenure.

INDIVIDUAL COUNTRIES

Australia

1219   Butlin, Sydney James. **War Economy.** Canberra, Australian War Memorial,
        1955. 2v. Maps, Bibliog.

These two volumes in the civil aspects of the series on Australia in the war of 1939-1945 cover the Australian war economy for these years from the formation of economic policy to its fruition. Areas covered include discussions of price control, external finance and trade, problems of supply, production and manpower and particularly Australia's importance as an Allied source of agricultural products.

China

1220   Young, Arthur Nichols. **China's Wartime Finance and Inflation, 1937-1945.** Cambridge, Harvard University Press, 1965. 421p. Bibliog.
This companion volume to *China and the Helping Hand* is an excellent documented history of China's wartime finance and its domestic politics. Topics covered include foreign aid, fiscal policy, monetary menagement and the country's serious inflationary problems. The author contends that China's inability to cope with her inflation played an important part in providing a base for revolution.

France

1221   Milward, Alan S. **The New Order and the French Economy.** Oxford, Clarendon Press, 1970. 320p. Maps, Bibliog.
A focus on Nazi efforts to integrate the French economy into the German economic sphere. This case study of the thorough economic domination of one nation by another delves into the conflicts in Nazi thought and practice between development of economic resources and outright exploitation. An interesting conclusion is that conquest pays only in the short run due to eventual high occupation costs and losses due to resistance and sabotage.

Germany

1222   Brandt, Karl. **Germany's Agricultural and Food Policies in World War II.** Stanford, Calif., Food Research Institute, Stanford University, 1953. 2v. Maps.
Volume one is titled *The Management of Agriculture and Food in Germany: A Study in Planned Economy* and volume two is *The Management of Agriculture and Food in the German-Occupied and Other Areas of Fortress Europe.* Both are concerned with Germany's attempts to utilize the agricultural resources of the homeland and the countries she overran. An evaluation and analysis of the policies applied, what they were meant to accomplish and how they were carried out to supply Germany with foodstuffs and related raw materials.

1223   Carroll, Berenice A. **Design for Total War: Arms and Economics in the Third Reich.** The Hague, Mouton, 1968. 312p. Bibliog.
This history of Germany's economy from the Weimar Republic to the end of the Third Reich notes the discrepancy betwen the propaganda pronouncements of gearing for total war and the actual avoidance of total economic mobilization. This is attributed to Hitler's Blitzkrieg theory and strategy which was expected to avoid prolonged conflict with its concomitant economic problems.

1224   Homze, Edward L. **Foreign Labor in Nazi Germany**. Princeton, N. J.,
        Princeton University Press, 1967. 350p. Bibliog.
A study of the inception, organization and administration of the Nazi foreign
labor program and its relationship to the war economy. A description of working
and living conditions and the status of these eight million workers recruited from
German allies, neutral areas and occupied countries. The study shows the effects
of unemployment in the home country on the availability of labor supply and
of the results of compulsory labor laws in occupied countries in forced labor
recruitment.

1225   Lochner, Louis Paul. **Tycoons and Tyrant: German Industry from Hitler
        to Adenauer**. Chicago, H. Regnery, 1954. 304p.
The Chief of the Berlin Bureau of the Associated Press described the relationship
between German industry, the government and the Nazi and other political parties.
Brief biographical sketches of figures in German industry are included. A revealing
insight into the attitudes of industrial leaders toward Hitler and his programs.

1226   Milward, Alan S. **The German Economy at War**. London, Athlone Press,
        1965. 214p. Map, Bibliog.
A study of Germany's wartime economic strategy set against its political background. This excellent work provides an understanding of Hitler's economic policy
based on his concept of the short term intensive military necessities of Blitzkrieg
warfare including descriptions of German war production and its administration.

1227   Schacht, Hjalmar Horace Greeley. **Confessions of the "Old Wizard."**
        Boston, Houghton Mifflin, 1956. 484p.
The frank memoirs of Hitler's foremost economic expert who played a leading
role in German economic life after World War I. Reveals the style of an old-line
capitalist whose sound economic principles were, however, accompanied by an
insensitivity to the methods employed.

1228   Schweitzer, Arthur. **Big Business in the Third Reich**. Bloomington,
        Indiana University Press, 1964. 739p. Bibliog.
An analysis of Nazi economic policies toward and relations with big and small
businesses against the setting of the total domestic economic picture. The structural changes in the German society and economy are shown in relation to the
role of the combined forces of big business, large landowners, the army and the
party. The problems of financing the war economy and the techniques used by
Hitler to further his policies in this area are well described.

Great Britain

1229   Hall, Hessel Duncan and C. C. Wrigley. **Studies of Overseas Supply**.
        London, H. M. Stationery Office, 1956. 537p. Bibliog.
A study and analysis of the different aspects of the problem of supplying Great
Britain. Describes the methods that were developed to turn policies into actions,
the contribution of the Commonwealth, the work of the Combined Boards relating
to supply, lend-lease procurement and the efforts of the British War Organization
office in the United States.

1230   Hammond, Richard James. **Food and Agriculture in Britain, 1939-45: Aspects of Wartime Control**. Stanford, Calif., Stanford University Press, 1954. 246p. Bibliog.
An analysis and interpretation of the decisions made by the British government in the wartime management and control of food supply and agricultural production. The author discusses among others the history and establishment of food controls (using the control of milk as a major example), the various rationing schemes, and the welfare subsidies of foods and vitamins.

1231   Hancock, William Keith and M. M. Gowing. **British War Economy**. London, H. M. Stationery Office, 1953. 583p. Bibliog.
A broad survey of the development of the British war economy as a whole in theory and in actual practice. These basic economic efforts are set against the strategy of wartime policies, governmental organization and inter-allied economic cooperation.

1232   Hargreaves, Eric Lyde and M. M. Gowing. **Civil Industry and Trade**. London, H. M. Stationery Office, 1952. 678p.
The main problems of production and distribution in areas outside of the aspects of war production. The three areas discussed include import and export policies, the transfer of civilian resources to war usage, and a search for some balance and equity in relation to the production of non-defense materiel in the consumer goods field.

1233   Hurstfield, Joel. **The Control of Raw Materials**. London, H. M. Stationery Office, 1953. 530p. Bibliog.
This is a study of the national requirements of raw materials in the inter-war and war years and the development of British policies in this general area. The specific areas covered include sources of supply, foreign exchange, import policies and programs, and the overall controlling machinery and problems thereof.

1234   Medlicott, William Norton. **The Economic Blockade**. London, H. M. Stationery Office, 1952-59. 2v. Bibliog.
Describes the attempt to deprive the Axis of economic materials from the neutral countries through contraband interception and control and diplomatic pressures. These administrative and diplomatic activities of the British Ministry of Economic Warfare cover the development of the policies of economic warfare up to and subsequent to U. S. entry into the war.

1235   Murray, Keith Anderson Hope. **Agriculture**. London, H. M. Stationery Office, 1955. 422p. Bibliog.
The war years are handled chronologically in describing agricultural planning and implementation to meet the changing circumstances of the war. Topics covered include food production, price controls, policy formulation, and changes in the structure and techniques of farming.

1236   Parker, Henry Michael Denne. **Manpower: A Study of War-Time Policy and Administration**. London, H. M. Stationery Office, 1957. 535p. Bibliog.

The methods used to mobilize the civilian population and how they were allocated to the military, civil defense and to industry. A description of the factors which determined British labor policy and administration during the Second World War. A companion volume describing the situation in a specific industry is P. Inman's *Labour in the Munitions Industry* HMSO, 1957).

1237   Payton-Smith, Derek Joseph. **Oil: A Study of War-Time Policy and Administration**. London, H. M. Stationery Office, 1971. 520p. Maps.
The direction of policy formed by a thirty-year vain search for self-sufficiency in oil is the focus of this work. The problems of wartime supply to the armed forces and the civilian population is seen against the background of the circumstances in which oil policy was made and how the resultant programs were administered. Another title of interest is William H. B. Court's *Coal* (HMSO, 1951).

1238   Postan, Michael Moissey. **British War Production**. London, H. M. Stationery Office, 1952. 512p.
A discussion of the strategic and economic factors affecting the trends of supply and demand from the interwar years and the efforts at rearmament from 1934 to 1938 to and through the war years. The author includes descriptions of the structure of the war industry, the blueprint of wartime production, the problems encountered until the U. S. entered the war, and the efforts to produce the equipment and weapons needed for a far flung war effort. A companion volume is J. D. Scott's and R. Hughes' *The Administration of War Production* (HMSO, 1955).

1239   Sayers, Richard Sidney. **Financial Policy, 1939-1945**. London, H. M. Stationery Office, 1956. 608p. Bibliog.
A description of the policies which were developed to resolve the complex problems of Britain's war finances. The main emphasis is on the internal aspects of budget policy, internal borrowing, interest rates, exchange control, and also on the financial relations with the Commonwealth, the dollar exchange problem and lend-lease obligations.

India

1240   Knight, Henry. **Food Administration in India, 1939-57**. Stanford, Calif., Stanford University Press, 1954. 323p. Maps, Bibliog.
A treatment in detail of the problems of food supply in India by the British advisor on food and agriculture to the Governor of Bombay. Drawing heavily on official documents, records and statistics the author describes government efforts to provide foodstuffs in times of crop failure and famine and the problems of rationing, black marketeering and supply.

Japan

1241   Bisson, Thomas Arthur. **Japan's War Economy**. New York, Macmillan, 1945. 267p. Bibliog.
A discussion of the various programs for the economic administration of the country's industrial resources which were developed during the war. The struggles

between the militarists and the large capitalist enterprises, the Zaibatsu, for control over the national economy and the roles played by these forces are set against a background of an ever-growing demand for increased production.

1242   Cohen, Jerome Bernard. **Japan's Economy in War and Reconstruction.**
        Minneapolis, University of Minnesota Press, 1949. 545p. Bibliog.
The author contends that economic strangulation, rather than the atom bombs, was the decisive weapon that defeated Japan. This comprehensive study of Japan's economy from the early 1930s through 1948 presents an exhaustive picture of the functioning of her wartime economy.

1243   Johnston, Bruce F., Mosaburo Hosada and Yoshio Kusumi. **Japanese Food
        Management in World War II.** Stanford, Calif., Stanford University Press,
        1953. 283p. Bibliog.
Food as a weapon of war was no more clearly evident than in Japan. The effects of the war were severe due to Japan's needs to import foodstuffs. The book describes the nature of Japan's wartime food problems, the measures adopted to deal with them, the characteristics of agricultural production, government policies which attempted to cope with food shortages and the impact of the war on the food supply.

Norway

1244   Milward, Alan S. **The Fascist Economy in Norway.** Oxford, Clarendon
        Press, 1972. 317p. Bibliog.
This history of the Norwegian wartime economy surveys the Nazi schemes to restructure it according to the German ideological and economic motives of the New European Order.

Russia

1245   Dobb, Maurice Herbert. **Soviet Economic Development Since 1917.**
        Rev. ed. New York, International Publishers, 1967. 515p. Maps, Bibliog.
The story of Soviet economic development and its relations between the planning, production and financial plans. The author analyzes the Five Year Plans and presents a reasoned justification of Soviet economic policies amid ideological conflicts. The work can be considered to be sympathetic to the policies of the Soviet Union.

1246   Voznesenskii, Nikolai Alekseevich. **The Economy of the U.S.S.R. During
        World War II.** Washington, D. C., Public Affairs Press, 1948. 115p.
This official statement of the Soviet war effort, its plans and development, provides an important revealing work on the methods and results of Soviet war production despite the somewhat heavy propaganda doses.

United States

1247   Chandler, Lester Vernon. **Inflation in the United States, 1940-1948.**
        New York, Harper, 1951. 402p. Bibliog.

A description of the causes and characteristics of inflation in the U. S. during World War II. An examination of the public and private policies which were responsible for wartime inflation, the methods adopted to deal with it, and the resultant consequences. The work provides a clear review of the monetary and financial aspects of the wartime economy.

1248   Connery, Robert Hough. **The Navy and the Industrial Mobilization in World War II**. Princeton, N.J., Princeton University Press, 1951. 527p. Bibliog.
A comprehensive contribution to the study of industrial and economic mobilization, public administration and government procurement and planning. This analytical history details the administrative problems of the U. S. Navy in its efforts to organize the acquisition of large amounts of needed materiel.

1249   Craf, John Riley. **A Survey of the American Economy, 1940-1945**. New York, North River Press, 1947. 217p.
The major wartime events on the economic front are discussed in terms of the organization and activities of the various governmental agencies involved with the making and execution of economic policy. Arranged topically the areas covered include national defense, war conversion, priorities and allocations, rationing, agriculture, finance, wages, manpower, raw materials and reconversion to peace.

1250   De Schweinitz, Dorothea. **Labor and Management in a Common Enterprise**. Cambridge, Harvard University Press, 1949. 186p. Bibliog.
An analysis of the wartime experiences of labor-management relations based on the work of the joint production committees sponsored by the War Production Board. The performance and potentialities of these labor-management production committees and their principles, procedures and functions are seen to be applicable to peacetime labor relations as well.

1251   Fairchild, Byron and Jonathan Grossman. **The Army and Industrial Manpower**. Washington, Office of Chief of Military History, Dept. of the Army, 1959. 291p. Bibliog.
The army's activities in the field of organized labor, as direct employers of civilian labor in government owned and operated plants, as the chief source of manpower and as one of the agencies called upon to enforce labor and manpower policies, is studied within the context of the problems involved and steps taken to deal with them.

1252   Gold, Bela. **Wartime Economic Planning in Agriculture: A Study in the Allocation of Resources**. New York, Columbia University Press, 1949. 594p.
A thorough study of how inadequately the production of the nations's agricultural resources were mobilized. This significant contribution examines the operational and theoretical difficulties of effective economic planning.

1253   Harris, Seymour Edwin. **The Economics of America at War**. New York, Norton, 1943. 418p. Bibliog.

A contemporary study detailing the basic economic problems of the war in terms of the fundamental principles of war economics. Includes a brief survey of the U. S. economy for the period 1933-1940.

1254　Hirsch, Julius. **Price Control in the War Economy**. New York, Harper, 1943. 311p. Bibliog.

An impartial explanation of the basic economic issues dividing the U. S. during this period including the theory and practice of price control. The author's views are based on his experience as a Weimar official during the inflation period after the First World War.

1255　Janeway, Eliot. **The Struggle for Survival: A Chronicle of Economic Mobilization in World War II**. New Haven, Yale University Press, 1951. 382p. Bibliog.

This study of the conversion of manpower and resources into military use stresses the administrative and personality problems that affected the various factors concerning industrial production, labor, agriculture and finance. The author traces the succession of mobilization agencies from the War Resources Board of 1939 to the Office of War Mobilization and Reconversion. One contention is that the New Deal bureaucracy saw the war as a way to continue their social programs under the banner of national defense.

1256　Johnson, Robert Wood. **"But, General Johnson—": Episodes in a War Effort**. Princeton, N. J., Princeton University Press, 1944. 160p. Bibliog.

An interesting personal account of the experiences in Washington bureaucracy of the Chairman of the wartime Smaller War Plants Corporation. Its primary purpose was to award subcontracts to small businesses who wished to engage in war work, to compel government procurement agencies to subcontract to these smaller war plants and to make loans to meet wartime conversion or expansion needs. The author discovered that essentially the Corporation became an agency to defend small business from the government's web of bureaucratic contradictions.

1257　Murphy, Henry Clifford. **The National Debt in War and Transition**. New York, McGraw-Hill, 1950. 295p.

A study of the merits of financing the war by borrowing or taxation with a major emphasis upon the public policy underlying governmental actions. This work discusses the development of borrowing techniques during the initial defense period of 1939-1941 and the various savings bonds programs and war loans.

1258　Nelson, Donald Marr. **Arsenal of Democracy: The Story of American War Production**. New York, Harcourt, Brace, 1946. 439p.

The Chairman of the War Production Board describes the remarkable achievement of the U. S. in supplying its own and the Allied war machine. The work details the difficulties encountered during the nation's conversion to a war economy, the planning problems, priority assignments, the accomplishments and the eventual reconversion to a peacetime economy. The author provides some insight into the question of the balance of power between the civil and military authorities during the war.

1259   Novick, David, Melvin Anshen and W. C. Truppner. **Wartime Production Controls**. New York, Columbia University Press, 1949. 441p.
A critical study of industrial production control through the shortcomings of the War Production Board. The author judges the relative effectiveness of these production controls and contends that the administering bureaucracy was somewhat indifferent to the detailed procedural aspects of stated policy.

1260   Riegelman, Carol. **Labour-Management Co-operation in United States War Production: A Study of Methods and Procedures**. Montreal, International Labor Office, 1948. 405p. Bibliog.
The U. S. experience in labor-management cooperation in the mobilization of manpower for war production is detailed by observers of the International Labor Office. The study describes how the cooperative machinery was set up, its composition, structure, functions and methods of operation.

1261   Rundell , Walter. **Black Market Money: The Collapse of U. S. Military Currency Control in World War II**. Baton Rouge, Louisiana State University Press, 1964. 125p. Bibliog.
An excellent history of the political-economic problem of currency control. Describes the problems of decision making and policy implementation amid the collapsing control mechanisms which allowed opportunities to engage in black market purchases of military currency and transferring the profits to the United States.

1262   Russell, Judith and Renee Fantin. **Studies in Food Rationing**. Washington, Office of Temporary Controls, Office of Price Administration, 1948. 404p.
This volume in the O.P.A.'s series of Historical Reports on War Administration provides an analytical narrative of the administration of food controls between 1942 and 1946. Covering major areas in food distribution and control, such as coffee rationing, processed food rationing, the plans for milk rationing and meat distribution controls, the study provides an understanding of the government's efforts to distribute equitably those food commodities in short supply.

1263   Seidman, Joel Isaac. **American Labor from Defense to Reconversion**. Chicago, University of Chicago Press, 1953. 307p.
Based on union source materials this is a study of the changes brought about by the war in union growth and strategy, especially in the area of collective bargaining.

1264   Smith, Ralph Elberton. **The Army and Economic Mobilization**. Washington, Office of the Chief of Military History, Dept. of the Army, 1959. 749p. Bibliog.
The wartime role of the army in the complex area of the procurement of materials and economic mobilization. Describes the basic policies and procedures that were developed for the administration and planning of economic mobilization and the issues it raised.

1265   Somers, Herman Miles. **Presidential Agency: OWMR, The Office of War Mobilization and Reconversion**. Cambridge, Harvard University Press, 1950. 238p. Bibliog.

A critical treatment of the OWMR, its predecessors and successors, which was established to coordinate executive policies in this area of economic mobilization. Describes the administrative infighting during the 1939-1946 period of defense planning, mobilization and reconversion.

1266   Spiegel, Henry William. **The Economics of Total War.** New York, Appleton-Century, 1942. 410p. Bibliog.
A careful analysis of the complex subject of the economic means of warfare. The author explains the economic causes of war, the factors of the quest for living space, the control of prices and war production. Includes discussions of the British and German war economies but the main emphasis is on the policies of the United States.

1267   U. S. Bureau of the Budget. **The United States at War: Development and Administration of the War Program by the Federal Government.** New York, Da Capo Press, 1972. 555p.
This is a reprint of a 1946 official analysis of the administration of the U. S. war effort in preparing for economic defense mobilization, war production, mobilizing labor, fighting inflation, food control, regulating the flow of war materials, and of the coordination of the various war agencies.

1268   U. S. Civilian Production Administration. **Industrial Mobilization for War: History of the War Production Board and Predecessor Agencies, 1940-1945.** Washington, 1947. 2v.
Volume one focuses on the overall problems of program and administration in the mobilization of U. S. industry and emphasizes the basic factors that determined goals, policies and the methods used in carrying them out. Volume two presents the basic problems of production and administrative control through the example of the record of the U. S. munitions program.

1269   Walton, Francis. **Miracle of World War II: How American Industry Made Victory Possible.** New York, Macmillan, 1956. 575p.
A description of the manner in which the necessary products to carry on the war were conceived and produced. Provides a good picture of political and industrial maneuvering, problems caused by material shortages, manpower problems and the production of wartime needs by large and small businesses.

1270   Wilcox, Walter William. **The Farmer in the Second World War.** New York, Da Capo Press, 1973. 410p. Maps, Bibliog.
A reprint of the 1947 comprehensive study of the wartime economic factors affecting U. S. farmers. Based on congressional committee hearings and statistical reports from various government agencies, the author brings into focus the wartime developments in agriculture. The study covers the orientation of agriculture to wartime goals, wartime agricultural production and marketing, price policies including controls and supports, farm manpower problems, technological developments and the influence of farm organizations. The work also covers the various production and controls in such areas as food crops, cotton, wool, livestock and dairy products.

RELATIONS BETWEEN TWO OR MORE COUNTRIES

Australia and New Zealand

1271   Crawford, John Grenfell. **Wartime Agriculture in Australia and New Zealand, 1939-50.** Stanford, Calif., Stanford University Press, 1954. 354p. Maps, Bibliog.

The wartime management of food and agriculture of these two countries is primarily focused on managing this production to meet the changing demands of the war. The work reviews the shortages in manpower, fertilizers, equipment, the experiences of the farming industries and the measures adopted to control the agricultural programs.

Canada and the United States

1272   James, Robert Warren. **Wartime Economic Co-operation: A Study of Relations Between Canada and the United States.** Toronto, Ryerson Press, 1949. 415p. Bibliog.

A history of the coordination of production and consumption, and of the various joint committees that were formed to deal with economic cooperation between the two countries. Describes the detailed aspects of production and price controls, agricultural planning, import and export controls, allocation of materials and financial cooperation that were the main areas of wartime economic cooperation.

Great Britain, United States, and Canada

1273   Hall, Hessel Duncan. **North American Supply.** London, H. M. Stationery Office, 1955. 559p. Bibliog.

A British account of the role played by the United States and Canada in the supply of raw materials, finished weapons and war stores. The economic and political aspects of these supply problems are seen against the background of the principal events of the war. The author describes U. S. economic preparation for war and how Britain's cash payment problem was eventually solved by the advent of Lend-Lease.

Middle East

1274   Lloyd, Edward Mayow Hastings. **Food and Inflation in the Middle East, 1940-45.** Stanford, Calif., Stanford University Press, 1956. 375p. Map, Bibliog.

The Anglo-American efforts at a regional management of food, agriculture and prices among the several political entities of the Middle East provide a picture of this vital aspect of World War II. Discusses the connection between inflation and food supply which posed such problems for the Allied Middle East Supply Center whose responsibilities included the supply of basic food and grains, restraining inflation, insect control (locusts) and the establishment of better farming methods.

1275   Wilmington, Martin W. **The Middle East Supply Centre**. Albany, State
        University of New York Press, 1971. 248p. Map, Bibliog.
An historical description and evaluation of the economic mobilization of the Middle
East by the British. An analysis of the evolution, responsibility, and activity of the
Middle East Supply Centre established in 1941 to supervise the civilian economy
of North Africa and the Middle East. Its areas of responsibilities included industrial
production, food distribution, insect control and health problems. Also noted is
the eventual association and role of the United States in the Centre.

CHAPTER 8–THE WAR YEARS, 1939-1945:
SOCIAL AND CULTURAL ASPECTS

GENERAL WORKS

1276   Frumkin, Grzegorz. **Population Changes in Europe Since 1939: A Study of Population Changes in Europe During and Since World War II As Shown by the Balance Sheets of Twenty-Four European Countries.** New York, A. M. Kelley, 1951. 191p. Bibliog.
A critical estimate of shifts in European population from the start of World War II through 1947. This demographic history investigates the magnitude and the determining factors of the changes for each country and for Europe as a whole.

1277   Grygier, Tadeusz. **Oppression: A Study in Social and Criminal Psychology.** London, Routledge and Paul, 1954. 362p. Bibliog.
Based on interviews of inmates of concentration camps, the author seeks to discover the psychological impact of various forms of oppression. The resulting structure of morality and conduct is laid bare in this systematic study of mankind under brutal conditions.

1278   Ikle, Fred Charles. **The Social Impact of Bomb Destruction.** Norman, University of Oklahoma Press, 1958. 250p. Bibliog.
This technical study of human responses to wartime bombing explores the resultant processes of adjustment and the resiliency of the social systems to physical destruction, disruptions and casualties. Based largely on the experiences of Great Britain, Germany and Japan this work provides an insight to World War II population behavior under stress.

1279   Janis, Irving Lester. **Air War and Emotional Stress: Psychological Studies of Bombing and Civilian Defense.** New York, McGraw-Hill, 1951. 280p. Bibliog.
An evaluation of the psychological effects of air warfare on civilian morale, disaster control and fear and emotional adaptation. The three major parts of the work cover the reactions at Hiroshima and Nagasaki, general effects of air warfare, and psychological aspects of civilian defense.

1280   LaFarge, Henry Adams. **Lost Treasures of Europe.** New York, Pantheon Books, 1946. 39p. (352p. of illus.)
A photographic survey of the great architectural and cultural monuments destroyed or damaged in World War II. The text gives brief histories of the buildings and monuments pictured and the amount of destruction involved.

1281   Roxan, David and Ken Wanstall. **The Rape of Art: The Study of Hitler's Plunder of the Great Masterpieces of Europe.** New York, Coward-McCann, 1965. 195p. Map.
A description of the efforts of the Allies to recover works of art looted by the Nazis and to restore this modern-day wholesale plunder to the owners.

222

1282   Schechtman, Joseph B. **European Population Transfers, 1939-1945.**
New York, Oxford University Press, 1946. 532p. Maps, Bibliog.
This study pertains to the transfer of ethnic groups from country of residence
to the sovereignty of its ethnic homeland. The book describes the exchanges of
population in the eastern European areas of Bulgaria, Hungary and Rumania
through interstate agreements and of Hitler's repatriation of the German minorities of Eastern Europe and South Tyrol.

1283   Snow, Edgar. **People on Our Side.** New York, Random House, 1944.
324p. Maps.
Descriptions, primarily of Russia, China and India, under the pressures of war.
A lucid and readable reflection on the effects of World War II on their people.

INDIVIDUAL COUNTRIES

Germany

1284   Grunberger, Richard. **The 12-Year Reich: A Social History of Nazi
Germany, 1933-1945.** New York, Holt, Rinehart and Winston, 1971.
535p. Bibliog.
A picture of daily living in Nazi Germany drawn from contemporary journals
and the author's interviews. Using a topical approach with subjects such as women,
army, youth, business and religion, this work is an interesting description of the
social structure of the German people and their reactions to Nazi ideology and
control.

1285   Guilleband, Claude William. **The Social Policy of Nazi Germany.**
Cambridge, Eng., The University Press, 1942. 134p. Bibliog.
An analysis of the achievements and underlying philosophy of Nazism in relation
to their social policies. Notes the reasons for the relative contentment of the
working class despite harsh Nazi control.

1286   Kardoff, Ursula von. **Diary of a Nightmare: Berlin, 1942-1945.** New
York, John Day, 1966. 256p.
A journalist for a Berlin non-Nazi paper gives her impressions of life in the German
capital during the last three years of the war. Describes the events and the reactions
of the people in a revealing account of the survival of humanity under adverse
conditions.

1287   Mayer, Milton Sanford. **They Thought They Were Free: The Germans,
1933-1945.** Chicago, University of Chicago Press, 1955. 345p.
A record of conversations by the author with ten Germans who had been party
members, to try to discern how they felt about Nazism. A penetrating and literate
discussion of Hitlerism and its effects on democracy and poeple.

1288   Mosse, George Lachmann. **Nazi Culture: Intellectual, Cultural and Social
Life in the Third Reich.** New York, Grosset and Dunlop, 1966. 386p.
Bibliog.

Using excerpts from plays, novels, government decrees, newspapers, and the speeches and writings of Hitler and other German leaders, the author interprets Nazi culture and explains how the selections illustrate what life was like under Nazi domination.

1289   Phillips, Peter. **The Tragedy of Nazi Germany**. New York, Praeger, 1969.
        241p. Bibliog.
A broad inquiry into the origins of the evil of Hitlerism that attempts to explain the deeper causes of the breakdown of German culture and the collapse of its character and morality.

Great Britain

1290   Beaton, Cecil Walter Hardy. **The Years Between: Diaries, 1939-1944**.
        New York, Holt, Rinehart and Winston, 1965. 352p.
The official photographer of the British Ministry of Information presents sensitive visual descriptions and word sketches of people at war. These wartime photographs along with his war reporting from a photographer's viewpoint comprise the second volume of his diaries.

1291   Calder, Angus. **The People's War: Britain, 1939-1945**. New York, Pantheon,
        1969. 656p. Bibliog.
A narrative of life in wartime Britain drawn from official documents, memoirs and newspapers. Pictures the reactions of the civilian population in the homes, offices, factories and shelters and from among evacuees, refugees and civil defense workers. An examination of the social currents and changes in the arts, industry, churches and other areas as a result of the war.

1292   Dean, Basil. **The Theatre at War**. London, Harrap, 1956. 573p.
An entertaining record of the seven years' existence of the British Entertainments National Service Association and their contribution to national morale. A picture of actors, singers and musicians and the efforts to bring their various performing groups to the fighting fronts.

1293   Hayes, Denis. **Challenge of Conscience: The Story of the Conscientious
        Objectors of 1939-1949**. London, Allen and Unwin, 1949. 406p. Bibliog.
The difficult work of the British Central Board for Conscientious Objectors in representing an unpopular minority during the tensions of war is the focus of this study. This coordinating body for regional and local organizations gave personal and legal advice and represented the conscientious objectors in Parliament and in negotiations with government departments.

1294   Longmate, Norman. **How We Lived Then: A History of Every-Day Life
        During the Second World War**. London, Hutchinson, 1971. 568p. Bibliog.
Concentrating on the ordinary and the typical, the author relates the ways in which the war affected everyday life on Britain's home front. The narrative is drawn from the personal recollections of differing sections of society, occupational groups and areas of the country.

1295   Mosley, Leonard. **Backs to the Wall: The Heroic Story of the People of London During World War II**. New York, Random House, 1971. 430p. Bibliog.

A vivid account of London's struggle for survival during World War II. Seen through the experiences of a people under the pressures of war. A story of heroism and integrity amid instances of government bungling.

1296   O'Brien, Terence Henry. **Civil Defence**. London, H. M. Stationery Office, 1955. 729p. Maps, Bibliog.

Civil defense planning and administration in Great Britain during World War II. The study provides an account of the preparation and application of passive defenses, air raid precautions, disposition of manpower and supply, provision of shelters and the effects of the air raids.

1297   Titmus, Richard Morris. **Problems of Social Policy**. London, H. M. Stationery Office, 1950. 596p. Bibliog.

Describes the social problems in Great Britain resulting from the effects of the war. The stresses within civilian society under bombardment are depicted against the background of the established social services. Topics discussed include the health services, public assistance, evacuation schemes, emergency care and all their interrelationships.

1298   Turner, Ernest Sackville. **The Phoney War**. New York, St. Martin's Press, 1962. 311p.

A description of life in Britain during the first year of the Second World War. This interpretation of the national community under the threat of war is seen against a background of the attitudes, controversies and efforts of a people attempting to cope with the situation.

Italy

1299   Tannenbaum, Edward R. **The Fascist Experience: Italian Society and Culture, 1922-1945**. New York, Basic Books, 1972. 357p. Bibliog.

All phases of life under the Italian fascist regime are included in this survey. Described are the effects of fascist influence and control on the cultural life, education, the church, economy, labor, propaganda and the party within the framework of the daily existence of the people.

United States

1300   Alexander, Charles C. **Nationalism in American Thought, 1930-1945**. Chicago, Rand McNally, 1969. 272p. Bibliog.

Using the concepts of nationalism this intellectual and cultural history describes these developments in every major phase and area of cultural life in the United States. The author relates this theme to depression-inspired demands for national economic planning, the reactions to the government's efforts at greater centralization, the response to involvement in the growing world conflict and to heightened awareness of national values and traditions.

1301   Bosworth, Allen R. **America's Concentration Camps**. New York, Norton,
        1967. 283p. Bibliog.
An angry history of the relocation of Japanese-Americans during the war and
the effects on individuals and family. The author raises some interesting questions
as to why other enemy nationalities were not interned and speculates on the
dangers of the McCarran Act.

1302   Broom, Leonard and John I. Kitsuse. **The Managed Casualty: The Japanese-
        American Family in World War II**. Berkeley, University of California Press,
        1956. 226p. Maps, Bibliog.
The impact of relocation on the family institution through ten family histories.
These case studies present insights into family, ethnic and community relations
and into civil rights problems. Interesting data is shown on the effects of accul-
turation, the transfer of cultural elements from one social group to another.

1303   Butler, Pierce, ed. **Books and Libraries in Wartime**. Chicago, University
        of Chicago Press, 1945. 159p.
A collection of lectures illustrating the effects of war on this cultural area. Areas
covered include the efforts to supply books to the U. S. armed forces, the effects
of war on journalism, the book trade, the reading public and on academic libraries.

1304   Dalfuime, Richard M. **Desegregation of the U. S. Armed Forces: Fighting
        on Two Fronts, 1939-1953**. Columbia, University of Missouri Press,
        1969. 252p. Bibliog.
This study of the development of the policy of desegration within the U. S. armed
forces traces the issues, events, forces and personalities involved in the broad
political and social contexts of the period. The author contends that the pressures
for and against desegregation were primarily civilian inspired and directed.

1305   Girdner, Audrie and Anne Loftis. **The Great Betrayal: The Evacuation
        of the Japanese-Americans During World War II**. New York, Macmillan,
        1969. 562p. Map, Bibliog.
Based on interviews and letters and told largely in the words of the people themselves this unbiased narration tells the story of the evacuation and internment of
over 100,000 West Coast Americans of Japanese ancestry.

1306   Goodman, Jack, ed. **While You Were Gone: A Report on Wartime Life
        in the United States**. New York, Simon and Schuster, 1946. 625p.
A collection of informative essays providing a good representation of the moods
and changes in wartime American civilian life. A recapitulation of the thoughts and
actions of the period.

1307   Havighurst, Robert J. and H. Gerthon Morgan. **The Social History of a
        War-Boom Community**. New York, Longmans, Green, 1951. 356p.
        Maps, Bibliog.
A penetrating sociological case study of the resulting problems when a small town
increases its population five fold in two years due to the influx of wartime industry.
A picture of social change, institutional inertia, and conflicts between old and
new mores.

1308   Kitagawa, Daisuke. **Issei and Nisei: The Internment Years.** New York,
        Seabury Press, 1967. 174p. Bibliog.
A deeply personal account of the internment years. Emphasizing the psychological
and emotional effects on the people and their attitudes toward each other and to
the United States and Japan. Though the internment was unnecessary and cruel
the author notes the decency and understanding of camp officials as a whole. He
also reminds one how hate on racial grounds can affect men of good will and that
laws are still in effect that could allow this to happen again.

1309   Koop, Theodore Frederic. **Weapon of Silence.** Chicago, University of
        Chicago Press, 1946. 304p.
A well documented story by the Assistant Director of the U. S. Office of Censorship of the voluntary censorship of the press and radio and of other aspects of
wartime civilian censorship.

1310   Lingeman, Richard R. **Don't You Know There's a War On? The American
        Home Front, 1941-1945.** New York, Putnam, 1970. 400p. Bibliog.
A carefully researched social history that interrelates domestic, social, economic
and political events with the changes and influences brought about by the war.
This detailed popular account describes the sights and sounds of the period,
letting the events speak for themselves with a human interest perspective, in
recounting the anxieties and frustrations of wartime society.

1311   Mauldin, William Henry. **Up Front.** Cleveland, World, 1945. 228p.
A collection of cartoons accompanied by interpretive text picturing with humor
and understanding the grim reality of the combat infantryman. He translates the
loneliness and sacrifice into a form which helped make a combat soldier's life
a little more bearable.

1312   Merrill, Francis Ellsworth. **Social Problems on the Home Front: A
        Study of War-Time Influences.** New York, Harper, 1948. 258p. Bibliog.
Social upheavals and disorganization in the area of human relationships during
World War II provide the basis for this study. It examines the role and influence
of the war in intensifying or reversing social trends and problems.

1313   Merton, Robert King. **Mass Persuasion: The Social Psychology of a War
        Bond Drive.** New York, Harper, 1946. 210p. Bibliog.
Using the Third War Loan appeal by Kate Smith as a case study, the author
attempts to uncover the dynamics of mass persuasion. He conducted intensive
interviews with a group of one hundred people, and shorter discussions with one
thousand more who heard the broadcasts.

1314   Myer, Dillon Seymour. **Uprooted Americans: The Japanese Americans
        and the War Relocation Authority During World War II.** Tucson, Univer-
        sity of Arizona Press, 1971. 360p. Map, Bibliog.
A portrayal of the problems of the relocation program both in human and administrative terms. A history of the internment of a people caught between an alliance
of political expedience and popular hysteria.

1315   Ogburn, William Fielding, ed. **American Society in Wartime.** Chicago,
        University of Chicago Press, 1943. 237p. Bibliog.
Discussions of the impact of war upon culture in the United States, racial ideologies,
domestic morale and its factors as observed by contemporary sociologists.

1316   Perrett, Geoffrey. **Days of Sadness, Years of Triumph: The American
        People 1939-1945.** New York, Coward, McCann and Geoghegan, 1973.
        512p. Bibliog.
An excellent summary and distillation of wartime society in the United States.
A society that saw massive fundamental social changes in six short years from a
confused and divided country to a strong united world power. This book is con-
cerned with ordinary people and the events which shaped their everyday lives.
An interesting and informative history of the times.

1317   Polenberg, Richard, ed. **America at War: The Home Front, 1941-1945.**
        Englewood Cliffs, N. J., Prentice-Hall, 1968. 175p.
A collection of source readings on the U. S. experience in World War II. Depicts
the problems created, how they were met and the changes in the life of the people
that the war fostered. The work surveys the creation of national unity, the transformation of a stagnant pre-war economy, the regroupings of political forces,
the issues of civil liberties and civil rights, the effects of the war on family life,
the overall social consequences of the war and the various conflicting positions
over U. S. war aims.

1318   Polenberg, Richard. **War and Society: The United States, 1941-1945.**
        Philadelphia, Lippincott, 1972. 298p. Bibliog.
The pattern of changes in the social and economic life of the United States,
brought about by the catalyst of World War II, is the focus of this work. The
author depicts the transformation of the country to a more urban technological
society through modernization and consolidation of agriculture, industry and
government.

1319   Sibley, Mulford Quickert, and Philip E. Jacobs. **Conscription of Conscience:
        The American State and the Conscientious Objector, 1940-1947.** Ithaca, N. Y.
        Cornell University Press, 1952. 580p. Bibliog.
A serious factual study of the treatment of conscientious objectors in the United
States during World War II and immediately thereafter. An analysis of the conflict
between the conscience of an individual and the demands of the state that believes
that it is fighting to protect its social and political values and its ideological ideals.
The authors discuss the role of the objector in the armed forces, alternative civilian
service, government prosecution and detention, and the legal framework of the
problem.

1320   **Studies in Social Psychology in World War II.** Princeton, N. J., Princeton
        University Press, 1949-50. 4v.
This attempt to deal with human behavior on a large scale was accomplished through
studies of the methods and effects of army programs on the soldier. This psycho-
analysis of the reactions of the soldier in the United States Army was designed to
determine how to prevent mistakes which could adversely affect morale. The four

volumes are titled: *The American Soldier: Adjustments During Army Life*; *The American Soldier: Combat and Its Aftermath; Experiments in Mass Communication;* and *Measurement and Prediction*.

1321   Susman, Warren, ed. **Culture and Commitment, 1929-1945.** New York, George Braziller, 1973. 372p. Bibliog.
A cultural study of the forms, patterns and symbols used by primarily middle class America to deal with the experiences of a deep economic depression and a long world war.

1322   Thomas, Dorothy Swaine. **Japanese Evacuation and Resettlement.** Berkeley, University of California Press, 1946-54. 3v. Bibliog.
These three distinct volumes study the social, psychological and legal aspects of the evacuation and resettlement of persons with Japanese ancestry in the United States during World War II. The first volume deals with those Japanese who were branded as disloyal and sent to a separate center. Volume two narrates the story of the one in three who were allowed to leave the camps in 1943 and 1944 to resettle in the Middle West and the East. Volume three investigates the whole question from historical, social, psychological and legal aspects of the effects of the surrender of democratic practices in times of national stress.

1323   White, Leonard Dupee, ed. **Civil Service in Wartime.** Chicago, University of Chicago Press, 1945. 253p.
Ten lectures on the recruitment of executive talent, the mobilization of the nation's professional manpower resources and the wartime administration and transformation of the civil service. This record of the problems faced by the U. S. government in its staffing problems points out the successes and failures encountered in meeting constant emergency situations and problems.

1324   Wyman, David S. **Paper Walls: America and the Refugee Crisis, 1938-1941.** Amherst, University of Massachusetts Press, 1968. 306p. Bibliog.
A documented and critical analysis of U. S. immigration and refugee policies. The study seeks to provide an understanding of the social forces and pressures behind official and unofficial policy.

CHAPTER 9–OCCUPATION AND RESISTANCE

OCCUPATION AND MILITARY GOVERNMENTS

General

1325   Friedrich, Carl Joachim, ed. **American Experiences in Military Government in World War II.** New York, Rinehart, 1948. 436p. Map, Bibliog.
The book deals with the broad general aspects of U. S. experience in military government with a contrasting picture, for comparison, of Axis occupation policies. More specific detail is provided in descriptive sections on the operations of the military governments of Austria, France, Germany, Italy and the Pacific areas.

1326   Holborn, Hajo. **American Military Government: Its Organization and Policies.** Washington, Infantry Journal Press, 1947. 243p. Maps, Bibliog.
This study of U. S. military government during and since World War II is especially useful in its description of the difficulties of coordinating the various occupation policies of the Allies. Extensive documentation is appended to the text.

Africa

1327   Rennell, Francis James Rennell Rodd. **British Military Administration of Occupied Territories in Africa During the War Years, 1941-1947.** London, H. M. Stationery Office, 1948. 637p. Maps, Bibliog.
The record of British military administration of the occupied territories in Africa and some of its environs. A description of the administrative organization, local agreement and directives regarding Ethiopia, Eritrea, the Somalilands, Madagascar, the northeast African areas, the Dodecanese Islands, the Middle East and East Africa. Separate chapters deal with international and internal laws, finance, trade, and custody of enemy property as they apply to the areas at large.

Belgium

1328   Goris, Jan Albert, ed. **Belgium Under Occupation.** New York, Moretus Press, 1947. 240p.
A description of German occupation policies and their effect on the Belgian economy, education, religion, and the judiciary. Nazi forced labor and deportation practices are reviewed along with national reactions to German occupation in the press and through the resistance movement.

Burma

1329   Nu, U. (Thakin). **Burma Under the Japanese: Pictures and Portraits.** New York, St. Martin's Press, 1954. 132p.
An account of the Japanese occupation from 1942 to 1945 by the wartime Minister of Foreign Affairs in the Japanese sanctioned Burmese government and of the conflicts which faced the country's nationalist leaders. This is also a defense of the puppet regime and his participation in it.

Czechoslovakia

1330   Mastny, Vojtech. **The Czechs Under Nazi Rule: The Failure of National Resistance, 1939-1942.** New York, Columbia University Press, 1971. 274p. Bibliog.
A study of German policy towards Bohemia and Moravia and Czech responses to the occupation. Notes the role of Benes and the Czech government in exile, the maneuvers of collaborationist elements in the country and the attitudes and behavior of Czech authorities. The author feels that the people were too accommodating, though essentially patriotic, in the face of German pressure.

Estonia

1331   Oras, Ants. **Baltic Eclipse.** London, V. Gollancz, 1948. 307p.
An account of the events and conditions in Estonia from 1939 to 1946. Their experiences in the Soviet occupation of this small Baltic nation to subsequent German occupation and the eventual Soviet re-occupation.

Europe

1332   Donnison, Frank S. V. **Civil Affairs and Military Government: Northwest Europe, 1944-1946.** London, H. M. Stationery Office, 1961. 518p. Maps, Bibliog.
A study of the British military responsibility for the civil administration of the liberated friendly countries and of conquered German territory. Well detailed is the organization created, the civil affairs agreements with the liberated nations, operational plans, the establishment of the military government for Germany and Austria and the preparations for the quadripartite Control Commission.

1333   Lemkin, Rafal. **Axis Rule in Occupied Europe: Laws of Occupation, Analysis of Government, Proposals for Redress.** Washington, Carnegie Endowment for International Peace, Division of International Law, 1944. 674p. Bibliog.
A study of organization of the Axis occupying government in each country, the texts of the basic laws and decrees promulgated by both the occupier and the puppet regime established and the purposes and application of these measures within the general scheme of conquest.

1334   Littlejohn, David. **The Patriotic Traitors: A History of Collaboration in German-Occupied Europe, 1940-45.** London, Heinemann, 1972. 391p. Maps, Bibliog.
Devoting a chapter to each of the occupied countries in the order of their invasion, the author sets out the story of the factors behind the incidences of collaboration with the Nazis and the puppet regimes.

1335   Toynbee, Arnold Joseph and Veronica Toynbee, eds. **Hitler's Europe.** New York, Oxford University Press, 1954. 730p.
This volume, in the series Survey of International Affairs, provides a comprehensive panorama of the government of Nazi Germany and the German occupied areas.

Delves into the political and economic structures of these occupied areas of western, eastern and southern Europe. This is considered to be one of the principal works of this period of history.

Far East

1336   Donnison, Frank S. V. **British Military Administration in the Far East, 1943-46.** London, H. M. Stationery Office, 1956. 483p. Maps.
One of the most interesting of the volumes in the United Kingdom Military Series in that it shows how the re-establishment of Allied authority was complicated by the nationalist aspirations fanned by the Japanese during their occupation. The areas discussed were all part of the territories of the Allied powers before the war and the reassertion of authority was a particular problem. The primary areas covered are Borneo, Burma, Hong Kong, and Malaya with smaller sections on Indo-China and Indonesia.

1337   Ward, Robert S. **Asia for the Asiatics? The Techniques of Japanese Occupation.** Chicago, University of Chicago Press, 1945. 204p. Map.
A systematic analysis of the techniques used by the Japanese to control, exploit and assimilate an area and their methods in using it as a base for continued expansion.

France

1338   Walter, Gerard. **Paris Under the Occupation.** New York, Orion Press, 1960. 209p. Bibliog.
An absorbing picture, derived from newspaper accounts, of life in Paris during the years of German occupation from 1940 into 1944. The translated extracts are introduced and joined together through the use of descriptive paragraphs.

Great Britain (Channel Islands)

1339   Wood, Alan, and Mary Wood. **Islands in Danger: The Story of the German Occupation of the Channel Islands, 1940-45.** New York, Macmillan, 1956. 255p. Maps.
An unusual sidelight on the war of the occupation of an English-speaking British area. Told with vivid human detail, it recounts the "correct" behavior between the population and the German occupiers of Guernsey, Alderney and Sark.

Greece

1340   Argenti, Philip Pandely. **The Occupation of Chios by the Germans and Their Administration of the Island.** Cambridge, Cambridge University Press, 1966, 375p. Maps, Bibliog.
Based on contemporary official and quasi-official documents, this is a description of the German occupying administration of one of the major islands of the Aegean Archipelago. Recounts the relations between the Germans and the local Greek authorities, life on the island under the occupation, the local resistance movement and the events leading to the island's liberation.

1341   Tsatsou, Ioanna. **The Sword's Fierce Edge: A Journal of the Occupation of
        Greece, 1941-1944.** Nashville, Tenn., Vanderbilt University Press, 1969. 131p.
An account of the struggle against the oppression of Italian and German rule.
Describes the life of civilian women during the years of occupation.

1342   Zotos, Stephanos. **Greece: The Struggle for Freedom.** New York, Crowell,
        1967. 194p. Bibliog.
A chronological narrative by an interpreter and liaison officer between the Greek
and British armies, of Greece's years of occupation, liberation and internal strife.
The emphasis is on the period to 1946 and is an eyewitness overview of the Greek
will to survive, their capacity for endurance and their basic individualism. The
account is laced with personal stories, conversations and impressions of the period.

Indonesia

1343   Benda, Harry Jindrich. **The Crescent and the Rising Sun: Indonesian
        Islam Under the Japanese Occupation, 1942-1945.** The Hague, W. Van
        Hoeve, 1958. 320p. Bibliog.
A well documented reinterpretation of pre-war Indonesian Islam under Dutch
rule and a study of the underlying motives of Japanese Islamic policy. The book
attempts to trace the evolution of Indonesian Islam and the complex role it
played in modern Indonesia's political history under foreign rule. Part one looks
at the subject in the context of Dutch colonial rule. Part two covers the eventful
forty months of Japanese occupation and their attempts to weld Islamic leadership
within a Japanese sponsored unity of all Islamic organizations in the interests of
a greater East Asia. This Muslim oriented direction served to strengthen Islamic
leadership to the detriment of political nationalistic groups.

1344   Benda, Harry Jindrich, James K. Irikura, and Koichi Kishi, eds.
        Japanese Military Administration in Indonesia: Selected Documents.
        New Haven, Yale University Press, 1965. 279p.
This volume of selected documents provides a significant picture of Japanese
administrative policies, their central guidelines on economic policy and the administrative rivalry between the Japanese army and navy. Of special interest is the documentation of the measures adopted by the military occupation administration
in support of Indonesian nationalism.

Italy

1345   Harris, Charles Reginald Schiller. **Allied Military Administration of Italy,
        1943-1945.** London, H. M. Stationery Office, 1957. 479p. Maps, Bibliog.
A description of the precedents established in the occupation of a non-colonial
enemy territory, that set the pattern for the rest of Western Europe. It describes
the formation and functioning of a jointly conducted Anglo-American military
government. The situation was further complicated when the Italians subsequently
became co-belligerents with the Allies.

Netherlands

1346   Maass, Walter B. **The Netherlands at War: 1940-1945.** New York, Abelard-
        Schuman, 1970. 264p. Map, Bibliog.
A first hand account of the German occupation by an active member of the Dutch
resistance. Particular attention is given to the Dutch underground movement and
to the work of Allied and German espionage.

1347   Meerloo, Joost Abraham Maurits. **Total War and the Human Mind: A
        Psychologist's Experiences in Occupied Holland.** New York, International
        Universities Press, 1945. 78p.
An interesting exploration of the effects of Nazi propaganda and terrorism on the
Dutch people.

1348   Warmbrunn, Werner. **The Dutch Under German Occupation, 1940-1945.**
        Stanford, Calif., Stanford University Press, 1963. 338p. Bibliog.
A detailed and well documented study of the behavior of a people under an occupying totalitarian rule, noting basic human reactions to the circumstances of their
occupation. The author contends that the Dutch traditional respect for bureaucratic authority tended to erode the spirit of resistance. Part one discusses events
prior to the occupation, part two the German administration and the Dutch
Nationalist Socialist movement, part three discusses Dutch reactions and part four
consists of the author's conclusions on Dutch response to the occupation.

Philippines

1349   Agoncillo, Teodoro A. **The Fateful Years: Japan's Adventure in the
        Philippines, 1941-1945.** Quezon City, Philippines, R. P. Garcia Pub. Co.,
        1965. 2v. Maps, Bibliog.
An assessment of the period of Japanese occupation from the Filipino point of
view. In sympathy with the Filipino wartime administration, the author describes
the hardships the country faced and the administrative measures forced upon the
Philippine government to support Japanese policies.

1350   Steinberg, David Joel. **Philippine Collaboration in World War II.** Ann
        Arbor, University of Michigan Press, 1967. 235p. Bibliog.
A valuable work for an understanding of the dimensions of Philippine collaboration
during the Japanese occupation. The focus of this history of wartime collaboration
is on the leadership supplied by the conservative Philippine oligarchy to the puppet
regime, the same group that had supplied Philippine political leadership to the
Americans.

Russia

1351   Dallin, Alexander. **German Rule in Russia, 1941-45: A Study of Occu-
        pation Policies.** New York, St. Martin's Press, 1957. 695p. Maps, Bibliog.
A basic work on German policies and actions in the occupied areas of the U.S.S.R.
during the German invasion, their occupation and retreat and the reaction of Soviet
citizens to these policies and actions.

1352   Kamenetsky, Ihor. **Hitler's Occupation of Ukraine, 1941-1944: A Study of Totalitarian Imperialism.** Milwaukee, Marquette University Press, 1956. 101p. Bibliog.

The account of one of the shortest occupations in the Ukraine's history but one with the heaviest losses in life and property. This area in Hitler's Lebensraum theory was one of his principal objectives for German agricultural colonization. The study is concerned with the character and procedure of the Nazi occupation, the background and circumstances of Germany's temporary success and the reasons for its eventual failure.

1353   Reitlinger, Gerald Roberts. **The House Built on Sand: The Conflicts of German Policy in Russia, 1939-1945.** New York, Viking Press, 1960. 459p. Maps, Bibliog.

A perceptive analysis of German occupation policies in the Soviet Union which resulted in the savage extermination of millions of people. A well documented study of Nazi civil government policy, the major partisan problem, and the treatment of Russian prisoners of war. Presents a good discussion of the German sponsored Russian Liberation Movement which ran counter to prevailing German policies toward Russians.

RESISTANCE AND UNDERGROUND ACTIVITIES

General

1354   Mao Tse-tung. **On Guerrilla Warfare.** New York, Praeger, 1961. 114p.

A primary source on guerrilla tactics, this analysis sets forth the principles, objectives, theory and operations of guerrilla warfare. A good introduction provides a succinct review of the subject as a whole.

Albania

1355   Amery, Julian. **Sons of the Eagle: A Study in Guerrilla War.** London, Macmillan, 1948. 354p. Maps.

The author, variously associated with resistance movements in the Balkans from 1940 to 1945, relates his experiences in one particular area of emphasis. He describes his role in organizing Albanian resistance to the occupying Italians and with his primary task of persuading the various political factions to work together toward a common purpose. The two main resistance groups were the communist directed partisans and the conservative Ballist faction.

Burma

1356   Fellowes-Gordon, Ian. **Amiable Assassins: The Story of the Kachin Guerrillas of North Burma.** London, Hale, 1957. 159p.

The story of the native Kachin Levies of Burma and their British led guerrilla war against the Japanese during the period 1942-1944.

China

1357   Miles, Milton E. **A Different Kind of War: The Little-Known Story of the Combined Guerrilla Forces Created in China by the U.S. Navy and the Chinese during World War II.** Garden City, N.Y., Doubleday, 1967. 629p. Maps.
A narrative of the Sino-American Co-operative Organization and its guerrilla war against the Japanese. The organizer and deputy commander under the Chinese Nationalists presents penetrating observations on U. S. policy towards China, towards the Chinese Communists, and the conflicts which developed between the author's group, the Office of Strategic Services and the U. S. Army.

Czechoslovakia

1358   Burgess, Alan. **Seven Men at Daybreak.** New York, Dutton, 1960. 231p.
A reconstruction, from records and interviews with the survivors, of the underground mission of a group of free Czechs to assassinate the Nazi Reinhard Heydrich. A picture of the courage, daring, frustrations, success and final tragedy of this episode in Czech resistance.

1359   Wiener, Jan G. **The Assassination of Heydrich.** New York, Grossman, 1969. 177p.
Traces the story behind the assassination, presenting a vivid picture of the courage and tenacity of Czech resistance. Describes in detail the events connected with the subsequent reprisal of the Germans and the destruction of Lidice.

Denmark

1360   Bennett, Jeremy. **British Broadcasting and the Danish Resistance Movement, 1940-1945: A Study of the Wartime Broadcasts of the B.B.C. Danish Service.** Cambridge, England, Cambridge University Press, 1966. 266p. Bibliog.
This is an analysis of the organization, work and effects of the wartime broadcasting of the Danish section of the British Broadcasting Corporation. A discussion also of the BBC's policies and their evolution toward German occupied Denmark. Their usefulness in fulfilling a deep psychological need of the people is seen within the general context of this type of political warfare.

1361   Flender, Harold. **Rescue in Denmark.** New York, Simon and Schuster, 1963. 281p. Bibliog.
An historical and sociological study of why Denmark, virtually alone in Europe, resisted Nazi designs on the Jews. This account of Danish resistance describes the thwarting in 1943 of Nazi plans to deport the Danish Jews to concentration camps and the successful exodus of the great majority of them to Sweden.

1362   Lampe, David. **The Savage Canary: The Story of Resistance in Denmark.** London, Cassell, 1957. 236p. Map.
The story of the work of five years of Danish underground resistance that was labeled by Field Marshal Montgomery as second to none. A description of a highly

effective underground press, accounts of sabotage operations, the liberation of captured resistance members and the aiding of the escape of 7,200 out of 7,770 Danish Jews.

Europe

1363   International Conference on the History of Resistance Movements. **European Resistance Movements, 1939-1945.** lst, Liege, 1958, New York, Pergamon Press, 1960, 410p. Maps, Bibliog. 2nd, Milan, 1961. New York, Macmillan, 1964. 663p. Bibliog. 3rd, Karlsbad, Bohemia, 1963, Karlovy Vary, 1963, pp. varies per translation of French, German, English or Russian. 4th, Vienna, 1965, Milano, Committee Secretariat c/o Institute Nazionale per la Storia del Movimento de Liberazione in Italia, 1965.

Multilingual presentations on the resistance movements and their role in Europe. The first conference includes topics on resistance in Germany and Italy, psychological warfare, concentration camps, Jewish resistance, guerrilla movements in France, Poland and Yugoslavia and relations between the Allies and the various resistance movements. This latter topic was used as the main theme of the second conference in which the relationships of the Allies to resistance movements in Europe are discussed separately by country. The third conference was held in Bohemia and the fourth in Vienna. This latter conference was concerned with the problems of documentation and method in the research on European resistance movements.

1364   Michel, Henri. **The Shadow War: European Resistance, 1939-1945.** New York, Harper and Row, 1972. 416p. Bibliog.

The author traces the development of resistance movements throughout Europe and their position in relation to the Allies and the occupying forces. Describes and analyzes its component parts, how and from where it drew its membership, how it was equipped, and the tactics used in the various countries the resistance was active in. The author notes the similarities and divergencies of operations using examples of individual and local actions. He concludes that if nothing else the moral importance of resistance was great.

1365   Seth, Ronald. **The Undaunted: The Story of Resistance in Western Europe.** London, Muller, 1956. 327p. Bibliog.

The purpose of this work is to provide an idea of the scope of the resistance movements in Western Europe, Yugoslavia and Greece. Essentially an account, for each country covered, of the origins, development and contribution to the Allied cause of resistance activities. An interesting chapter is the description of the resistance movement in Luxembourg whose Grand Duchess, on fleeing from the German invasion, found the time to declare war on Germany.

France

1366   Benouville, Guillain de. **The Unknown Warriors: A Personal Account of the French Resistance.** New York, Simon and Schuster, 1949. 372p. Map.

The history of the gradual development of the French resistance from July 1940 by the holder of a top post in the movement. In this manual on large-scale guerrilla operations in occupied territory he writes about the figures in the movement, its adventures and despairs.

1367   Bird, Michael J. **The Secret Battalion**. New York, Holt, Rinehart and
        Winston, 1964. 189p.
The narrative of the disastrous set piece battle fought between the 500 Free French Maquis and the 10,000 Germans and Vichy forces in March of 1944. The work describes the cleavages betwen various resistance groups and their relations with Vichy France. This is also basically an account of the heroism, honor, cowardice and treachery that culminated in the defeat of this band of Maquis.

1368   Braddon, Russell. **The White Mouse**. New York, Norton, 1956. 255p.
A vivid picture of the experiences of a member of the Maquis who helped prisoners to escape. Her work against the Nazis in France and with the resistance is told with verve. Provides a good picture of some of the resistance leadership.

1369   Collier, Richard. **Ten Thousand Eyes**. New York, Dutton, 1958. 320p.
The story of the activities of the French undergound movement called the Century Network which gave the Allies the Atlantic Wall defense plans, plotted gun positions and strong points for the D-Day invasion. The group was made up of people in all walks of life led by a few full-time resistance leaders.

1370   Ehrlich, Blake. **Resistance: France 1940-1945**. Boston, Little, Brown,
        1965. 278p. Maps.
A systematic and factual account of French resistance and the disparate efforts of the British, American and Free French to direct and supply them. Covers the period from the collapse of France into the last months of the war. Notes the role of the communist partisan group, the FTP (Francs-Tireurs et Partisans).

1371   Fuller, Jean Overton. **Madeleine: The Story of Noor Inayat Khan, George
        Cross, M.B.E., Croix De Guerre with Gold Star**. London, Gollancz,
        1952. 192p.
For annotation, see item 1450.

1372   Liebling, Abbot Joseph. **The Republic of Silence**. New York, Harcourt,
        Brace, 1947. 522p. Maps.
A chronicle of the actions of the French underground giving a contemporary history of the movement through articles, essays and short stories written by some of its members.

1373   Marshall, Bruce. **The White Rabbit.** Boston, Houghton Mifflin, 1953.
        262p.
This story of adventure and suspense, a chronicle of man's spirit and ability to
survive and succeed, tells of the role of Wing Commander F. F. E. Yeo-Thomas
of the R.A.F. in the French resistance. The qualities of his courage and leadership
are portrayed in this skillful recording of the events he was involved in.

1374   Millar, George Reid. **Waiting in the Night: A Story of the Maquis, Told
        by One of its Leaders.** Garden City, N. Y., Doubleday, 1946. 377p.
The story of a British officer who was specially trained to work with the French
Maquis to train them in the use of the new weapons being supplied to them just
prior to D-Day. An exciting account of adventure and sabotage.

1375   Novick, Peter. **The Resistance Versus Vichy: The Purge of Collaborators
        in Liberated France.** New York, Columbia University Press, 1968. 245p.
        Bibliog.
An excellent detailed study of the struggles of the resistance against the Vichy
regime and the subsequent actions against Vichy and Nazi collaborationists upon
France's liberation.

1376   Vomecourt, Philippe de. **An Army of Amateurs.** Garden City, N. Y.,
        Doubleday, 1961. 307p.
A lively account of the crises and strains of the operations of the group of the
French underground directed by the British Special Operations Executive. Details
their relations with other groups of the French resistance.

Italy

1377   Battaglia, Roberto. **The Story of the Italian Resistance.** London, Odhams
        Press, 1957. 287p.
A history of the active anti-German partisan movements in Italy from 1943 to
the end of the German occupation. The events are seen from the Italian point of
view.

Malaya

1378   Chapman, Frederick Spencer. **The Jungle Is Neutral.** New York, Norton,
        1949. 384p. Maps.
The description of resistance in Japanese occupied Malaya by a leading authority
on the subject. An incredible adventure describing three years in the life of a
Chinese guerrilla unit. A well written honest and effective personal narrative of
organized guerrilla resistance.

Netherlands

1379   Martens, Allard and Daphne Dunlop. **The Silent War: Glimpses of the
        Dutch Underground and Views on the Battle of Arnhem.** London, Hodder
        and Stroughton, 1961. 318p. Bibliog.

The story of the Dutch resistance movement and the different tactics it had to develop due to the terrain and dense population of the country. The situation posed another major problem in that the occupying administration was not under the German army as in France or Belgium but under the Nazi Party whose purpose was to eventually incorporate the country in the Third Reich. The Dutch resistance excelled in passing intelligence to the Allies and in maintaining the morale of the population through an excellent underground press.

Norway

1380   Astrup, Helen and B. L. Jacot. **Oslo Intrigue: A Woman's Memoir of the Norwegian Resistance.** New York, McGraw-Hill, 1954. 237p.
The record of a personal experience with the Norwegian underground that presents a good picture of the inside operations of a resistance movement and of German reactions in dealing with Norwegian resistance.

1381   Haukelid, Knut Anders. **Skis Against the Atom.** London, Kimber, 1954. 201p. Maps.
The story of the destruction of the German heavy water plant in Norway and the sinking of the ferry carrying a crucial shipment of this vital ingredient for Germany's atomic research. The author describes the work involved in organizing resistance in Norway along with excellent descriptions of operations in the snow covered Norwegian mountains.

1382   Manus, Max. **9 Lives Before 30.** Garden City, N. Y., Doubleday, 1947. 328p.
An account of absorbing interest of the author's experiences as a leader in the Norwegian underground that harried the Gestapo in Norway for five wartime years.

Philippines

1383   Harkins, Philip. **Blackburn's Headhunters.** New York, Norton, 1955. 326p.
The experiences of a U. S. Army officer in the organization of guerrilla operations in the Philippines. In this personal narrative he describes the tactics of evasion, escapes, endless pursuit and security problems in the face of constant enemy counter activity.

1384   Ingham, Travis. **Rendezvous by Submarine: The Story of Charles Parsons and the Guerrilla-Soldiers in the Philippines.** Garden City, N. Y., Doubleday, Doran, 1945. 255p.
This account of the planning and execution of guerrilla operations in the Philippines describes the tasks of military and morale building that faced one of the noted leaders of Philippine resistance.

1385   Volckmann, Russell W. **We Remained: Three Years Behind the Enemy Lines in the Philippines.** New York, Norton, 1954. 244p.

A U. S. Army colonel's experiences as a guerrilla leader in the Philippines. A vivid description of the problems of supply and security and of the techniques employed by the guerrillas against the Japanese forces.

1386   Wolfert, Ira. **American Guerrilla in the Philippines**. New York, Simon and
         Schuster, 1945. 222p. Map.
A swift-paced story of the exploits of a U. S. Navy officer with the guerrilla
band of Philippine Colonel Kangleon. This narrative, told with journalistic crisp-
ness, tells of the courage, initiative and cunning required in combatting the Japanese
and in the task of keeping General MacArthur informed of the situation in Leyte.

Poland

1387   Komorowski, Tadeusz. **The Secret Army**. New York, Macmillan, 1951.
         407p.
The explicit account of the Warsaw rising by one of the organizers of the Polish
underground movement and the Commander of the Home Army.

1388   Korbonski, Stefan. **Fighting Warsaw: The Story of the Polish Underground
         State, 1939-1945**. New York, Macmillan, 1956. 495p.
A description of the Polish underground movement from 1939 to 1945 by its last
head. He portrays the rise and feeling of the Polish national spirit, the conspira-
torial atmosphere, and the complicated relations between the Polish government
in exile in London and the underground leadership in Warsaw. An absorbing account
conveying the sense of the resistance in vivid detail.

1389   Zagorski, Waclaw. **Seventy Days**. London, Muller, 1957. 267p.
The daily story from July 30 to October 7, 1944 of the uprising and struggles of
the Polish Home Army in the battle to rid Warsaw of German troops upon the
approach of Soviet forces. Despite assurances of Soviet aid and support, the Soviet
troops stopped at the Vistula which was all that separated them from the Poles.
This abandoned the Home Army, and its potential postwar source of Polish leadership, to an aroused and reinforced German force.

Russia

1390   Armstrong, John Alexander. **Soviet Partisans in World War II**. Madison,
         University of Wisconsin Press, 1964. 792p. Maps, Bibliog.
A comprehensive analytical work on the Soviet partisan movement based on a
wide range of Soviet materials. Describes the movement's role in Soviet political
strategy including specific studies of the experiences and significance of the movement, its origins, doctrine, operations and effectiveness. Also contributes to the
understanding of the social and political aspects of Soviet irregular warfare.

1391   Dixon, Cecil Aubrey, and Otto Heilbrunn. **Communist Guerrilla Warfare**.
         New York, Praeger, 1962. 229p. Maps, Bibliog.
A reprint of a 1955 publication, this general study of Soviet partisan and German
anti-partisan activity shows clearly the political importance of the movement and
the principles both sides followed. Describes the principles of guerrilla warfare as

advanced by Mao Tse-tung and further perfected by the Soviets during the German occupation of Russia. A very good description of Soviet guerrillas in action, their organization and tactical tasks, the German formed anti-guerrillas and the final integration of the Soviet guerrillas into regular army units.

Thailand

1392   Smith, Nicol and Blake Clark. **Into Siam, Underground Kingdom.**
        Indianapolis, Bobbs-Merrill, 1946. 315p. Maps.
The formation of an underground system in Thailand in World War II by U. S. educated Thai. This is the story of their training and preparation by the O.S.S. and of their subsequent activities.

Yugoslavia

1393   Deakin, Frederick William. **The Embattled Mountain.** New York,
        Oxford University Press, 1971. 284p. Maps, Bibliog.
The account of the joint commander of the first British military mission to establish liaison with Tito and to report on the potential of this partisan movement to the Allied cause. Set in the mountains of Montenegro this is a vivid description of the Yugoslav Communist partisan's struggle against the German occupation. The author's dispatches helped to swing British support from the royalist Mihailovic to Tito.

1394   Dedijer, Vladimir. **With Tito Through the War: Partisan Diary, 1941-1944.**
        London, Hamilton, 1951. 403p.
A narrative of the events and the personal reactions of a member of the Yugoslav Communist Party whose work brought him in constant contact with Tito and other partisan leaders. Describes the long struggle against the Italians, Germans and Royalist forces. Provides an insight into internal conditions and fortunes of the partisan movement from their point of view.

1395   Maclean, Fitzroy. **Escape to Adventure.** Boston, Little, Brown, 1950.
        419p. Maps.
The first part is a narrative of the author's travels in the Central Asian regions of the Soviet Union in the last three years of the 1930s. An excellent picture of an area rarely seen by foreigners, especially a member of the British Foreign Service stationed in Moscow. The second section describes his adventures in the western desert of North Africa as an officer in the British Special Services in World War II. However, about half of this interesting book is concerned with his participation in the Yugoslav guerrilla war as Churchill's envoy to Tito. His mission was initially to form an estimate of the possible contributions to the Allied cause of Tito's partisans and subsequently to direct Allied aid to Tito and his forces. Altogether good reading with much excitement and suspense.

1396   Roberts, Walter R. **Tito, Mihailovic and the Allies, 1941/1945.** New
        Brunswick, N.J., Rutgers University Press, 1973. 406p. Map, Bibliog.
The origins and development of the two resistance movements in Yugoslavia and their relationship to the Allies, the Yugoslav government-in-exile and between

each other. A very thorough study of one of the most active resistance movements
in World War II. Describes the aims and aspirations of the Royalist Cetniks and
the Communist Partisans. Emphasis is given to Yugoslav-U. S. relations.

1397   Rootham, Japer. **Miss Fire: The Chronicle of a British Mission to
        Mihailovich, 1943-1944**. London, Chatto and Windus, 1946. 224p. Map.
A record of events in Eastern Serbia between May 1943 and June 1944. The
author found that the policy of British support to anyone who was against the
Axis and said they were willing to act did not take into account the complicated
Yugoslav question of nationalities and religious rivalry between the Serbs, Croats
and Slovenes. This is the story of the steady loss of confidence by the British
in Mihailovich and his movement and in the growth of a basic suspicion of each
other due to the subsequent British policy of—no action against the Germans—no
support.

ANTI-FASCIST, ANTI-NAZI, AND ANTI-SOVIET MOVEMENTS

Anti-Fascist Movements in Italy

1398   Delzell, Charles F. **Mussolini's Enemies: The Italian Anti-Fascist
        Resistance**. Princeton, N. J., Princeton University Press, 1961. 620p.
        Bibliog.
An assessment of the development and significance of anti-fascism in Italy from
1924 to 1946. Covers the periods of clandestine opposition to the Fascist regime
from 1924 to 1943 and the armed resistance by various anti-fascist groups from
1943 to 1945.

1399   Rosengarten, Frank. **The Italian Anti-Fascist Press (1919-1945): From
        the Legal Opposition Press to the Underground Newspapers of World
        War II**. Cleveland, Case Western Reserve University, 1968. 253p.
        Bibliog.
A well balanced account and analysis of the Italian resistance press in terms of
its ideological variety and programs within the political climate of the Fascist
state. This active and lively oppostition to the regime thrived underground for
two decades and was composed of various competing anti-fascist groups each with
its own interpretation of fascism. These various ideological components of anti-
fascist thought arose from the Christian Democratic, Communist, Republican and
Socialist political groups.

Anti-Nazi Movements in Germany

1400   Andreas-Friedrich, Ruth. **Berlin Underground, 1938-1945**. New York,
        Holt, 1947. 312p.
A testimony to the fact that there were people in Germany willing to help Jews,
helping men to dodge the draft, and in spreading defeatism, all activities which
carried the death penalty or shipment to a concentration camp. The group written
about were people who could have easily left the country earlier but chose to
remain and help those in need for the love of their country.

1401   Balfour, Michael Leonard Graham, and Julian Frisby. **Helmuth Von Moltke:**
        A Leader Against Hitler. New York, St. Martin's Press, 1973. 388p. Bibliog.
The life and political career of a member of a famous German military family who
led anti-Nazi and anti-Hitler underground groups. Their approach differed in that
they disapproved of any assassination attempts. Recounts the part Moltke played
in the resistance movement known as the Kreisau Group. Provides the flavor of
daily life in wartime Germany. The Count served in the German Abwehr as an
international law expert and was arrested in January 1944 and subsequently
executed.

1402   Bethge, Eberhard. **Dietrich Bonhoeffer: Man of Vision, Man of Courage.**
        New York, Harper and Row, 1970. 867p.
An early member of the resistance movement within the German Evangelical
Church. Describes another aspect of anti-Nazi resistance and Bonhoeffer's involvement in the various plots against Hitler and the Nazi regime. Traces the development
of his theology as an academic theologian and of his career which was fundamentally
affected by the Nazi rise to power, reflecting the dilemma of many Germans of the
time. He was eventually executed in a Nazi concentration camp.

1403   Boehm, Eric H., ed. **We Survived: Fourteen Histories of the Hidden and**
        the Hunted of Nazi Germany. Santa Barbara, Calif., Clio Press, 1966.
        316p.
This reprint of the 1949 edition includes a new epilogue. It presents the stories
of fourteen people hiding from persecution in Nazi Germany. People from many
walks of life and persuasion who had to lead underground "illegal" existences
either because they were Jews or because of their anti-Nazi stand.

1404   Brandt, Willy. **In Exile: Essays, Reflections and Letters, 1933-1947.**
        London, Wolff, 1971. 264p. Bibliog.
A lucid record of the thoughts of an outspoken advocate of freedom and
democracy. Firmly anti-Nazi but never anti-German he defines the difference
between Nazism as an ideology and Germany as a state. He describes his clandestine experiences in resistance work with the Norwegian underground during his
exile in Norway.

1405   Deutsch, Harold Charles. **The Conspiracy Against Hitler in the Twilight**
        War. Minneapolis, University of Minnesota Press, 1968. 394p. Bibliog.
A carefully researched study of the clandestine effort from September 1939 to
May 1940 to find some way to overthrow Hitler and stop the war. A prime concern
was to insure a functioning government through the crisis. The failure to gain the
support of the army's leadership doomed these efforts to failure.

1406   Donohoe, James. **Hitler's Conservative Opponents in Bavaria, 1939-1945:**
        A Study of Catholic, Monarchist, and Separatist Anti-Nazi Activities.
        Leiden, Brill, 1961. 348p. Bibliog.
Details the extent and influence of the opposition of Catholic conservatives in
Bavaria to the Nazi regime. The author's thesis is that in defending the liberty
of the Catholic Church, its laymen found themselves advocating political

opposition to the regime. The author also gives some good detail on the Munich Student Revolt in 1943.

1407   Dulles, Allen Welsh. **Germany's Underground.** New York, Macmillan, 1947. 207p.
An authoritative account of German anti-Hitler activities showing the parts played by the military, politicians, church and academic circles in the movement. The author was the World War II O.S.S. station chief for Germany operating out of Switzerland from November 1942 to the end of the war. He theorizes that the conspiracy to assassinate Hitler was a ramification of a growing moral resistance to Nazism within Germany.

1408   FitzGibbon, Constantine. **20 July.** New York, Norton, 1956. 285p. Bibliog.
A scholarly reappraisal of the German officers' conspiracy to overthrow Hitler that culminated in the attempt to assassinate the German leader. The earlier failures of the conspiracy are well detailed.

1409   Gallin, Mary Alice. **German Resistance to Hitler: Ethical and Religious Factors.** Washington, Catholic University of America Press, 1962. 259p. Bibliog.
A perceptive analysis of the German Christian anti-Hitler movement. Probes the ethical problems involved of those who turned against their government distinguishing also between peacetime and wartime attitude differences in the issues involved.

1410   **The German Resistance to Hitler.** Berkeley, University of California Press, 1970. 281p. Bibliog.
A collection of five essays on various aspects of the German resistance movement in the nation's foreign policy, in the labor movement, and of the movement's general political, social, moral and constitutional motives and plans.

1411   Gisevius, Hans Bernd. **To the Bitter End.** Boston, Houghton Mifflin, 1947. 632p.
An account of the anti-Hitler movement within Germany from 1933 to 1945 by one of the few survivors of the assassination plot. A revealing inside story of the fight waged by men and women of conscience. The author was one of a small group who were against Hitler from the beginning of his accession to power. The narrative also details the cooperation of Admiral Wilhelm Canaris, Chief of the German Abwehr in the conspiracy against Hitler.

1412   Gollwitzer, Helmut, Kathe Kuhn, and Reinhold Schneider, eds. **Dying We Live: The Final Messages and Records of the Resistance.** New York, Pantheon, 1956. 285p.
A collection of the farewell messages of victims of Nazi Germany between 1933 and 1945. Includes brief factual introductions giving age, occupation, circumstances of arrest and death. Serves to provide a reaffirmation of the strength and nobility of humanity.

1413   Hassell, Ulrich von. **Von Hassell Diaries, 1938-1944: The Story of Forces Against Hitler Inside Germany as Recorded by Ambassador Ulrich von Hassell, a Leader of the Movement.** Garden, City, N. Y., Doubleday, 1947. 400p.

One of the leading conspirators against Hitler describes life and the state of mind under Nazi Germany and the conspirators' long, patient, despairing attempts to overthrow Hitler. A morally impressive picture of enduring courage.

1414   Kramarz, Joachim. **Stauffenberg: The Architect of the Famous July 20th Conspiracy to Assassinate Hitler.** New York, Macmillan, 1967. 255p. Bibliog.

The story of the July 20th conspiracy, centering on Stauffenberg's role within the circle of those conspirators who sought a path to peace and to save Germany through the elimination of Hitler. An account, through letters and interviews, of how this highly regarded officer turned from passive acceptance of Hitler to an active role in the assassination attempt.

1415   Manvell, Roger and Heinrich Fraenkel. **The Canaris Conspiracy: The Secret Resistance to Hitler in the German Army.** New York, McKay, 1969. 267p. Bibliog.

Competent historical journalism serves to present an accurate story of the German resistance in military intelligence circles. This is a critical view of the conspirators' plans and mistakes.

1416   Manvell, Roger and Heinrich Fraenkel. **The July Plot: The Attempt in 1944 on Hitler's Life and the Men Behind It.** London, Bodley Head, 1964. 272p. Bibliog.

An exciting account of the July 20th plot to assassinate Hitler. The authors traced the plot from its inception through its end, pointing out the weaknesses and strengths of these few courageous men. This high drama investigates the complexities and consequences of the plot and the procedural and philosophical conflicts of the conspirators.

1417   Prittie, Terence Cornelius Farmer. **Germans Against Hitler.** Boston, Little, Brown, 1964. 291p. Bibliog.

An overview of the development of opposition to Hitler from within various factions in Germany such as the army, the Protestant and Catholic churches, the underground communists, the universities and the Kreisau Circle. A coherent, sober and readable account of German resistance.

1418   Ritter, Gerhard. **The German Resistance: Carl Goerdeler's Struggle Against Tyranny.** New York, Praeger, 1959. 330p. Bibliog.

The history and significance of the German resistance movement as told by a noted German historian, himself a member of the resistance. This is an account of the various individuals and groups who were involved in the German resistance and specifically of one of its principal members. The story of a courageous man and the ill-fated results of his conscience-driven activities.

1419   Roon, Ger van. **German Resistance to Hitler: Count Von Moltke and the Kreisau Circle**. New York, Van Nostrand Reinhold, 1971. 400p. Bibliog.

The author explores the significant aspects of the origins, activities and lives of the members of one of the most important groups of German opposition to Hitler. They were primarily civilians whose goal was the regeneration of Germany and their task was not so much the removal of Hitler but to determine the direction in which to start anew.

1420   Rothfels, Hans. **The German Opposition to Hitler: An Appraisal**. Hinsdale, Ill., Regnery, 1948. 172p. Bibliog.

A judicious analysis of the German resistance movement and its personalities. He defends the conspirators of the July 20th plot against Hitler against charges that they were nationalist reactionaries and contends that this was an effort by dedicated Germans to restore the dignity of humanity to the nation.

1421   Schlabrendorff, Fabian von. **The Secret War Against Hitler**. New York, Pitman, 1965. 438p.

A moving saga and detailed personal account of the author's experiences with German resistance operations. One of the few survivors of the movement traces the first awakening of anti-Nazi activities during the 1920s to the disastrous final attempt on Hitler's life. The participation of the resisters, in the author's mind, were the reactions of individuals with religious and moral convictions. He also relates his involvement in an earlier abortive attempt on Hitler's life.

1422   Scholl, Inge. **Students Against Tyranny: The Resistance of the White Rose Munich 1942-1943**. Middletown, Conn., Weslyan University Press, 1970. 160p.

The story of the small resistance group, the White Rose, in Germany, who first joined together to discuss what was happening to Germany and to then speak out against the Nazis. The group consisted of four medical students, one of their sisters, and a professor of psychology and philosophy at the University of Munich. They were subsequently arrested, tried for high treason against the state and executed.

1423   Schramm, Wilhelm. **Conspiracy Among Generals**. New York, Scribner, 1957. 215p.

The author, a military reporter attached to Rommel's headquarters and an eye-witness to some of the events, documents the account of the 1944 bomb attempt on Hitler's life. The story presents a sense of atmosphere in which the events took place and an insight into the code and psychology of the German military. The author emphasizes the role of the key figures in the German military command in Paris in the initial planning and in the confusion after the attempt.

1424   Zeller, Eberhard. **The Flame of Freedom: The German Struggle Against Hitler**. Coral Gables, Fla., University of Miami Press, 1969. 471p. Bibliog.

A detailed narrative of the July 20, 1944 plot on Hitler's life, its background and motivation. A scholarly defense of the conspirators emphasizing their courage and nobility.

Anti-Soviet Movements in Russia

1425   Armstrong, John Alexander. **Ukrainian Nationalism.** 2nd ed. New York,
        Columbia University Press, 1963. 361p. Maps, Bibliog.
A chronicle and evaluation of the resistance to the Soviet government of the
Ukrainian nationalists and the effects on their movement of the German occupation. The author's research was grounded largely on German sources at the Nuremberg Trials and on interviews with participants.

1426   Fischer, George. **Soviet Opposition to Stalin: A Case Study in World
        War II.** Cambridge, Harvard University Press, 1952. 230p. Bibliog.
An evaluation of the Vlasov movement. This study interprets the political significance of the only major organized opposition against the Soviet state during
World War II within the framework of the strengths and tensions of Soviet
society.

1427   Steenberg, Sven. **Vlasov.** New York, Knopf, 1970. 230p. Bibliog.
Describes the career of the Soviet general who after his capture joined the Germans
to form a Russian army as a means to rid Russia of Stalin. This account from the
German viewpoint attempts to refute charges that Vlasov was a traitor. Vlasov
is seen clearly to be more of a symbol of this anti-Soviet movement. Its failure
was inherent due to the nature of Nazi doctrine whose racial overtones made the
full successful exploitation of Stalin's weaknesses, through the use of properly
equipped and led anti-Soviet Russian troops, an almost impossible task.

1428   Strik-Strikfeldt, Wilfried. **Against Stalin and Hitler: Memoirs of the
        Russian Liberation Movement, 1941-5.** New York, John Day, 1973.
        270p. Map.
The military career of the Soviet Lieutenant General Andrei A. Vlasov, defender
of Moscow. By 1943 he was behind German lines and the titular head of an
anti-Stalin Russian army fighting with the Germans to overthrow Stalin. A
description of the motivations behind one of the more intriguing political
anomalies of World War II.

CHAPTER 10—ESPIONAGE

1429   Accoce, Pierre, and Pierre Quet. **A Man Called Lucy, 1939-1945.** New York, Coward-McCann, 1967. 250p.
This is the story of Rudolf Roessler a Soviet agent based in Switzerland. Known as "Lucy," Roessler was one of the most successful espionage agents in history based on the quality of the military information he supplied. He supplied the data to both the Swiss intelligence and Soviet intelligence. Roessler and Sorge were probably the two outstanding espionage agents of the war. The book is not always well documented, but all the truth may never be known about a man like "Lucy."

1430   Alcorn, Robert Hayden. **No Banners, No Bands: More Tales of the OSS.** New York, McKay, 1965. 275p.
An exciting well written series of stories about spies and saboteurs. Most of the action takes place in France, Italy and Norway. Alcorn was himself an officer in the Office of Strategic Services (OSS). This work is a sequel to the author's earlier *No Bugles for Spies: Tales of the OSS.*

1431   Alcorn, Robert Hayden. **No Bugles for Spies: Tales of the OSS.** New York, McKay, 1962. 209p.
A popular account of various Office of Strategic Services (OSS) espionage and sabotage operations. The action takes place in Europe, North Africa and the Far East. There is some material on the OSS's troubles with General MacArthur who did not want OSS operating in this area of command. A flattering picture of General Donovan, the head of the OSS.

1432   Alsop, Stewart Johonnot Oliver, and Thomas Braden. **Sub Rosa: The OSS and American Espionage.** New York, Harcourt and Brace, 1964. 264p.
One of the first, but unfortunately not the best, studies of the Office of Strategic Services. Nonetheless, this journalistic account of parachute jumps, sabotage and organizing resistance movements is almost always exciting. There is little analysis and nothing about the important Research and Analysis Branch of the OSS. First published in 1946.

1433   Babington-Smith, Constance. **Air Spy: The Story of Photo Intelligence in World War II.** New York, Harper, 1957. 266p.
An interesting story of the role of photo intelligence during World War II in the European theater. Some events affected by photo intelligence were the chase of the Bismark, commando raids, the Normandy Invasion, aircraft and U-boat production and the V-weapon attack on England.

1434   Buckmaster, Maurice J. **Specially Employed: The Story of British Aid to French Patriots of the Resistance.** London, Batchworth, 1952. 200p.
A personal view of the S.O.E.'s (Special Operations Executive) work with French resistance groups. The author says all the events described did in fact happen, but

admits the details are not always accurate because of the very nature of clandestine operations. A good view of S.O.E., their recruits and their methods.

1435   Buckmaster, Maurice J. **They Fought Alone: The Story of British Agents in France.** New York, Norton, 1958. 255p.
An account of British Special Operations Executive (S.O.E.) in France. Buckmaster tells about the beginnings of SOE in 1940, the recruiting of agents, training and operational procedures. The initial idea of gathering intelligence later developed into espionage, sabotage and cooperation with the French Resistance. Corrects some earlier errors about SOE operations. The author was the wartime head of SOE's French Section.

1436   Churchill, Peter. **Duel of Wits.** New York, Putnam, 1955. 368p.
A sequel to the author's *Of Their Own Choice* in which he tells the story of his second, third and fourth missions to France for S.O.E. All of the danger, boredom and excitement of these missions which lasted some 200 days come through. Churchill was attempting to organize French resistance for the S.O.E.

1437   Churchill, Peter. **Of Their Own Choice.** London, Hodder and Stoughton, 1952. 218p.
An exciting personal story of an S.O.E. agent's clandestine twenty-eight day mission to France in 1941-42. Good view of the dangers faced by the French underground. Churchill returned safely and went on three more missions which he describes in a sequel, *Duel of Wits*. One of the better first hand accounts by an S.O.E. agent.

1438   Colvin, Ian Goodhope. **Master Spy: The Incredible Story of Admiral Wilhelm Canaris, Who, While Hitler's Chief of Intelligence, Was a Secret Ally of the British.** New York, McGraw-Hill, 1952. 286p.
A biographical study of Admiral Canaris, the Chief of Intelligence of the German General Staff from 1935 to 1944. Colvin claims that Canaris and the Abwehr fed false intelligence information to Hitler and the General Staff. Interesting, but Colvin offers no proof for many of his assertions. Colvin was a chief of British Intelligence. Published in England under the title *Chief of Intelligence.*

1439   Cowburn, Benjamin. **No Cloak, No Dagger.** London, Jarrolds, 1960. 192p.
A personal account of the adventures of an SOE agent in France. One of the more accurate accounts by an agent. Not dramatic, but interesting and well written.

1440   Dallin, David J. **Soviet Espionage.** New Haven, Yale University Press, 1956. 558p. Bibliog.
A scholarly historical survey of Soviet intelligence operations with emphasis on World War II and the pre-war years. Concentrates on the development of espionage networks in France, Germany and Switzerland. An interesting introduction to the development of a highly successful espionage operation.

1441   Deakin, Frederick William, and G. R. Storry. **The Case of Richard Sorge.** New York, Harper & Row, 1966. 373p. Bibliog.

Two British scholars have written a well documented account of one of the most successful Soviet spies of the war. Based on interviews and Japanese and German sources. Tells of Sorge's earlier assignments in Europe, China, Berlin and the United States before his final assignment to Tokyo.

1442   Downes, Donald C. **The Scarlet Thread: Adventures in Wartime Espionage.**
        London, Verschoyle, 1953. 207p.
A personal story by an OSS civilian operative who served in various countries all over the world. Most of the story is concerned with activities in the Middle East, the Balkans and Italy. Many personal tales, but an honest account with many criticisms of U. S. policies. Downes is, however, very complimentary about General William Donovan, the head of the O.S.S.

1443   Farago, Ladislas. **The Broken Seal: The Story of Operation Magic and the
        Pearl Harbor Disaster.** New York, Random House, 1967. 439p. Bibliog.
A popular history of American and Japanese efforts at code breaking from 1921 to December 7, 1941. Tells of the efforts to crack secret codes, the high point being the breaking of Japanese "Purple" code by Colonel William F. Friedman. Farago concentrates on the events leading up to Pearl Harbor and attempts to determine why the Americans were surprised.

1444   Farago, Ladislas. **Burn After Reading: The Espionage History of World
        War II.** New York, Walker, 1961. 319p.
A popular comprehensive account of wartime espionage, but often not well documented. Besides individual spies the book is concerned with the national intelligence bureaus—Abwehr, M.I.5., Deuxime Bureau, O.S.S. and the O.N.I.— and spy networks and resistance movements. However, many topics are treated briefly or left out. The author is a former Chief of Research and Planning in the Navy's Special Warfare Branch.

1445   Farago, Ladislas. **The Game of the Foxes: The Untold Story of German
        Espionage in the United States and Great Britain During World War II.**
        New York, McKay, 1972. 696p. Bibliog.
Based on records of the Abwehr, the German secret service, the book concentrates on German espionage efforts against the United States and Great Britain. Every aspect of the Abwehr operations, including fiscal records, biographies of agents and other secret transactions is reconstructed. Farago acknowledges the importance of deception and counter espionage.

1446   Feldt, Eric Augustus. **The Coastwatchers.** New York, Oxford University
        Press, 1946. 264p. Maps.
An account of the men organized by the Australian Navy to gather intelligence about the Japanese. The men were largely recruited and organized before the war began. The coastwatchers included planters, missionaries and government workers, and they succeeded in obtaining important information under difficult circumstances.

1447   Foot, Michael Richard Daniel. **SOE in France: An Account of the Work of the British Special Operations Executive in France, 1940-1944**. London, H. M. Stationery Office, 1966. 550p. Maps, Bibliog.
The official history of the Special Operations Executive based on official and "less official" records. S.O.E. was formed in 1940 to encourage underground resistance on continental Europe. Foot explains what "SOE was, where it fitted into the allied war machine, and how it worked into France." Included are narrative accounts of the adventures of many agents operating in France. An interesting scholarly history.

1448   Foote, Alexander. **Handbook for Spies**. Garden City, N. Y., Doubleday, 1949. 273p.
Foote, an English communist, was involved in Soviet espionage activities in Switzerland during the war. The information gathered by the Swiss network was of exceptionally high quality. Describes the Rossler-Rado networks which apparently had sources in the German high command. An honest memoir which tells of the hard work and long hours involved in spying with no glorification.

1449   Ford, Corey. **Donovan of OSS**. Boston, Little, Brown, 1970. 366p. Bibliog.
A biography of General William ("Wild Bill") Donovan, the creator and wartime head of the Office of Strategic Services (O.S.S.). Ford is perhaps too uncritical of Donovan. Tells of Donovan's wartime missions to see Mussolini and to some of the occupied countries. A little weak on the theory of intelligence as practiced by the O.S.S. A good, but not a definitive work.

1450   Fuller, Jean Overton. **Madeleine: The Story of Noor Inayat Khan**. London, Gollanz, 1952. 192p.
The story of Noor-un-Nisa Inayat-Khan who served as an S.O.E. agent in occupied France. Inayat-Khan operated under the code name "Madeleine" and was a successful agent until the betrayal which led to her death. One of the more mysterious operatives employed by S.O.E.

1451   Fuller, Jean Overton. **No. 13, BOB**. Boston, Little, Brown, 1954. 240p.
The adventures of Captain John Starr, an S.O.E. agent in France. Known by the code names "Bob" and "Emile," he served as an organizer of French resistance groups. Starr worked with "Madeleine" (Inayat-Khan). After the war Starr was suspected of betraying his trust, but was exonerated. The English edition is titled *The Starr Affair*.

1452   Garlinski, Jozef. **Poland, S.O.E. and the Allies**. London, Allen and Unwin, 1969. 248p. Maps, Bibliog.
A personal account of S.O.E.'s Polish Section by a former agent. Tells about the training of Polish agents, secret parachute drops into Poland, organizing resistance, sabotage and the development of the Polish Home Army. There is also material on the various political problems the English and Poles had with the Russians over the development and extent of the Polish resistance movement.

1453   Gilchrist, Andrew. **Bangkok, Top Secret: Being the Experiences of a British Officer in the Siam Country Section of Force 136.** London, Hutchinson , 1970. 231p. Map.

A story of the activities of the British S.O.E. in Japanese occupied Siam. The mission organized anti-Japanese resistance, gathered some intelligence and was involved in various clandestine operations. S.O.E. worked closely with the Free Siamese Movement.

1454   Giskes, H. J. **London Calling North Pole.** London, Kimber, 1953. 208p.

A well told account of the successful German counter espionage radio operation to subvert the S.O.E. operations in the Netherlands. Called "Operation Northpole" by the Germans, the S.O.E. was seriously hampered and lost over fifty agents. The author was Chief of German Military Counter Intelligence in Holland, Belgium and Northern France.

1455   Hepburn, Sybil. **Wingless Victory.** London, Allan-Wingate-Baker, 1969. 190p.

An autobiographical account of an English woman trapped in France by the German invasion in May 1940. Hepburn almost immediately set up an underground operation to help downed R.A.F. pilots and later Allied pilots escape the Germans. She was successful for five years and was never detected by the Germans. An exciting story.

1456   Hoettl, Wilhelm. **The Secret Front: The Story of Nazi Political Espionage.** New York, Praeger, 1954. 327p. Map.

The story of the Central European Section of the Sicherheitsdienst (S.D.), or the German Secret Service. Deals primarily with the atrocities committed by the S.D. between 1933 and 1945. Mostly undocumented; however, the documentation was nearly all destroyed. Shows how German intelligence attempted to help the war effort.

1457   Hohne, Heinz. **Codeword Direktor: The Story of the Red Orchestra.** New York, Coward, McCann & Geoghegan, 1971. 310p. Bibliog.

A carefully researched history of the "Red Orchestra." The Red Orchestra was a Russian spy network composed of Germans and Polish Jews which operated successfully in Western Europe from 1941 to 1944. Hohne concludes that the "Red Orchestra" was not a resistance movement, but traitors who sought a Russian victory and not just a German defeat.

1458   Howarth, David Armine. **We Die Alone.** New York, Macmillan, 1955. 231p.

An exciting story of the Norwegian born saboteur Jan Baalsrud. Tells of Nazi sadism and the dangers of operating behind German lines. One part tells of Baalsrud's escape from Norway to Sweden in a reindeer stampede. He was the only one of twelve who succeeded in escaping.

1459   Hyde, Harford Montgomery. **Room 3603: The Story of the British Intelligence Center in New York During World War II.** New York, Farrar, Straus, 1963. 257p.

A biography of William Stephenson, the wartime director of British Security operations in New York. Tells of the British attempt to destroy U. S. neutrality, partly by fraud and counterfeit letters and documents. Little concern over ethics— the end simply justifies the means. The English edition is titled *The Quiet Canadian*.

1460   Ind, Allison. **Allied Intelligence Bureau: Our Secret Weapon in the War Against Japan.** New York, McKay, 1958. 305p.
This is the story of the Allied Intelligence Bureau (A.I.B.) which operated in the Southwest Pacific under MacArthur's command. A.I.B. was engaged in intelligence gathering and sabotage activities. Many individual exploits are covered. Some of the best sections are on the underground in the Philippines. Not a definitive history, but one of the few works available.

1461   Irving, David John Cawdell, ed. **Breach of Security: The German Secret Intelligence File on Events Leading to the Second World War.** London, Kimber, 1968. 216p.
A compilation of documents which illustrate the work of one of the most secret German intelligence agencies—the Forschungsamt (Research Office). The reports of the Research Office were called brown pages ("Braune Blatter") and covered a wide range of domestic and foreign political intelligence. Includes material on the background of the Forschungsamt and its relations with the Nazis.

1462   Johnson, Chalmers A. **An Instance of Treason: Ozaki Hotsumi and the Sorge Spy Ring.** Stanford, Calif., Stanford University Press, 1964. 278p. Bibliog.
A scholarly account of Ozaki Hotsumi, a respected Japanese journalist who served as Richard Sorge's assistant. Sorge was, of course, an outstanding Russian spy and possibly their most successful one. Includes background material on Japanese nationalism and the political atmosphere of the times.

1463   Jong, Louis de. **The German Fifth Column in the Second World War.** Chicago, University of Chicago Press, 1956. 308p. Maps, Bibliog.
A well documented analysis of the threat posed by an allegedly powerful German fifth column. The author concludes that the fifth column did exist, but it played little part in the defeat of any country. A study of fear and the psychology of the masses in a stressful war situation. Traces fifth column activities in the U. S., England, Norway, Denmark, France, Belgium, Latin America and other selected countries.

1464   Kahn, David. **The Codebreakers: The Story of Secret Writing.** New York, Macmillan, 1967. 1164p. Bibliog.
A comprehensive history of cryptology with chapters on World War II. A fascinating book that combines a simple narrative along with highly technical sections on the development of codes and the methods used to break them. An excellent introduction to cryptology and the highlights of cryptology during World War II.

1465   Kemp, Peter Kemp. **Alms for Oblivion.** London, Cassell, 1961. 188p. Maps.
A personal memoir of a Special Operations Executive (S.O.E.) agent in Siam. Initially Kemp parachuted into Siam in May 1945 to organize guerrilla operations

against the Japanese. Eventually he began gunrunning for the French who were starting their unsuccessful fight against the Communist Viet-Minh.

1466   Kimche, Jon. **Spying for Peace: General Guisan and Swiss Neutrality.** London, Weidenfeld and Nicolson, 1961. 168p.
An interesting account of the relationships of the Allies and Axis intelligence services in Switzerland. Kimche argues that the German resistance to Hitler was just as interested in breaking up the Allies as overthrowing Hitler. A good view of the difficulties of trying to remain neutral. General Guisan was Switzerland's General from 1939 to 1945.

1467   Kirkpatrick, Lyman B. **Captains Without Eyes: Intelligence Failures in World War II**. New York, Macmillan, 1969. 303p. Maps, Bibliog.
The author, a former U. S. Army intelligence officer, analyses five major battles where intelligence failed. The five battles are Pearl Harbor, Barbarossa, Dieppe Raid, the airborne assault on Arnheim and the Ardennes Offense (Battle of the Bulge). Kirkpatrick offers some suggestions on how these failures might have been prevented.

1468   Klein, Alexander. **The Counterfeit Traitor**. New York, Holt, 1958. 301p.
The story of Eric Erickson, a businessman who became a valuable Allied spy. He was most successful in obtaining information on the locations of German petroleum refineries. An exciting story, but unfortunately the reader must be careful because the author has manufactured many conversations. An exciting movie of the same title has been made.

1469   Leverkuehn, Paul. **German Military Intelligence**. New York, Praeger, 1954. 209p. Maps.
A personalized account of Abwehr operations in the Balkans, Russia, Poland and Western Europe. The most effective parts of the book tell of Nazi interference which made the Abwehr under Admiral Canaris an ineffective organization. In many ways only an average book, but there has not been much published on the topic.

1470   McLachlan, Donald. **Room 39: A Study in Naval Intelligence**. New York, Atheneum, 1968. 438p. Bibliog.
An excellent account of British Naval Intelligence in World War II and the philosophy and principles upon which it operated. Shows "how raw facts were molded into prime orders to ships at sea, how code-breakers pitted their brains against the enemy, and how scholarship was matched against violence." Tells the sources of intelligence and how it is evaluated. Removes many false impressions about intelligence work—it's not all cloak and dagger and danger. First rate study.

1471   Martelli, George. **The Man Who Saved London: The Story of Michel Hollard**. Garden City, N. Y., Doubleday, 1961. 258p.
The exciting story of Michel Hollard who sent much vital information on the "flying bombs" to England. Hollard contacted British Intelligence and offered to set up a network. He succeeded in getting data on the construction and

location of many launch sites. Hollard was eventually betrayed and sent to a concentration camp where he survived the war. Also published under the title *Agent Extraordinary*.

1472   Masterman, John Cecil. **The Double-Cross System in the War of 1939 to 1945**. New Haven, Yale University Press, 1972. 203p.
An official "internal memorandum" first written in 1945 describing the successful efforts to control German agents in Britain. Describes how every German agent was turned into a double agent and transmitted only pre-screened or fabricated intelligence back to Germany. A sober account of the war's most successful counter espionage operation.

1473   Maugeri, Franco. **From the Ashes of Disgrace**. New York, Reynal & Hitchcock, 1948. 376p.
The autobiography of Italy's wartime Chief of Naval Intelligence. An honest account that includes much information on Italian naval history. Tells of the activities of the Rome underground which was composed largely of naval personnel and led by Maugeri. Maugeri had a long record of opposition to Mussolini and fascism.

1474   Montagu, Ewen. **The Man Who Never Was**. New York, Lippincott, 1954. 160p. Map.
A well written account of the successful British plan to plant a corpse with fake identification papers and fake orders to deceive the Germans about Allied plans to invade Sicily. The corpse was identified only as "Major Martin" and his real identity was known only to his family. Montagu, who was involved in "Operation Mincemeat," tells the story of a truly professional intelligence operation.

1475   Moss, William Stanley. **Ill Met by Moonlight**. New York, Macmillan, 1950. 192p. Maps.
The author, who participated in the operation, gives "an account of the abduction of Major General Karl Kreipe, commander of the German forces on Crete on April 26, 1944." Kreipe was captured by two English officers leading a group of Cretan guerrillas. An exciting "typical plot" type spy story.

1476   Perrault, Giles. **The Red Orchestra**. New York, Simon and Schuster, 1969. 496p. Bibliog.
An exciting well paced study of the Russian intelligence network which operated in France, Belgium and the Netherlands from 1941 to 1944. The network was called the Rote Kapelle or Red Orchestra. The story centers primarily around the Polish Jew, Leopold Trepper, who was in charge of the network. Although not always well documented, this is a generally accurate and readable work by a well known French journalist.

1477   Pirie, Anthony. **Operation Bernhard**. New York, Morrow, 1962. 303p. Bibliog.
A detailed study of the Nazi counterfeit ring responsible for the forgery of millions of dollars in British pound notes between 1940 and 1945. The idea was originally Reinhard Heydrich's and other SS leaders. Details of intrigue, self-enrichment and

murder. The pound notes were allegedly dumped in an Austrain lake after the war. The author admits to manufacturing some undocumented events in order to fill in the story.

1478   Pitt, Roxane. **The Courage of Fear**. New York, Duell, Sloan and Pearce, 1957. 242p.
The personal story of an S.O.E. agent who operated in occupied France and in Italy. Tells how she became an agent and her work in gathering intelligence and helping Allied prisoners escape. The author posed as an artist, singer and once as her own sister. Good view of life in Paris and Rome during the war.

1479   Rachlis, Eugene. **They Came to Kill: The Story of Eight Nazi Saboteurs in America**. New York, Random House, 1961. 306p.
The story of "Operation Pastorius" the plan to land Nazi spies in the United States by submarine. The eight agents who landed on Long Island and in Florida were captured almost immediately. The Germans thought this attempt necessary after the FBI broke the German spy network in 1941. The spies were tried in secret and their conviction was appealed to the Supreme Court and President Roosevelt. Good materials on the constitutional issues of the trial.

1480   Renault-Roulier, Gilbert. **Courage and Fear**. London, Barker, 1950. 320p.; **The Silent Company**. London, Barker, 1948. 406p.
A personal story of a Frenchman sent back to France in 1940 as an S.O.E. agent. His first assignment was to observe the Atlantic Coast for German invasion preparations. Later under the code name "Raymond," he organized a major espionage network called the Confrerie Notre-Dame. Good explanation of the organization and work of a spy network. These two volumes were written under the pseudonym Remy.

1481   Renault-Roulier, Gilbert. **Portrait of a Spy**. New York, Roy, 1955. 224p.
The story of Georges Henri Delfane, a Belgian who acted as a German agent. Delfane, known usually as Henri Masuy, worked for the Germans in counter-espionage operations to break up resistance organizations. The story is full of brutality and excitement. Masuy enriched himself in black market operations and was tried as a traitor after the war.

1482   Schellenberg, Walter. **The Labyrinth: Memoirs**. New York, Harper, 1956. 423p.
The memoirs of the Chief of the German Secret Service who rose from the lower ranks over the years. An inside view of Heydrich, Mueller, Kaltenbrunner and the Byzantine politics of the Secret Service. The atmosphere is one of total corruption. An interesting story, but also a self-serving apology for Schellenberg's wartime activities. Not an entirely trustworthy source. The English edition is titled *The Schellenberg Memoirs*.

1483   Seth, Ronald. **Forty Years of Soviet Spying**. London, Cassell, 1965. 294p. Bibliog.
A general introduction to Soviet espionage with one section on World War II. Good for a quick review of the major Soviet spy networks of the war. Includes

information on the "Red Orchestra," the Swiss network, the Canadian network and the Japanese network. Seth concludes that Rudolf Rossler and Richard Sorge were possibly the greatest spies in history based on the value of their information.

1484   Seth, Ronald. **Secret Servants: A History of Japanese Espionage**. New York, Farrar, Straus, Cudahy, 1957. 278p. Bibliog.
There is not much on World War II here, but then little has been written on Japanese espionage during the war. Mostly concerned with Japanese spies in Hawaii and the events leading to Pearl Harbor and with Japanese espionage in Southeast Asia.

1485   Smith, Richard Harris. **OSS: The Secret History of America's First Central Intelligence Agency**. Berkeley, University of California Press, 1972. 458p. Bibliog.
Not a definitive history of the O.S.S., but one of the best to date. The O.S.S. was organized to gather intelligence and conduct special operations. Includes material on the organization of the O.S.S. by General Donovan and many individual operations throughout the world. Smith argues that the O.S.S. was successful because of its liberal political elements.

1486   Spiro, Edward. **Set Europe Ablaze**. New York, Crowell, 1967. 410p. Bibliog.
A popular history of the SOE which was established in 1940 to collect intelligence data, perform sabotage and assist underground resistance movements. With SOE Churchill hoped to "set Europe ablaze." Describes the setting up of SOE and the training of agents. Includes many stories of agents' adventures. The author was an SOE agent who spent time in Dachau and Buchenwald. Published also under the title *Inside S.O.E.*

1487   Spiro, Edward. **They Came from the Sky**. New York, Crowell, 1967. 257p. Bibliog.
The exciting story of three SOE agents who worked with the French Resistance movement in 1943-44. The three agents were Roger Landes, Harry Ree and Francis Cammaerts who were still alive to verify the accuracy of the stories in this book. One weakness is the author's manufacturing of conversations when he does not have any documentation.

1488   Stead, Philip John. **Second Bureau**. London, Evans, 1959. 212p.
A history of the Special Services section—the Second Bureau—of the French Army which remained in occupied France. The Second Bureau carried on the struggle against France's enemies—Allied and Axis. The history centers on activities in Vichy France and North Africa and their cooperation with the Allies. The function of the Second Bureau was to gather and interpret intelligence for the French High Command.

1489   Stephan, Enno. **Spies in Ireland**. Harrisburg, Stackpole, 1965. 311p. Map, Bibliog.
A detailed and thorough history of German espionage in Ireland. It is the story of a German failure. Only two of twelve known agents escaped arrest and they

accomplished nothing of importance. Among the reasons for failure explored
are the squabbles and inability to coordinate with the I.R.A. and poor leadership
from Berlin.

1490   Strong, Kenneth. **Intelligence at the Top: The Recollections of an Intel-
        ligence Officer.** Garden City, N. Y., Doubleday, 1969. 366p. Maps, Bibliog.
Memoirs of the man who held posts as Director General of Intelligence of the
British Ministry of Defense, head of M.I. 14—the German section of British
Military Intelligence—and later as Eisenhower's intelligence chief in North Africa
and Europe. Tells of the impact of intelligence on wartime military and political
planning and what exactly is intelligence information. Views of the personalities
of Patton, Bradley and Montgomery.

1491   Sweet-Escott, Bickham. **Baker Street Irregular.** London, Methuen, 1965.
        278p. Maps.
A superb general survey of the Special Operations Executive (S.O.E.) by a former
middle level staff officer. Based in part on the author's personal experiences. Tells
of the formation of S.O.E. and its early difficulties when the members were considered young "upstarts." Covers various operations of the S.O.E., primarily in
Western Europe, Eastern Europe and the Middle East.

1492   Tickell, Jerrard. **Moon Squadron.** Garden City, N. Y., Doubleday, 1958.
        204p.
The seldom told story of the special duties squadrons of the R.A.F. used in many
S.O.E. operations. The two better known groups were 138 Squadron and 161
Squadron which used both British and Polish pilots. These special squadrons
dropped agents in occupied territory, made pickups of escaping agents and flyers,
and dropped supplies and weapons to agents and underground organizations. An
exciting well told story.

1493   Tompkins, Peter. **A Spy in Rome.** New York, Simon and Schuster, 1962.
        347p.
A story of an O.S.S. spy in Rome in 1944. Based on a diary and contemporary
notes, Tompkins recounts the exciting experiences he lived through as the
Allies approached Rome. At the time Tompkins was young and some of his
criticisms of the O.S.S. are probably unfair.

1494   Walker, David Esdaile. **Lunch with a Stranger.** New York, Norton, 1957.
        223p.
The personal story of a foreign correspondent for the London *Daily Mirror* who
served as an agent and S.O.E. operative for seven years. Walker served in the
Balkans and later in Berlin. Not a glamorous danger-filled tale by a highly successful spy, but an honest account of an "average" spy.

1495   Whaley, Barton. **Codeword Barbarossa.** Cambridge, MIT Press, 1973. 376p.
        Bibliog.
An excellent well researched account of the warnings given to the Russians that
the Germans were planning an invasion. The author lists eighty-four separate
incidents that could be interpreted as signs of the impending start of the German

intentions to invade Russia—"Operation Barbarossa." Whaley shows why Stalin was completely fooled and how Hitler achieved a total surprise. A fascinating study.

1496   Wighton, Charles. **Pin-Stripe Saboteur: The Story of "Robin," British Agent and French Resistance Leader.** London, Odhams, 1959. 253p.
A biography of a then anonymous Swiss Jew who served as a British S.O.E. agent gathering intelligence and acting as a resistance leader. "Robin" gathered valuable information which was of help at El Alamein and in combatting the V-bomb attacks on England. Later "Robin" was an active resistance leader.

1497   Zacharias, Ellis M. **Secret Missions: The Story of an Intelligence Officer.** New York, Putnams, 1946. 433p.
An account of intelligence operations in the Far East by a former U. S. naval intelligence officer. Tells of spies, saboteurs and counterspies in Japan. Some emphasis is given to breaking the Japanese codes and psychological warfare. Tells how the navy developed and used intelligence information. The author possibly overestimates the overall effects of intelligence.

CHAPTER 11–THE "FINAL SOLUTION," CONCENTRATION CAMPS AND OTHER MAJOR ATROCITIES

THE "FINAL SOLUTION" AND CONCENTRATION CAMPS

[Materials on the Jewish Question, the "Final Solution" and other atrocities will also be found in the chapter on War Crimes Trials. The testimony and documents presented at the Nuremberg Trials and other war crimes trials are invaluable primary materials.]

1498   American Jewish Conference. **Nazi Germany's War Against the Jews.** New York, American Jewish Conference, 1947. 857p.
A massive documentary presentation of Nazi Germany's anti-semitic campaign. The horrifying nature of the material is overwhelming and the reader would probably only want to read selected segments. Much of this documentary material was presented as evidence at the Nuremberg Trials.

1499   Apenszlak, Jakob. **The Black Book of Polish Jewry: An Account of the Martyrdom of Polish Jewry Under the Nazi Occupation.** New York, Roy, 1943. 343p.
A collection of documents and pictures comprising evidence of Nazi anti-semitism. There is a narrative account of Nazi atrocities and the beginning of the mass exterminations of the "final solution." An interesting wartime account of the developing holocaust.

1500   Barkai, Meyer, ed. **The Fighting Ghettos.** Philadelphia, Lippincott, 1962. 407p.
The seldom told story of Jewish resistance is related in this volume. Based on personal recollections of survivors and notes and diaries of those who died. The three sections of the book are: "Within the Walls," "In the Forests" and "In the Concentration Camps."

1501   Bartoszewski, Wladyslaw, and Zofia Lewinowna. **The Samaritans: Heroes of the Holocaust.** New York, Twayne, 1970. 442p.
The story of the "Polish Council for Aid to Jews" and its efforts to help save Polish Jewry from the holocaust. The author was one of the Council's founders and leaders from 1942 to 1944. This work is based on personal memories, first-hand accounts, newspapers and archival materials.

1502   Bettelheim, Bruno. **The Informed Heart: Autonomy in a Mass age.** Glencoe, Ill., Free Press, 1960. 309p.
The author, a famous psychoanalyst, tells of his personal experiences at pre-war Dachau and Buchenwald. With the eye of a professional analyst, Bettelheim discusses the German psychological techniques used to break camp inmates. Bettelheim claims a lack of Jewish resistance and "sheep to the slaughter" mentality which is hotly disputed by the newer writers on the subject.

1503   Cohen, Elie Aron. **Human Behavior in the Concentration Camp.** New
        York, Norton, 1953. 295p. Bibliog.
An interesting personal interpretation of what happened to human beings in concentration camps. The author, who spent 1942 to 1945 in a concentration camp, does
not relate his personal experiences but attempts to present a broad picture. Sections
of the book cover the establishment of a camp, the medical problems in the camps,
the psychology of the prisoners and the psychology of the SS. Based on the author's
experiences primarily at Auschwitz.

1504   D'Harcourt, Pierre. **The Real Enemy.** New York, Scribners, 1967. 186p.
A personal memoir by a person who spent five years in the French underground
and in German prisons and concentration camps. D'Harcourt concludes that the
"real enemy" is inside a person and is reflected in his reactions under pressure.
Insight into men's psychological and physiological needs in situations of great
stress. The author is a Catholic.

1505   Donat, Alexander. **The Holocaust Kingdom: A Memoir.** New York, Holt,
        Rinehart and Winston, 1965. 361p. Maps.
An emotional personal account of a family brutally separated with the parents
sent to different concentration camps and a son hidden by non-Jews. The story
centers around the father's experiences which give a view of the hell he experienced.
Based on experiences at Maidanek, Auschwitz, Dachau and Ravensbruck. One of
a number of newer works refuting the contention that the Jews were slaughtered
"like sheep" and without a struggle.

1506   Feingold, Henry L. **The Politics of Rescue: The Roosevelt Administration
        and the Holocaust, 1938-1945.** New Brunswick, N. J., Rutgers University
        Press, 1970. 394p. Bibliog.
A scholarly study of the failure of any effective intervention by the United States
to save European Jews from destruction. Highlights the tragic chasm between good
intentions and the inability to implement them. A penetrating analysis of the U. S.
State Department and Assistant Undersecretary Breckinridge Long show their
roles in the failure of U. S. policy.

1507   Frank, Anne. **The Diary of a Young Girl.** Garden City, N. Y., Doubleday,
        1952. 285p.
This is a now classic diary describing how a young Jewish girl and her family hid
for over two years from the Nazis in Holland. A penetrating look into daily life
and human emotions under extreme conditions. When discovered Anne was sent
to Bergen-Belsen where she was killed—only her father survived the war. The fact
that the Franks made no attempts to escape has subjected them to some criticism
from revisionists who also do not hold Anne to be a heroine.

1508   Frankl, Viktor Emil. **Man's Search for Meaning: An Introduction to
        Logotherapy.** Boston, Beacon Press, 1962. 142p. Bibliog.
These are the personal experiences in a concentration camp of a trained psychiatrist.
Frankl's experiences were not unique, but occurred to millions of other prisoners.

The author attempts to answer the question, "How was everyday life in a concentration camp reflected in the mind of the average prisoner?" An excellent analysis. An earlier edition was titled *From Death Camp to Existentialism.*

1509   Friedlander, Albert H., comp. **Out of the Whirlwind: A Reader of Holocaust Literature.** Garden City, N. Y., Doubleday, 1968. 536p. Bibliog.
A collection of thirty-two pieces of the best Holocaust literature. The selections include diaries, works of scholarship and fiction. Good for getting a broad "feel" for the impact of the holocuast on the individual.

1510   Friedman, Philip, ed. **Martyrs and Fighters: The Epic of the Warsaw Ghetto.** New York, Praeger, 1954. 325p.
This selection of eyewitness accounts of the Warsaw ghetto give the reader a realistic picture of the Nazi efforts to annihilate the Jews. There is an attempt to be objective and both Jewish heroism and discreditable acts are shown. The book also describes the resistance to the Nazis by the ghetto's Jewish Fighting Organization.

1511   Glatstein, Jacob, and others, comps. **Anthology of Holocaust Literature.** Philadelphia, Jewish Publication Society of America, 1969. 412p. Bibliog.
This anthology attempts to present a general overview of the Jewish experience in the Holocaust. Eyewitness accounts include concentration camp experiences, resistance movements, the underground movement and the role of non-Jews. A good selection of materials.

1512   Hilberg, Raul. **The Destruction of the European Jews.** Chicago, Quadrangle, 1961. 788p. Maps, Bibliog.
One of the standard general accounts of the almost successful Nazi attempt to kill all of Europe's Jews. There is a great amount of detail on every European country where the Germans operated against the Jews. The study is actually about the Germans—not the Jews. In spite of justified criticism that Hilberg's study is flawed because of almost exclusive reliance on German sources, it remains a valuable introduction.

1513   Hoess, Rudolf. **Commandant of Auschwitz: Autobiography.** Cleveland, World Publishing, 1960. 285p.
The frightening personal document of a man who oversaw the death of millions at Auschwitz. Hoess shows little emotion as he was simply following his orders; hence, he never felt he did anything wrong. Hoess tells us what he did, but not why he did it. Some have concluded Hoess was not a monster, but just a follower who would have obeyed any order.

1514   Iranek-Osmecki, Kazimierz. **He Who Saves One Life.** New York, Crown, 1971. 336p. Bibliog.
This is an account of the efforts of many non-Jewish Poles to save the Jews from Nazi genocide in occupied Poland. The story of Polish heroism is often overlooked or ignored. The author relies on official documents, post-war official investigations and reports of clandestine and underground organizations. Harsh but enlightening reading.

1515   Jewish Black Book Committee. **The Black Book: The Nazi Crime Against the Jewish People.** New York, Duell, Sloan and Pearce, 1946. 560p. Bibliog.
A compilation of documents and personal accounts illustrating the sufferings of the Jews under Nazi persecution. A useful overview of the immensity of the Holocaust. Most of the documents were used in evidence at the Nuremberg Trials.

1516   Kaplan, Chaim Aron. **Scroll of Agony: The Warsaw Diary of Chaim A. Kaplan.** New York, Macmillan, 1965. 350p. Maps.
This diary of a simple Hebrew school principal is a vivid well written story of one person's struggle for survival under Nazi occupation. The insight and feeling for life under the most trying conditions comes through strongly. Kaplan died in 1942.

1517   Kogon, Eugen. **The Theory and Practice of Hell: The German Concentration Camps and the System Behind Them.** New York, Farrar, Straus, 1950. 307p.
One of the best general accounts of the Nazi concentration camp system. Kogon covers nearly every aspect of camp life. There are many eyewitness accounts of the brutalities and atrocities which were daily occurences in camp life. Kogon, a Catholic, remains a detached unemotional observer in spite of the fact that he spent six years in Buchenwald. A good introduction.

1518   Korman, Gerd. **Hunter and Hunted: Human History of the Holocaust.** New York, Viking Press, 1973. 320p. Bibliog.
A collection of 17 essays which attempt to give the flavor of the "Jewish problem" from Hitler's assumption of power in 1933 to the destruction of his Reich in 1945. Includes selections on the Jews at the start of the war, the deportations, concentration camps, the Warsaw Ghetto uprising and the Allied liberation of the camps.

1519   Kowalski, Isaac. **A Secret Press in Nazi Europe: The Story of a Jewish United Partisan Organization.** New York, Central Guide Publishers, 1969. 416p. Map, Bibliog.
A personal view of life in Vilna, Poland, during the German occupation and the development and activities of a Jewish resistance movement. The United Partisan Organization was active in underground activities and the publication of clandestine anti-Hitler newspapers. An example of some of the works being translated from Yiddish and Hebrew which tell of Jewish efforts at resisting the Germans.

1520   LeChene, Evelyn. **Mauthausen: The History of a Death Camp.** London, Methuen, 1971. 296p. Maps, Bibliog.
A very detailed serious study of Mauthausen concentration camp. Every aspect of the construction of the camp, its method of operation and life in the camp is fully covered. Complete statistics from 1938 to 1945 are included. The work also gives information on a number of sub-camps attached to Mauthausen. Gruesome but essential reading for trying to understand the mechanisms of an amoral dictatorship.

1521   Lengyel, Olga. **Five Chimneys: The Story of Auschwitz.**Chicago, Ziff-
        Davis, 1947. 213p.
One of the best personal accounts of life in a concentration camp. The author was
confined in Birkenau-Auschwitz where she worked in the camp hospital. Her
husband, a Jew, was killed but Olga, who was a Christian, luckily managed to
survive. Harsh reading, but an accurate protrayal of man's inhumanity to man.

1522   Levi, Primo. **Survival in Auschwitz: The Nazi Assault on Humanity.**
        New York, Collier-Macmillan, 1961. 157p.
A sensitive intelligent personal account of the author's two years in Auschwitz.
Levi, a trained chemist, managed to survive only because he was able to work.
When he did become too ill to work, he was saved by the on-coming Russians who
caused the SS to abandon Auschwitz. A clear unemotional account of life in an
insane world. One of the best personal memoirs of camp life. An earlier edition
is titled *If This Is a Man.*

1523   Levin, Nora. **The Holocaust: The Destruction of European Jewry, 1933-
        1945.** New York, Crowell, 1968. 768p. Maps, Bibliog.
A popular well written general survey of the Holocaust from Hitler's coming to
power in 1933 to the defeat of Germany in 1945. Part I of the book covers the
preparation and background of the "final solution"; part II covers the deportations
and killings which were the culmination of the "final solution." Every European
country is covered. Levin disputes the Hilberg-Arendt thesis that the Jews did
not resist and gives much evidence to show that there was indeed much Jewish
resistance considering the circumstances. An excellent introduction.

1524   Levy, Claude and Paul Tillard. **Betrayal at the Vel D'Hiv.** New York,
        Hill and Wang, 1969. 284p. Bibliog.
This is the sad story of Vichy France's cooperation in the extermination of
French Jews. Specifically the book is mostly concerned with the roundup of
13,000 Jews in Paris on July 16, 1942 and their ultimate fate in Auschwitz.
There were few survivors of this "Black Thursday." Vel d'Hiv (Velodrome
d'Hiver) was a sports place in Paris where the victims were held pending deportation. The authors were French resistance leaders and spent time in Nazi prisons.

1525   Mitscherlich, Alexander and Fred Mielke. **Doctors of Infamy: The Story
        of the Nazi Medical Crimes.** New York, Schuman, 1949. 172p.
The story of Nazi medical experiments carried out on concentration camp inmates.
The details are horrifying and sometimes it is difficult to accept that it could
really have happened. Harsh reading.

1526   Nyiszli, Miklos. **Auschwitz: A Doctor's Eyewitness Account.** New York,
        Fell, 1960. 222p.
An account of life in Auschwitz by a Jewish doctor who chose to work with the SS
as a way to survive. An unforgettable account of some of the medical horrors which
were part of the "final solution." The story of a man who accepted his fate rather
than fight it and as a consequence became a collaborator in order to survive. There
is an interesting account of the revolt of a sonderkommando unit—the only one at
Auschwitz.

1527   Pinkus, Oscar. **The House of Ashes.** Cleveland, World Publishing, 1964.
        243p. Map.
A personal narrative of one man's sturggle for survival. Pinkus emphasizes that
he speaks for thousands for he is not unique. Pinkus places the blame for thousands
if not millions of Jewish deaths on two factors: (1) the Jews were surrounded by
non-Germans who were anti-semitic and would not help, and (2) the refusal of
the Allies to give any aid (i.e., bombing concentration camps). In particular, the
Polish underground comes off badly for their lack of concern for helping Polish
Jews.

1528   Poliakov. Leon. **Harvest of Hate: The Nazi Program for the Destruction
        of the Jews of Europe.** Syracuse, Syracuse University Press, 1954. 338p.
        Maps, Bibliog.
Perhaps the best general introduction to the Nazi attempt to destroy European
Jews. There is background material on the origins of the Nazi's Jewish policy and
the various proposals to remove the Jews from Europe before a "final solution"
was chosen. Some other topics discussed include the ghettos, massacres on the
Eastern Front, deportations to the death camps, the death camps, Jewish resistance and Nazi plans for other "inferior peoples." A balanced and unemotional
scholarly work.

1529   Presser, Jacob. **The Destruction of the Dutch Jews.** New York, Dutton,
        1969. 556p. Map, Bibliog.
A lengthy detailed and definitive study of the Nazi program to destroy the Dutch
Jews. Covers from May 10, 1940, when the Netherlands was occupied, through the
later deportations to death camps. Presser is critical not only of the Germans, but
also of the Dutch and the Jews when their inaction or collaboration was of help
to the Germans. Based on documents and personal narratives, many of which have
been available only a few years. The English edition is titled *Ashes in the Wind:
The Destruction of Dutch Jewry.*

1530   Reitlinger, Gerald Roberts. **The Final Solution: The Attempt to
        Exterminate the Jews of Europe, 1939-1945.** 2nd ed. rev. and augm.
        ed. South Brunswick, N.J., Yoseloff, 1968. 667p. Maps, Bibliog.
A general historical survey of the fate of Europe's Jews under Nazi rule. The first
part of the study is concerned with the "search for the final solution" and the
decision for genocide. The second part traces "the final solution in practice" in
each European country. A comprehensive "Statistical Summary of the Final
Solution" is a useful source of data. This was a pioneer work in the area of the
Holocaust and laid the groundwork for further research. Recently it has been
subjected to some criticism by revisionist historians.

1531   Ringelblum, Emanuel. **Notes from the Warsaw Ghetto: The Journal of
        Emmanuel Ringelblum.** New York, McGraw-Hill, 1958. 369p. Maps.
A classic standard work on life in the Warsaw Ghetto. The *Notes* cover the period
from October 1939 to the end of 1942. Ringelblum, a professional historian, became the archivist for the ghetto and took these notes for historical reasons—they
are not a diary. The *Notes* ". . . are really notes toward a history of the times,
and nothing else." Ringelblum's information came from his own observations

and interviews, and conversations with a great variety of important and common
people. Ringelblum was killed in 1944 along with his family. In part Hersey's
novel *The Wall* is based on the *Notes.*

1532   Robinson, Jacob, and Philip Friedman. **Guide to Jewish History Under
        Nazi Impact.** New York, KTAV Publishing House, 1960. 425p.
The standard bibliographic guide to the study of the impact of the Nazis on
Europe's Jews. Every aspect of Jewish history is covered and the materials cited
are in English, Yiddish and most modern European languages. This is a primary
guide for anyone studying the Holocuast and the fate of European Jewry from
1933 to 1945. Unfortunately, the bibliography is now fourteen years old and
in need of some updating. Nonetheless, the guide remains the basic bibliographic
tool for the Holocaust.

1533   Rousset, David. **The Other Kingdom.** New York, Reynal and Hitchcock,
        1947. 173p.
A vivid yet unemotional account of the author's sixteen months in Buchenwald,
Neuengamme and several other concentration camps. Many specific incidents of
camp life are cited, but Rousset is mainly concerned with an analysis of how the
tragic results of a criminal government happened.

1534   Trunk, Isaiah. **Judenrat: The Jewish Councils in Eastern Europe Under
        Nazi Occupation.** New York, Macmillan, 1972. 664p. Bibliog.
An imposing definitive work on the Jewish Councils, or Judenrat, in Eastern
Europe primarily in Poland. This is an analysis of the "self-government" imposed
on the Jews by the local Nazi governments. Trunk is concerned with the conditions
under which the Councils were forced to operate, the motivations of Council
leaders and the results of the "self-government."

1535   Wells, Leon Weliczker. **The Janowska Road.** New York, Macmillan,
        1963. 305p. Maps.
One of the best personal memoirs of a concentration camp inmate. Wells spent
from 1941 to 1945 in Nazi concentration camps. The memoirs are based at least
in part on a secret diary Wells managed to keep in the camps, and he quotes
liberally from notes made at the time events actually occurred. Good psychological
and sociological insights into life in a concentration camp.

1536   Wiesel, Eliezer. **Night.** New York, Hill and Wang, 1960. 116p.
A short moving account of a Jewish family's brief but disastrous ordeal in a concentration camp. Wiesel, now a well established author, wrote this work as a child's
view of camp life. Wiesel's account of his relationship with his father, who died
only days before the liberation, is particularly moving. Wiesel also describes how
he lost his belief in God.

1537   Yahil, Leni. **The Rescue of Danish Jewry: Test of a Democracy.**
        Philadelphia, Jewish Publication Society of America, 1969. 536p. Bibliog.
A history of the heroic escape of Denmark's Jews to Sweden to prevent their
annihilation by the Nazis. Yahil gives a short history of the Jews in Denmark prior
to the Nazi occupation. There is coverage of Jewish life during the occupation and

of the activities of a small number of native Danish anti-semites. The main part of the study is concerned with the planning for the escape and the escape itself of the Danish Jews. Some emphasis is placed on the part played by non-Jewish Danes. The Danes were a singularly shining example in Europe of a people attempting—and succeeding—to prevent a human disaster.

ATROCITIES AND PRISON CAMPS

Europe

1538   Bradley, John. **Lidice: Sacrificial Village**. New York, Ballantine Books, 1972. 160p. Maps, Bibliog.
An account of the tragic destruction of the village of Lidice and the murder of many of its inhabitants as a reprisal for the assassination of Reinhard Heydrich in 1942. After S.O.E. operatives successfully murdered Heydrich the Nazis decided on a dramatic display of vengeance. Lidice was leveled, the soil salted, the men inhabitants executed, the women and some children sent to concentration camps and the remainder of the children scattered.

1539   Dicks, Henry Victor. **Licensed Mass Murder: A Socio-Psychological Study of Some SS Killers**. New York, Basic Books, 1972. 283p. Bibliog.
A psychological and sociological study based on interviews of a number of SS killers. The subjects include both actual killers and high ranking "arm Chair" killers. The conceptual approach of the study tries to answer five questions: (1) Were the killers insane? (2) How do humans descend so low as to serve in murder squads, etc.? (3) What pressures made such acts acceptable? (4) What happened to these men when Hitler's power collapsed? (5) How did these men's conduct indirectly reflect on the mentality of Nazi leadership?

1540   Katz, Robert. **Death in Rome**. New York, Macmillan, 1967. 334p. Map, Bibliog.
The story of the Ardeatine Massacre in 1944 of 335 Italian civilians in retaliation for the death of some German SS troops. Katz delves into the reasons for the massacre and the German reaction. There is attention given to the political reasons behind the silence of Pius XII.

1541   Kenrick, Donald, and Grattan Puxon. **The Destiny of Europe's Gypsies**. New York, Basic Books, 1972. 256p. Bibliog.
A scholarly well researched study of Europe's Gypsies. Most of the book is concerned with the period 1939-1945 and the Nazis' attempt to exterminate the Gypsies. Attention is given to the fate of the Gypsies in the concentration camps. There is a good section which attempts to explain why society, and Nazi society in particular, needs victims.

1542   Macardle, Dorothy. **Children of Europe: A Study of the Children of Liberated Countries; Their War-Time Experiences, Their Reactions, and Their Needs, With a Note on Germany**. Boston, Beacon Press, 1951. 349p.

A study of the tragic fate of many European children trapped in a war they could not understand. The author is primarily concerned with the psychological impact of war on children. The study involved travel to many countries and interviews with child psychologists. Twenty countries are covered.

1543   Paris, Edmond. **Genocide in Satellite Croatia, 1941-1945: A Record of Racial and Religious Persecutions and Massacres.** Chicago, American Institute of Balkan Affairs, 1961. 306p. Map, Bibliog.
A study of the crimes of the Croatian fascists—the Ustashi—under Ante Pavelic. Paris claims that over 800,000 people were killed by the Ustashi including 700,000 Serbs, 60,000 Jews and 26,000 Gypsies. Interesting material on the role of the Catholic Church in war-time Croatia.

1544   Russell, Edward Frederick Langley Russell. **The Scourge of the Swastika: A Short History of Nazi War Crimes.** New York, Philosophical Library, 1954. 259p.
A carefully done study of the entire scope of the Nazis' crimes against humanity. Only in parts does the objectivity of the book become blurred by the author's emotions. Strong reading, but a good general introduction.

1545   U. S. Congress. House. Select Committee on the Katyn Forest Massacre. **The Katyn Forest Massacre.** Washington, Government Printing Office, 1952. 7pts. (2362p.) Maps.
A massive compilation of testimony and documents relating to the massacre of thousands of Polish officers in the Katyn Forest near Smolensk, Russia. The hearings were held in Washington and Germany. Witnesses and documents include American, Polish and Russian sources. The charge to the House committee was "to conduct a full and complete investigation and study of the facts, evidence and extenuating circumstances both before and after the massacre of thousands of Polish officers . . . ." The Committee concluded that the Russians, not the Germans, were responsible for the massacre.

1546   U. S. Congress. Senate. Committee on Armed Services. **Malmedy Massacre Investigation.** Washington, Government Printing Office, 1949. 2pts. (1639p.)
An official U. S. investigation of the massacre of American troops in December 1944 during the Battle of the Bulge. A number of Belgian civilians were also killed by German troops. Includes testimony of people directly involved and official documentary evidence. A further investigation on the evidence presented at the War Crimes Trial held at Dachau in 1946. These hearings were held in Washington and in Germany.

1547   Whiting, Charles. **Massacre at Malmedy: The Story of Jochen Peiper's Battle Group, Ardennes, December 1944.** New York, Stein and Day, 1971. 198p. Bibliog.
A popular well researched account of the massacre of American troops and Belgian civilians in Malmedy, Belgium, during the Battle of the Bulge. There is good detail of the events preceding the atrocity and the actions of the German troops.

1548   Yoors, Ian. **Crossing**. New York, Simon and Schuster, 1971. 224p.
A study of the Gypsies' experiences during the war with the Nazis. Yoors, who
worked for Allied intelligence, includes many of his personal experiences with
the Gypsies. Well written interesting reading about often forgotten victims of
Nazi genocide policies. An autobiographical study.

1549   Zawodny, Janusz Kazimierz. **Death in the Forest: The Story of the Katyn
        Forest Massacre**. Notre Dame, University of Notre Dame Press, 1962.
        235p. Bibliog.
A standard scholarly account of the Katyn Forest massacre. The author, who
fought in the Polish underground, presents an objective unemotional account of
the disappearance or massacre of some 15,000 Poles including some 8,000 officers.
The book tries to answer three questions: "Who killed these men? How were they
killed? Why were they killed?"

Far East

1550   Falk, Stanley Lawrence. **Bataan: The March of Death**. New York, Norton,
        1962. 256p.
The story of the infamous Philippines "death march." The Japanese forced
nearly 90,000 American and Filipino troops to march long distances to prisoner
of war camps. The cruelty of many Japanese troops combined with lack of supplies
led to numerous deaths and injuries. Probably the most publicized and worst single
atrocity committed against Americans.

1551   Fletcher-Cooke, John. **The Emperor's Guest, 1942-45**. London, Hutchin-
        son, 1971. 318p. Maps.
The memoirs of an English prisoner of war from late 1942 to 1945 when the war
ended. Good for details of the camp life of a prisoner. Fletcher-Cooke maintains
that based on his experiences with the Japanese the use of the atomic bomb
probably saved more lives than it killed in the long run.

1552   Gilkey, Langdon Brown. **Shantung Compound: The Story of Men and
        Women Under Pressure**. New York, Harper & Row, 1966. 242p.
The story of the author's experiences at a civilian internment camp in North China.
The inmates suffered no extreme hardships and no physical brutality. The author,
a theologian, is interested in the behavior of individuals in stressful situations.
Good psychological insights into people stripped of their basic dignity. Based on
a journal kept in the camp.

1553   Hartendorp, A. V. H. **The Santo Tomas Story**. New York, McGraw-Hill,
        1964. 446p. Maps.
A first hand account of the Santo Tomas internment camp established in the
Philippines under the Japanese occupation. The author, an inmate, tells of conditions in the camp, camp government and makes "observations on the sociological, psychological and medical aspects of camp life." Based primarily on notes
and diary entries kept at the time. This work is part of the author's unpublished
history of Santo Tomas and the Japanese occupation of the Philippines.

1554   McDougall, William H. **By Eastern Windows: The Story of a Battle of Souls and Minds in the Prison Camps of Sumatra.** New York, Scribner, 1949. 349p. Map.
An exciting account of the author's experiences in four Japanese prison camps over a three year period. Good on the Japanese treatment of Allied prisoners and the harshness and dullness of camp life. Unfortunately, while never dull, the book tends to be weak when discussing the psychological adaptation of the prisoners.

1555   Pavillard, Stanley S. **Bamboo Doctor.** New York, St. Martin's Press. 1960. 206p. Maps.
A well written memoir of a British medical officer who served with the Malayan Volunteer Force. Insights into camp life of prisoners of war and the brutalities of the Japanese in Southeast Asia. Pavillard, like many other medical officers, helped to ease the life of many prisoners under the most trying conditions.

1556   Russell, Edward Frederick Langeley Russell. **The Knights of bushido: The Shocking History of Japanese War Atrocities.** New York, Dutton, 1958. 334p.
A good general introduction to the atrocities committed by the Japanese against military prisoners of war and civilians. Harsh reading about a seemingly unending series of atrocities. Based primarily on materials and testimony at the International Military Tribunal for the Far East.

1557   Stewart, Sidney. **Give Us This Day.** New York, Norton, 1957. 254p.
A personal narrative by an American soldier who was a Japanese prisoner more than three years. Stewart was held prisoner under very cruel conditions and there are good insights into prison camp life. There is equally good insight into the Japanese soldier's mentality. Stewart was in the Philippines when the war started and was captured in Bataan and was involved in the infamous death march.

CHAPTER 12–WAR CRIMES TRIALS

GENERAL

1558   Appleman, John Alan. **Military Tribunals and International Crimes.**
        Indianapolis, Bobbs-Merrill, 1954. 421p.
A clearly written comprehensive treatise on the war crimes trials. The author
discusses the major trials held at Nuremberg and Tokyo and the other lesser
trials. The main purpose of the book is to determine "the legal right to conduct
these proceedings . . . the fairness or unfairness of the procedures employed and
sentences handed down." An excellent introduction.

1559   Hankey, Maurice Pascal Alers Hankey. **Politics, Trials, and Errors.**
        Chicago, Regnery, 1950. 150p.
A critical essay on the Nuremberg and Tokyo war crimes trials. Hankey, a respected
British statesman, criticizes the concepts of "unconditional surrender" and the
principles behind the war crimes trials. He contends that the political nature of
the trials led to victor's justice. However, the conclusions are not always documented.
A stimulating book. Part of the book is an argument against the conviction of
Mamoru Shigemitsu at the Tokyo trial.

1560   International Conference on Military Trials. **Report of Robert H. Jackson,
        United States Representative to the International Conference on Military
        Trials, London, 1945.** Washington, Government Printing Office, 1949.
        441p.
The official proceedings and documents of the conference held from June to
August 1945 by the United States, Great Britain, France and Russia to establish
the machinery for the European war crimes trials. This work represents the
"formal statement of the principles of substantive law and agreed upon methods
of procedure for the prosecution and trial of the major European war criminals."
A basic resource for understanding the principles upon which the trails were held.

1561   Maugham, Frederic Herbert Maugham. **U.N.O. and War Crimes.** London,
        Murray, 1951. 143p.
The author, a former Lord Chancellor of Great Britain, is critical of the basic
principles on which the war crimes trials were held. The object of the book is
to establish the principle that in the future the only persons who can be tried
fairly are those guilty of violating "the laws and usages of war" and not "crimes
against peace" or "crimes against humanity."

1562   United Nations War Crimes Commission. **History of the United Nations
        War Crimes Commission and the Development of the Laws of War.**
        London, H. M. Stationery Office, 1948. 592p. Bibliog.
A detailed history of the origin and work of the United Nations War Crimes Commission. The Commission was established to investigate and record the evidence
of war crimes, to identify the individuals responsible, and to report the cases to

the Allied governments. The Commission also developed the procedures to prose-
cute war criminals and defined the terms "major" and "minor" war criminals.
There is basic background material on the laws of war and the concepts of "War
Crimes," "Crimes Against Humanity," and "Crimes Against Peace." A basic work
on the laws of war as applied at the war crimes trials.

1563   United Nations War Crimes Commission. **Law Reports of War Criminals.**
        London, H. M. Stationery Office, 1947-49. 15v.
A series of analyses of the various cases of the "minor" war criminals tried before
British and U. S. military courts. Includes trials held in Europe and the Far East.
Each case is summarized with a brief section on the crimes committed, applicable
laws and the legal issues involved. Rather complex and legalistic, but basic for
studying the legal aspects of the trials.

GERMAN

1564   Benton, Wilbourn E. and Georg Grimm, eds. **Nuremberg: German Views
        of the War Trials.** Dallas, Southern Methodist University Press, 1955.
        232p. Bibliog.
A compilation of twelve essays on the Nuremberg Trials mostly by German lawyers.
In general the contributors agree with the need to punish war criminals, but are
critical of the trials. An introductory essay by the editors tends to reinforce the
German view and introduce the reader to the place of the trials in the law of
nations.

1565   Bosch, William J. **Judgment on Nuremberg: American Attitudes Toward
        the Major German War-Crime Trials.** Chapel Hill, University of North
        Carolina Press, 1970. 272p. Bibliog.
A scholarly study of American public opinion of the Nuremberg Trials. With a
few exceptions most Americans favored the trials and the punishment of war
criminals. The exceptions were mostly historians and experts in international
affairs.

1566   Calvocoressi, Peter. **Nuremberg: The Facts, the Law and the Consequences.**
        New York, Macmillan, 1948. 176p.
An interpretation of the Nuremberg Trials by a member of the British prosecution
staff. The weakest sections of the book are those in which Calvocoressi comments
on the defendants' personalities. A good general introduction to the trials.

1567   Davidson, Eugene. **The Trial of the Germans: An Account of the Twenty-
        Two Defendants Before the International Military Tribunal.** New York,
        Macmillan, 1966. 636p. Bibliog.
A popular biographical introduction to twenty-two of the major German war
criminals tried in person or *in absentia* at Nuremberg. There is background
material on the purpose and scope of the trials. The biographical materials give
a brief sketch of the person's role in the war, the reasons for being on trial and
their general background. Davidson captures well the atmosphere of the trials.
Also, six criminal organizations (i.e., SS, Gestapo) and their role in the Third
Reich are discussed.

1568   DuBois, Josiah Ellis and Edward Johnson. **The Devil's Chemists: 24 Conspirators of the International Farben Cartel Who Manufacture Wars.** Boston, Beacon Press, 1952. 374p.

A very readable account of the 1947 trial of twenty-four high ranking officials of the I. G. Farben Company. These men were tried as war criminals at the International Tribunal at Nuremberg. Good for understanding the wartime activities of a business' relationship with waging war. The English edition is titled *Generals in Grey Suits.*

1569   Eck, Heinz, defendant. **Trial of Heinz Eck, August Hoffman, Walter Weisspfennig, Hans Richard Lenz and Wolfgang Schwender (The Peleus Trial).** London, Hodge, 1948. 247p.

The account of the trial of the crew of the German submarine U-852 for deliberately attempting to murder the surviving crewmen of the merchant ship Peleus. After torpedoing the Peleus, U-852 remained in the area instead of fleeing and eventually attempted to murder helpless seamen for very questionable reasons. Eck and most of the defendants were sentenced to death.

1570   Falkenhorst, Nikolaus von, defendant. **Trial of Nikolaus von Falkenhorst, Formerly Generaloberst in the German Army.** London, Hodge, 1949. 278p. Maps.

This is an account of the proceedings of the trial of General von Falkenhorst, the German Commander-in-Chief in Norway from 1940 to 1944. There were nine charges against von Falkenhorst but essentially the question was: "whether von Falkenhorst had decreed the deaths of Allied fighting men taken prisoner . . . contrary to the laws and usages of war; and if he had, was there any lawful justification or excuse for his actions." The court found von Falkenhorst guilty.

1571   Gerike, Heinrich, defendant. **Trial of Heinrich Gerike and Others (The Velpke Baby Home Trial).** London, Hodge, 1950. 356p.

The proceedings of the trial of eight German civilians charged "with having been concerned in the killing by wilful neglect of a number of children, Polish nationals." Unlike most of the other trials the issue here was not waging aggressive war but rather violation of individual rights. The court found most of the defendants guilty. Gruesome reading showing the degree to which men can sink in a criminal society.

1572   Germany (Territory Under Allied Occupation, 1945– . U. S. Zone) Military Tribunals. **Trials of War Criminals Before the Nuremberg Military Tribunals Under Control Council Law No. 10, Nuremberg, October 1946- April 1949.** Washington, Government Printing Office, 1949-53. 15v.

The official compilation of the trial proceedings and related documents of German war criminals—these are *not* the trials of the major criminals. The twelve trials included are: (1) The Medical Cases, (2) The Milch Case, (3) The Justice Case, (4) The Pohl Case, (5) The Flick Case, (6) I. G. Farben Case, (7) Hostage Case, (8) The Ru SHA Case, (9) The Einsatzgruppen Case, (10) The Krupp Case, (11) The Ministries Case, and (12) The High Command Case.

1573   Gilbert, G. M. **Nuremberg Diary.** New York, Farrar, Straus, 1947. 471p.

An examination of the attitudes and personalities of the defendants at the Nuremberg Trials. The author was the prison psychologist at Nuremberg and had numerous conversations and other contacts with the defendants. Many verbatim quotations are given and Gilbert refrains from "manufacturing conversations." Good psychological insights. An interesting book.

1574   Glueck, Sheldon. **The Nuremberg Trial and Aggressive War.** New York, Knopf, 1946. 121p. Bibliog.

The author, a criminal law expert, has written a defense and justification of the Nuremberg Trials of German war criminals. Glueck argues that "aggressive war" is unlawful and criminal. An insight into a contemporary American view of the trials.

1575   Goering, Hermann, defendant. **Trial of the Major War Criminals Before the International Military Tribunal, Nuremberg, 14 November 1945- 10 October 1946.** Nuremberg, 1947-49. 42v.

The official record of the proceedings and related documents of the trial of the twenty-three major German war criminals. Among the defendants were Goering Hess, Speer, Von Ribbentrop, Kaltenbrunner, Streicher and others. Membership in certain organizations was also declared criminal—Reich Cabinet, Leadership Corps of Nazi Party, SS, SD, Gestapo, SA and the General Staff. The volumes include: v.1, Official Documents; v.2-22, Proceedings; v.23, Chronological and Subject Index; v.24, Document and Name Index; v.25-42, Documents and Other Material in Evidence. The basic source for the German war crimes trials.

1576   Harris, Whitney R. **Tyranny on Trial: The Evidence at Nuremberg.** Dallas, Southern Methodist University Press, 1954. 608p. Map, Bibliog.

A detailed scholarly analysis of the Nuremberg Trials and the evidence presented. The study examines the evidence used to show the Nazi rise to power, the war crimes and the crimes against humanity. A study of aggression and crimes against humanity in international law.

1577   Jackson, Robert Houghwout. **The Nuremberg Case, as Presented by Robert H. Jackson, Chief of Counsel for the United States, Together with Other Documents.** New York, Knopf, 1947. 268p.

A good summary of the U. S. case at the Nuremberg Trials. Includes the opening statement and closing statement of the United States counsel and excerpts from the cross examinations of Goering, Speer, Schacht and others. Jackson was the United States' Chief prosecutor at Nuremberg.

1578   Joyce, William, defendant. **Trial of William Joyce.** London, Hodge, 1946. 312p.

This volume "consists of a verbatim record of the trial . . . at the Central Criminal Court . . . . A summary of the arguments . . . the full text of the judgments in the appeals to the Court of Criminal Appeal and to the House of Lords . . . ." Also included are the text of the Treason Act, 1945, and some of the wartime broadcasts made by Joyce. Joyce was accused of treason for his wartime broadcasts from Germany. The introduction includes some material on the problem of Joyce's citizenship.

1579   Killinger, Erich, defendant. **Trial of Erich Killinger, Heinz Junge, Otto Boehringer, Heinrich Eberhardt, Gustav Bauer-Schlichtegroll (The Dulag-Luft Trial).** London, Hodge, 1952. 255p.
The verbatim account of the trial of five German Air Force officers accused of crimes relating "to endeavors to extract operational information from Allied airmen by torture . . . ." Durlag Luft was the name given to the German Air Force Interrogation Centre where many Allied airmen were taken to gather intelligence information.

1580   Kline, Alfons, defendant. **Trial of Alfons Kline, Adolf Wahlmann, Heinrich Ruoff, Karl Willig, Adolf Merkle, Irmgard Huber, and Philipp Blum (The Hadamar Trial).** London, Hodge, 1949. 250p.
An account of the trial of seven German civilians charged "with the deliberate murder of over 400 Polish and Russian nationals at Hadamar Institution by injections or poisonous drugs." A view of some of the "little men" who just followed their orders. Without this type Hitler could not have carried out most of his murderous plans. Not pleasant reading.

1581   Knieriem, August von. **The Nuremberg Trials.** Chicago, Regnery , 1959. 561p.
An analysis of the Nuremberg Trials by a German defense lawyer. Not primarily concerned with the trails of major war criminals, but with twelve further trials of lesser criminals held between 1946 and 1949. Knieriem argues that the concept of war crimes trials is reasonable, but these particular trials were unfair.

1582   Kramer, Josef, defendant. **Trial of Josef Kramer and Forty-Four Others (The Belsen Trial).** London, Hodge, 1949. 749p. Map.
"This book tells a story which, in its horrible account of 'man's inhumanity to man,' has perhaps never been surpassed." The forty-five accused "were charged with having either personally killed or ill-treated Allied nationals, or with having been concerned with such killing or ill-treatment as to share in the responsibility for it." Although called the Belsen Trial, the defendants were involved at both Bergen-Belsen and Auschwitz. Unpleasant reading.

1583   Musmanno, Michael Angelo. **The Eichmann Kommandos.** Philadelphia, Macrae Smith, 1961. 268p.
The story of the Einsatzgruppen Trial. These were the special units employed on the Eastern Front to murder the racial or political undesirables as defined by the Nazis. An insight into mass murder carried out by men with tortured minds. Musmanno, a judge, discusses the philosophy behind Nuremberg and the preparation and scope of the Einsatzgruppen Trial.

1584   Naumann, Bernd. **Auschwitz: A Report on the Proceedings Against Robert Karl Ludwig Mulka and Others Before the Court at Frankfurt.** New York, Praeger, 1966. 433p.
An account of the "show trial" held from 1963 to 1965 of twenty-two SS officers and officials who served at Auschwitz. Mulka, the main defendant, was adjutant to the camp commander Hoess. The defendants were mostly lower echelon cold blooded killers, not armchair planners far removed from Auschwitz, Hannah

Arendt's introduction covers some of the contemporary legal, political and public opinion aspects of the trial.

1585   Paget, Reginald Thomas. **Manstein: His Campaigns and His Trial.** London, Collins, 1951. 239p. Maps.

An account of the trial of Field-Marshal Erich von Manstein for alleged war crimes committed by himself and men under his command in Poland and Russia. Manstein was found guilty and sentenced finally to 12 years in prison. The background material on his campaigns relates to his later trial. This was a controversial trial which many thought should never have been held. The author, a member of the defense, presents a sympathetic account.

1586   U. S. Chief of Counsel for the Prosecution of Axis Criminality. **Nazi Conspiracy and Aggression.** Washington, Government Printing Office, 1946-48. 10v.

A massive collection of "documentary evidence and guide materials" used by the Americans and British in the trial of the major German war criminals at Nuremberg. The materials are in English. These materials are not part of the official trial documents, but were used to prepare the case for the prosecution.

1587   West, Rebecca. **The New Meaning of Treason.** New York, Viking Press, 1964. 374p.

The first section of this book is concerned with the treason trials of William Joyce and William Amery. William Joyce was known as "Lord Haw Haw." In separate trials each was accused of treason for their propaganda broadcasts made from Nazi Germany during the war years. The author covers the men's backgrounds, their wartime activities and their trial. A beautifully written book which keeps the reader's interest.

1588   Woetzel, Robert K. **The Nuremberg Trials in International Law.** New York, Praeger, 1960. 287p. Bibliog.

A scholarly analysis of the Nuremberg trials which concludes that the trials indeed had "a legal character and a legal basis." Woetzel places the Nuremberg trials in historical perspective by discussing some historical precursors beginning in the Middle Ages. There is discussion of the responsibility of the individual under international law, crimes against peace and humanity and criminal organizations.

1589   Zeuss, Wolfgang, defendant. **Trial of Wolfgang Zeuss, Magnus Wochner, Emil Meier, Peter Straub, Fritz Hartjenstein, Franz Berg, Werner Rohde, Emil Bruttel, Kurt Aus Dem Bruch and Harberg (The Natzweiler Trial).** London, Hodge, 1949. 233p.

The verbatim official record of the trial of nine members of the staff at the Struthof-Natzweiler Concentration Camp. They were charged with "the cold-blooded killing of four women by injection followed by cremation, in circumstances which gave rise to suspicions whether or not the victims were dead or even unconscious when they were put into the crematorium oven." The four women were spies working for the British Special Operations Executive (SOE). The defense claimed it was legal to execute captured spies.

EICHMANN TRIAL

1590   Arendt, Hannah. **Eichmann in Jerusalem: A Report on the Banality of**
         Evil. Rev. and enl. ed. New York, Viking Press, 1964. 312p. Bibliog.
A controversial analysis of Adolf Eichmann, his trial and the totalitarian state
which conceived the "final solution." Arendt questions the fairness of trial, but
not the need for justice. Blame for the death of five million Jews is placed on the
Germans and on the Jews for not escaping after 1933 or resisting later. Stimulating reading.

1591   Hausner, Gideon. **Justice in Jerusalem.** New York, Harper & Row, 1966.
         528p. Bibliog.
A justification of the Eichmann trial by the Attorney General of Israel who was
the chief trial prosecutor. The background materials present a general record of
the "final solution" and particularly where Eichmann was involved. Hausner is
critical of the attitude on the Jewish problem of the Vatican and Pope Pius XII.

1592   Papadatos, Petros Achilleos. **The Eichmann Trial.** New York, Praeger,
         1964. 129p. Bibliog.
A brief clear interpretation of the major issues and problems involved in the
Eichmann trial. Some of the topics discussed include the case against Eichmann,
main problems of the trial, the Israeli judges, the right of Israel to try Eichmann,
the abduction and the evidence. Excellent analysis by a scholar of international
law.

1593   Pearlman, Moshe. **The Capture and Trial of Adolf Eichmann.** New York,
         Simon and Schuster, 1963. 666p.
Possibly the most objective study of the capture and trial of Adolf Eichmann.
There is material on the tracking and capture of Eichmann in South America
and a full account of the trial. Pearlman defends the trial and cites legal precedent
in his support. The transcript of the trial is quoted at length.

1594   Robinson, Jacob. **And the Crooked Shall be Made Straight: The Eichmann**
         Trial, the Jewish Catastrophe, and Hannah Arendt's Narrative. New York,
         Macmillan, 1965. 406p. Bibliog.
The author, an international law authority, was a prosecution consultant at the
Eichmann trial. The book covers Eichmann's background and war crimes, the
legal basis for the trial, the trial itself, Jewish behavior and resistance in the holocaust and the fate of Europe's Jews in a country by country survey. Robinson is
critical of Arendt's thesis and defends the trial and Jewish behavior during the
holocaust. A good critical analysis.

JAPANESE

1595   Dull, Paul S. and Michael Takaaki Umemura. **The Tokyo Trials: A**
         Functional Index to the Proceedings of the International Military Tri-
         bunal for the Far East. Ann Arbor, University of Michigan Press, 1957.
         94p.

An index and guide to the 50,000 pages of evidence taken at the International Military Tribunal for the Far East. Of course, you probably will not be able to find a set of the proceedings! Unlike the ubiquitous Nuremberg trials set, the Tokyo trials proceedings were never printed, but only mimeographed.

1596   Gozawa, Sadaichi, defendant. **Trial of Gozawa Sadaichi and Nine Others.** London, Hodge, 1948. 245p. Map.
The verbatim report of the trial of ten Japanese officers and men charged with the mistreatment of over 500 Indian troops. The prisoners were placed under the control of a special Japanese unit called the "Gozawa Butai." What followed was a brutal confinement with beatings, starvation and inhuman labor assignments. The introduction includes an information section on life in the Japanese Army.

1597   Hanayama, Shinsho. **The Way of Deliverance: Three Years with the Condemned Japanese War Criminals.** New York, Scribner, 1950. 297p.
The author was a Buddhist chaplain to the accused Japanese war criminals and was with them during the trials. He gives his impressions of the accused's mental state and their reactions to the legal proceedings. He maintains that religion was an important part of their discussions. A very human compassionate story.

1598   Keenan, Joseph Berry, and Brendan Francis Brown. **Crimes Against International Law.** Washington, Public Affairs Press, 1950. 226p. Bibliog.
This book "constitutes, in effect, the position taken by the United States at the historic Tokyo war crimes trials ending in 1948." The authors are principally concerned with the law involved in the Tokyo trails. They further contend that "the Tokyo and Nuremberg trials were manifestations of an intellectual and moral revolution . . . ." Both authors served on the U. S. prosecution team at the Tokyo trials.

1599   Minear, Richard H. **Victors' Justice: The Tokyo War Crimes Trial.** Princeton, N.J., Princeton University Press, 1971. 229p. Bibliog.
The author presents a scholarly study whose major concern is "to challenge this prevailing image of the trial, to demolish the credibility of the Tokyo trial and its verdict." Minear argues that Tojo and others were legally innocent. Twenty-five military and political prisoners were tried at Tokyo. There is coverage of the background of the trials, the proceedings and the verdicts.

1600   Pal, Radhabinod. **International Military Tribunal for the Far East: Dissentient Judgment.** Calcutta, Sanyal, 1953. 701p.
A scholarly and lengthy minority legal opinion arguing against the concept of the war crimes trials as conceived by the International Military Tribunal for the Far East. Pal holds that most of the so-called criminal acts were in fact legal and carried out by representatives of a legally recognized government. There are lengthy discussions on aggressive war, crimes against peace, murder, conventional war crimes and crimes against humanity. Pal concludes that the victor cannot offer the vanquished justice, and in the Far East trials, justice was merely the interest of the stronger power.

1601   Reel, Adolf Frank. **The Case of General Yamashita.** Chicago, University
        of Chicago Press, 1949. 323p.
An eloquent well researched account of General Yamashita's trial. Reel is sympathetic to Yamashita, but nonetheless objective. A call for conscience, Reel presents a frightening view of "victors' justice" and its future implications. An
appendix gives the opinion of the U. S. Supreme Court to which Yamashita's
sentence was appealed. Reel served as a defense counsel at the trial.

1602   Sumida, Haruzo, defendant. **Trial of Sumida Haruzo and Twenty Others
        (The "Double Tenth" Trial).** London, Hodge, 1951. 324p.
The record of the trial of Lt. Colonel Sumida Haruzo, the chief of the Singapore
Kempei Tai, and twenty other officers and enlisted men. The defendants were
charged with responsibility for fifteen deaths and the torture and beating of many
other civilians while trying to gather intelligence information at Changi Gaol.

1603   U. S. Dept. of State. **Trial of Japanese War Criminals. Documents:**
        1. Opening Statement by Joseph B. Keenan, Chief of Counsel.
        2. Charter of the International Military Tribunal for the Far East.
        3. Indictment. Washington, Government Printing Office, 1946. 104p.
A compilation of important documents basic to the conduct of the International
Military Tribunal for the Far East. This is one of the few items on the Tokyo
trials that has been printed. The proceedings of the IMTFE have not been printed
as have the Nuremberg trials. So far they are only in mimeograph format and are
held by only a few libraries. [See Richard H. Minear, *Victors' Justice: The Tokyo
War Crimes Trial* (Princeton, Princeton University Press, 1971) p.213.]

AUTHOR-TITLE-BIOGRAPHEE INDEX

The materials are cited by item number. Entries for biographical material have been made both under the author's name and under the subject's name.

Abel, T. F., 217
Abraham Lincoln Brigade, 143
Accoce, P., 1429
Aces High, 745
Acheson, D. G., 1104
Ack-Ack, 742
Addington, L. H., 461
Adler, S., 321
Administration of War Production, 1238
Admiral Ambassador to Russia, 1199
Admiral Halsey's Story, 817
Admiral Kimmel's Story, 417
Admiral Raymond A. Spruance, USN, 814
After Imperialism, 364
After Victory, 1208
Aftermath, 262
Against Stalin and Hitler, 1428
Agar, H., 1035
Agar-Hamilton, J. A. I., 629-30
Age of Roosevelt, 348
Ageton, A. A., 1199
Agoncillo, T. A., 1349
Agricultural Economy of the Danubian Countries, 1935-1945, 1218
Agriculture, 1235
Aid to Russia, 1941-1946, 1195
Air Marshals, 726
Air Spy, 1433
Air War and Emotional Stress, 1279
Aircraft in Profile, 848
Aircraft of the Royal Air Force since 1918, 872
Aircraft of World War II, 846
Aircraft Versus Submarine, 867
Airpower and Russian Partisan Warfare, 750
Airwar, 719
Alamein, 646
Albrecht-Carrie, R., 209
Alcorn, R. H., 1430-31
Alexander, C. C., 1300
Alexander, H., 584
Alexander of Tunis as Military Commander, 584
Alfieri, D., 1170
Allen, G. E., 1105
Allen, W. S., 218
Alliance Against Hitler, 368
Allied Bayonets of World War II, 876

Allied Intelligence Bureau, 1460
Allied Military Administration of Italy, 1943-1945, 1345
Allied Wartime Diplomacy, 1086
Alms for Oblivion, 1465
Alperovitz, G., 913
Alsop, J. W., 322
Alsop, S. J. O., 1432
Ambrose, S. E., 497, 612
American at War: A Geographical Analysis, 1148
America at War: The Home Front, 1941-1945, 1317
America, Britain and Russia, 1207
America Encounters India, 1941-1947, 1189
America First, 179
American Aid to France, 1938-1940, 406
American Appeasement, 163
American Battleships, Carriers and Cruisers, 877
American Combat Planes, 893
American Crisis Diplomacy, 352
American Diplomacy and the Spanish Civil War, 148
American Diplomacy during the Second World War, 1941-1945, 1144
American Diplomacy in the Great Depression, 337
American Experiences in Military Government in World War II, 1325
American Fleet and Escort Destroyers, 877
American Foreign Policy in the Making, 1932-1940, 324
American Guerrilla in the Philippines, 1386
American Heritage Picture History of World War II, 460
American Historical Association, 4
American Jewish Conference, 1498
American Labor from Defense to Reconversion, 1263
American Liberalism and World Politics, 1931-1941, 186
American Military Government, 1326
American Peace, 927
American Policy and the Division of Germany, 1197

American Policy in the Far East, 1931-1941, 428
American Secretaries of State and Their Diplomacy, 338, 343
American Society in Wartime, 1315
American Strategy in World War II, 473
American Submarines, 877
American Way of War, 496
American White Paper, 322
Americans and Chinese Communists, 1927-1945, 205
Americans Betrayed, 1124
America's Concentration Camps, 1301
America's Failure in Chines, 1940-1950, 1182
America's Second Crusade, 1113
America's Strategy in World Politics, 349, 1145
Amery, J., 1355
Amiable Assassins, 1356
Amphibians Came to Conquer, 813
Amrine, M., 894
Anatomy of the SS State, 1008
And the Crooked Shall Be Made Straight, 1594
Andenaes, J., 529
Andreas-Friedrich, R., 1400
Andrews, A., 726
Andrews, E. M., 200
Anglin, D. G., 976
Anglo-American Relations at the Paris Peace Conference of 1919, 94
Annual Register of World Events, 45
Anschluss: The Rape of Austria, 157
Ansel, W., 462, 538
Anshen, M., 1259
Anthology of Holocaust Literature, 1511
Anti-Appeasers, 166
Anzio: The Gamble That Failed, 579
Apenszlak, J., 1499
Appeasement, 165
Appeasement on Trial, 164
Appeasers, 160
Apple of Discord, 1050
Appleman, J. A., 1558
Appleman, R. E., 672
Approach of War, 1938-1939, 85
Approach to the Philippines, 705
Ardennes, Battle of the Bulge, 614
Arendt, H., 1590
Argenti, P. P., 1340
Armed Forces in Peacetime, 268
Armoured Fighting Vehicles, 848
Arms, Autarky and Aggression, 222
Armstrong, A., 952
Armstrong, H. F., 49
Armstrong, J. A., 1390, 1425
Army Air Forces in World War II, 723
Army and Economic Mobilization, 1264

Army and Industrial Manpower, 1251
Army of Amateurs, 1376
Arndt, H. W., 50
Arnold, H. H., 485, 716
Aron, R., 605-606, 977
Arsenal of Democracy, 1258
Ashes in the Wind, 1529
Asia for the Asiatics?, 1337
Assassination of Heydrich, 1359
Assignment to Catastrophe, 989
Assize of Arms, 102
Aster, S., 192
Astrup, H., 1380
Atomic Bomb and the End of World War II, 914
Atomic Diplomacy, 913
Attempts to Form an Anglo-French Alliance, 1919-1924, 388
Auchinleck, C., 648
Augsburg Eagle, 852
Auphan, G. A. J. P., 780
Auschwitz, 1584
Auschwitz: A Doctor's Eyewitness Account, 1526
Austria from Hapsburg to Hitler, 201
Austria, Germany and the Anschluss, 155
Ayro Lancaster, 889
Axis Alliance and Japanese-American Relations, 1941, 423
Axis Rule in Occupied Europe, 1333

B-24 Liberator, 881
Babington-Smith, C., 1433
Backdoor to War, 350
Backs to the Wall, 1295
Badoglio, P., 1056
Baer, G. W., 127
Baillie-Grohman, H. T., 552
Baker, L., 411
Baker Street Irregular, 1491
Balance of Power in the Interwar Years, 1919-1939, 75
Balcony Empire, 1066
Baldwin, H. W., 434, 464
Balfour, M. L. G., 1401
Ball, A., 193
Ball, M. M., 154
Ballantine, D. S., 762
Baltic Eclipse, 1331
Bamba, N., 297
Bamboo Doctor, 1555
Bangkok, Top Secret, 1453
Bankwitz, P. C. F., 210
Barbarossa, 556
Barber, N., 673
Barbey, D. E., 810
Barkai, M., 1500
Barker, A. J., 128, 668, 674, 811, 876

Barnes, G. M., 879
Barnes, H. E., 323
Barnett, C., 631
Barron, G. J., 194
Barros, J., 95, 112
Bartoszewski, W., 1501
Bassett, R., 117
Bastogne, 621
Bataan: The March of Death, 1550
Battaglia, R., 1377
Battle Against Isolation, 183
Battle for Asia, 152
Battle for Germany, 616
Battle for Guadalcanal, 690
Battle for Italy, 585
Battle for Moscow, 570
Battle for Normandy, 595
Battle for North Africa, 653
Battle for Rome, 586
Battle for Stalingrad, 555
Battle for the Ardennes, 625
Battle for the Mediterranean, 797
Battle of Cassino, 588
Battle of Greece, 1940-1941, 553
Battle of Huertgen Forest, 617
Battle of Kohima, 709
Battle of the Atlantic, 798
Battle of the Java Sea, 830
Battle of the River Plate, 801
Battle of the V-Weapons, 1944-1945, 731
Battle, The Story of the Bulge, 627
Battles Lost and Won, 434
Baumbach, W., 727
Baxter, J. P., 880
Beans, Bullets and Black Oil, 812
Beard, C. A., 324-25
Beaton, C. W. H., 1290
Beaverbrook, 1st Baron, 1046
Beaverbrook, 1046
Beginning of the Road, 555
Behemoth, 1017
Behind Japan's Surrender, 1069
Behind the Japanese Mask, 300
Behind the Steel Wall, 1002
Beitzell, R. E., 1204
Belden, J., 675
Belfield, E. M. G., 595
Belgian Foreign Policy between Two Wars, 1919-1940, 202
Belgium under Occupation, 1328
Bell, L. V., 326
Beloff, M., 312
Belot, R. D., 781
Belote, J. H., 676-77
Belote, W. M., 676-77
Belsen Trial, 1582
Benda, H. J., 1343-44
Benes, E., 969
Bennett, E. W., 219

Bennett, J., 1360
Benouville, G. D., 1366
Benton, W. E., 1564
Berenbrok, H. D., 728
Bergamini, D., 298
Berlin Diary, 253
Berlin Underground, 1938-1945, 1400
Bethell, N. W., 523
Bethge, E., 1402
Betrayal at Vel D'Hiv, 1524
Betrayal from Within, 95
Betrayal in Central Europe, 358
Bettelheim, B., 1502
Between Two Empires, 1083
Between War and Peace, 915
Bevin E., 1036
Bialer, S., 463
Bibliographic Index, 10
Big Business in the Third Reich, 1228
Big Lie, 950
Big Three, 1205
Binchy, D. A., 289
Biographical Dictionary of World War II, 32
Biography Index, 30
Bird, M. J., 1367
Birdsall, P., 87
Birdsall, S., 881
Birth of the Bomb, 895
Birth of the Missile, 856
Bisson, T. A., 149, 428, 1241
Bitter Woods, 615
Black Book, 1515
Black Book of Polish Jewry, 1499
Black Boomerang, 943
Black Market Money, 1261
Black Thursday, 730
Blackburn's Headhunters, 1383
Blast of War, 1939-1945, 1043
Blau, G. E., 554
Blitzkrieg Era and the German General Staff, 1865-1941, 461
Blitzkrieg to Defeat, 471
Bloch, M. L. B., 533
Blood, Sweat and Tears, 1038
Bloody River, 580
Blore, T., 832
Blum, J. M., 327
Blumenson, M., 579-81, 607-608, 632
Boca, A. D., 129
Boehm, E. H., 1403
Boeing B-17 Flying Fortress, 889
Boelcke, W. A., 939
Bohlen, C. E., 1106
Bomber Offensive, 737
Bomber's Eye, 871
Bombing of Germany, 744
Bones of Contention, 935
Bonhoeffer, D., 1402

Book Review Digest, 15
Books and Libraries in Wartime, 1303
Books: Subjects: A Cumulative List of Works
  Represented by Library of Congress
  Printed Cards, 14
Borg, D., 412, 429
Bosch, W. J., 1565
Bosworth, A. R., 1301
Bowers, C. G., 133
Boyce, J. C., 882
Boyle, J. H., 1156
Bracher, K. D., 993
Braddon, R., 1368
Braden, T., 1432
Bradley, J., 1538
Bradley, O. N., 498
Bragadin, M. A., 782
Bramsted, E. K., 994
Brandt, K., 1222
Brandt, W. , 1404
Brassey's Annual, 46
Brassey's Naval Annual, 46
Breach of Security, 1461
Breaking Wave, 545
Breakout and Pursuit, 607
Brereton, L. H., 717
Brereton Diaries, 717
Bretton, H. L., 220
Brickhill, P., 729
Briggs, A., 940
Brighter Than a Thousand Suns, 898
Britain and France Between Two Wars, 389
Britain and Germany Between the Wars, 390
Britain and the Dictators, 284
Britain and the Second World War, 445
Britain and the Sino-Japanese War, 1937-
  1939, 395
Britain Between the Wars, 1918-1940, 277
Britain Divided, 287
British and American Infantry Weapons of
  World War II, 876
British and American Tanks of World War
  II, 833
British Battleships and Aircraft Carriers, 877
British Broadcasting and the Danish Resis-
  tance Movement, 1940-1945, 1360
British Commonwealth and International
  Security, 261
British Cruisers, 877
British Fleet and Escort Destroyers, 877
British Foreign Policy in the Inter-War
  Years, 282
British Foreign Policy in the Second World
  War, 1048
British Foreign Policy since Versailles, 276
British Military Administration in the Far
  East, 1943-46, 1336

British Military Administration of Occu-
  pied Territories in Africa during the
  War Years, 1941-1947, 1327
British Naval Aircraft since 1912, 872
British Press and Germany, 1936-1939,
  265
British Strategy in the Far East, 1919-
  1939, 396
British Submarines, 877
British Tanks and Fighting Vehicles,
  1914-1945, 833
British War Economy, 1231
British War Production, 1238
British Warships of the Second World
  War, 890
Broken Seal, 1443
Broken Swastika, 727
Broken World, 1919-1939, 83
Brome, V., 134
Brooks, L., 1069
Broom, L., 1302
Broszat, M., 995
Broue, P., 135
Brown, B. F., 1598
Brown, E. F., 25
Browne, C., 1070
Bruegel, J. W., 158
Brutal Friendship, 1171
Brutal Takeover, 156
Bryan, J., 817
Bryant, A., 465-66
Buchanan, A. R., 435, 1107
Buckley, C., 549, 633
Buckmaster, M. J., 1434-35
Budurowycz, B. B., 399
Buhite, R. D., 405
Bulletin (Public Affairs Information
  Service), 18
Bullitt, W. C., 1139
Bullock, A. L. C., 996, 1036
Bundy, M., 1146
Bunker, G. E., 150
Bunker, J. G., 883
Burchard, J. E., 884
Burden, H. T., 221
Burden of Guilt, 1033
Burdick, C. B., 467
Burgess, A., 1358
Burma under the Japanese, 1329
Burn after Reading, 1444
Burns, J. M., 328, 1108
Business of War, 481
Buss, C. A., 363
"But, General Johnson–", 1256
But Not in Shame, 711
Butler, J. R. M., 468
Butler, P., 1303

Butlin, S. J., 1219
Butow, R. J. C., 299, 1071
By Eastern Windows, 1554
Byrnes, J. F., 1109

Cadogan, A., 1037
Caidin, M., 730, 753, 759, 841
Cain, C. W., 848
Calculated Risk, 582
Calder, A., 1291
Calvocoressi, P., 436, 1556
Cameron, E. R., 211
Campaign for Guadalcanal, 680
Campaign in Italy, 587
Campaign in Norway, 530
Campaign in the Marianas, 682
Campaigns of Wavell, 1939-1943, 657
Campbell, T. M., 1110
Canada in World Affairs, 901
Canaris Conspiracy, 1415
Cannon, M. H., 678
Captains Without Eyes, 1467
Captive Press in the Third Reich, 1004
Capture and Trial of Adolf Eichmann, 1593
Carew, J. M., 679
Carlton, D., 260
Carr, E. H., 51-52, 380, 921
Carr, R., 136
Carr, W., 222
Carroll, B. A., 1223
Carroll, W., 941
Carse, R., 783
Carsten, F. L., 53, 223
Carter, G. M., 261
Carter, J. A., 876
Carter, W. R., 784, 812
Carthaginian Peace, 91
Cartwheel: The Reduction of Rabaul, 694
Carver, M., 634-35
Case of General Yamashita, 1601
Case of Richard Sorge, 1441
Cassels, A., 290, 1057
Cassidy, H. C., 1089
Catholic Church and Nazi Germany, 1212
Cattell, D. T., 137-38
Catton, B., 1111
Cause of Japan, 1078
Causes of the War, 162
Cave, F. A., 54
Cecil, R., 997
Central Blue, 746
Cervi, M., 550
Chadwin, M. L., 177
Challener, R. D., 178
Challenge of Conscience, 1293
Challenge of War, 863
Challenge to Isolation, 1937-1940, 185
Chalmers, W. S., 785

Chamberlain, J., 667
Chamberlain, N., 274
Chamberlain, P., 833,885
Chamberlain, W. H., 1113
Chandler, D. G., 28
Chandler, L. V., 1247
Chapman, F. S., 1378
Charles De Gaulle, 980
Chennault, C. L., 754
Chiang, K., 958
Chief of Intelligence, 1438
Chief of Staff, 495
Children of Europe, 1542
China and Japan at War, 1937-1945, 1156
China and the Helping Hand, 1937-1945, 1185
China Reader, 204
China Tangle, 1180
China, The Struggle for Power 1917-1972, 967
China's Crisis, 964
China's Wartime Finance and Inflation, 1937-1945, 1220
China's Wartime Politics, 1937-1944, 965
Chinese High Command, 715
Christopher, J. W., 430
Chronology, 1941-1945, 35
Chronology of the Navy's War in the Pacific, World War II, 34
Chronology of the Second World War, 33
Chuikov, V. I., 555, 613
Church and State in Fascist Italy, 289
Churchill, P., 1436-37
Churchill, W. L. S., 55, 262-63, 271, 437, 455, 1038, 1045
Churchill: A Study in Failure, 1900-1939, 271
Churchill and the Montgomery Myth, 655
Churchill, Roosevelt, Stalin, 1206
Churchill Tank, 885
Ciano, G., 291, 1058
Ciano Diaries, 1939-1943, 1058
Ciechanowski, J., 1084
Cienciala, A. M., 308
Civil Affairs and Military Government, 1332
Civil Defence, 1296
Civil Industry and Trade, 1232
Civil Service in Wartime, 1323
Civilizing Mission, 128
Clark, A., 556
Clark, B., 1392
Clark, D., 907
Clark, M. W., 582
Clark, R. W., 895
Clifford, N. R., 394
Cline, R. S., 469
Closing of the Door, 1184
Coakley, R. W., 483

Coal, 1237
Coastwatchers, 1446
Cocchia, A., 786
Code Names Dictionary, 39
Codebreakers, 1464
Codeword Barbarossa, 1495
Codeword Direktor, 1457
Coffey, T. M., 1072
Coggins, J., 680, 834
Cohen, B. C., 1114
Cohen, E. A., 1503
Cohen, J. B., 1242
Cold Corner of Hell, 783
Cole, H. M., 609, 614
Cole, J. A., 942
Cole, W. S., 179, 329
Collapse of the Third Republic, 536
Collier, B., 397, 438, 451, 539, 731
Collier, R., 1059, 1369
Collins, L., 610
Collis, M. S., 957
Colvin, I. G., 56, 1438
Combat, 439
Combat and Command, 733
Combined Boards of the Second World
    War, 1217
Combined Food Board, 1216
Combined Operations, 542
Coming of the Italian-Ethiopian War, 127
Coming of the New Deal, 348
Command and Leadership in the German
    Air Force, 750
Command Decisions, 494
Command Decisions: A Personal Story, 520
Commandant of Auschwitz, 1513
Commando, 548
Commissioned Barges, 832
Communism and the Spanish Civil War, 137
Communist Guerrilla Warfare, 1391
Communist Subversion of Czechoslovakia,
    970
Community of Fate, 385
Company Commander, 618
Complacent Dictator, 1168
Compton, J. V., 407
Conditions of Peace, 921
Confessions of the "Old Wizard", 1227
Conflict in the Far East, 430
Congdon, D., 439
Congressional Politics in the Second World
    War, 1150
Connery, R. H., 1248
Conscription of Conscience, 1319
Consolidated B-24D-M Liberator, 889
Conspiracy Against Hitler in the Twilight
    War, 1405
Conspiracy Among Generals, 1423
Conspiracy at Mukden, 124
Constable, T. J., 732

Control of Germany and Japan, 929
Control of Japanese Foreign Policy, 305
Control of Raw Materials, 1233
Conversations with Stalin, 1213
Convoy Escort Commander, 792
Conway, J. S., 998
Cooper, B., 841
Cooper, D., 1039
Coox, A. D., 452
Cordell Hull, 1933-1944, 343
Corfu Incident of 1923, 112
Corregidor: The Saga of a Fortress, 676
Corwin, E. S., 1115
Counterfeit Traitor, 1468
Courage and Fear, 1480
Courage of Fear, 1478
Court, W. H. B., 1237
Cowburn, B., 1439
Cowie, J. S., 862
Craf, J. R., 1249
Craig, G. A., 57
Craig, J., 881
Craig, W., 557, 681
Craigie, R. L., 300
Crankshaw, E., 999
Crawford, J. G., 1271
Cremona, P., 293
Crescent and the Rising Sun, 1343
Creswell, J., 764
Crete 1941, The Battle at Sea, 654
Cretzianu, A., 1088
Crimes Against International Law, 1598
Crisis in the Desert, 629
Crisis of German Ideology, 240
Crisis of the Old Order, 1919-1933, 348
Crocker, G. N., 1190
Cross-Channel Attack, 597
Crossing, 1548
Crow, D., 848
Crowl, P. A., 659, 682-83
Crowley, J. B., 301
Crucible of Power, 641
Crusade in Europe, 500
Culture and Commitment, 1929-1945,
    1321
Cumulative Book Index, 11
Cunningham, A. B., 787
Cunningham, W. S., 684
Current, R. N., 1116
Current Biography, 31
Curtiss Kitty Hawk MKI-V, 889
Curtiss P-40, 889
Curtiss P-40D-N Warhawk in USSAF-
    French and Foreign Service, 889
Curzon: The Last Phase, 1919-1925, 278
Czechoslovak-Polish Confederation and
    the Great Powers, 1940-1943, 1157
Czechoslovakia Before Munich, 158
Czechs Under Nazi Rule, 1330

D-Day: The Normandy Invasion in Retro-
spect, 596
Dahlerus, J. B. E., 195
Dalfuime, R. M., 1304
Dallek, R., 330, 1117
Dallin, A., 1351
Dallin, D., 1090, 1205, 1440
Dalton, H., 1040
Dam Busters, 729
Dangerfield, R., 1214
Danzig Dilemma, 377
Dark December, 622
Dark Side of the Moon, 1177
Darkest Year, 1035
Davidson, E., 1567
Davies, J. E., 427
Davis, B. L., 850
Davis, F., 331
Davis, G. T., 332
Davis, K. S., 440
Davis, M. S., 1060
Dawn of Liberation, 1038
Dawn Over Zero, 900
Dawson, R. H., 1191
Day, D., 866
Day of Infamy, 669
Day of Trinity, 899
Days of Emperor and Clown, 130
Days of Sadness, Years of Triumph, 1316
Deadly Stroke, 809
Deakin, F. W., 1171, 1393, 1441
Dean, B., 1292
Deane, J. R., 1192
Death in Rome, 1540
Death in the Forest, 1549
Death of the Battleship, 821
Debicki, R., 309
Decade of American Foreign Policy, 42
Decision to Aid Russia, 1941, 1191
Decision to Drop the Bomb, 1122
Decisive Battles of World War II, 506
Dedijer, V., 1394
Defeat in the East, 573
Defeat in Victory, 1084
Defeat into Victory, 704
Defense of the United Kingdom, 539
Defiance in Manchuria, 119
DeGaulle, C., 504, 978, 980, 1187
De Gaulle Before Paris, 605
De Gaulle Triumphant, 606
De Gaulle's Foreign Policy, 1944-1946, 978
Degras, J. T., 313
De Guingand, F. W., 499
Deichmann, P., 750
Delarue, J., 1000
Delbos, Y., 212
Delmer, S., 943
Delzell, C. F., 58, 1398
Democracy and Foreign Policy, 117

Democrat and Diplomat, 330
Demster, D. D., 547
Dennett, R., 1193
DePorte, A. W., 978
Derry, T. K., 530
De Schweinitz, D., 1250
Desegregation of the U.S. Armed Forces,
1304
Desert Generals, 631
Design and Development of Weapons,
866
Design for Total War, 1223
Design for War, 347
Destiny of Europe's Gypsies, 1541
Destruction of Convoy PQ17, 795
Destruction of Dresden, 739
Destruction of the Dutch Jews, 1529
Destruction of the European Jews, 1512
Deutsch, H. C., 1405
Development of the German Air Force,
1919-1939, 750
Devereux, J. P. S., 685
Devices of War, 864
Devil's Chemists, 1568
Dexter, B. V., 96
Dexter, D., 686
d'Harcourt, P., 1504
Diaries of Sir Alexander Cadogan, 1037
Diary of a German Soldier, 563
Diary of a Nightmare, 1286
Diary of a Young Girl, 1507
Dicks, H. V., 1539
Dictators Face to Face, 1170
Dictionary of American Naval Fighting
Ships, 892
Dictionary of Battles, 29
Dictionary of Forces' Slang, 1939-1945
38
Dieppe: The Same and the Glory, 544
Dietrich Bonhoeffer, 1402
Different Kind of War, 1357
Dilas, M., 1213
Dilemmas of Growth in Prewar Japan,
306
Diplomacy for Victory, 955
Diplomacy in a Whirlpool, 1053
Diplomacy in the Near and Middle East,
1174
Diplomacy of Appeasement, 159
Diplomacy of Illusion, 392
Diplomacy of the Winter War, 1159
Diplomat Among Warriors, 1135
Diplomat Between Wars, 354
Diplomat in Berlin, 1933-1939, 376
Diplomat in Paris, 1936-1939, 398
Diplomatic Prelude, 1938-1939, 72
Diplomatic Twilight, 1930-1940, 283
Diplomats: 1919-1939, 57
Dirksen, H., 224

Disarmament and Security since Locarno, 1925-1931, 106
Divine, A. D., 540
Divine, R. A., 180-81, 1118-19
Divine Wind, 756
Dixon, C. A., 1391
Dobb, M. H., 1245
Dr. Goebbels, His Life and Death, 1012
Doctors of Infamy, 1525
Documentary Background of World War II, 61
Documents on American Foreign Relations, 902
Documents on British Foreign Policy, 1919-1939, 65
Documents on German Foreign Policy, 1918-1945, 64
Documents on International Affairs, 903
Documents on Polish-Soviet Relations, 1939-1945, 1178
Dodd, W. E., 330
Donat, A., 1505
Doenitz, K., 788
Donnison, F. S. V., 1332, 1336
Donohoe, J., 1406
Donovan, W., 1449
Donovan of OSS, 1449
Don't Blame the Generals, 643
Don't You Know There's a War On?, 1310
Doolittle's Tokyo Raiders, 755
Doomed Democracy, 207
Dornberger, W., 851
Dorpalen, A., 225
Double-Cross System in the War of 1939 to 1945, 1472
"Double Tenth" Trial, 1602
Douglas, S., 733
Douglas-Hamilton, J., 1160
Douglas DC-3, 881
Dowding, H., 752
Dowding and the Battle of Britain, 752
Downes, D. C., 1442
Dream of Empire, 251
Dreifort, J. E., 212
Drum, K., 750
Drummond, D. F., 182
Drury, A., 1120
DuBois, J. E., 1568
Duce!, 1059
Duel for France, 1944, 608
Duel of Wits, 1436
Dugan, J., 130, 734
Dulag-Luft Trial, 1579
Dull, P. S., 1595
Dulles, A. W., 953, 1407
Dunlop, D., 1379
Dunn, F. S., 922
Dupuy, R. E., 36
Dupuy, T. N., 36

Duroselle, J. B., 1121
Dutch under German Occupation, 1940-1945, 1348
Duvall, E. E., 784
Dyck, H. L., 381
Dyer, G. C., 813
Dying We Live, 1412

Eagles East, 741
East Wind Rising, 365
Eastern Europe Between the Wars, 1918-1941, 362
Eck, H., 1569
Economic Blockade, 1234
Economic Consequences of the Peace, 89
Economic Lessons of the Nineteen Thirties, 50
Economics of America at War, 1253
Economics of Total War, 1266
Economy of the U.S.S.R. During World War II, 1246
Eden, A., 264, 1041-42
Education of a General, 1880-1939, 489
Eggleston, W., 849
Ehrenburg, I. G., 1091
Ehrlich, B., 1370
Eichelberger, R. L., 658
Eichmann in Jerusalem, 1590
Eichmann Kommandos, 1583
Eichmann Trial, 1592
Eight Years Overseas, 1939-1947, 656
Eisenhower, D. D., 500-501, 517, 612
Eisenhower, J. S. D., 615
Eisenhower and Berlin, 1945, 612
Eisenhower as Military Commander, 517
El Alamein, 634
El Alamein to the River Sangro, 512
Ellis, C., 833, 835, 885
Ellis, L. E., 333-34
Ellis, L. F., 534, 592
Elsbree, W. H., 1073
Embattled Mountain, 1393
Emperor's Guest, 1942-45, 1551
Encyclopedia of Military History, 36
End in Africa, 643
End of an Alliance, 1172
End of Glory, 68
End of the Beginning, 1038
End of the Imperial Japanese Navy, 823
End of the Third Reich, 613
Enemy at the Gates, 557
Engle, E. K., 525
English History, 1914-1945, 285
Erickson, J., 314
Escape to Adventure, 1395
Esch, P. A. M. v. d., 139
Essame, H., 595, 616
Essay and General Literature Index, 12

Estrangement of Great Britain and Japan, 1917-1935, 393
Ethiopian War, 1935-1941, 129
Eubank, K., 59-60, 167
Eudin, X. J., 315
Europe in Decay, 73
Europe Leaves the Middle East, 1936-1954, 1176
Europe of the Dictators, 1919-1945, 86
Europe on the Eve, 82
European Democracy Between the Wars, 74
European Diplomacy Between Two Wars, 1919-1939, 63
European Peace Treaties after World War II, 924
European Population Transfers, 1939-1945, 1282
European Resistance Movements, 1939-1945, 1363
Evans, G. C., 687
Eve of War, 1939, 199
Expansion and Coexistence, 320
Experience of War, 440
Explaining Munich, 168
Eyck, E., 226

F. D. R.'s Undeclared War, 1939-1941, 336
Face of the Third Reich, 1001
Facing the Dictators, 264
Failure of a Mission, 391
Fairchild, B., 1251
Falange, 1101
Falconi, C., 1151
Falk, S. L., 1550
Falkenhorst, N. v., 1570
Fall of Berlin, 613
Fall of Fortress Europe, 598
Fall of Japan, 681
Fall of Mussolini, 1065
Fall of the Philippines, 697
Famous Aircraft, 881
Famous Bombers of the Second World War, 837
Famous Fighters of the Second World War, 838
Fantin, R., 1262
Far Eastern Crisis, 432
Far Eastern Front, 121
Far Eastern Policy of the United States, 431
Far Eastern War, 1937-1941, 151
Farago, L., 502, 789, 1443-45
Farmer, P., 979
Farmer in the Second World War, 1270
Fascism: Doctrine and Institutions, 294
Fascism in Italy, 296
Fascist Economy in Norway, 1244
Fascist Experience, 1299
Fascist Italy, 1057
Fast Carriers, 828

Fatal Decisions, 503
Fateful Years: Japan's Adventure in the Philippines, 1941-1945, 1349
Fateful Years: Memoirs of a French Ambassador in Berlin, 1931-1939, 366
Fateful Years: Memoirs, 1931-1945, 1040
Faulkner, H. U., 335
Federal Records of World War II, 23
Fehrenbach, T. R., 336
Feingold, H. L., 1506
Feis, H., 413, 915, 1100, 1180, 1206
Feldt, E. A., 1446
Felix, D., 109
Fellowes-Gordon, I., 688, 1356
Fenyo, M. D., 1169
Ferrell, R. H., 114, 337-38
Fest, J. C., 1001
Fiercest Battle, 807
Fifty Ships That Saved the World, 189
Fighter Pilots, 722
Fighters and Bombers Between the Wars, 847
Fighters and Bombers, 1939-45, 847
Fighting Ghettos, 1500
Fighting Mustang, 887
Fighting Vehicles of the Red Army, 878
Fighting Warsaw, 1388
Final Secret of Pearl Harbor, 424
Final Solution, 1530
Financial Policy, 1939-1945, 1239
Finland and the Great Powers, 973
Finland and World War II, 1939-1944, 972
Finland, Germany and the Soviet Union, 1940-1941, 974
Finland in Crisis, 1940-1941, 975
Finland in the Second World War, 526
Fioravanzo, G., 782
Fireside, H., 916
First and the Last, 735
First Offensive, 1942, 492
First Summit, 1188
Fischer, G., 1426
Fischer, L., 316-17, 1092
FitzGibbon, C., 1408
Five Chimneys, 1521
Five Ventures, 633
Flame of Freedom, 1424
Fleet Admiral King, 766
Fleet That Faced Both Ways, 793
Fleming, D. F., 97-98, 908
Fleming, P., 541
Flender, H., 1361
Fletcher-Cooke, J., 1551
Flight in the Winter, 573
Flower, D., 441
Flying Fortress, 888
Food Administration in India, 1939-47, 1240

Food and Agriculture in Britain, 1939-45, 1230
Food and Inflation in the Middle East, 1940-45, 1274
Foot, M. R. D., 1447
Foote, A., 1448
Force Mulberry, 604
Ford, B., 841
Ford, C., 1449
Forecast for Overlord, June 6, 1944, 603
Foreign Affairs Bibliography, 5
Foreign Affairs 50-Year Bibliography, 6
Foreign Labor in Nazi Germany, 1224
Foreign Policy of Czechoslovakia, 1918-1935, 208
Foreign Policy of Hitler's Germany, 257
Foreign Policy of Poland, 1919-39, 309
Foreign Policy of Soviet Russia, 1929-1941, 312
Foreign Policy of the Soviet Union, 319
Foreign Policy of the Third Reich, 1005
Forgotten Fleet, 831
Forgotten Soldier, 565
Forrestel, E. P., 814
Fortress That Never Was, 623
Forty Years of Soviet Spying, 1483
Fotitch, C., 1155
Four Power Pact, 1933, 125
Four Samurai, 710
Fox, A. B., 917
Foxes of the Desert, 651
Fraenkel, H., 1012-14, 1415-16
France and Her Eastern Allies, 1919-1925, 215
France and Munich, 175
France and the Italo-Ethiopian Crisis 1935- 1936, 132
France, Europe and the Two World Wars, 209
France 1940-1955, 991
France Reborn, 606
France: The Tragic Years, 1939-1947, 983
Francillon, R. J., 874
Francois-Poncet, A., 366
Frank, A., 1507
Frank, W., 790, 804
Frank B. Kellogg and American Foreign *Relations, 1925-1929, 333*
Frank B. Kellogg. Henry L. Stimson, 338
Frankl, V. E., 1508
Frankland, N., 751
Franklin D. Roosevelt and Foreign Affairs, 345
Franklin D. Roosevelt's World Order, 1136
Fredbord, A., 1002
Free City, 373
Freed, F., 1122
Freedom and Order, 1041
Freeman, R. A., 886

Freidin, S., 503
French Navy, 877
French Navy in World War II, 780
French Right and Nazi Germany, 1933- 1939, 367
Freund, G., 382
Friedlander, A. H., 1509
Friedlander, S., 408, 1211
Friedman, P., 1510, 1532
Friedrich, C. J., 1325
Friend, T., 1083
Friendship Under Stress, 1202
Frisby, J., 1401
From Death Camp to Existentialism, 1508
From Down Under to Nippon, 661
From Isolation to Containment, 1921- 1952, 178
From Lenin to Khrushchev, 1095
From Prague After Munich, 206
From the Ashes of Disgrace, 1473
From the Diaries of Henry Morgenthau, *Jr., 327*
From the Marco Polo Bridge to Pearl *Harbor, 304*
From Versailles to the New Deal, 335
From Wilson to Roosevelt, 1121
Frumkin, G., 1276
Frye, A., 409
Fuchida, M., 815
Fuehrer: Hitler's Rise to Power, 232
Fuehrer Conference on Matters Dealing *with the German Navy, 1939-1945, 470*
Fuller, J. F. C., 442
Fuller, J. O., 1450-51
Funk, A. L., 980
Furnia, A. H., 159

Gaddis, J. L., 1194
Gafencu, G., 196
Galland, A., 735
Gallin, M. A., 1409
Gallo, M., 1061
Game of the Foxes, 1445
Gannon, F. R., 265
Gantenbein, J. W., 61
Gardner, B., 909
Garfield, B. W., 689
Garland, A. N., 583
Garlinski, J., 1452
Gathering Storm, 55, 437
Gathorne-Hardy, G. M., 62
Gatzke, H. W., 63, 227
Gedye, G. E. R., 358
Gehl, J., 155
General Kenney Reports, 757
General Sikorski Historical Institute, 1178
General Stilwell in China, 1942-1944, 960

General Wainwright's Story, 714
Generals in Grey Suits, 1568
Genocide in Satellite Croatia, 1941-1945,
1543
Gentlemen Talk of Peace, 938
Geography of the Peace, 932
George, A. L., 944
George, M., 266
George C. Marshall, 489
Georges Mandel and the Third Republic,
214
Geraud, A., 981
Gerike, H., 1571
German Air Force, 740
German Air Force Airlift Operations, 750
German Air Force Fighters of World War
Two, 861
German Air Force General Staff, 750
German Air Force Operations in Support of
Army, 750
German Air Force Versus Russia, 1941-1943,
750
German Army and the Nazi Party, 1933-
1939, 244
German Army Uniforms and Insignia, 1933-
1945, 850
German Atomic Bomb, 897
German Campaign in Poland, 1939, 524
German Campaign in Russia, 554
German Campaigns in the Balkans, Spring,
1941, 551
German Catastrophe, 1015
German Catholics and Hitler's Wars, 1034
German Combat Planes, 860
German Delegation at the Paris Peace
Conference, 90
German Democracy and the Triumph of
Hitler, 242
German Dictatorship, 993
German Economic Policy in Spain during the
Spanish Civil War, 1936-1939, 379
German Economy at War, 1226
German Fifth Column in the Second World
War, 1463
German Financial Policies, 1932-1939, 246
German Generals Talk, 509
German Infantry Weapons of World War II,
876
German-Japanese Relations, 1936-1940
German Military Intelligence, 371, 1469
German National Socialism, 1919-1945,
995
German Northern Theater of Operations,
1940-1945, 522
German Opposition to Hitler, 1420
German-Polish Relations, 1918-1933, 378
German Radio Propaganda, 945
German Raider Atlantis, 804
German Research in World War II, 858

German Resistance, 1418
German Resistance to Hitler, 1410
German Resistance to Hitler: Count von
Moltke and the Kreisau Circle, 1419
German Resistance to Hitler: Ethical and
Religious Factors, 1409
German Rule in Russia, 1941-1945, 1351
German Secret Weapons, 841
German Secret Weapons of World War II,
854
German Social Democracy, 1918-1933,
235
German-Soviet Relations Between the
Two World Wars, 1919-1939, 380
German Strategy Against Russia, 1939-
1941, 482
German Submarines, 877
German Surface Vessels, 877
German Tank and Antitank in World War
II, 847
German Tanks of World War II, 857
German Warships of World War II, 890
Germans Against Hitler, 1417
Germany. Auswartiges Amt., 64, 1162
Germany and American Neutrality,
1939-1941, 410
Germany and Japan, 372
Germany and the Diplomacy of the
Financial Crisis, 1931, 219
Germany and the Soviet Union, 1939-
1941, 386
Germany Is Our Problem, 928
Germany, Kriegsmarine. Oberkommando,
470
Germany (Territory Under Allied Occu-
pation, 1945– . U.S. Zone) Military
Tribunals, 1572
Germany Tried Democracy, 230
Germany. Wehrmacht. Oberkommando,
471-72
Germany's Agricultural and Food Poli-
cies in World War II, 1222
Germany's Economic Preparations for
War, 236
Germany's Foreign Indebtedness, 231
Germany's Military Strategy and Spain
in World War II, 467
Germany's Underground, 1407
Germino, D. L., 1062
Gestapo: A History of Horror, 1000
Gestapo, Instrument of Tyranny, 999
Gilbert, F., 57
Gilbert, G. M., 1573
Gilbert, M., 160-61, 390
Gilchrist, A., 1453
Gilkey, L. B., 1552
Giovannitti, L., 1122
Girdner, A., 1305
Gisevius, H. B., 1411

Giskes, H. J., 1454
Give Us This Day, 1557
Glatstein, J., 1511
Gleason, S. E., 185, 340
Glines, C. V., 755
Global Logistics and Strategy, 1940-1945, 483
Global Mission, 716
Glueck, S., 1574
Goebbels, J., 994, 1003, 1012
Goebbels and National Socialist Propaganda, 1925-1945, 994
Goebbels Diaries, 1942-1943, 1003
Goerdeler, C., 1418
Goering, 1013
Goering, H., 1013, 1575
Goerlitz, W., 558
Gold, B., 1252
Gollwitzer, H., 1412
Golovko, A. G., 791
Gonella, G., 1152
Goodhart, P., 189
Goodman, J., 1306
Gordon, D. L., 1214
Gordon, H. J., 228-29
Goris, J. A., 1328
Gott, R., 160
Goure, L., 559
Government and the People, 956
Gowing, M. M., 1231-32
Gozawa, S., 1596
Graf Spee, 801
Grand Strategy, 468
Gravediggers of France, 981
Graves, R., 267
Great Betrayal, 1305
Great Britain. Central Statistical Office, 43
Great Britain. Combined Operations Command, 542
Great Britain. Foreign Office, 65
Great Britain, France and the German Problem: 1918-1939, 387
Great Britain. Public Record Office, 22
Great Decision, 894
Great Mistakes of the War, 464
Great Powers and Eastern Europe, 1158
Great Sea War, 770
Great Weapons of World War II, 845
Greatest Treason, 174
Greece and Crete, 1941, 549
Greece: The Struggle for Freedom, 1342
Greek Tragedy, 1941, 552
Green, W., 836-38, 852-53
Greenfield, K. R., 473
Greet, W. C., 37
Grenfell, R., 816
Gretton, P., 792
Grew, J. C., 414, 1123
Griffith, S. B., 690

Griffiths, R. M., 982
Grimm, G., 1564
Gripenberg, G. A., 973
Griswold, A. W., 431
Grodzins, M., 1124
Grossman, J., 1251
Groves, L. R., 896
Gruenhagen, R. W., 887
Grumman, F6F3/5 Hellcat, 889
Grunberger, R., 1284
Grygier, T., 1277
Guadalcanal Diary, 712
Guadalcanal: The First Offensive, 695
Guderian, H., 505
Guedalla, P., 736
Guide to Historical Literature, 4
Guide to Jewish History Under Nazi Impact, 1532
Guide to the Sources of British Military History, 8
Guilleband, C. W., 1285
Guisan, H., 1466
Gulick, C. A., 201
Guns, 1939-45, 841
Gurney, G., 881

Hadamar Trial, 1580
Haight, J. M., 406
Haines, C. G., 66
Halder, F., 474-75
Halder Diaries, 474
Hale, O. J., 1004
Hall, H. D., 1229, 1273
Halperin, S. W., 230
Halsey, W. F., 817
Hammond, R. J., 1230
Hamzavi, A. H., 1055
Hanayama, S., 1597
Hancock, W. K., 1231
Handbook for Spies, 1448
Handlin, O., 7
Hankey, M. P. A. H., 1559
Hara, T., 818
Harbottle, T. B., 29
Hargreaves, E. L., 1232
Harkins, P., 1383
Harper, G. T., 379
Harris, A. T., 737
Harris, B., 131
Harris, C. R. S., 231, 1345
Harris, S. E., 1253
Harris, W. R., 1576
Harrison, G. A., 597
Hartcup, G., 863
Hartendorp, A. V. H., 1553
Hartley, A. B., 839
Hartmann, F. H., 1102
Harvard Guide to American History, 7

Harvest of Hate, 1528
Hashimoto, M., 819
Hasluck, P., 956
Hassell, U. v., 1413
Hatlem, J. C., 456
Haukelid, K. A., 1381
Hausner, G., 1591
Havighurst, R. J., 1307
Hawaii's War Years, 1941-1945, 1105
Hawker Hurricane MKI-IV, 889
Hawks of World War II, 177
Hayabusha I-III, 889
Hayashi, S., 452
Hayes, C. J. H., 1201
Hayes, D., 1293
Hayes, P. M., 1081
He Who Saves One Life, 1514
Headlam-Morley, J., 88
Heckstall-Smith, A., 552, 636, 793
Heiden, K., 232
Heilbrunn, O., 1391
Helmuth Von Moltke, 1401
Henderson, N. M., 391
Henry Stimson and Japan, 1931-1933, 422
Hepburn, S., 1455
Herrick, R. W., 794
Herring, G. C., 1195
Hess, G. R., 1189
Hess, W. N., 887
Hess, R., 1160, 1513
Hewins, R., 1082
Hidden Diary, 1937-1938, 291
Hidden Weapon, 1214
Higgins, T., 476-77
Higham, R., 8-9, 268-69
Hilberg, R., 1512
Hildebrand, K., 1005
Hilger, G., 383
Himmler, 1014
Himmler, H., 1014
Hindenburg and the Weimar Republic, 225
Hinshaw, D., 1125
Hinsley, F. H., 478
Hirohito, 1076
Hirohito, Emperor of Japan, 1076
Hirsch, J., 1254
Hirszowicz, L., 1165
Historic Documents of World War II, 41
Historical Abstracts, 16
*Historical Turning Points in the German
  Air Force War Effort, 750*
*History of Broadcasting in the United
  Kingdom, 940*
*History of Marine Corps Aviation in World
  War II, 761*
*History of the Czechoslovak Republic,
  1918-1948, 971*
History of the League of Nations, 99
History of the Nazi Party, 1018

History of the Second World War
  (Liddell Hart), 444
History of the Second World War
  (United Kingdom Series), 443
*History of the United Nations Charter,
  1142*
*History of the United Nations War
  Crimes Commission and the Development
  of the Laws of War, 1562*
*History of the U.S. Marine Corps
  Operations in World War II, 665*
History of the Weimar Republic, 226
*History of United States Naval Opera-
  tions in World War II, 768*
Hitler, A., 228, 232-34, 237, 247, 475,
  478, 493, 996, 1006, 1021, 1025
Hitler: A Study in Tyranny, 996
Hitler and Japan, 1161
Hitler and the Beer Hall Putsch, 228
Hitler and the Middle Sea, 462
Hitler as Military Commander, 493
Hitler as Warlord, 475
Hitler Confronts England, 538
Hitler Directs His War, 472
Hitler, Horthy and Hungary, 1169
Hitler: Legend, Myth and Reality, 237
Hitler Moves East, 1941-1943, 567
Hitler's Battles for Europe, 493
*Hitler's Conservative Opponents in
  Bavaria, 1939-1945, 1406*
Hitler's Europe, 1335
Hitler's Free City, 375
Hitler's Interpreter, 1026
Hitler's Mein Kampf, 238
*Hitler's Occupation of Ukraine, 1941-
  1944, 1352*
*Hitler's Pre-War Policy and Military
  Plans, 1933-1939, 250*
Hitler's Rise to Power, 247
Hitler's Social Revolution, 252
Hitler's Strategy, 478
Hitler's War Aims, 1025
Hitler's War Directives, 1939-1945, 471
Hitler's War on Russia, 567
Hjalmar Schacht, 1022
Hoag, C. L., 101
Hodge, A., 267
Hoehling, A. A., 415
Hoess, R., *See* Hess, R.
Hoettl, W., 1456
Hofer, W., 197
Hoffman, R. J. S., 66
Hoffschmidt, E. J., 748, 840, 847
Hogg, I. V., 841, 854
Hohne, H., 1007, 1457
Holborn, H., 1326
Hollard, M., 1471
Hollow Legions, 550
Holmes, W. J., 820

Holocaust, 1523
Holocaust Kingdom, 1505
Home Front, 1125
Homze, E. L., 1224
Hopkins, H., 1143
Hoptner, J. B., 355
Horikoshi, J., 759
Horne, A., 535
Horrido!, 732
Horthy, M., 1051
Horton, M. K., 785
Hosada, M., 1243
Hostile Allies, 1187
Hotsumi, O., 1462
Hough, F. O., 453
Hough, R. A., 821
House Built on Sand, 1353
House of Ashes, 1527
How the Far East Was Lost, 1181
How We Lived Then, 1294
Howarth, D. A., 1458
How They Won the War in the Pacific, 822
How War Came, 331
Howard, M. E., 479
Howe, G. F., 637
Howe, Q., 67
Howell, E. M., 560
Hoyt, E. P., 822
Huang, C., 715
Huddleston, S., 983
Hughes, R., 1238
Hull, C., 339, 343
Human Behavior in the Concentration
    Camp, 1503
Hungarian Premier, 1052
Hungary and Her Successors, 288
Hunt, R. N., 235
Hunter, K. E. 456-58
Hunter and Hunted, 1518
Hunters and the Hunted, 786
Hunting of Force Z, 821
Hurewitz, J. C., 1174
Hurstfield, J., 1233
Huston, J. A., 718
Huzar, E., 1126
Huzel, D., 855
Hyde, H. M., 1459
Hytier, A. D., 984

I Saw the Fall of the Philippines, 702
I Was There, 1130
Icon and the Swastika, 916
If This Is a Man, 1522
Ike, N., 302
Ikle, F. C., 1278
Ikle, F. W., 371
Ill Met by Moonlight, 1475
Illusion and Necessity, 918

Illusion of Neutrality, 180
Imperial Japan: 1926-1938, 307
Imperial Tragedy, 1072
In Allied London, 1085
In Exile, 1404
In Hitler's Shadow, 326
In the Nazi Era, 241
In the Thick of the Fight, 1930-1945,
    213
Imcompatible Allies, 383
Incredible Victory, 827
Ind, A., 1460
Independent Eastern Europe, 361
Index to the Times, 21
Industrial Mobilization for War, 1268
Infantry Brigadier, 638
Infield, G. B., 738
Inflation in the United States, 1940-
    1948, 1247
Information on the Reduction of
    Armaments, 107
Information on the Renunciation of
    War, 1927-1928, 116
Informed Heart, 1502
Ingham, T., 1384
Inman, P., 1236
Inoguchi, R., 756
Inside Hitler's Headquarters, 1939-1945,
    521
Inside S.O.E., 1486
Inside the Third Reich, 1029
An Instance of Treason, 1462
Institute fur Zeitgeschichte, Munich,
    1008
Instruments of Darkness, 868
Intelligence at the Top, 1490
International Brigades, 134
International Conference on Military
    Trials, 1560
International Conference on the History
    of Resistance Movements, 1363
International Index, 20
International Law and Diplomacy in the
    Spanish Civil Strife, 144
International Military Tribunal for the
    Far East, 1600
International Relations Between the Two
    World Wars, 1919-1939, 51
Into Battle, 1038
Into Siam, Underground Kingdom, 1392
Invasion, 1940, 541
Invasion—They're Coming!, 602
Iranek-Osmecki, K., 1514
Irikura, J. K., 1344
Iriye, A., 364
Ironside, E., 270
Irving, D. J. C., 739, 795, 842, 897, 1461
Is Paris Burning?, 610
Isakov, I. S., 796

Isely, J. A., 659
Island Victory, 693
Island War, 453
Islands in Danger, 1339
Ismay, H. L., 480
Isolationism and Appeasement in Australia, 200
Isolationism in America, 1935-1941, 184
Isolationism in America, 1939-1945, 1127
Issei and Nisei, 1308
Italian Anti-Fascist Press (1919-1945), 1399
Italian Campaign, 1943-45, 591
Italian Fascist Party in Power, 1062
Italian Foreign Policy under Mussolini, 295
Italian Navy in World War II, 782
Italy and the Allies, 1064
Italy Betrayed, 1068
Italy in the Second World War, 1056
Italy's Austrian Heritage, 1919-1946, 1067
Italy's Foreign and Colonial Policy, 1914-1937, 293
Ito, M., 823

Jablonski, E., 719, 888
Jackson, G., 140
Jackson, R. H., 1577
Jackson, W. G. F., 584-86
Jacobs, P. E., 1319
Jacobsen, H. A., 506
Jacobson, J., 113
Jacoby, A., 968
Jacot, B. L., 1380
Jakobson, M., 1159
James, R. R., 271
James, R. W., 1272
Jane's All the World's Aircraft, 1945-1946, 843
Jane's Fighting Ships, 1942, 844
Janeway, E., 1255
Janis, I. L., 1279
Janowska Road, 1535
Japan and Her Destiny, 1077
Japan in China, 149
Japan Subdued, 914
Japanese Aircraft Carriers and Destroyers, 877
Japanese Aircraft of the Pacific War, 874
Japanese Battleships and Cruisers, 877
Japanese Destroyer Captain, 818
Japanese Diplomacy in a Dilemma, 297
Japanese Evacuation and Resettlement, 1322
Japanese Food Management in World War II, 1243
Japanese Military Administration in Indonesia, 1344
Japanese Navy in World War II, 824
Japanese Thrust, 666
Japanese Warships of World War II, 875

Japan's Decision for War, 302
Japan's Decision to Surrender, 1071
Japan's Economy in War and Reconstruction, 1242
Japan's Imperial Conspiracy, 298
Japan's New Order in East Asia, 303
Japan's Quest for Autonomy, 301
Japan's Radio War on Australia, 1941-1945, 949
Japan's Role in Southeast Asian Nationalist Movements, 1940 to 1945, 1073
Japan's War Economy, 1241
Japan's World War II Balloon Bomb Attacks on North America, 758
Jarausch, K. H., 125
Jarman, T. L., 1009
Jedrzejewicz, W., 1167
Jewish Black Book Committee, 1515
Johnson, C. A., 959, 1462
Johnson, E., 1568
Johnson, J. E., 1193
Johnson, N. T., 405
Johnson, R. W., 1256
Johnson, W., 183
Johnston, B. F., 1243
Johnston, G. H., 691
Johnston, S., 825
Johnston, V. B., 141
Johnstone, W. C., 416
Jonas, M., 184, 1127
Jones, F. C., 118, 303
Jones, R. H., 1196
Jong, L., 1463
Jordan, W. M., 387
Journey to the Missouri, 1075
Joyce, W., 942, 1578
Judenrat, 1534
Judgment on Nuremberg, 1565
Jukes, G., 561-62
July Plot, 1416
Junger, E., 923
Jungk, R., 898
Jungle Is Neutral, 1378
Justice in Jerusalem, 1591

Kahn, D., 1464
Kallay, M., 1052
Kamenetsky, I., 1352
Kaplan, C. A., 1516
Kardoff, U. v., 1286
Kase, T., 1075
Kasserine Pass, 632
Katyn Forest Massacre, 1545
Katz, R., 1540
Kawasaki Ki.61-I/III Hein/Ki.100, 889
Kecskemeti, P., 954
Keenan, J. B., 1598
Keitel, W., 507

Keith, A. B., 162
Kellogg, F. B., 333, 338
Kemp, N., 864
Kemp, P. K., 765, 1465
Kennan, G. F., 206, 318, 1128
Kennedy, J., 481
Kennedy, J. F., 272
Kennedy, M. D., 393
Kennedy, R. M., 524
Kenney, G. C., 757
Kenrick, D., 1541
Kersten, F., 1010
Kersten Memoirs, 1940-1945, 1010
Kertesz, I., 1053
Kesselring, A., 508
Kesselring: A Soldier's Record, 508
Key to Victory, 765
Keynes, J. M., 89
Killinger, E., 1579
Kimball, W. F., 190
Kimche, J., 1466
Kimmel, H. E., 417
Kimmich, C. M., 373
King, E. J., 485, 766
Kings Depart, 256
Kintner, R., 322
Kippenberger, H., 638
Kirby, S. W., 660, 692
Kirk, G. E., 1175
Kirk, J., 845
Kirkpatrick, I., 1063
Kirkpatrick, L. B., 1467
Kishi, K., 1344
Kitagawa, D., 1308
Kitsuse, J. I., 1302
Klee, E., 856
Klein, A., 1468
Klein, B. H., 236
Kleine-Ahlbrandt, W. L., 142
Kline, A., 1580
Knieriem, A. v., 1581
Knight, H., 1240
Knights of Bushido, 1556
Koehl, R. L., 1011
Kogan, N., 1064
Koginos, M. T., 418
Kogon, E., 1517
Kogun, 452
Kolko, G., 1129
Komorowski, T., 1387
Koop, T. F., 1309
Korbel, J., 310, 970
Korbonski, S., 1388
Korman, G., 1518
Kousoulas, D. G., 1049
Kowalski, I., 1519
Kramarz, J., 1414
Kramer, J., 1582
Kris, E., 945

Krosby, H. P., 974
Krueger, W., 661
Kubek, A., 1181
Kuhn, K., 1412
Kuklick, B., 1197
Kursk: The Clash of Armour, 561
Kusumi, Y., 1243

Labor and Management in a Common
    Enterprise, 1250
Labour in the Munitions Industry, 1236
Labour-Management Co-operation in
    United States War Production, 1260
Labyrinth, 1482
La Farge, H. A., 1280
Lafore, L. D., 68, 130
Lammers, D. N., 168
Lamont, L., 899
Lampe, D., 1362
Landis, A. H., 143
Lane, F. C., 767
Langer, R., 69
Langer, W. L., 185, 340, 1186
Langsam, W. C., 41
Language of World War II, 40
Lapierre, D., 610
Last and First in Burma (1941-48), 957
Last Attempt, 195
Last Battle, 564
Last Day of the Old World, 193
Last Days of Europe, 196
Last Days of Hitler, 1032
Last 100 Days, 628
Last Train from Berlin, 1028
Laurence, W. L., 900
Laurens, F. D., 132
Laval, P., 990
Law Reports of War Criminals, 1563
Leach, B. R., 482
Leadership in Crisis, 194
League of Nations and the Rule of Law,
    1918-1935, 100
Leahy, W. D., 1130
LeChene, E., 1520
Lederer, I. J., 356
Lee, A., 740
Lee, B. A., 395
Lee, D. E., 70
Legal Effect of World War II on Treaties
    of the United States, 1132
Legions of Babel, 141
Leighton, R. M., 483
Leiss, A. C., 924
Le May, C. E., 720
Lemkin, R., 1333
Lend-Lease, Weapon for Victory, 191
Lengyel, O., 1521
Lensen, G. A., 1173

Lenton, H. T., 877
Leonhardt, H. L., 374
Lerner, D., 946-47
Leverkuehn, P., 1469
Levi, P., 1522
Levin, N., 1523
Levine, H. S., 375
Levy, C., 1524
Lewin, R., 639
Lewinowna, Z., 1501
Lewy, G., 1212
Leyte: The Return to the Philippines, 678
Liang, C., 960
Liberty Ships, 883
Licensed Mass Nurder, 1539
Liddell Hart, B. H., 273, 444, 484, 509, 640
Liddell Hart Memoirs, 273
Lidice: Sacrificial Village, 1538
Liebling, A. J., 1372
Life (Chicago), 455, 459
Life and Death of Adolf Hitler, 1021
Life and Death of the Luftwaffe, 727
Life and Times of Ernest Bevin, 1036
Limits of Foreign Policy, 122
Limits of Hitler's Power, 1023
Lin Yutang, 961
Lindley, E. K., 331
Linebarger, P. M. A., 948
Lingeman, R. R., 1310
Linklater, E., 587
Lion and the Eagle, 397
Lippmann, W., 925
Lipski, J., 376
Lithuania in Crisis, 1079
Littlejohn, D., 1334
Liu, C., 203
Lloyd, E. M. H., 1274
Locarno Diplomacy, 113
Lochner, L. P., 1225
Lockheed P-38 Lightening, 889
Lockwood, C. A., 826
Loewenheim, F. L., 169
Loftis, A., 1305
Logistical Support of the Armies, 515
London Calling North Pole, 1454
Long, B., 1131
Long, G. M., 662
Long Generation, 1016
Long Week End, 267
Longest Day, June 6, 1944, 601
Longest Retreat, 679
Longmate, N., 1294
Lord, W., 669, 827
Lord Haw-Haw—And William Joyce, 942
Lorraine Campaign, 609
Lost Opportunity, 1088
Lost Treasures of Europe, 1280
Lost Victories, 510
Louis, W. R., 396

Love, E. G., 683
Lu, D. J., 304
Luckau, A. M., 90
Luftwaffe War Diaries, 728
Lukacs, J. A., 1158
Lukas, R. C., 741
Lukasiewicz, J., 398
Lunch with a Stranger, 1494
Lundin, C. L., 526
Luza, R., 359, 971
Lyttelton, A., 292

ME 109, 841
Maass, W. B., 1346
Macardle, D., 1542
MacArthur, D., 662-63, 667
MacArthur as Military Commander, 662
MacArthur, 1941-1951, 667
MacArthur's Amphibious Navy, 810
Macartney, C. A., 288, 361, 1054
Macartney, M. H. H., 293
MacDonald, C. B., 448, 617-20
MacDonald Versus Henderson, 260
McDougall, W. H., 1554
McDowell, E. R., 881
Macintyre, D. G. F. W., 531, 797-99
McIntyre, S. H., 1132
MacIver, R. M., 926
Macksey, K. J., 641
McLachlan, D., 1470
McLane, C. B., 963
Maclean, F., 1395
Macleod, I., 274
Macmillan, H., 275, 1043
MacNeil, N., 927
McNeill, W. H., 1207
Macrae, R. S., 863
McSherry, J. E., 384, 1163
Madeleine, 1450
Magic War, 688
Magnificent Mitscher, 829
Main Fleet to Singapore, 816
Maisky, I. M., 1093
Majdalany, F., 588, 598
Making the Peace, 1941-1945, 930
Making the Peace Treaties, 1941-1947, 934
Malmedy Massacre Investigation, 1546
Mamatey, V. S., 971
Man Called Lucy, 1939-1945, 1429
Man Who Never Was, 1474
Man Who Saved London, 1471
Man Who Won the Battle of Britain, 752
Managed Casualty, 1302
Manchuria since 1931, 118
Manchurian Crisis, 1931-1932, 120
Mandel, G., 214
Mannerheim, C. G. E., 527

Manpower, 1236
Man's Search for Meaning, 1508
Manstein, E. v., 510, 1585
Manstein, His Campaigns and His Trial, 1585
Mantoux, E., 91
Manus, M., 1382
Manvell, R., 1012-1016
Mao, T., 962, 1354
Marauders, 698
March of Conquest, 519
March on Delhi, 674
March to Tunis, 643
Mare's Nest, 842
Marlio, L., 929
Marshal Zhukov's Greatest Battles, 577
Marshall, B., 1373
Marshall, G. C., 485, 489, 1133
Marshall, S. L. A., 599, 621, 693
Martelli, G., 1471
Martens, A., 1379
Martin, J. J., 186
Martyrs and Fighters, 1510
Maser, W., 237-381
Mason, D., 841
Mason, H. M., 239
Mason, J. B., 377
Masquerade Peace, 1110
Mass Persuasion, 1313
Massacre at Malmedy, 1547
Masterman, J. C., 1472
Master Spy, 1438
Mastny, V., 1330
Mathews, S. T., 620
Matloff, M., 486
Maugeri, F., 1473
Maugham, F. H. M., 1561
Maughan, B., 642
Mauldin, W. H., 1311
Mauthausen, 1520
Max Horton and the Western Approaches, 785
Maxime Weygand and Civil-Military Relations in Modern France, 210
Maxon, Y. C., 305
Mayer, A. J., 92
Mayer, M. S., 1287
Meaning of Yalta, 1209
Mediterranean and the Middle East, 647
Mediterranean Fascism, 1919-1945, 58
Mediterranean Front, 643
Mediterranean Strategy in the Second World War, 479
Medlicott, W. N., 276, 1234
Meerloo, J. A. M., 1347
Meier, H. K., 1202
Mein Kampf, 233
Meinecke, F., 1015
Meister, J., 877

Mellenthin, F. W. v., 511
Memoir of the Paris Peace Conference, 1919, 88
Memoirs of a Soviet Ambassador, 1093
Memoirs of Cordell Hull, 339
Memoirs of Field Marshal Keitel, 507
Memoirs of Field Marshal Kesselring, 508
Memoirs: Ten Years and Twenty Days, 788
Men, Years—Life, 1091
Mengin, R., 985
Meo, L. D., 949
Merk, O., 856
Merriam, R. E., 622
Merrill, F. E., 1312
Merton, R. K., 1313
Meskill, J. M. M., 1161
Messerschmitt Bf. 109, 881
Meyer, A. G., 383
Meyer, H. C., 1016
Micaud, C. A., 367
Michel, H., 1364
Middle East in the War, 1175
Middle East, 1940-1942, 736
Middle East Supply Centre, 1275
Middlemas, R. K., 392
Middleton, D., 543, 910
Midway, the Battle That Doomed Japan, 815
Midway: The Turning Point, 811
Mielke, F., 1525
Mighty Eighth, 886
Mighty Endeavor, 448
Mikesh, R. C., 758
Miles, M. E., 1357
Military History of Modern China, 1924-1949, 203
Military Intellectuals in Britain, 1918-1939, 269
Military Transport of World War II, 835
Military Tribunals and International Crimes, 1558
Millar, G. R., 1374
Miller, J., 694-95
Miller, J. K., 202
Millis, W., 419
Milner, S., 696
Milward, A. S., 1221, 1226, 1244
Minear, R. H., 1599
Mines, Minelayers and Minelaying, 862
Minott, R. G., 623
Miracle of World War II, 1269
Miss Fire, 1397
Mission to Moscow, 427
Mission with Le May, 720
Mitscherlich, A., 1525
Mitsubishi Abm-Zero-Sen, 889
Moltke, H. v., 1401, 1419
Montagu, E., 1474

Montgomery, B. L., 512-13, 593, 626, 655
Montgomery Legend, 655
Montgomery: The Field Marshal, 626
Monthly Catalog of United States Government Publications, 24
Moon Squadron, 1492
Moore, H. L., 403
Moorehead, A., 643
Mordal, J., 780
Morgan, F. E., 600
Morgan, H. G., 1307
Morgan, J. H., 102
Morgan, L., 881
Morganthau, H., 327, 928
Morgenstern, G. E., 420
Morin, R., 365
Morison, S. E., 487, 768-69
Morley, J. W., 306
Morse, A. D., 1134
Morton, L., 1, 488, 697
Morzik, F., 750
Moscow Dateline, 1941-1943, 1089
Moscow, Tokyo, London, 224
Moscow War Diary, 574
Mosley, L., 71, 1076, 1295
Moss, W. S., 1475
Mosse, G. L., 240, *1288*
Most Unsordid Act, 190
Motive for a Mission, 1160
Motter, T. H. V., 1198
Moulton, H. G., 929
Moulton, J. L., 532
Mowat, C. L., 277
Mufti and the Fuehrer, 1166
Munich, 167
Munich: Before and After, 171
Munich Conspiracy, 173
Munich 1938, 172
Munich: "Peace for Our Time", 170
Munich, Prologue to Tragedy, 176
Munson, K. G., 846-47
Murphy, A., 589
Murphy, H. C., 1257
Murphy, R. D., 1135
Murphy, W. E., 644
Murray, K. A. H., 1235
Musmanno, M. A., 1583
Mussolini, B., 290, 294, 1063, 1065
Mussolini: A Study in Power, 1063
Mussolini's Early Diplomacy, 290
Mussolini's Enemies, 1398
Mussolini's Italy, 1061
Mustang, 887
Muther, J., 1142
Myer, D. S., 1314
My Life, 803
My Mission to Spain, 133
Myth of the Master Race, 997

Nakajima, T., 756
Nakajima Ki.43, 889
Nakajima Ki.27, 889
Namier, L. B., 72-73, 241
Narrow Margin, 547
Narvik, 531
National Debt in War and Transition, 1257
Nationalism in American Thought, 1300
Natzweiler Trial, 1589
Naumann, B., 1584
Naval Policy Between the Wars, 104
Naval War Against Hitler, 799
Navy and the Industrial Mobilization in World War II, 1248
Navy at War, 1939-1945, 774
Navy Second to None, 332
Nazi Conquest of Danzig, 374
Nazi Conspiracy and Aggression, 1586
Nazi Culture, 1288
Nazi Germany and the American Hemisphere, 1933-1941, 409
Nazi Germany's War Against the Jews, 1498
Nazi Movement, 217
Nazi Persecution of the Churches, 1933-1945, 998
Nazi Propaganda, 951
Nazi Seizure of Power, 218
Nazi-Soviet Relations, 1939-1941, 1162
Nazi Victory: Crete, 1941, 654
Nazis and Fascists in Europe, 1918-1945, 912
Nazis in the Balkans, 1019
Negotiating with the Russians, 1193
Nelson, D. M., 1258
Nelson T. Johnson and American Policy Toward China, 1925-1941, 405
Nemesis of Power, 259
Netherlands at War, 1346
Neumann, F. L., 1017
Neumann, W. L., 930, 1208
Neville Chamberlain, 274
Nevins, A., 341-42
New Deal and World Affairs, 341
New Guinea Offensive, 686
New Meaning of Treason, 1587
New Order and the French Economy, 1221
New Weapons for Air Warfare, 882
New York Times Index, 17
New Zealand People at War, 1080
Newman, K. J., 74
Newman, W. J., 75
Nicholls, A. J., 242-43, 936
Nicolson, H. G., 93, 278-79, 1044
Nielson, A., 750
Night, 1536
Night Drop, 599

Night Over Europe, 198
Nimitz, C. W., 770, 822
Nine Days of Dunkirk, 540
900 Days, 566
9 Lives Before 30, 1382
Nine Troubled Years, 286
1940, 1047
1939: The Making of the Second World War, 192
No Banners, No Bands, 1430
No Bugles for Spies, 1431
No Clear and Present Danger, 346
No Cloak, No Dagger, 1439
No Laurels for De Gaulle, 985
Nogueres, H., 170
Nolte, E., 76
None So Blind, 56
Normandy to the Baltic, 593
North American B-25 A/J Mitchell, 889
North American Mustang MKI-IV, 889
North American P-51D Mustang, 889
North American Supply, 1273
Northedge, F. S., 280
Northwest Africa, 637
Norway and the Second World War, 529
Notes from the Warsaw Ghetto, 1531
Novick, D., 1259
Novick, P., 1375
Now It Can Be Told, 896
Nowarra, H., 860
Nu, U., 1329
No. 13, BOB, 1451
Nuremberg Case . . ., 1577
Nuremberg Diary, 1573
Nuremberg: German Views of the War Trials, 1564
Nuremberg Party Rallies, 221
Nuremberg: The Facts, the Law and the Consequences, 1566
Nuremberg Trial and Aggressive War, 1574
Nuremberg Trials, 1581
Nuremberg Trials in International Law, 1588
Nye, P., 329
Nyiszli, M., 1526

OSS, 1485
O'Brien, T. H., 1296
Occupation of Chios by the Germans, 1340
O'Connor, R. G., 103, 955
October Fifteenth, 1054
Of Their Own Choice, 1437
Official Histories, 9
Official Index (London, Times), 21
Offner, A. A., 163
Ogata, S., 119
Ogburn, C., 698
Ogburn, W. F., 1315
Oil, 1237

Okamoto, S., 412
Okinawa: The Last Battle, 672
Okumiya, M., 759, 815
Old Men Forget, 1039
Olivova-Pavava, V., 207
On Active Service in Peace and War, 1146
On Borrowed Time, 71
On Guerrilla Warfare, 1354
One Story of Radar, 870
O'Neill, R. J., 244
Onwards to Victory, 1038
Operation Bernhard, 1477
Operation Sea Lion: The Projected Invasion of England in 1940, 541
Operation Sea Lion: German Plans for the Invasion of England, 1939-1942, 546
Operation Victory, 499
Oppression, 1277
Oras, A., 1331
Ordeal and Hope, 1939-1942, 489
Ordeal of Total War, 1939-1945, 450
Order of the Death's Head, 1007
Organizer of Victory, 1943-1945, 489
Organizing Scientific Research for War, 891
Origins and Background of the Second World War, 66
Origins and Consequences of World War II, 54
Origins of Intervention, 188
Origins of the Pact of Steel, 369
Origins of the Second World War, 80
Origins of the Second World War, 84
Origins of World War II, 59
Orlow, D., 1018-19
Orton, W. A., 77
Oslo Intrigue, 1380
Other Kingdom, 1533
Other Side of the Hill, 509
Our Jungle Road to Tokyo, 658
Our Share of Night, 910
Our Vichy Gamble, 1186
Out of the Blue, 718
Out of the Whirlwind, 1509
Overture to Overlord, 600
Oxford War Atlas, 26

P-51 Mustang, 881
P-40 Kitty Hawk, 881
P-47 Thunderbolt, 881
P-38 Lightning, 881
PT Boats, 841
Paananen, L., 525
Packard, E., 1066
Packard, R., 1066
Padelford, N. J., 144
Paget, R. T., 1585
Pal, R., 1600

Palmer, A. W., 361
Panay Incident: Prelude to Pearl Harbor, 421
Panay Incident: Prelude to War, 418
Panzer Battles, 511
Panzer Leader, 505
Papacy and World Peace, 1152
Papadatos, P. A., 1592
Papagos, A., 553
Papen, F. v., 1020
Paper Walls, 1324
Paperbound Books in Print, 13
Papers of Dwight David Eisenhower, 501
*Papers Relating to the Foreign Relations of
the United States, 905*
Parades and Politics at Vichy, 986
Paris, E., 1543
Paris Under the Occupation, 1338
Parker, H. M. D., 1236
Parkinson, R., 281
Parsons, C., 1384
Partridge, E., 38
*Passing of American Neutrality, 1937-1941,
182*
Path to Dictatorship, 1918-1933, 245
Patriotic Traitors, 1334
Pattern of Soviet Power, 1096
Patton, G. S., 502, 514
Patton: Ordeal and Triumph, 502
Paulus and Stalingrad, 558
Pavillard, S. S., 1555
Pawle, G., 865
Paxton, R. O., 986-87
Payne, D. G., 800
Payne, P. S. R., 1021
Payne, S. G., 1101
Payton-Smith, D. J., 1237
Peace, 923
Peace and Counterpeace, 49
Peace and War, 351
Peace Conspiracy, 150
Peace for Our Time, 281
Peace in Their Time, 114
*Peace-Making and the Settlement with
Japan, 922*
Peace or Appeasement?, 169
Peacemaking 1919, 93
Pearl Harbor, 420, 668
Pearl Harbor as History, 412
Pearl Harbor Attack, 670
Pearl Harbor: Warning and Decision, 426
Pearlman, M., 1593
*Peasant Nationalism and Communist
Power, 959*
Pedestal, 808
Peenemunde to Canaveral, 855
Peleus Trial, 1569
Pelling, H., 445
People on Our Side, 1283
People's War, 1291

Percival, A. E., 699, 707
*Percival and the Tragedy of Singapore,
707*
Perilous Equilibrium, 103
Perowne, S., 645
Perpetual War for Perpetual Peace, 323
Perrault, G., 1476
Perrett, B., 878
Perrett, G., 1316
Perry, H. D., 421
Persia and the Powers, 1055
Persian Corridor and Aid to Russia, 1198
Persuade or Perish, 941
Petain, 982
Petain, P., 981-82
Peterson, E. N., 1022-23
*Philippine Collaboration in World War II,
1350*
Phillips, C. E. L., 646
Phillips, P., 1289
Phoney War, 1298
Picture History of World War II, 459
*Pierre Laval and the Eclipse of France,
990*
Pile, F. A., 742
Pin-Stripe Saboteur, 1496
Pinkus, O., 1527
Pipe Dream of Peace, 108
Pirie, A., 1477
Pitt, R., 1478
Pius XII, 1151, 1203, 1211
Pius XII and the Third Reich, 1211
Playfair, I. S. O., 647
Plehwe, F. K., 1172
Plocher, H., 750
Ploesti, 734
Pogue, F. C., 489-90
*Poland and the Western Powers 1938-
1939, 308*
Poland Between East and West, 310
*Poland in the British Parliament,
1939-1945, 1167*
Poland, S.O.E. and the Allies, 1452
Polenberg, R., 1317-18
Poliakov, L., 1528
Policy of Simmering, 142
Polish-Soviet Relations, 1932-1939, 399
Political Process and Foreign Policy, 1114
*Politics and Diplomacy of Peacemaking,
92*
*Politics in Independent Poland 1921-
1939, 311*
Politics of Cultural Despair, 254
Politics of Rescue, 1506
Politics of Upheaval, 348
Politics of War, 1129
Politics, Trials, and Errors, 1559
Polonsky, A., 311
Poltava Affair, 738

Pond, H., 590
Poole, K. E., 246
Pope, D., 801-802
Population Changes in Europe since 1939,
1276
Portrait of a Spy, 1481
Postan, M. M., 866, 1238
Post-War German-Austrian Relations, 154
Potter, E. B., 770
Power of Small States, 917
Pratt, J. W., 343
Preface to Preparedness, 101
Prelude to Calamity, 258
Prelude to Downfall, 408
Prelude to Pearl Harbor, 433
Prelude to Victory, 1137
Prelude to War, 139
Prelude to World War II, 81
Preparing for Ulysses, 1141
Prescription for Permanent Peace, 931
Present at the Creation, 1104
President Roosevelt and the Coming of the
War, 1941, 325
Presidential Agency: OWMR, 1265
Presseisen, E. L., 372
Presser, J., 1529
Prest, A. R., 1215
Price, A., 867-68
Price Control in the War Economy, 1254
Price of Freedom, 1049
Pridham, G., 247
Prittie, T. C. F., 1417
Problems of Social Policy, 1297
Prologue to Appeasement, 211
Propaganda Analysis, 944
Propaganda in War and Crisis, 946
Pruller, W., 563
Psychological Warfare, 948
Public Affairs Information Service, 18
Public Opinion, 1935-1946, 911
Public Papers and Addresses of Franklin D.
Roosevelt, 1140
Pulse of Radar, 873
Purse and the Sword, 1126
Puxon, G., 1541
Puzzo, D. A., 145

Queen of the Flat-Tops
Quest for Peace since the World War, 78
Quet, P., 1429
Quiet Canadian, 1459
Quigley, H. S., 151
Quisling, V.. 1081-82
Quisling, 1081
Quisling, Prophet without Honor, 1082

RKFDV, 1011
Rachlis, E., 1479
Raczynski, E., 1085
Raeder, E., 803
Ragged, Rugged Warriors, 753
Range, W., 1136
Rape of Art, 1281
Rappaport, A., 422
Rappard, W. E., 78
Rauch, B., 344
Rauschning, H., 248-49
Ravan, A., 890
Readers' Guide to Periodical Literature,
19
Real Enemy, 1504
Recalled to Service, 537
Reckoning, 1042
Records and Documents of the Holy See
Relating to the Second World War, 1153
Red Duster, White Ensign, 800
Red Fleet in the Second World War, 796
Red Orchestra, 1476
Red Star Over China, 966
Reel, A. F., 1601
Reeves, J., 441
Reichswehr and Politics, 223
Reichswehr and the German Republic,
1919-1926, 229
Reitlinger, G. R., 1024, 1353, 1530
Relief of Tobruk, 644
Reluctant Belligerent, 181
Renault-Roulier, G., 1480-81
Rendezvous by Submarine, 1384
Rennell, F. J. R. R., 1327
Renouvin, P., 79
Report by the Supreme Commander to
the Combined Chiefs of Staff on the
Operations in Europe, 594
Report of Robert H. Jackson, 1560
Republic and the Civil War in Spain, 136
Republic of Silence, 1372
Republic P-47 Thunderbolt, 889
Republican China, 204
Republican Foreign Policy, 1921-1933,
334
Rescue in Denmark, 1361
Rescue of Danish Jewry, 1537
Resistance and Reconstruction, 958
Resistance: France 1940-1945, 1370
Resistance Versus Vichy, 1375
Reston, J. B., 1137
Retreat from China, 394
Retreat with Stilwell, 675
Revolution and the Civil War in Spain,
135
Revolution of Nihilism, 248
Reynaud, P., 213
Reynolds, C. G., 828
Reynolds, P. A., 282

Rhodes, A., 1154
Rich, N., 1025
Richards, D., 721
Richardson, W., 503
Riegelman, C., 1260
Ringelblum, E., 1531
Ripka, H., 171
Rise and Fall of Nazi Germany, 1009
Rise and Fall of the German Air Force, 1933-1945, 748
Rise and Fall of the Third Reich, 516
Rise of Fascism, 53
Rise of the Luftwaffe, 239
Rising Sun, 454
Riste, O., 529
Ritter, G., 1418
Road to Pearl Harbor, 413
Road to World War II, 60
Road to Yalta, 1092
Roads to Russia, 1196
Robbins, K., 172
Roberts, J., 890
Roberts, W. R., 1396
Robertson, B., 869
Robertson, E. M., 80, 250
Robertson, J. H., 648-49
Robertson, T., 544
Robichon, J., 611
Robinson, E. E., 1138
Robinson, J., 1532, 1594
Rock, W. R., 164
Rockets, Guns and Targets, 884
Rogge, B., 804
Rohwer, J., 506
Roll, E., 1216
Romanus, C. F., 491, 700-701
Rome-Berlin Axis, 370
Rommel, E., 632, 639, 650
Rommel as Military Commander, 639
Rommel Papers, 650
Rommel's Last Victory, 632
Romulo, C. P., 702
Room 39, 1470
Room 3603, 1459
Roon, G. v., 1419
Roosevelt, F. D., 328, 345, 1108, 1136, 1138-40, 1143, 1187, 1203
Roosevelt and Hopkins, 1143
Roosevelt and Pearl Harbor, 411
Roosevelt and the Russians, 1200
Roosevelt and World War II, 1118
Roosevelt Diplomacy and World War II, 1117
Roosevelt: From Munich to Pearl Harbor, 344
Roosevelt Leadership, 1933-1945, 1138
Roosevelt: The Lion and the Fox, 328
Roosevelt: The Soldier of Freedom, 1108
Roosevelt's Road to Russia, 1190

Rootham, J., 1397
Roots of Appeasement, 161
Roscoe, T., 771-72
Rosen, S. M., 1217
Rosenbaum, K., 385
Rosengarten, F., 1399
Rosinger, L. K., 964-65
Roskill, S. W., 104, 773-74
Ross, D. R. B., 1141
Rothfels, H., 1420
Rothstein, A., 173, 1094
Rousset, D., 1533
Rowe, A. P., 870
Rowse, A. L., 165
Roxan, D., 1281
Roy, J., 988
Royal Air Force, 1939-1945, 721
Royal Institute of International Affairs, 33
Royal Netherlands Navy, 877
Rozek, E. J., 1086
Rubinstein, A. Z., 319
Rudel, H. U., 743
Ruffner, F. G., 39
Ruge, F., 805
Rumpf, H., 744
Rundell, W., 1261
Ruppenthal, R. G., 515
Rusinow, D. I., 1067
Russell, E. F. L. R., 1544, 1556
Russell, J., 1262
Russell, R., 1142
Russett, B. M., 346
Russia and the West Under Lenin and Stalin, 318
Russia at War, 1941-1945, 575
Russian Air Force in the Eyes of German Commanders, 750
Russian and Soviet Policy in Manchuria and Outer Mongolia, 1911-1931, 404
Russian Convoys, 806
Russian Infantry Weapons of World War II, 876
Russian Reactions to German Airpower in World War II, 750
Russia's Road from Peace to War, 316
Russo-German Alliance, August 1939-June 1941, 1164
Russo-German War, 1941-1945, 571
Ryan, C., 564, 601

SOE in France, 1447
S.S., Alibi of a Nation, 1922-1945, 1024
Saar Plebiscite, 126
Sabaliunas, L., 1079
Sachar, H. M., 1176
Sadler, W. S., 931
Sailor's Odyssey, 787

St. Pierre and Miquelon Affaire of 1941, 976
Sajer, G., 565
Sakai, S., 760
Salerno, 590
Salerno to Cassino, 581
Salisbury, H. E., 566
Salvemini, G., 81
Samaritans, 1501
Samurai!, 760
Sanborn, F. R., 347
Santo Tomas Story, 1553
Saunders, H. A. S., 721
Savage Canary, 1362
Saward, D., 871
Sayers, R. S., 1239
Scarlet Thread, 1442
Schacht, H. H. G., 1022, 1227
Schechtman, J. B., 1166, 1282
Schell, O., 204
Schellenberg, W., 1482
Schellenberg Memoirs, 1482
Schlabrendorff, F. v., 1421
Schlesinger, A. M., 348
Schmidt, P., 1026
Schmidt, P. K., 567-68, 602, 651
Schmidt, R. J., 111
Schmokel, W., 251
Schneider, R., 1412
Schoenbaum, D., 252
Schoenfeld, M. P., 1045
Schofield, B. B., 806
Scholl, I., 1422
Schramm, W., 1423
Schroeder, P. W., 423
Schroter, H., 569
Schuman, F. L., 82, 198
Schurmann, H. F., 204
Schuschnigg, K. v., 156
Schwabedissen, W., 750
Schwartz, H., 1179
Schweitzer, A., 1228
Scientists Against Time, 880
Scientists at War, 849
Scorched Earth, 568
Scott, J. D., 866, 1238
Scott, W. E., 368
Scourge of the Swastika, 1544
Scroll of Agony, 1516
Sea Warfare, 1939-1945, 764
Sea Warfare, 1939-1945: A German View-point, 805
Sea Wolves, 790
Seabury, P., 1027
Seaton, A., 570-71
Second Bureau, 1488
Second Chance, 1119
Second D-Day, 611
Second World War, 437

Second World War (Life), 455
Second World War: A Guide to Documents in the Public Record Office, 22
Second World War: A Military History from Munich to Hiroshima, 438
Second World War Combat Weapons, 840
Second World War, 1939-1945, 442
Secret Army, 1387
Secret Battalion, 1367
Secret Conferences of Dr. Goebbels, 939
Secret Conversations, 1941-1944, 1006
Secret Front, 1456
Secret Missions, 1497
Secret Press in Nazi Europe, 1519
Secret Raiders, 779
Secret Servants, 1484
Secret Surrender, 953
Secret War Against Hitler, 1421
Secret War, 1939-1945, 865
Secret Weapons of the Third Reich, 854
Secretary Stimson, 1116
Seeds of Discord, 992
Seekrieg, 805
Seidman, J. I., 1263
Seizure of Power, 292
Seizure of Territory, 69
Seizure of the Gilberts and Marshalls, 683
Selby, W., 283
Selected Speeches and Statements of General of the Army George C. Marshall, 1133
Selsam, J. P., 388
Semblance of Peace, 936
Senate Journal, 1943-1945, 1120
Senator Gerald P. Nye and American Foreign Relations, 329
Senger und Etterlin, F. M. v., 857
Set Europe Ablaze, 1486
Seth, R., 807, 1365, 1483-84
Seton-Watson, H., 362, 1095
Seton-Watson, R. W., 284
Seven Decisions That Shaped History, 1149
Seven Men at Daybreak, 1358
Seventy Days, 1389
73 North, 802
Shadow War, 1364
Shantung Compound, 1552
Shepherd, G., 157
Shepperd, G. A., 591
Sherman, 885
Sherrod, R. L., 703, 761
Sherwood, J. M., 214
Sherwood, R. E., 1143
Shewmaker, K. E., 205
Shigemitsu, M., 1077
Ships for Victory, 767
Ships, Salvage, and Sinews of War, 784

Shirer, W. L., 253, 516, 536
Shores, C. F., 745, 889
*Short History of International Affairs,
1920-1939, 62*
Shotwell, J. T., 115
Sibley, M. Q., 1319
Sicily and the Surrender of Italy, 583
Sidi Rezeg Battles, 1941, 630
Siege of Leningrad, 559
Siege within the Walls, 645
Siegfried Line Campaign. 619
Silence of Pius XII, 1151
Silent War, 1379
Silverstone, P. H., 890
Simon, L. E., 854, 858
Sims, E. H., 722
Singapore: The Chain of Disaster, 692
Singapore: The Japanese Version, 713
Sinister Twilight, 673
Sink 'em All, 826
*Sino-Japanese Controversy and the League
of Nations, 123*
Sixsmith, E. K. G., 517
Skis Against the Atom, 1381
Skodvin, M., 529
Sky Suspended, 543
Slessor, J. C., 746
Slim, W., 687, 704
Slim as Military Commander, 687
Slusser, R. M., 315
*Small Unit Actions during the German
Campaign in Russia, 572*
Smith, G., 1144
Smith, G. S., 187
Smith, H. K., 1028
Smith, N., 1392
Smith, P. C., 808, 859
Smith, R. E. 1264
Smith, R. H., 1485
Smith, R. R., 705-706
Smith, S. E., 664, 775
Smith, S. R., 120
Smyth, H. M., 583
Smyth, J. G., 707
Snell, E. M., 486
Snell, J. L., 918-19, 1209
Snow, E., 121, 152, 966, 1096, 1283
Sobel, R., 188
*Social History of a War-Boom Community,
1307*
Social Impact of Bomb Destruction, 1278
Social Policy of Nazi Germany, 1285
Social Problems on the Home Front, 1312
Social Sciences & Humanities Index, 20
Soft Underbelly, 476
Soldier's Story, 498
Somers, H. M., 1265
Sons of the Eagle, 1355
Sontag, R. J., 83

Soviet Air Force in World War II, 747
Soviet Combat Tanks, 1939-1945, 885
*Soviet Diplomacy and the Spanish Civil
War, 138*
*Soviet Documents on Foreign Policy,
313*
*Soviet Economic Development since
1917, 1245*
Soviet Espionage, 1440
*Soviet Far Eastern Policy, 1931-1945,
403*
*Soviet Foreign Policy during the
Patriotic War, 1094*
Soviet Foreign Policy, 1928-1934, 315
Soviet High Command, 314
Soviet Naval Strategy, 794
Soviet Navy, 877
Soviet Opposition to Stalin, 1426
*Soviet Partisan Movement, 1941-1944,
560*
Soviet Partisans in World War II, 1390
Soviet Policies in China, 1917-1924, 402
*Soviet Policy and the Chinese Commun-
ists, 1931-1946, 963*
*Soviet Policy Toward the Baltic States,
1918-1940, 357*
Soviet-Polish Relations, 1917-1921, 400
*Soviet Russia's Foreign Policy 1939-1942,
1090*
Soviets in World Affairs, 317
*Spain and the Great Powers, 1936-1941,
145*
Spanish Civil War, 147
*Spanish Republic and the Civil War,
1931-1939, 140*
Spanish Story, 1100
Speaking Frankly, 1109
Spears, E. L., 989
Specially Employed, 1434
Speeches of Adolf Hitler, 234
Speer, A., 1029
Speier, H., 945
Spiegel, H. W., 1266
Spies in Ireland, 1489
Spiro, E., 1486-87
Spitfire, 841
*Spitfire—The Story of a Famous
Fighter, 869*
Spruance, R. A., 814
Spy in Rome, 1493
Spying for Peace, 1466
Spykman, N. J., 349, 932, 1145
Stacey, C. P., 624
Stagg, J. M., 603
Stalin, I., 1097, 1099, 1210
Stalin and His Generals, 463
*Stalin, Hitler and Europe: The Imbalance
of Power, 1939-1941, 1163*

Stalin, Hitler and Europe: The Origins of World War II, 1933-1939, 384
Stalin: The Man and His Era, 1099
Stalingrad, 569
Stalingrad: The Turning Point, 562
Stalingrad to Berlin, 578
Stalin's Correspondence with Churchill, Attlee, Roosevelt and Truman, 1941-1945, 1210
Standley, W. H., 1199
Stanford, A. B., 604
Starr Affair, 1451
Statesman's Yearbook, 47
Statistical Abstract of the United States, 44
Statistical Digest of the War, 43
Stauffenberg, C. v., 1414
Stauffenberg, 1414
Stead, P. J., 1488
Steele, R. W., 492
Steenberg, S., 1427
Stein, G. H., 518
Steinberg, D. J., 1350
Steinert, M. G., 1030
Stembridge, J. H., 26
Step By Step, 1936-1939, 263
Stephan, E., 1489
Stern, F. R., 254
Stern, H. P., 1087
Stettinius, E. R., 191, 1200
Stewart, C., 734
Stewart, I., 891
Stewart, I. M. G., 652
Stewart, S., 1557
Stilwell, J. W., 491, 700, 708, 1183
Stilwell and the American Experience in China, 1183, 1911-45
Stilwell Papers, 708
Stilwell's Command Problems, 491
Stilwell's Mission to China, 700
Stimson, H. L., 338, 432, 1146
Storry, G. R., 1441
Story of the Italian Resistance, 1377
Story of Wake Island, 685
Strange Alliance, 1192
Strange Defeat, 533
Strange Neutrality, 1173
Strategic Air Offensive Against Germany, 751
Strategic Planning for Coalition Warfare, 1941-1944, 486
Strategic Surrender, 954
Strategy, 484
Strategy and Command, 488
Strategy and Compromise, 487
Strategy of Peace, 937
Strawson, J., 493, 625, 653
Stresemann, G., 220, 227
Stresemann and the Rearmament of Germany, 227

Stresemann and the Revision of Versailles, 220
Strik-Strikfeldt, W., 1428
Strong, K., 1490
Struggle for Crete, 652
Struggle for Europe, 449
Struggle for North China, 153
Struggle for Poland, 1941-1947, 1087
Struggle for Survival, 1255
Struggle for the Mediterranean, 1939-1945, 781
Students Against Tyranny, 1422
Students in Food Rationing, 1262
Studies in Social Psychology in World War II, 1320
Studies of Overseas Supply, 1229
Study of Warfare in Three Dimensions, 532
Stuka at War, 859
Stuka Pilot, 743
Sub Rosa, 1432
Subject Guide to Books in Print, 13
Submarine Attacking, 786
Submarine Victory, 776
Suchenwirth, R., 750
Sulzberger, C. L., 460
Sumida, H., 1602
Sunderland, R., 491, 700-701
Sunk: The Story of the Japanese Submarine Fleet, 1941-1945, 819
Supermarine Spitfire MKI-IV, 889
Supreme Command, 490
Supreme Commander, 497
Supreme Headquarters Allied Expeditionary Force, 594
Surrender of Italy, Germany and Japan, World War II, 933
Survey of International Affairs, 904
Survey of the American Economy, 1940-1945, 1249
Survival in Auschwitz, 1522
Susman, W., 1321
Swastika and the Eagle, 407
Sweet-Escott, B., 1491
Swinson, A., 709-710
Swiss Press and Foreign Affairs in World War II, 1102
Sword and Swastika, 1031
Sword's Fierce Edge, 1341
Sykewar, 947

Tackley, M. E., 458
Tang, P. S., 404
Tanks, 640
Tanks and Other A.F.V.'s of the Glitzkrieg Era, 1939 to 1941, 847
Tannenbaum, E. R., 1299
Tanner, V. A., 528

Tansil, C. C., 350
Tantum, W. H., 748
Tantum, W. J., 840, 847
Tarawa: The Story of a Battle, 703
Tarulis, A. N., 357
Tasca, A. R., 1164
Taste of Courage, 441
Tate, M., 105
Taylor, A. J. P., 84, 285, 1046
Taylor, A. M., 40
Taylor, F. J., 146
Taylor, G. E., 153
Taylor, J. C., 890
Taylor, T., 519, 545, 829, 1031
Tedder, A. W., 749
Temime, E., 135
Templewood, S. J. G. H., 286, 1168
Ten Thousand Eyes, 1369
Ten Years, 70
Ten Years in Japan, 414
Tenth Fleet, 789
Theatre at War, 1292
Theobald, R. A., 424
Theory and Practice of Hell, 1517
Thetford, O. G., 872
They Came From the Sky, 1487
They Came to Kill, 1479
They Fought Alone, 1435
They Thought They Were Free, 1287
Third Reich and the Arab East, 1165
This is Pearl!, 419
Thomas, D. A., 654, 776-77, 830
Thomas, D. S., 1322
Thomas, H., 147
Thomas, R. C., 39
Thompson, L. V., 174, 1047
Thompson, R. W., 626, 655
Thompson, N., 166
Thorne, C., 85, 122
Thornton, R. C., 967
Thorwald, J., 573
Thousand Mile War, 689
*Three Battles: Arnaville, Altuzzo,
  and Schmidt, 620*
Three Days to Catastrophe, 907
Three Faces of Fascism, 76
Thunder Out of China, 968
Tickell, J., 1492
Tillard, P., 1524
Tillman, S. P., 94
Time for Decision, 353
Time Runs Out in CBI, 701
Time Unguarded, 270
Times, London, 21
Titmus, R. M., 1297
Tito, J. B., 1394
*Tito, Mihailovic and the Allies, 1941/1945,
  1396*
To Hell and Back, 589

To Lose a Battle, 535
To Save a Nation, 187
To the Bitter End, 1411
Tobruk, 635
Tobruk and El Alamein, 642
Tobruk, the Story of a Siege, 636
Togo, S., 1078
Tojo and the Coming of the War, 299
Tojo: The Last Banzai, 1070
Tokyo Trials, 1595
Toland, J., 454, 627-28, 711
Toliver, R. F., 732
Tompkins, P., 1068, 1493
Toscano, M., 369
Total War, 436
Total War and the Constitution, 1115
Total War and the Human Mind, 1347
Toughest Fighting in the World, 691
Towards an Abiding Peace, 926
Toynbee, A. J., 199, 920, 1335
Toynbee, V., 199, 920, 1335
Tragedy of Nazi Germany, 1289
Traina, R. P., 148
Transfer of the Sudeten Germans, 359
*Traveller's Guide to the Battlefields of
  Europe, 28*
Trefousse, H. L., 410, 425
Tregaskis, R. W., 712
Trevor-Roper, H. R., 1032
Trial of Alfons Kline . . ., 1580
Trial of Erich Killinger . . ., 1579
*Trial of Gozawa Sadaichi and Nine
  Others, 1596*
Trial of Heinrich Gerike, 1571
Trial of Heinz Eck, 1569
Trial of Japanese War Criminals, 1603
Trial of Josef Kramer . . ., 1582
Trial of Marshal Petain, 988
Trial of Nikolaus Von Falkenhorst, 1570
*Trial of Sumida Haruzo and Twenty
  Others, 1602*
Trial of the Germans, 1567
*Trial of the Major War Criminals Before
  the International Military Tribunal,
  Nuremberg . . ., 1575*
Trial of William Joyce, 1578
Trial of Wolfgang Zeuss . . ., 1589
*Trials of War Criminals before the
  Nuremberg Military Tribunals, 1572*
Triumph in the Philippines, 706
Triumph in the West, 466
Troubled Giant, 280
Truman, H. S., 1147
Trunk, I., 1534
Truppner, W. C., 1259
Truscott, L. K., 520
Tsars, Mandarins and Commissars, 1179
Tsatsou, I., 1341
Tsou, T., 1182

Tsuji, M., 713
Tuchman, B., 1183
Tunny, C., 32
Turbulent Era, 1123
Turkish Foreign Policy, 1943-1945, 1103
Turn of the Tide, 465
Turner, E. S., 1298
Turner, L. C. F., 629-30
Turner, R. K., 813
Tute, W., 809
12-Year Reich, 1284
20 July, 1408
23 Days, 1030
Twenty Years' Armistice 1918-1938, 77
Twenty Years' Crisis, 1919-1939, 52
Twilight of France, 1933-1940, 216
Two-Ocean War, 769
Two World Wars, 2
Two Years of French Foreign Policy, 984
Tycoons and Tyrant, 1225
Typhoon of Steel, 677
Tyranny on Trial, 1576

U-Boat, 841
U.N.O. *and War Crimes, 1561*
USAF Historical Studies, 750
Uebe, K., 750
Ukrainian Nationalism, 1425
Ulam, A. B., 320, 1099
Umemura, M. T., 1595
Uncertain Giant: 1921-1941, 321
Unconditional Surrender, 952
Undaunted, 1365
Undeclared War, 1940-1941, 340
Undersea Victory, 820
Uneasy Alliance, 1204
Unexploded Bomb, 839
Unholy Alliance, 382
United Nations, 933
United Nations War Crimes Commission,
  1562-63
U.S. Air Force. USAF Historical Division,
  723
United States and Armaments, 105
U.S. and Japan's New Order, 416
*United States and the Far Eastern Crisis of
  1933-1938, 429*
*United States and the Italo-Ethiopian
  Crisis, 131*
*United States and the League of Nations,
  1918-1920, 97*
*United States and the Origins of the Cold
  War, 1941-1947, 1194*
United States and the Spanish Civil War, 146
*United States and World Organization,
  1920-1933, 98*
United States and World War II, 435

*United States and World War II: Military
  and Diplomatic Documents, 1107*
*United States Army in World War II,
  446*
United States at War, 1267
U.S. Bureau of the Budget, 1267
U.S. Bureau of the Census, 44
U.S. Chief of Counsel for the Prosecu-
  tion of Axis Criminality, 1586
U.S. Civilian Production Administration,
  1268
U.S. Coast Guard in World War II, 778
U.S. Congress. House. Select Committee
  on the Katyn Forest Massacre, 1545
U.S. Congress. Joint Committee on the
  Investigation of the Pearl Harbor
  Attack, 670-71
U.S. Congress. Senate. Committee on
  Armed Services, 1546
U.S. Congress. Senate. Committee on
  Foreign Relations, 42
U.S. Department of State, 351, 905,
  934, 1603
U.S. Department of the Army. Office
  of Military History, 494
*United States Destroyer Operations in
  World War II, 771*
United States in a Chaotic World, 342
United States in World Affairs, 906
U.S. Library of Congress, 14
U.S. Marine Corps, 665
U.S. Marines and Amphibians War, 659
*United States Marine Corps in World
  War II, 664*
U.S. Military Academy, West Point, 27
U.S. National Archives, 23
U.S. Naval History Division, 892
*U.S. Naval Logistics in the Second
  World War, 762*
*United States Navy in World War II,
  775*
U.S. Office of Naval History, 34
*United States Strategic Bombing
  Survey, 724*
*United States Submarine Operations
  in World War II, 772*
U.S. Superintendent of Documents, 24
U.S. War Aims, 925
U.S. Warships of World War II, 890
Unknown Warriors, 1366
Unrelenting Struggle, 1038
Up Front, 1311
Uprooted Americans, 1314
Upton, A. F., 975

V-2, 851
Vader, J., 841
Van Alstyne, R. W., 352
Vanguard of Nazism, 255
Vansittart, R. G. V., 56, 935
Van Valkenburg, S., 1148
Varg, P. A., 1184
Vatican in the Age of the Dictators, 1922-1945, 1154
Velpke Baby Home Trial, 1571
Versailles and the Ruhr, 111
Versailles Twenty Years After, 87
Vichy France, 987
Vichy: Political Dilemma, 979
Vichy Regime, 1940-1944, 977
Victors' Justice, 1599
Victory, 1038
Victory at Sea, 1939-1945, 765
Victory Campaign, 624
Victory in Papua, 696
Victory in the West, 592
Vigil of a Nation, 961
Villari, L., 295
Viorst, M., 1187
Virus House, 897
Vlasov, A., 1427-28
Vlasov, 1427
Vogt, H., 1033
Voice of Destruction, 249
Volckmann, R. W., 1385
Vomecourt, P. d., 1376
Vondracek, F. J., 208
Von Hassell Diaries, 1938-1944, 1413
Von Riekhoff, H., 378
Vought F4U-1/7 Corsair, 889
Voznesenskii, N. A., 1246

Waffen SS, 518
Wagner, R., 860, 893
Wainwright, J. M., 714
Waite, R. G. L., 255
Waiting in the Night, 1374
Wake Island Command, 684
Walker, D. E., 1494
Walter, G., 1338
Walter, J., 876
Walter Rathenau and the Weimar Republic, 109
Walters, F. P., 99
Walton, F., 1269
Wambaugh, S., 126
Wandycz, P. S., 215, 400, 1157
Wang, Ching-Wei, 150
Wanstall, K., 1281
War Against Germany and Italy, 456
War Against Germany: Europe and Adjacent Areas, 457
War Against Japan, 458, 660

War and Diplomacy in Eastern Asia, 363
War and Society, 1318
War and the Neutrals, 920
War As an Instrument of National Policy and Its Renunciation in the Pact of Paris, 115
War As I Knew It, 514
War at Sea, 1939-1945, 773
War Diary of Breckinridge Long, 1131
War Economics of Primary Producing Countries, 1215
War Economy, 1219
War Hitler Won, 523
War in France and Flanders, 1939-1940, 534
War in Malaya, 699
War in Maps, 25
War in the Far East, 1941-1945, 451
War Lords of Washington, 1111
War Memoirs, 504
War Ministry of Winston Churchill, 1045
War: 1941-1945, 1091
War Planes of the Second World War, 836
War Premeditated, 1939, 197
War Reports of General of the Army George C. Marshall . . . H. H. Arnold . . . Ernest J. King, 485
War Speeches, Orders of the Day . . ., 1097
War Speeches (Churchill, W. L. S.,), 1038
War We Lost, 1155
War Words, 37
Ward, R. S., 1337
Warlimont, W., 521
Warmbrunn, W., 1348
Warner, G., 990
Warped Vision, 266
Warplanes of the Third Reich, 853
Warships in Profile, 848
Wartime Agriculture in Australia and New Zealand, 1939-1950, 1271
Wartime Correspondence Between President Roosevelt and Pope Pius XIII, 1203
Wartime Economic Co-operation, 1272
Wartime Economic Planning in Agriculture, 1252
Wartime Mission in Spain, 1942-1945, 1201
Wartime Origins of the East-West Dilemma over Germany, 919
Wartime Production Controls, 1259
Washington Command Post, 469
Watkins, K. W., 287
Watson, M. S., 495
Watson-Watt, R. A., 873
Watt, R. M., 256
Watts, A. J., 875
Wavell, A., 649, 657

Wavell, Scholar and Soldier, 649
Way of a Fighter, 754
Way of Deliverance, 1597
We Remained, 1385
We Survived, 1403
Weapon of Silence, 1309
Weapons of World War II, 879
Webster, C. K., 751
Wedemeyer, A. C., 725
Wedemeyer Reports!, 725
We Die Alone, 1458
Week Before Pearl Harbor, 415
Weigley, R. F., 496
Weimar and the Rise of Hitler, 243
Weimar Germany and Soviet Russia,
  1926-1933, 381
Weinberg, G. L., 257, 386
Weisband, E., 1103
Weiss, J., 912
Welles, S., 353, 1149
Wells, L. W., 1535
Werth, A., 175, 216, 574-76, 991
West, R., 1587
West Point Atlas of American Wars, 27
Weygand, M., 210, 537
Whaley, B., 1495
What Happened to Pearl Harbor?, 425
Wheatley, R., 546
Wheaton, E. B., 258
Wheeler, G. E., 433
Wheeler-Bennett, J. W., 106-108, 110, 116,
  176, 259, 936
While America Slept, 908
While Six Million Died, 1134
While You Were Gone, 1306
White, B. T., 833, 847
White, D. S., 992
White, J. B., 950
White, L. D., 1323
White, T. H., 968
White Ensign, 774
White Mouse, 1368
White Rabbit, 1373
Whitehill, W. M., 766
Whiting, A. S., 402
Whiting, C., 1547
Whitson, W. W., 715
Who Defends Rome?, 1060
Why England Slept, 272
Wiener, J. G., 1359
Wiesel, E., 1536
Wighton, C., 1496
Wigmore, L., 666
Wilcox, W. W., 1270
Wilhelmstrasse, 1027
Williams, C., 745
Williams, M. H., 35
Willoughby, C. A., 667
Willoughby, M. F., 778

Willoughby, W. W., 123
Wilmington, M. W., 1275
Wilmot, C., 449
Wilson, H. M., 656
Wilson, H. R., 354
Wilson, T. A., 1188
Windrow, M. C., 848, 861
Winds of Change, 1914-1939, 275
Wingate, J., 848
Wingless Victory, 1455
Winston Churchill and the Second Front,
  1940-1943, 477
Winston Churchill's Toy Shop, 863
Wint, G., 436
Winter War: Finland Against Russia,
  1939-1940, 528
Winter War: The Russo-Finish Conflict,
  1939-1940, 525
Winton, J., 831
Wiskemann, E., 86, 296, 370
With Ensigns Flying, 777
With Prejudice, 749
With the Red Fleet, 791
With Tito Through the War, 1394
Witness to History, 1929-1969, 1106
Woetzel, R. K., 1588
Wohlstetter, R., 426
Wolfers, A., 389
Wolfert, I., 1386
Wood, A., 1339
Wood, D., 547
Wood, F. L. W., 1080
Wood, M., 1339
Woodhouse, C. M., 1050
Woodward, D., 779
Woodward, E. L., 1048
Woollcombe, R., 657
World Almanac and Book of Facts, 48
World Between the Wars, 67
World War, 1939-1945, 447
World War II and Its Origins, 79
World War II: Books in English,
  1945-1965, 3
World Words, Recommended Pronuncia-
  tions, 37
Wreck of Reparations, 110
Wright, G., 450
Wright, R., 752
Wrigley, C. C., 1229
Wriston, H. M., 937
Writings on World War II, 1
Wuorinen, J. H., 972
Wyman, D. S., 1324

Yahil, L., 1537
Year of Stalingrad, 576
Year That Changed the World: 1945, 909
Years Between, 1290

Years of Combat, 733
Years of Command, 733
Years of Opportunity, 96
Yoors, I., 1548
Yoshihashi, Takehiko, 124
Young, A. M., 307
Young, A. N., 1185, 1220
Young, P., 447, 548
Young, R., 845, 1150
Yugoslavia at the Paris Peace Conference, 356
Yugoslavia in Crisis, 1934-1941, 355
Yvon Delbos at the Quai D'Orsay, 212

Zacharias, E. M., 1497
Zagorov, S. D., 1218
Zagorski, W., 1389
Zahn, G. C., 1034
Zawodny, J. K., 1549
Zeller, E., 1424
Zeman, Z. A. B., 951
Zero! 759, 841
Zeuss, W., 1589
Zhukov, G. K., 577
Ziegler, J., 3
Ziemke, E. F., 522, 578
Ziff, W. B., 938
Zimmern, A. E., 100
Zotos, S., 1342